WAGNER ON MUSIC
AND
DRAMA

WAGNER ON MUSIC

A compendium of
Richard Wagner's
prose works

AND

DRAMA

Selected and arranged, and with an introduction, by
Albert Goldman and Evert Sprinchorn

Translated by H. Ashton Ellis

A DA CAPO PAPERBACK

Library of Congress Cataloging in Publication Data

Wagner, Richard, 1813-1883.
   [Literary works. English. Selections]
   Wagner on music and drama: a compendium of Richard Wagner's prose
works / selected and arranged, with an introduction, by Albert Goldman and
Evert Sprinchorn; translated by H. Ashton Ellis.
   (Da Capo paperback)
   Reprint. Originally published: New York: Dutton, 1964.
   Bibliography: p.
   ISBN 0-306-80319-4 (pbk.)
   1. Music — History and criticism. 2. Drama. I. Goldman, Albert Harry, 1927-
II. Sprinchorn, Evert.
ML410.W1A128   1988
782.1 — dc19   87-34666
                                                                              CIP

ACKNOWLEDGMENT

      Grateful acknowledgment is made to the following
for permission to quote from copyright material:
      "Adolphe Appia's Tristan and Isolde" as translated
by Lee Simonson in *The Art of Scenic Design.* Copyright 1950 by Lee Simonson. Reprinted by permission
of Lee Simonson and Harper & Row, Publishers, Incorporated.

Published by Da Capo Press, Inc.
A Subsidiary of Plenum Publishing Corporation
233 Spring Street, New York, N.Y. 10013

Contents

PART III
The Origins of Modern Opera, Drama, and Music

PART IV
The Artwork of the Future

PART V
Wagner's Development

PART VI
The Art of Performance

PART VII
Bayreuth

PART VIII
Politics

Introduction

No musician, perhaps no artist in the history of Western art, has ever had so much to say about his own life, works, and ideas as did Richard Wagner. And with the possible exception of Beethoven, no musician has ever exercised such influence over men and even nations as has Wagner in the past one hundred years. In his own lifetime alone, Wagner was the subject of ten thousand articles and books attacking, defending, and explaining his system and his cult. Today students of drama, music, and politics contemplate with astonishment the impact of this one man on a civilization so old, so rich, and so sophisticated as to seem immune to wonder.

Both in his promises and in his demands Wagner was extravagant; but he performed what he promised, received what he demanded. In an age when drama was dead, the theatre reduced to melodrama and spectacle, Wagner deliberately set out to revive the spirit of tragedy. At a time when music was in decline after the great achievements of the Viennese School, he sought to reconstitute the art in a radically new form. And in a period when Germany was still a congeries of petty states, Wagner addressed himself to the German nation as the prophet and celebrant of its future greatness.

His success in this last role has clouded in modern times the brilliance of his artistic and intellectual achievements. But now —one hundred and fifty years after his birth and eighty years after his death—it may be hoped that we have finally attained the detachment necessary for a clear and untroubled vision of this extraordinary man, one of the seminal forces in modern European culture.

WAGNER'S LIFE

Richard Wilhelm Wagner was born on May 22, 1813, at Leipzig. Like his hero Siegfried, Wagner was troubled (at least in his later years) by the uncertainty of his paternity. His putative father was a police actuary who died shortly after

Wagner's birth. Soon afterward his mother married an intimate friend of the family, Ludwig Geyer, an assimilated Jew, a theatrical performer whose family for many generations had been organists and town musicians. In his fifties, Wagner obtained by means of some family letters a "penetrating glimpse" into the early relations between Geyer and his mother; he concluded evidently that Geyer was his natural father, an idea that was then bruited about by Nietzsche, his quondam disciple and later enemy.[1]

Wagner received a sound academic education, passing through the *Gymnasium* and even spending some time at the University of Leipzig; but his formal training in music did not amount to much—hardly more than a year with competent instructors. At nineteen he wrote a symphony and an opera, and in 1833 he obtained his first professional appointment, as chorusmaster at Würzburg. For a number of years, he served as conductor in several provincial German opera houses until, in 1839, he went with his wife, Mina Planer, to Paris, where he suffered two and a half years of grinding poverty while he sought to advance his career as composer. In 1842 *Rienzi* was successfully performed at Dresden, and Wagner's fortunes suddenly improved. Appointed royal music director, his next three operas—*The Flying Dutchman* (1843), *Tannhäuser* (1845), and *Lohengrin* (1850)—were received with acclaim.

But after becoming involved in the Dresden May Revolution of 1849, Wagner had to flee Germany. He settled in Zurich, where he remained until 1859. Here he composed two-thirds of *The Ring*, and began *Tristan*. Again in Paris in 1861, he saw an elaborately prepared production of *Tannhäuser* end in fiasco because of the machinations of his political enemies.

Once more Wagner's fortunes declined, but several years later his future was assured when Ludwig II of Bavaria became the composer's patron. *Tristan* was performed at Munich in 1865, *Die Meistersinger* in 1868. But, having aroused the anger of the court, Wagner was compelled to withdraw. In 1870 he married Cosima Liszt von Bülow, and two years later he established his residence in Bayreuth. Here, in 1876, the entire *Ring* was performed; *Parsifal* was given at the next festival, in 1882. Wagner died in Venice, at the age of seventy, on February 13, 1883.

[1] See Ernest Newman, *The Life of Richard Wagner*, 4 vols., New York, 1933–1947, I, 3–18; III, 558–562.

The Prose Writings

Wagner's principal prose writings were produced between the years 1848 and 1851, a period of profound crisis in both his external circumstances and his development as artist. Still burning with impotent revolutionary rage after his flight from Germany, baffled in his schemes for operatic success in Paris, in these years Wagner could neither ignore the world nor come to terms with it. At the same time, his gradually unfolding vision of the artwork of the future deeply engaged his thoughts and feelings while denying him the fixity of intention necessary for composition. Consequently, for almost six years —from the completion of *Lohengrin* in 1847 to the commencement of *The Ring* late in 1853—he wrote no music.

With no practical outlets for his energies and ideas, Wagner turned to speculation, writing a series of theoretical treatises designed to explain the nature of his projected artwork and the circumstances, political, cultural, and artistic, which made its realization necessary. *The Artwork of the Future* (1849), *Opera and Drama* (1850–1851), and *A Communication to My Friends* (1851), are all parts of a single sustained effort of reflective consciousness. In later years, Wagner described the state of mind in which he wrote these theoretical works as "abnormal," because "it drove me to treat as a theorem a thing that had become quite positive and certain to me in my artistic intuition." But his urgent need for intellectual clarity and literary expression hardly seems abnormal now; it was merely a temporary intensification of a lifelong habit of philosophic speculation, a habit that in later years continued unabated, though it found its outlet more often in letters and conversation than in systematic exposition.

Indeed, in the fullest and most modern sense of the word, Wagner was an intellectual. It was never enough for him to conceive an idea and act upon it: he had to formulate it in philosophic terms, demonstrate its internal logic or necessity. And he liked to support or enlarge his ideas by setting them in a framework of related concepts, causes, and conditions. It is to this inveterate practice of rationalization, as much as to his extraordinary circumstances during these years of crisis, that we owe Wagner's major critical writings.

As a thinker, Wagner is both original and derivative. But even when his root ideas were borrowed from pure philosophers—Feuerbach in his early writings, Schopenhauer in his later work—Wagner assimilated these ideas in such a manner as to make them not merely parts of his system, but formulations of what he had most deeply experienced. What is more, in his proper sphere as a critic and theorist of the arts of theatre and music, Wagner was an enormously resourceful and versatile thinker. He pioneered in the study of symbols, myths, and primitive legends; he was a shrewd, if not disinterested, critic of opera, a brilliant exponent of Beethoven, and a penetrating analyst of the technical problems of conducting, acting, musical declamation, and theatre design.

But the real fascination of Wagner's writings lies not so much in the light they shed on philosophy and the arts, but on himself. They provide profound insight into his mind and art, and cannot be ignored by anyone who wishes to understand his compositions and his place in modern culture. This is such an obvious truth that one wonders how, with so many recent books and articles devoted wholly or in part to Wagner's life, works, and ideas, Wagner should have been allowed so rarely to speak for himself, at least in English.

Perhaps the chief reason for this neglect lies in the character of Wagner's style and his habits of argument and exposition. Wagner was not a writer so much as a talker or monologuist. Most of his writings were hastily and impatiently composed in the manner of improvised lectures, and they have the faults of all such work: they are terribly prolix and often oblique in their approach to problems, the talker sliding into his theme instead of attacking it directly from the start. There is often a great deal of backtracking because a talker is naturally digressive and repetitive and also because ideas often occur to him after the proper time for their introduction has passed. Reading Wagner can be a trying experience. Often we feel his idea within our grasp only to see it slip away on the endless stream of verbiage or become lost in irrelevant disquisition. He was not the kind of writer who has difficulty expressing himself; quite the contrary, he was highly articulate. His difficulty rather lay in the very superfluency of his style that allowed everything to be said so immediately that it was never really said, but rather skimmed or quaintly illustrated, the depth and fullness of the thought left unrealized.

Wagner had some bad mental habits. He was always generalizing about subjects that have long and complicated histories, without taking much heed of these histories except to choose a point here and there with which to support his contention. Consequently, we never really know what he is talking about in historical terms, which would not be so bad if he generalized from the universal nature of art and did not concern himself with developmental processes. The very opposite is the case, however: Wagner almost always presents his ideas in one of those idealized histories familiar to us from the writings of eighteenth-century political theorists. Like Rousseau, he must always begin with some ideal primitive condition, trace down vaguely our descent from this early Eden, and then turn about to point the way up the ideal incline of the future.

Another obvious fault is the result of a naturally imaginative mind working in a world of abstract thought. Wagner is an inveterate personifier of ideas. Abstractions like poetry, music, speech, and melody assume in his mind personal identities and sexes. His presentation of ideas in terms of human relations is so primitive as to be at times absurd.

Finally, one is distracted by the tangled involution of his thought. At times he seems constitutionally incapable of simple and direct utterance. This is partly the vice of his nation and period, but it is also a flaw in his own mind. His ideas are so unripe that they have not yet assumed a definite form; we see them only in their developmental flux.

In general, Wagner's writings suffer from a lack of *composition*. To be easily understood, they require editing, cutting, and rearranging, not simply selection and anthologizing. *Wagner on Music and Drama* is designed to make the substance of the composer's thought both accessible and coherent. It is not an anthology of the usual kind, made up of individual works complete or cut; rather, it is an integrated presentation of the whole of Wagner's thought by means of an arrangement of key pieces and passages drawn from many sources—books, articles, and letters—fitted together so that they can be read as continuous systematic exposition. This arrangement, the editors believe, faithfully reflects Wagner's own intentions. For, as previously noted, most of his theoretical writings were produced in one brief period, and, despite certain minor differences in emphasis, represent successive stages in the development of a unified theory. As his subjects, principles, and arguments remained the same, while his various statements of them differed considerably in clarity, force, and fullness, it is desirable to have available the best formulation of each idea and to have this material assembled in a logical and convenient arrangement. At the same time, those matters on which

Wagner changed his mind without discussing the change in his published writings are represented here by selections from his correspondence.

The anthology is arranged in eight major divisions. Part I presents, as background for his later reforms, Wagner's criticism of art and culture in his own day. Part II offers a contrasting vision—Wagner's historical ideal, the Greek theatre. Part III, a critical history of opera, drama, and music, leads to the famous specifications for the artwork of the future (Part IV). These theoretical projections are then supplemented by the facts of Wagner's artistic development (Part V); by discussions of the practical problems of conducting, orchestration, acting, and singing (Part VI); and by Wagner's own accounts of the founding of the *Festspielhaus* and the first performance of *Parsifal* in 1882 (Part VII). The important essay by Adolphe Appia on the staging of *Tristan* is provided at the end of Part VII. The final section (Part VIII) is devoted to Wagner's late political writings.

CULTURAL DECADENCE OF THE NINETEENTH CENTURY

Wagner's criticism of cultural conditions in the mid-nineteenth century—given symbolic form in the character of Alberich, the ugly dwarf who renounces love and beauty for gold—is essentially no different (and a good deal less subtle and searching) from that of many other critics of his day. Like Heine, Balzac, Stendhal, Carlyle, and Arnold, Wagner saw his age sinking into a morass of philistinism as everywhere the burgher class triumphed over the decadent aristocracy and the fettered proletariat. But unlike other critics, who took as evidence of the degeneracy of the age changes in manners, morals, and literary values, Wagner concentrated on the condition of the theatre. This characteristic emphasis can be associated with several factors: with his own immediate experience as conductor and composer; with the assumption—common to German cultural criticism since the time of Lessing—that the theatre as the principal form of public art must be necessarily a powerful agency of social influence; and, most important, with Wagner's belief in the redemptive power of art, the theatre being in his view the supreme art, the crown of civilization.

Theatre for Wagner and his age meant opera; not primarily the Italian opera of Bellini and Rossini (in which Wagner found a genuine but limited value), but the brilliant genre of

Parisian grand opera, initiated by Auber and Halévy and brought to its culmination in the enormously successful collaborations of Scribe and Meyerbeer. These once-famous operas—*Robert le Diable* (1831), *Les Huguenots* (1836), and *Le Prophète* (1849)—were aimed directly at the pretentious bourgeois public of the time. They were gigantic celebrations of the materialistic spirit, performed on stages crammed with elaborate and costly objects. Every material resource of the theatre was employed in their production. For *Robert le Diable*, according to William Crosten, "No effort was spared. . . . The English stage traps were introduced, gas illumination was used for the first time on the French opera stage and advantage was taken of the varied effects of perspective, illusion, and chiaroscuro which had been developed in the Boulevard theatres. . . . We are assured that the *mise en scène* . . . cost nearly 200,000 francs."

Meyerbeer's main talent lay in his mimicry, his ability to assimilate and reproduce a variety of styles. During the Venice Carnival of 1815, he heard Rossini's *Tancredi*. Enraptured by it, he immediately altered his own style and in practically no time produced a series of highly successful Italian operas. His friend and fellow pupil, Carl Maria von Weber, wrote to him, "My heart bleeds to see a German composer of creative power stoop to become an imitator in order to win favor with the crowd," but the facile Meyerbeer was undeterred. Next, he moved to Paris, where he devoted seven years to a thorough study of everything French, especially French opera from Lully on. A visitor to his library was surprised to find "hundreds of scores great and small, many of which were hardly known by name even to the most initiated." His preparation complete, Meyerbeer launched his career in French opera.

Meyerbeer drove himself to win fame and prestige. (Heine quipped that he fulfilled the true Christian ideal, for he could not rest while there remained a single unconverted soul.) As we might expect from both his motives and his methods of working, the music of his operas is incredibly, monumentally inane—a hodgepodge of nondescript themes and devices taken over from other composers, garish orchestral brilliance, and dreary letter-perfect declamation. Meyerbeer was so passionless and empty a musician that Donald Francis Tovey once remarked that he could not "regard him as a real person at all," and could not be bothered to argue with people who could.

The sudden prominence of Jewish composers, like Halévy,

Meyerbeer, and Mendelssohn, after the "emancipation" of the Jews in the early nineteenth century, soon attracted attention, and in time a Jewish "question" arose. In 1850, *Die Neue Zeitschrift für Musik* published a discussion of "Hebrew Artistic Taste," which included Wagner's famous, or infamous, piece, "Das Judentum in der Musik" (Jews in Music), an essay that is still the primary document of its kind.

"Jews in Music" is usually considered the work of a violent anti-Semite, but it is unwise to dismiss Wagner's ideas simply on these grounds, for his basic argument contains as much truth on the subject as anyone could have seen during the nineteenth century. The strength of this argument lies in its perception that the newly assimilated Jewish composer, being alienated both from Jewish life and from the life of his adopted nation, lacked the prime requisite of the true artist: the deep cultural roots that provide an instinctive grasp of the unconscious aspirations and conflicts of his society and that enable an individual writing out of his own being to bring forth at the same time a true expression of the spirit of his nation. This, according to Wagner, the Jewish artist can never do. Where the Jew *is* equipped to excel is in intellectual activity, for his precarious social position requires, above all, that he understand the society in order to overcome his problems within it.

In his early writings, Wagner is even more antagonistic to orthodox Christianity than he is toward Judaism; or rather, like most of the Romantics, he condemned Christianity precisely for its failure to purge itself of its Judaic inheritance: the stone tablets inscribed with "forbiddals" and the primitive image of a wrathful, tyrannical God. But Wagner was equally incensed by the Christian character as it had developed through history, particularly during the Middle Ages. "Hypocrisy" was his epithet for Christianity: hypocrisy not in the sense of conscious duplicity but rather in the sense of a profound split between the normal healthy desires of mankind (especially sexual desires) aiming instinctively at happiness in this world and the morbid, otherworldly yearnings inspired by the Christian religion.

Wagner's accumulated frustrations and anger against Christianity, against the Jews, against the bourgeois supremacy, and against the degradation of art into entertainment finally impelled him to call for a revolution that should end "the dominion of Death over Life." When fighting actually broke out in the streets of Dresden, Wagner was in the thick of it, his attitude toward the hostilities being "a playful exhilaration." In later years he recalled how as he was passing through a barricade a common soldier had shouted to him, "*Herr Kapellmeister! Der Freude schöner Götterfunken* has set fire to things!"

Though Wagner's revolutionary ardor was real enough to make him take arms and risk his life, it sprang from sources so deep that when political action failed him, he immediately carried the same spirit into the world of art, substituting an art revolution for a political upheaval.

THE GREEK IDEAL

Wagner's denunciations of the modern theatre are balanced and relieved by his idealized vision of the Greek theatre, a theatre that incorporated all the conditions of great art: a religious occasion, the participation of the entire community, and the cooperation of all the arts in the dramatic representation of a mythic action. To Wagner, enthralled by the Romantic dream of "Hellas" (nowhere more vividly experienced than in the Germany of Winckelmann, Lessing, Goethe, Schiller, and Hölderlin), Greek drama appeared a noble and beautiful celebration of "the purely human." And so intent was he on this sunlit vision of the Greek stage that reading him one almost forgets that this theatre exists for us principally in the form of tragic dramas. In his period of "Hellenic optimism," Wagner was curiously indifferent to the specific character of tragedy, being concerned rather with those general values he found wanting in the theatre of his own day: community, myth, mimesis, and the synthesis of the arts.

SYNTHESIS OF THE ARTS

Wagner's doctrine that every art reaches its fulfillment in a union with the other arts appears extremely dubious when it is abstracted from the cultural conditions that fostered its development. Indeed, there appears to be a baffling paradox in Wagner's arguments, for while limiting each art individually (and complaining about its inadequacies), at the same time he seeks the illimitable combination of all the arts. But when we turn from the consideration of this doctrine merely as idea to reflect upon the peculiar character of Romantic art, we see the whole question in a different light.

Both Romantic poetry and Romantic music, it has often been observed, exhibit a tendency to transcend their natural limitations as arts and to pass over into the sphere of the complementary art. Romantic poetry seems to aspire to the condition of music by subordinating the plastic and delineative function of language to the lyrical and suggestive. Nor is this tendency confined to the use of language; it is apparent in the very substance of Romantic poetry. Wordsworth's "Nature" is not so much a landscape filled with carefully observed and accurately delineated details, as an evocation of spiritual "presences" and "powers" that hover mysteriously around and above the observable features of his world. Beethoven's music is likewise distinguished by an unmistakable poetic tendency, an effort to render through the tonal medium the abstracted essence of certain "root experiences," analogous to the moods and myths that are the subjects of Romantic literature.

This tendency to overstep the traditional limits of the various art media is unquestionably a reflection of the Romantic sense of reality, a reality that often seems to lie in that obscure region where the arts share common borders. Seen from this perspective, Wagner's synthetic artwork appears as the ultimate endeavor totally to encompass Romantic reality.

MYTH AND MIMESIS

The nature of Romantic reality also explains in large measure the great importance that Wagner attributed to myth, as well as the great importance subsequently ascribed by the Symbolists (who shared much the same subjective orientation) to Wagner's successful employment of myth.

When the Romantics located reality in the mind rather than in the external world—the world of character, action, and locale—they created an enormous problem for art. None of the traditional genres, neither epic, romance, drama, nor the novel (at least in their received forms), were really suitable for the representation of a totally subjective reality. Consequently, a wholly new mode of representation had to be found that would faithfully reflect the new subjective reality and at the same time provide the externalization and objectification indispensable for mimetic art. Blake, Keats, and Shelley experimented with mental allegories, thus in a manner returning to the practice of the Middle Ages, when a comparable stirring of psychological interest prompted a modification of romance. But allegory was not really in keeping with the spirit of the age, and so the search for a new mode of representation had to be extended.

The rediscovery of myth provided the Romantic artist with an ideal solution to his problem, for myth arose from psychological depths even more profound than those plumbed by self-reflection, and myth likewise provided character, action, and locale of a kind suitable for epic or tragic treatment while remaining distinct from even the most idealized representation of actual life. Myth, as a symbolist critic has said, could "satisfy the intellect while safeguarding the rights of the dream."

ROMANTIC OPTIMISM AND ROMANTIC PESSIMISM

When in the early 1850's, Wagner stopped theorizing about the artwork of the future and began composing *The Ring of the Nibelung*, he suddenly realized that he was involved in a fundamental philosophic contradiction. As artist he was intent on projecting a tragic vision of life; yet as a prophetic thinker, he had committed himself to an optimistic faith in Utopia. The immediate practical result of this realization was not another theoretical statement but some significant changes in the design of the final opera of *The Ring*. Consequently, the vigorous controversy that has gone on for many decades concerning the revolution in Wagner's thinking centers upon the nature of these changes and the motives that prompted them.

Many of the older commentators—most notably Kurt Hildebrandt—argued that the shift from an optimistic to a pessimistic philosophy in *The Ring* (the original Siegfried was "The new man who springs from the communistic paradise"; he was modeled on Bakunin, who was "fearless, full of childlike confidence, utterly regardless of consequences to himself, tender in spite of his passion for destruction") was the result of growing political disillusionment after 1848, culminating, after the *coup d'état* of Napoleon III in 1851, with a denial of the world and an attitude of resignation.

Most modern critics, led by Ernest Newman, do not agree: they see the problem in a wider context. For the fact is that Wagner had always been unsure about the central moral problem embodied in Wotan's guilt. At first he held with the Romantics that the evil of the world was the effect of an evil god (Wotan) and that a new and righteous world could be created by new men without fear. Then, after reading Schopenhauer (in 1854), Wagner began to understand how his essential artistic nature had for long been functioning in opposition to the willed optimism of his intellect. Writing to August Röckel two years later, he confessed to "having arrived at a clear understanding of my own works of art through the help of another, who has provided me with reasoned conceptions corresponding to my intuitive principles." *The Flying Dutchman, Tannhäuser,* and *Lohengrin*—all his early works—were actually, he now maintained, expressions of "the sublime tragedy of renunciation." The strange thing was that "in all my intellectual ideas on life, and in all the conceptions at which I had arrived in the course of my struggles to understand the world with my conscious reason, I was working in direct opposition to the intuitive ideas expressed in these works."[2]

The evil of the world, in this new view, was irremediable. The artwork of the future, therefore, could redeem the world only by illustrating with inevitable logic the necessity for the world's destruction. This conviction produced a reversal in *The Ring* from "a final scene in which Siegfried and Brynhilde reestablish the power of the Gods by the death of the former and the restoration of the Ring to the Rhine Maidens by the latter, to a final scene in which the restoration of the Gold to the Rhine brings with it the destruction of the Gods."[3]

Having reversed himself on the question of the value of life, Wagner, in his late writings, no longer conceives of art as a celebration of triumphant humanity. Art is now a "noble illusion, a turning away from reality, a cure for life which is indeed not real, which leads one wholly outside life, but thereby raises one above it."

It is very important to keep this radical alteration in philosophic values in mind when reading Wagner's published writings—which for the most part reflect his earlier attitude—lest one be misled into thinking that Wagner the optimist is Wagner entire.

TRAGEDY REBORN FROM MUSIC

Wagner's philosophical predicament at the time of the composition of *The Ring* arose from the incompatibility of tragedy and the Romantic spirit. Romantic tragedy had been tragedy inverted: the heroes of *Prometheus Unbound* and *Faust* pursued a course that led through suffering and conflict to ulti-

[2] See *post* p. 279.
[3] Newman, *op. cit.,* II, 358.

mate triumph and repose. Wagner aimed, in contrast, at the revival of genuine tragedy. What is more, he determined— despite his enthusiasm for the Greek drama—to employ only those legends that could be made to embody the sufferings and the moral dilemmas of the modern sensibility; neoclassicism of any sort he regarded as vain and regressive. Lacking any literary precursor in this bold endeavor, he took his warrant from a musician: Beethoven. Wagner's hopes for a rebirth of tragedy in the modern world sprang ultimately from his awareness of the great new power that had been released into that world through Beethoven's music.

Beethoven's contribution to the artwork of the future was twofold: he had demonstrated the unique capacity of music to project the inmost content of the tragic myth—the myth of the hero's struggles, victories, and death—and he had pointed the way in the final movement of his Ninth Symphony to the use of language in conjunction with symphonic music.

But Beethoven, in Wagner's eyes, was actually a musical Columbus, who seeking one world had accidentally discovered another and far greater one. Though he had invested music with undreamed-of powers of dramatic and philosophic implication, Beethoven remained to the end an absolute musician. When, as in the *Leonora* Overture, the progressive development of his dramatic subject could not be accommodated within his recapitulatory form, Beethoven betrayed the subject for the sake of the form. Reasoning from examples like these —as well as from Beethoven's evident need for language in the Ninth—Wagner concluded that instrumental music could go no further in the direction of poetic representation.

The artwork of the future, therefore, was intended as an enormous extension of that portentous moment when Beethoven brought the Word out of the depths of music. In the new artwork, the Beethoven symphony orchestra would sound again the mighty themes of the hero's sufferings, triumphs, loves, and death; but instead of these themes conjuring up phantasms in the listeners' minds, the figures of the hero and the heroine would actually appear, acting out the content of the music in verbally pointed pantomime. And the music freed, in turn, from the necessity to create its own abstract unity through formal devices of repetition and recapitulation, would flow on in "endless melody," enfolding the entire drama in a rich fabric of closely woven symphonic motifs. Freed likewise from the arbitrary system of key relations indispensable to sonata form, the music would be tonally, as well as melodically, unbounded—endlessly modulating in accordance with the shifting moods and unfolding action of the drama.

DRAMA VERSUS MUSIC DRAMA

As a playwright and dramatic theorist, Wagner set himself the task of finding a new solution to the main problem that confronts the writer of serious drama. A situation must be created that will stir the audience profoundly, and the situation must be arrived at in such a way that the audience will not only accept it but be overwhelmed by it. The solution adopted by the writers of melodrama was to string together a series of strong but spurious situations, none of them adequately motivated. The sophisticated spectator would at best be merely titillated by the hectic adventures of the hero and villain, and even the naïve spectator would let himself be moved only so far as it pleased him. The solution adopted by the practitioners of the well-made play lay in emphasizing a single strong situation and motivating it thoroughly. To Dumas *fils* the whole art of the drama consisted in the art of preparation. The trouble with this solution was that the playwright was compelled to devote most of his script to preparing for the big scene, the climax.

But the serious dramatist wanted to do more than construct a machine that would set off an emotional explosion of a certain magnitude at precisely the right moment. He wanted to bring the audience to a state of wider or deeper awareness by exploring the depths out of which the emotions arose. Like a surgeon, he wanted to open up his patient, clear away the covering tissue, and expose the sensitive nerves or the source of the pain as quickly as possible. Since the patient could be anesthetized in the operating theatre for only a limited period of time, the preliminaries would have to be held to a minimum. Wagner's solution to the dramatist's main problem was to reduce motivation in order to spend most of the time exploring a single strong emotional situation.

Recognizing the power of music to create excitement instantly, Wagner relied upon the orchestra to warm up the audience for the dramatic climaxes that would otherwise have to be prepared through one or more acts. Furthermore, he knew music could add enormous weight to the climax itself as long as it seemed to represent an overflowing of the emotions contained in the scene. However, it would not do to eliminate the preparation altogether, for although music by itself could express emotion it could not express the reason for the emotion. As Wagner pointed out, if the emotion in a symphony became too intense, the audience would react against it by asking, "Why this intensity?" Consequently, musical expression and dramatic motivation had to be made to serve each other.

As for the crucial situation around which the drama was to be built, Wagner wanted it to provide the spectators with a degree of insight denied them in realistic drama dealing with contemporary or historical subjects. A realistic situation in the theatre set motives and characters clearly before the audience in terms that it could understand. The audience was not content merely to see a thing happen; it wanted to see how and why it happened. Consider the situation in which the cuckolded husband decides to kill his wife. To make this situation as real as possible, the playwright explains why the wife took a lover, how the husband found out about them, and why the husband had no recourse but to slay his wife. To Wagner this "absolute disclosing of intentions disturbed true insight." Giving a completely realistic cast to a subject meant covering it with a veil of illusion, for the truth lay less in the motives than in the emotions. What Wagner sought to capture was the movements of the soul. What he wanted to seize upon was jealousy itself, or love itself, and not the complicated actions in everyday life that gave rise to it.

The realistic situation was inevitably anchored in a certain moment of time, and its horizons were consequently limited. The typical situation, the mainstay of the neoclassic drama, was at best only the sum of all similar realistic situations. Only the archetypal situation, which existed at the beginning of time and which would always exist, could serve Wagner's purpose of presenting life as the "resultant not of arbitrary forces but of eternal laws." And the archetypal situations could be found only in myths. The neoclassic dramatist and the realistic dramatist, both of whom were primarily concerned with verisimilitude, tried to modernize the myths, if they dealt with them at all. They thought of themselves as wiser than the inventors of the myths, wiser than the folk. In contrast, Wagner's attitude was reverential. He confronted the old mythographers not to bring them up to date but to learn from them, to share their wisdom, and to make us their coevals.

Wagner's attitude is the key to an understanding of his whole system of thought. For him the universe was composed

of forces rather than of things. Seeing the truth meant understanding these forces, and understanding meant merging with
the world will, the force that is the universe. In the depths of
our individual minds and souls are the roots and tentacles that
link us to the primordial unity. What we share with every
other living creature is the energy that drives us. What each
of us shares with every other human being is a similar network
of roots and tentacles; and whatever produces a certain response in the depths of one of us should produce much the
same response in all the rest of us. On this premise Wagner
could formulate his theory of "folk" art in which communion
of feeling counted for more than communication of ideas.

Consequently, the Wagnerian drama has the depths of the
soul as its setting. Explaining the genesis of *Tristan and Isolde*,
Wagner said,

Here, in perfect trustfulness, I plunged into the inner depths of soul
events, and from out this inmost center of the world I fearlessly
built up its outer form [of the drama]. A glance at the *volumen* of
this poem will show you at once the exhaustive detail-work which
a historical poet is obliged to devote to clearing up the outward
bearings of his plot, to the detriment of a lucid exposition of its
inner motives, I now trusted myself to apply to these latter alone.
Life and death, the whole import and existence of the outer world,
here hang on nothing but the inner movements of the soul. The
whole affecting action comes about for reason only that the inmost
soul demands it, and steps to light with the very shape foretokened
in the inner shrine.[4]

Wagner's most original contribution to dramaturgy in the nineteenth century was the perfection of the demotivated drama, a
drama that speaks to us in anagogical terms and in which the
story and characters are meant to serve as mediums between
us and a larger, profounder, and truer world. Dramatists before Wagner—Byron, for example—had tried to do something
similar, but Wagner provided his plays with a firmer philosophical basis by combining and amplifying the ideas of early
German romanticists like Novalis, Görres, Schelling, G. H.
von Schubert, and the Schlegel brothers. In addition to regarding myths as the repositories of eternal truths and the folk as
mythmakers, these German writers tended to share one key
thought that is crucial for an understanding of the Wagnerian
drama and its influence in the last quarter of the nineteenth

[4] See *post* p. 270.

century. They assumed that the heart of the universe lay within each man's soul. For Friedrich Schlegel the spirit of love in its broadest sense was the fuel that ran the universe and was piped into each human breast; and a poem was romantic to the extent that it was suffused with this spirit. According to him, a romantic work presents a sentimental content in the form of fantasy:

> What is sentimental? Whatever is addressed to our feelings, and not, indeed, to our sensual but to our spiritual sides. The source and soul of all these impulses is love, and over romantic poetry the spirit of love must everywhere be seen hovering invisibly. It is the holy breath that stirs us through the sounds of music. . . . It is an infinite presence, and it by no means seeks to cling and cleave exclusively to persons, events and situations, and to individual propensities: for the true poet all this, no matter how deeply it may be embedded in his soul, is only the intimation of something higher, something infinite, only the token or hieroglyph of the one true love, of the fullness of life, the creativity of nature.[5]

Allowing for a brief excursion back to Kant, it is only a short journey from Schlegel's hypostasis of an irradiating and infinite love to Schopenhauer's concept of a universal will or force, basically erotic in nature, that is ceaselessly and senselessly spawning and destroying life. Schopenhauer urged man not to cooperate with this force, but to withdraw from it or to make it the object of intellectual contemplation. Schopenhauer entered Wagner's life when the composer was in the midst of his most passionate romance, a romance that seemed to offer no prospect of a happy end. Said Wagner, Schopenhauer's

> chief idea, the final negation of the desire of life . . . shows the only salvation possible. To me of course that thought was not new, and it can indeed be conceived by no one in whom it did not pre-exist, but this philosopher was the first to put it clearly before me. . . . I have at least found a quietus that in wakeful nights helps me to sleep. This is the genuine, ardent longing for death, for absolute unconsciousness, total non-existence. Freedom from all dreams is our only final salvation.[6]

Tristan and Isolde, the artistic product of Wagner's romance, is built entirely on the dualism of life and death, of truth and

---

[5] Quoted in *Die deutschen Romantiker,* Gerhard Stenzel, Salzburg, 1954, I, 251.
[6] See *post* p. 271.

illusion, with the everyday world being represented as an illusion. The ambivalent feelings of love and hate felt by Isolde for Tristan adumbrate the dualism in its first form. At the end of the first act the love potion is exchanged for the death potion, suggesting not only the transformation of hate into love but also the equivalence of love and death. In the second and central act of the drama, a long and explicit depiction of the sex act itself, physical passion carries the two lovers through the night to the point where the coming of morning and a return to the everyday world of individual existences is unthinkable. Eternal night, eternal love, pure feeling, unconsciousness suggest the primordial unity out of which the individual emerges briefly to live his "strange interlude" before sinking back whence he came. When day dawns, Tristan allows himself to be wounded, and exacts a promise from Isolde that she will follow him into night's realm. In the final, sublime moments of the drama, Isolde, standing over Tristan's body, sinks ecstatically into oblivion:

In dem wogenden Schwall,	In the sea of pleasure's
in dem tönenden Schall,	Billowing roll,
in des Welt-Atems	In the ether waves'
wehendem All—	Knelling and toll,
ertrinken,	In the world-breath's
versinken—	Wavering whole—
unbewusst—	To drown in, go down in—
höchste Lust!	Lost in swoon—greatest boon![7]

This final scene reveals a radical difference between Schopenhauer's way of dealing with the universal will and Wagner's. Where Schopenhauer advocates withdrawal and noncooperation in order to impose one's own meaning on the essential meaninglessness of life, Wagner's lovers rush to embrace this will with such abandon and vigor that it is difficult to tell whether the force is overcoming the individuals or the individuals are momentarily mastering the force. It was impossible for Wagner to go much further in this direction, and in his subsequent works he sought to escape the anguish of individual existence by methods more in tune with Schopenhauer and with Christian thinking. In 1870 Wagner wrote of redeeming oneself from the guilt of phenomenal existence through the spirit of music. To Nietzsche, Wagner's later attitude meant a return to pessimism and a betrayal of the heroic, life-affirming attitude of the true Dionysian spirit.

[7] Francis Golffing translation.

THEATRE OF NARCOSIS

In the romantic view, the thought of submerging one's self in the waves of the world will—whether to escape life or to experience it more fully—was as terrifying as it was attractive. But art provided a vicarious and socially acceptable way of attaining simultaneously the heights of ecstasy and the depths of self-annihilation or self-degradation. The romantic theatre, especially, aimed at reducing the audience to an unthinking, highly suggestible mass in which the individual was transported out of himself and made to drift with the tides of the universe. In both its realistic and antirealistic aspects the nineteenth-century theatre sought to render the spectator incapable of passing impartial judgment or controlling his senses. It was a theatre of narcosis, and Wagner was its chief architect.

To make the spectator utterly responsive to the movements of the soul that were being shadowed forth on the stage, Wagner had to hypnotize him. He used every means at his disposal to heighten audience response and to make all responses subservient to the artist. First, music. Then he reduced plot development and let the action revolve around one or two crucial scenes. Then he built his own theatre at Bayreuth with the seats so arranged that the spectators would have to look at the stage and not at each other, as in an Italian opera house. Then he put the orchestra in a sunken pit so that the players would not distract the attention of the audience and so that the music would seem as sourceless as the universal will it expressed. Then he turned the house lights completely off—something of an innovation in his time—in order to focus all the lights and all the attention on the stage. And finally he filled the stage with all sorts of magnificent mummery, including fire-breathing dragons and Rhine-swimming maidens.

Looking at pictures of the sets used at Bayreuth, the awkward dragon, the strange swimming-machines for the Rhine maidens,[8] we might wonder how anyone could be hypnotized by this cluttered scenery and these creaking machines. After Wagner's death there were many stage designers who felt that the soul drama required an abstract set, as abstract as the music itself—a set in which shifting lights and shadows would convey as much of the mood as tones of music. In the 1890's the Swiss designer Adolphe Appia put his dreams of a perfect Wagner production on paper. These designs exercised an enor-

[8] See Adolphe Jullien, *Richard Wagner, sa vie et ses œuvres,* Paris, 1886, pp. 218–219.

mous influence on the theatre of the twentieth century when the development of electric lighting made it possible to realize Appia's dreams. It should be borne in mind, however, that Wagner himself would almost certainly have disapproved of Appia's sets. He would have preferred to have the light fall on something solid and tangible than on amorphous shapes or on nothing at all. Like the *maître des feyntes* of the medieval Bible plays, Wagner strove for reality on the stage. The spirit world speaks most forcefully when it moves real objects. And before reproaching Wagner the theatrical magician with being old-fashioned in his stage designs, we should also bear in mind that nineteenth-century gas lighting lent a warm, glowing, almost ectoplasmic quality to the scene that electric lighting has never been able to achieve. The barely perceptible flickering characteristic of gas lighting endowed everything, even the most inanimate papier-mâché rock, with a life of its own.

Wagner and the Symbolists

In 1860 Baudelaire became the first French poet to succumb to Wagner's mesmeric spell. *Tannhäuser,* he said, affected him like drugs. He led Villiers de l'Isle-Adam to Wagner, and Villiers was completely subdued, not so much by the music as by Wagner's story material, his handling of myths, the symbols arising from them, and the projection of the soul-states of the protagonists. Inspired by Wagner, Villiers wrote his strange drama *Axël* in the early 1870's, though it did not find its audience until twenty years later. In 1885 the *Revue Wagnérienne,* under the editorship of Edouard Dujardin,[9] began to appear, its express purpose being to present "Wagner as the great poet, Wagner as the great thinker, and Wagner as the creator of a new art form."[10] From that time on, there was scarcely a

[9] Dujardin's play *La Fin d'Antonia,* performed in 1893 by Lugné-Poe's troupe, made use of the "recurrence of motifs based on consonant or vowel sounds." In addition to borrowing the idea of leitmotifs from Wagner, Dujardin imitated Bayreuth in dimming all the house lights and concentrating all the lights on the stage. See Gertrude R. Jasper, *Adventure in the Theatre: Lugné-Poe and the Théâtre de l'Œuvre to 1899,* New Brunswick, 1947, p. 108. Dujardin is best known for introducing the interior monologue to modern literature in his novel *Les lauriers sont coupés,* printed 1887.

[10] Cited by Werner Vordtriede, *Novalis und die französischen Symbolisten,* Stuttgart, 1963, p. 166.

single French Symbolist who was not directly influenced by Wagner's theoretical writings.[11] Many of them attempted to create their own form of the synthetic artwork by using words as notes of music and by stressing sound at the expense of sense—though they were good students of Wagner in never abandoning conscious control over their material as their off-spring, the surrealists, were to do. Mallarmé, *doyen* of the Symbolists, was drawn to Wagner because he appreciated the composer's use of myth to give substance to ineffable emotions, and of music to suggest an object or a state without naming it. In the most famous of Symbolist pronouncements, Mallarmé declared that "to name an object is to suppress three-fourths of the enjoyment of the poem." The symbolic method should "evoke an object little by little to reveal a state of soul *[état d'âme]*, or, conversely, select an object and disengage from it a state of soul by a series of decipherings."[12]

Here we are confronted by the central concern of the Symbolists—the attempt to evoke a state of soul. It was this concern that united them with the German Romanticists as regards basic aims and principles. It was their need to find a method for evoking this state of soul that made them disciples of Wagner. For Wagner had found a way, the way of the myth. The myth could corporealize the world of the spirit. The myth could put our dreams, our vague intimations of another existence, into tangible shape.

THE WORLD STAGE

The key to understanding Wagner lies in the fact that he gave himself entirely to art, particularly to the art of the theatre. Art was his religion and the theatre its temple. Moral and spiritual values existed for him only in so far as his art might benefit from them. His art was not created to serve any patriotic, racial, or religious causes; the causes were opportunistically appropriated by Wagner to serve his art.

[11] See Vordtriede, *op. cit.;* Max Nordau, *Degeneration,* New York, 1895; Rodolphe Palgen, *Villiers de l'Isle-Adam, auteur dramatique,* Reims, 1925; Grange Wooley, *Richard Wagner et le Symbolisme français,* Paris, 1931; Kurt Jäckel, *Richard Wagner in der französischen Literatur,* 2 vols., Breslau, 1931–1932; Guy Michaud, *Message poétique du Symbolisme,* Paris, 1947; Haskell M. Block, *Mallarmé and the Symbolist Drama,* Detroit, 1963.

[12] Reply to an *enquête* conducted by Jules Huret and printed in *l'Echo de Paris* in 1891. Reprinted in Mallarmé, *Œuvres complètes,* edited by H. Mondor and G. Jean-Aubry, Paris, 1945, p. 869.

All too often his admirers as well as his detractors insisted on turning Wagner upside down in order to make him serve their causes. Bernard Shaw, whose two gods were Ibsen and Wagner, attempted to give Wagner's drama a moral significance by reading socialism and economics into it. The racists, the Nazis, and other Wagner idolaters made Bayreuth into a center of anti-Semitism and hero worship, as if Wagner had built the Bayreuth *Festspielhaus* with the express purpose of breeding the blond superman, founding the Third Reich, and exterminating the Jews, all in the name of Teutonic mysticism.

Both those who worshiped him and those who despised him did so all too often because they took Wagner's political and racial ideas as the main planks in his platform.

Actually, they were only ancillary to his main concern, only ways by which he might achieve his own kind of theatre. Which is not to say that we can ignore his political writings or shroud his racist pronouncements in silence. We can neither exculpate him from sharing the blame for their pernicious effect nor minimize their importance to those who wish to understand our times and the forces that rule our lives. Hence the inclusion in this volume of an extensive section from these writings.

Nietzsche, who both idolized and hated the man, understood him best. He saw early in the game that the driving force behind Wagner was histrionicism and that the mainspring of his genius was the ability to create illusions that would draw out man's hidden desires and reflect his inner dreams. All Wagner wanted was the chance to display his genius.[13] The will to power within him was the need to subve the world to his art. Once this is understood, his polemica writings acquire a meaning different from that ascribed to them by cultural historians.

A born illusionist, he extended the principles that operate within the theatre to the world outside the theatre. For him the world was divided into two camps, the movers and the moved, those who performed and those who watched, those who created effects and those who were imposed on. The theatre was a place where man might attain to the sublimest truths, that is, the highest pitch of emotion, on the wings of

---

[13] After breaking with Wagner, Nietzsche described him as "essentially . . . a man of the theatre and an actor, the most enthusiastic mimomaniac, perhaps, who ever existed, even as a musician."—"Nietzsche contra Wagner" in *The Portable Nietzsche*, tr. Walter Kaufmann, New York, Viking, 1954, p. 665.

illusion. The state was essentially the same—an artwork, an illusion (*Wahn*), in which the reverence offered to the throne, the respect paid to officialdom, and the patriotism felt by the people for a mysterious entity called a fatherland were nothing more or less than theatrical effects, feats of levitation conjured up on the political stage. What was life itself to him but an unrehearsed piece of theatre in need of a stage manager?

Everything he did was determined by his need to create theatre. If he scorned Scribe and Meyerbeer for producing effects without causes, he did so because he knew that profounder, more brilliant, and more disturbing effects could be created by Wagnerian methods. If he was a socialist and revolutionist in his youth, it was because he felt he had to reconstruct society in order to win an audience for his art. If he sank down at the foot of the cross in his old age, he did so in part to exploit Christian prejudices for theatrical purposes. If he resurrected the old heroes and revived the old myths, if he adulated the king and eulogized the state, if he stirred up race prejudice and raked up the coals of a dying religion, he did so, in the final analysis, in order that he might take the stage and bend to his will the emotions he had unleashed. He was a demagogue of the arts to whom the art of moving and stirring the people was the highest art, an all-inclusive art, a religion; and beneath its Juggernaut he was prepared to sacrifice everything except the audience that had to be on hand when he took his curtain call.

ALBERT GOLDMAN and EVERT SPRINCHORN

New York, N.Y.
        and
Poughkeepsie, N.Y.
January, 1964

PART I

*Cultural Decadence of the
Nineteenth Century*

1. Mercury, god of merchants, reigns over modern culture.

THE Romans had a god, Mercury, whom they likened to the Grecian Hermes. But with them his winged mission gained a more practical intent. For them it was the restless diligence of their chaffering and usurious merchants, who streamed from all the ends of the earth into the heart of the Roman world; to bring its luxurious masters, in barter for solid gain, all those delights of sense which their own immediately surrounding Nature could not afford them. To the Roman, surveying its essence and its methods, commerce seemed no more nor less than trickery; and though, by reason of his ever-growing luxury, this world of trade appeared a necessary evil, he cherished a deep contempt for all its doings. Thus Mercury, the god of merchants, became for the Roman the god withal of cheats and sharpers.

This slighted god, however, revenged himself upon the arrogant Romans, and usurped their mastery of the world. For, crown his head with the halo of Christian hypocrisy, decorate his breast with the soulless tokens of dead feudal orders, and ye have in him the god of the modern world, the holy-noble god of "five per cent," the ruler and the master of the ceremonies of our modern "art." Ye may see him embodied in a strait-laced English banker, whose daughter perchance has been given in marriage to a ruined peer. Ye may see him in this gentleman, when he engages the chief singers of the Italian Opera to sing before him in his own drawing room rather than in the theatre, because he will have the glory of paying higher for them here than there; but on no account, even here, on the sacred Sunday. Behold Mercury and his docile handmaid, Modern Art!

This is art, as it now fills the entire civilized world! Its true essence is industry; its ethical aim, the gaining of gold; its æsthetic purpose, the entertainment of those whose time hangs heavily on their hands. From the heart of our modern society, from the golden calf of wholesale speculation, stalled at the meeting of its crossroads, our art sucks forth its life juice, borrows a hollow grace from the lifeless relics of the chivalric conventions of medieval times, and—blushing not to fleece the poor, for all its professions of Christianity—descends to the depths of the proletariat, enervating, demoralizing, and dehumanizing everything on which it sheds its venom.

Its pleasaunce it has set up in the theatre, as did the art of Greece in its maturity; and, indeed, it has a claim upon the theatre: for is it not the expression of our current views of present life? Our modern stage materializes the ruling spirit of our social life, and publishes its daily record in a way that no other branch of art can hope to rival; for it prepares its feasts, night in, night out, in almost every town of Europe. Thus, as the broad-strewn art of drama, it denotes, to all appearance, the flower of our culture; just as the Grecian tragedy denoted the culminating point of the Grecian spirit; but ours is the efflorescence of corruption, of a hollow, soulless, and unnatural condition of human affairs and human relations.

This condition of things we need not further characterize here; we need but honestly search the contents and the workings of our public art, especially that of the stage, in order to see the spirit of the times reflected therein as in a faithful mirror; for such a mirror public art has ever been.

Thus we can by no means recognize in our theatrical art the genuine drama; that one, indivisible, supreme creation of the mind of man. Our theatre merely offers the convenient *locale* for the tempting exhibition of the heterogeneous wares of art manufacture. How incapable is our stage to gather up each branch of art in its highest and most perfect expression—the drama—it shows at once in its division into the two opposing classes, play and opera; whereby the idealizing influence of music is forbidden to the play, and the opera is forestalled of the living heart and lofty purpose of actual drama. Thus on the one hand, the spoken play can never, with but few exceptions, lift itself up to the ideal flight of poetry; but, for very reason of the poverty of its means of utterance—to say nothing of the demoralizing influence of our public life—must fall from height to depth, from the warm atmosphere of passion into the cold element of intrigue. On the other hand, the opera becomes a chaos of sensuous impressions jostling one another without rhyme or reason, from which each one may choose at will what pleases best his fancy; here the alluring movements of a dancer, there the bravura passage of a singer; here the dazzling effect of a triumph of the scene painter, there the astounding efforts of a Vulcan of the orchestra. Do we not read from day to day that this or that new opera is a master-

piece because it contains a goodly number of fine arias and
duets, the instrumentation is extremely brilliant, and so on?
The aim which alone can justify the employment of such complex means—the great dramatic aim—people never give so
much as a thought.

Such verdicts as these are shallow, but honest; they show
exactly what is the position of the audience. There are even
many of our most popular artists who do not in the least con-
ceal the fact that they have no ambition other than to satisfy
this shallow audience. They are wise in their generation; for
when the prince leaves a heavy dinner, the banker a fatiguing
financial operation, the workingman a weary day of toil, and
go to the theatre, they ask for rest, distraction, and amusement, and are in no mood for renewed effort and fresh expenditure of force. This argument is so convincing that we can
only reply by saying: It would be more decorous to employ
for this purpose any other thing in the wide world, but not the
body and soul of art. We shall then be told, however, that if
we do not employ art in this manner, it must perish from out
our public life, that is, that the artist will lose the means of
living.

On this side everything is lamentable, indeed, but candid,
genuine, and honest; civilized corruption, and modern Christian dullness!

But, affairs having undeniably come to such a pass, what
shall we say to the hypocritical pretense of many an art hero
of our times, whose fame is now the order of the day?—when
he dons the melancholy counterfeit of true artistic inspiration:
when he racks his brains for thoughts of deep intent, and ever
seeks fresh food for awe, setting heaven and hell in motion; in
short, when he behaves just like those honest journeymen of
art who avowed that one must *not* be too particular if one
wishes to get rid of one's goods. What shall we say, when these
heroes not only seek to entertain, but expose themselves to all
the peril of fatiguing, in order to be thought profound; when,
too, they renounce all hope of substantial profit, and even—
though only a rich man, born and bred, can afford that!—
spend their own money upon their productions, thus offering
up the highest modern sacrifice? To what purpose this enormous waste? Alas! there yet remains one thing other than gold,
a thing that nowadays a man may buy for gold like any other
pleasure; that thing is *fame!* Yet what sort of fame is there to
reach in our public art? Only the fame of the same publicity
for which this art is planned, and which the fame-lusting man

can never obtain but by submission to its most trivial claims. Thus he deludes both himself and the public, in giving it his piebald artwork; while the public deludes both itself and him, in bestowing on him its applause. But this mutual lie is worthy of the lying nature of modern fame itself; for we are adepts in the art of decking out our own self-seeking passions with the monstrous lies of such sweet-sounding names as "patriotism," "honor," "law and order," and so on.

Yet, why do we deem it necessary so publicly to cheat each one the other? Because, mid all the ruling evils, these notions and these virtues are present still within our conscience; though truly in our *guilty* conscience. For it is sure that where honor and truth are really present, there also is true art at hand. The greatest and most noble minds—whom Æschylus and Sophocles would have greeted with the kiss of brotherhood—for centuries have raised their voices in the wilderness. We have heard their cry, and it lingers still within our ears; but from our base and frivolous hearts we have washed away its living echo. We tremble at their fame, but mock their art. We admit their rank as artists of lofty aim, but rob them of the realization of their artwork; for the one great, genuine work of art they cannot bring to life unaided: we, too, must help them in its birth. The tragedies of Æschylus and Sophocles were the work of Athens!

What boots, then, the fame of these masters? What serves it us that Shakespeare, like a second Creator, has opened for us the endless realm of human nature? What serves it that Beethoven has lent to music the manly, independent strength of poetry? Ask the threadbare caricatures of your theatres, ask the street-minstrel commonplaces of your operas: and ye have your answer! But do ye need to ask? Alas, no! Ye know it right well; indeed, ye would not have it otherwise; ye give yourselves only in the air as though ye knew it not!

What then is your art, and what your drama?

The Revolution of February deprived the Paris theatres of public support; many of them were on the brink of bankruptcy. After the events of June, Cavaignac, busied with the maintenance of the existing order of society, came to their aid and demanded a subvention for their continuance. Why? Because the breadless classes, the prolétariat, would be augmented by the closing of the theatres. So, this interest alone has the state in the stage! It sees in it an industrial workshop, and, to boot, an influence that may calm the passions, absorb the excitement, and divert the threatening agitation of the heated public mind; which broods in deepest discontent, seeking for the way by which dishonored human nature may return to its true self, even though it be at cost of the continuance of our so appropriate theatrical institutions!

Well! the avowal is candid; and on all fours with the frankness of this admission stands the complaint of our modern artists and their hatred for the revolution. Yet what has art in common with these cares and these complaints?

2. The rabble and the Philistines set artistic standards.

OUR theatrical institutions have, in general, no end in view other than to cater for a nightly entertainment, never energetically demanded, but forced down people's throats by the spirit of speculation, and lazily swallowed by the social ennui of the dwellers in our larger cities. Whatever, from a purely artistic standpoint, has rebelled against this mission of the stage has always shown itself too weak for any good. The only regulator of distinctions has been the section for whom this entertainment was to be provided: for the rabble, brought up in tutored grossness, coarse farces and crass montrosities were served; the decorous Philistines of our bourgeoisie were treated to moral family pieces; for the more delicately cultured, and art-spoiled higher and highest classes, only the most elegant art viands were dished up, often garnished with æsthetic quips. The genuine poet, who from time to time sought to make good his claim, among those of the three above-named classes, was always driven back with a taunt peculiar to our theatre public, the taunt of ennui—at least until he had become an antiquarian morsel wherewith conveniently to grace that art repast.

Now, the special feature of our greater theatrical institutions consists in this, that they plan their performances to catch the taste of all 'three classes of the public; they are provided with an auditorium wherein those classes range themselves entirely apart, according to the figure of their entrance money, thus placing the artist in the predicament of seeking out his hearers now among the so-called "gods," now in the pit, and again in the boxes. The director of such institutions, who proximately has no concern other than to make money, has therefore to please each section of his public in its turn: this he arranges, generally with an eye to the business character of the day of the week, by furnishing the most diverse products of the playwright's art, giving today a vulgar burlesque, tomorrow a piece of Philistine sensationalism, and the day after, a toothsome delicacy for the epicures. This still left one thing to be aimed at, namely, from all three mentioned genera to concoct a genre of stage piece which should satisfy the whole public at one stroke. That task the modern opera has with great energy fulfilled; it has thrown the vulgar, the philistinish, and the exquisite into one common pot, and now sets the broth before the entire public, crowded head on head. The opera has thus succeeded in fining down the mob, in vulgarizing the genteel, and finally in turning the whole conglomerate audience into a superfinely mobbish Philistine; who now, in the shape of the theatre public, flings his confused demands into the face of every man who undertakes the guidance of an art institute.

This position of affairs will not give a moment's uneasiness to that stage director whose only business is to charm the money out of the pockets of the "public"; the said problem is solved, even with great tact and never-failing certainty, by every director of the unsubventioned theatres of our large or smaller cities. It operates confusingly, however, upon those who are called by a royal court to manage an exactly similar institution, differing only in that it is lent the court ægis to cover any contingent deficiency in the "takings." In virtue of this protecting ægis, the director of such a court theatre ought to feel bound to look aside from any speculation on the already corrupted taste of the masses, and rather to endeavor to improve that taste by seeing to it that the spirit of the stage performances be governed by the dictates of a higher art intelligence. And, as a matter of fact, such was originally the good intention of enlightened princes, like Joseph II of Austria, in founding their court theatres; as a tradition, it has also been transmitted to the court-theatre intendants even of our later days. Two practical obstacles, however, have stood in the way of realizing this—in itself more munificently chimerical than actually attainable—object: first, the personal incapacity of the appointed intendant, who is chosen from the ranks of court officials mostly without any regard to acquired professional skill, or even so much as natural disposition to artistic sensibility; and second, the impossibility of really dispensing with speculation on the public's taste. In fact, the ampler monetary support of the court theatres has led only to an increase in the price of the artistic matériel, the systematic cultivation whereof, so far as concerns theatric art, has never occurred to the else so education-rabid leaders of our state; and thus the expenses of these institutions have mounted so high that it has become a sheer necessity to the director of a court theatre, beyond all others, to speculate upon the paying public, without whose active help the outlay could not possibly be met. But on the other hand, a successful pursuit of this speculation, in the same sense as that of any other theatrical manager, is made impossible to the distinguished court-theatre intendant by the feeling of his higher mission; a mission, however, which—in his personal incapacity for rightly fathoming its import—has been taken only in the sense of a shadowy court dignity, and could be so interpreted that, for any particularly foolish arrangement, the intendant would excuse himself by saying that in a court theatre this was nobody's business. Thus a modern court theatre intendant's skill can only, and inevitably, result in the perpetual exhibition of a conflict between a second-rate spirit of speculation and a courtier's red-tape arrogance.

3. Criticism of the Vienna Opera House

IF we view the operations of one of the chief musico-dramatic institutes in all Germany, the Imperial Opera House, from *without*, we are faced with a piebald medley of the most diverse products from the most contrasted realms of style; the only thing that clearly comes to sight at first is that not one of these performances bears the stamp of correctness in any respect, and therefore each appears to take the reason for its existence, by no means from anything within itself, but from a fatal outer necessitation. It would be impossible to name a single performance in which end and means had been in thorough harmony: thus in which the lack of talent, the faulty training, or the unfit employment of individual singers; insufficient preparation, and consequent uncertainty of others; raw and spiritless delivery of the choruses, gross blunders in

the staging; an almost total want of balance in the dramatic
action, clumsy and senseless byplay on the part of individuals;
and finally, grave faults and negligences in the reading and
rendering of the music itself, carelessness in its nuancing, want
of harmony between the phrasing of the orchestra and that of
the singers—had not made themselves felt somewhere or other
in a more or less disturbing, and even an offensive manner.
Most of these performances bear the character of a heedless
devil-may-care, against which, as background, the efforts of
single singers to force themselves out of the artistic frame, in
order to gain particular applause for patches of their execution, seem all the more repulsive and give the whole a something of the downright laughable. If the public has grown too
used to the nature of those performances to be aware of anything amiss, so that the faults I complain of may be denied by
habitual operagoers, then we should only have to ask the singers and bandsmen of the theatre themselves, to hear them
admit with one consent how demoralized they feel, how well
they know the ill character of their work in common, and with
what disheartenment they mostly embark on such performances—aware that, insufficiently prepared, they are doomed to
turn out full of faults.

For if we view this theatre from *within*, where we had anticipated laziness and leisure we are suddenly amazed to find a
factory-like excess of labor, overwork, and often an altogether
wonderful endurance beneath the utmost burden of fatigue. I
believe that the abuses practiced on artistic forces at such an
opera house are comparable with no other kind; and among
the most grievous memories of my life I number the experiences reaped in my own person, and especially in that of the
members of the orchestra, under similar circumstances. Just
reflect that the personnel of a first-class band consists, for no
little part, of the only truly musically cultured members of an
opera company; bear in mind again what this means with
German musicians, familiar as they are with the flower of all
musical art, in the works of our great German masters; note
that *these* are the people employed for the lowest uses of art-
industry, for hundredfold rehearsals of the musically emptiest
operas, simply for the toilsome underpropping of unmusical
and ill-trained singers! For my part I avow that in such en-
forced activity in my time, both suffering in myself and suffering with others, I have often learned to mock the torments of
the damned in Dante.

First-rate members of the singing personnel, no doubt, often find themselves exposed to similar tortures; but they have already grown so used to placing themselves outside the general frame that they are less affected by these common griefs. As a rule with them the personal craving for approbation swallows up everything else; and even the better of them at last accustom themselves, amid the general confusion, to shake off any sense of how the singing and acting is going on around them, and pay sole heed to playing their own hand as best they can. In this they are supported by the public, which, consciously or unconsciously, turns its attention away from the ensemble, and devotes it purely to the doings of this or that chief favorite. The first result is that the public losing more and more its feeling for the artwork placed before it, and regarding nothing but the performance of the individual virtuoso, the whole remaining apparatus of an operatic representation is degraded to the level of a superfluous adjunct. The further evil consequence, however, is that the individual singer, now regarded to the exclusion of the whole, arrives at that overbearing attitude toward the institute and its directors which has been known in every age as prima-donna tyranny and suchlike.

4. Italic opera—an excuse for conversation and social gatherings

In the shrill and freqeunt outcry of our shallow musical dilettanti for "Melody, melody!" I find evidence that they take their idea of melody from musical works in which, by side of the melody, there stretches an expanse of unmelodiousness, setting the melody they mean in the light they love so dearly. In the opera house of Italy there gathered an audience which passed its evenings in amusement; part of this amusement was formed by the music sung upon the stage, to which one listened from time to time in pauses of the conversation; during the conversation and visits paid from box to box the music still went on, and with the same office as one assigns to table music at grand dinners, namely, to encourage by its noise the otherwise timid talk. The music which is played with this object, and during this conversation, fills out the virtual bulk of an Italian operatic score; whereas the music which one really listens to makes out perhaps a twelfth part thereof. An Italian opera must contain at least *one* aria to which one is glad to listen; if it is to have a success, the conversation must be broken, and the music listened to with interest, at least six times; whilst the composer who is clever enough to attract the audience's attention a whole twelve times is lauded as an inexhaustible melodic genius. Now, how are we to blame this public if, suddenly confronted with a work which claims a like attention throughout its whole extent and for each of its parts, it sees itself torn from all its habits at musical performances, and cannot possibly take as identical with its beloved melody a thing which in the luckiest event may pass for a mere refinement of that musical noise—that noise whose naïve use before had facilitated the most agreeable interchange of small talk, whereas it now obtrudes the upstart claim of being really heard? It must cry out again and again for its six to twelve melodies, if only to gain the stimulating and protective intervals for conversation, the main end and object of the opera evening.

5. *Paris demanded a ballet in* Tannhäuser.

MY first conference with the director of the Grand Opéra showed me that the introduction of a ballet into *Tannhäuser,* and indeed in the second act, was considered a *sine qua non* of its successful performance. I couldn't fathom the meaning of this requirement, until I had declared that I could not possibly disturb the course of just this second act by a ballet, which must here be senseless from every point of view; while on the other hand I thought the first act, at the voluptuous court of Venus, would afford the most apposite occasion for a choreographic scene of amplest meaning, since I myself had not deemed possible to dispense with dance in my first arrangement of that scene. Indeed, I was quite charmed with the idea of strengthening an undoubtedly weak point in my earlier score, and I drafted an exhaustive plan for raising this scene in the Venusberg to one of great importance. This plan the director most emphatically rejected, telling me frankly that in the production of an opera it was not merely a question of a ballet, but of a ballet to be danced in the middle of the evening's entertainment; for it was only at about this time that the subscribers, to whom the ballet almost exclusively belonged, appeared in their boxes, as they were in the habit of dining very late; a ballet in the opening scene would therefore be of no use to them, since they were never by any chance present for the first act. These and similar admissions were subsequently repeated to me by the Cabinet minister himself, and all possibility of a good result was made so definitely dependent on the said conditions being fulfilled that I began to believe I should have to renounce the whole undertaking. I most carefully revised the score afresh, entirely rewrote the scene of Venus and the ballet scene preceding it, and everywhere sought to bring the vocal parts into closest agreement with the translated text.

Now, as I had made the performance my unique aim, and left every other consideration out of count, so my real trouble at last began with the perception that this performance itself would not attain the height expected by me. It would be hard for me to tell you exactly on what points I had finally to see myself undeceived. The most serious, however, was that the singer of the difficult chief role fell into greater and greater disheartenment the nearer we approached the actual production, in consequence of interviews it had been thought necessary for him to hold with the reporters, who assured him of the inevitable failure of my opera. The most promising hopes, which I had harbored in the course of the pianoforte rehearsals, sank deeper and deeper the more we came in contact with the stage and orchestra. I saw that we were getting back to the dead level of ordinary operatic performances, that all the requirements meant to bear us far above it were doomed to stay unmet. Yet in this sense, which I naturally had disallowed from the first, we lacked the only thing that could confer distinction on such an operatic show: some noted "talent" or other, some tried and trusted favorite of the public; whereas I was making my debut with almost absolute novices. Finally, what most distressed me was that I had not been able to wrest the orchestral conductorship, through which I might still have exercised a great influence on the spirit of performance, from the hands of the official *chef d'orchestre*; and my being thus compelled to mournfully resign myself to a dull and spiritless rendering of my work (for my wish to withdraw the score was not acceded to) is what makes out my genuine trouble even to this day.

Under such circumstances it became almost a matter of indifference to me, what kind of reception my opera would meet
at the hands of the public; the most brilliant could not have
moved me personally to attend a longer series of performances, for I found far too little satisfaction in the thing. But
hitherto you have been diligently kept in ignorance of the true
character of that reception, as it seems to me, and you would
do very wrong if you based thereon a judgment of the Paris
public in general, however flattering to the German, yet in
reality incorrect. On the contrary, I abide by my opinion that
the Paris public has very agreeable qualities, in particular
those of a quick appreciation and a truly magnanimous sense
of justice. A public, I say: a whole audience to which I am a
total stranger, which day by day has heard from the journals
and idle chatterers the most preposterous things about me,
and has been deliberately set against me with well-nigh unexampled care—to see such a public repeatedly taking up the
cudgels in my behalf against a clique, with demonstrations of
applause a quarter of an hour long, must fill me with a warmth
of heart toward it, were I even the most indifferent of men.
But, through the admirable foresight of those who have the
sole distribution of seats on first nights, and who had made it
almost impossible for me to gain admission for my handful of
personal friends, there was assembled on that evening in the
Grand Opera house an audience which every dispassionate
person could see at once was prejudiced in the extreme against
my work; add to this the whole Parisian press, which is always
invited officially on such occasions, and whose hostile attitude
toward me you have simply to read its reports to discover, and
you may well believe that I have a right to speak of a great
victory, when I tell you in all sober earnest that this by no
means exquisite performance of my work met with louder and
more unanimous applause than ever I experienced personally
in Germany.

The actual leaders of an opposition perhaps almost universal at first—several, nay, very likely all of the musical reporters here—who up to then had done their utmost to distract
the attention of the public, were seized toward the end of the
second act by manifest terror of having to witness a complete
and brilliant success of *Tannhäuser*; and now they fell on
the expedient of breaking into roars of laughter after certain
cues, prearranged among themselves at the general rehearsals,
whereby they created a diversion sufficiently disturbing to
damp a considerable manifestation of applause at the curtain's

second fall. These selfsame gentlemen, however, had observed at the stage rehearsals, which I had also not been able to hinder them from attending, that the opera's real success lay guaranteed in the execution of its third act.

At the rehearsals an admirable "set" by Monsieur Despléchin, representing the Wartburg Valley in the light of an autumn evening, had already exerted on everyone present a charm which irresistibly gave birth to the *Stimmung* (mood) requisite for taking in the following scenes; on the part of the performers these scenes were the bright spot in the whole day's work; quite insurpassably was the Pilgrims' Chorus sung and managed; the Prayer of Elisabeth, delivered in its entirety by Fräulein Sax with affecting expression, the "fantasie" to the evening star, rendered by Morelli with perfect elegiac tenderness, so happily prepared the way for the best part of Niemann's performance, his narration of the Pilgrimage— which has always won this artist the liveliest commendation— that a quite exceptional success seemed assured for just this third act, even in the eyes of my most determined adversaries. So this was the act the aforesaid leaders fastened on, trying to hinder any onset of the needful mood of absorption by outbursts of violent laughter, for which the most trivial occasion had to afford the childish pretext. Undeterred by these adverse demonstrations, neither did my singers allow themselves to be put out, nor the public refrain from devoting its sympathetic attention, and often its profuse applause, to their valiant exertions; and at the end, when the performers were vociferously called before the curtain, the opposition was at last entirely beaten down.

That I had made no mistake in viewing this evening's outcome as a complete victory was proved to me by the public's demeanor on the night of the second performance; for here it became manifest with what opposition alone I should have to do in the future, to wit, with that of the Paris Jockey Club— whose name I need not scruple to give you, as the public itself, with its cry "*à la porte les Jockeys*," both openly and loudly denounced my chief opponents. The members of this club— whose right to consider themselves the rulers of the Grand Opéra I need not here explain to you—feeling their interests deeply compromised by the absence of the usual ballet at the hour of their arrival, that is, toward the middle of the representation, were horrified to discover that *Tannhäuser* had *not* made a fiasco, but an actual triumph at its first performance. Henceforth it was their business to prevent this ballet-less opera from being given night after night; to this end, on their way from dinner they had bought a number of dog calls and suchlike instruments, with which they maneuvered against *Tannhäuser* in the most unblushing manner directly they had entered the opera house. Until then, that is to say from the beginning of the first to about the middle of the second act, not a single trace of the first night's opposition had been shown, and the most prolonged applause had undisturbedly accompanied those passages of my opera which had become the speediest favorites. But from now on, no acclamation was of the least avail: in vain did the Emperor himself, with his Consort, demonstrate for a second time in favor of my work; by those who considered themselves masters of the house, and all of whom belong to France's highest aristocracy, the condemnation of *Tannhäuser* was irrevocably pronounced. Whistles and flageolets accompanied every plaudit of the audience, down to the very close.

In view of the management's utter impotence against this powerful club, in view of even the state minister's obvious dread of making serious enemies of its members, I recognized that I had no right to expect my proved and faithful artists of the stage to expose themselves any longer to the abominable agitation put upon them by unscrupulous persons (naturally with the intention of forcing them to throw up their engagements). I told the management that I must withdraw my opera, and consented to a third performance only upon condition that it should take place on a Sunday: that is to say, on a night outside the subscription, and thus under circumstances which would not incur the subscribers' wrath, while on the other hand the house would be left completely clear for the public proper. My wish to have this performance announced on the posters as "the last" was not allowed, and all I could do was personally to inform my acquaintances of the fact.

These precautionary measures, however, were powerless to dissipate the Jockey Club's alarm; on the contrary, it fancied that it detected in this Sunday performance a bold stratagem against its dearest interests, after which—the opera once brought to an unqualified success—the hated work might be forced quite easily down its throat. In the sincerity of my assurance, that in case of such a success I should still more certainly withdraw my work, people hadn't the courage to believe. So the gentlemen forsook their other pleasures for this evening, returned to the Opéra in full battle array, and renewed the scenes of the second night. This time the public's exasperation, at the downright attempt to hinder it from following the opera at all, reached a pitch unknown before, as people have assured me; and it was only the, as it would seem, unassailable social standing of Messieurs Disturbers-of-the-Peace, that saved them from positive rough handling. To put the matter briefly: astonished as I am at the outrageous behavior of those gentlemen, I am equally touched and moved by the real public's heroic exertions to procure me justice; and nothing can be more distant from my mind, than to entertain the smallest doubt of the Paris public whenever it shall find itself on a neutral terrain of its own.

6. Jews in music

IN the *Neue Zeitschrift für Musik* not long ago, mention was made of an "Hebraic art taste": an attack and a defense of that expression neither did, nor could, stay lacking.

Of quite decisive weight for our inquiry is the effect the Jews produce on us through his speech; and this is the essential point at which to sound the Jewish influence upon music. The Jew speaks the language of the nation in whose midst he dwells from generation to generation, but he speaks it always as an alien. As it lies beyond our present scope to occupy ourselves with the cause of this phenomenon, too, we may equally abstain from an arraignment of Christian civilization for having kept the Jew in violent severance from it, as on the other hand, in touching the sequelæ of that severance we can scarcely propose to make the Jews the answerable party. Our only object, here, is to throw light on the æsthetic character of the said results.

In the first place, then, the general circumstance that the Jew talks the modern European languages merely as learned, and not as mother tongues, must necessarily debar him from all capability of therein expressing himself idiomatically, independently, and conformably to his nature. A language, with its expression and its evolution, is not the work of scattered units, but of a historical community; only he who has unconsciously grown up within the bond of this community takes also any share in its creations. But the Jew has stood outside the pale of any such community, stood solitarily with his Jehova in a splintered, soilless stock, to which all self-sprung evolution must stay denied, just as even the peculiar (Hebraic) language of that stock has been preserved for him merely as a thing defunct. Now, to make poetry in a foreign tongue has hitherto been impossible, even to geniuses of highest rank. Our whole European art and civilization, however, have remained to the Jew a foreign tongue; for, just as he has taken no part in the evolution of the one, so has he taken none in that of the other; but at most the homeless wight has been a cold, nay more, a hostile looker-on. In this speech, this art, the Jew can only after-speak and after-patch—not truly make a poem of his words, an artwork of his doings.

Now, if the aforesaid qualities of his dialect make the Jew almost incapable of giving artistic enunciation to his feelings and beholdings through *talk*, for such an enunciation through *song* his aptitude must needs be infinitely smaller. Song is just talk aroused to highest passion: Music is the speech of passion.

The Jew, who is innately incapable of enouncing himself to us artistically through either his outward appearance or his speech, and least of all through his singing, has nevertheless been able in the widest spread of modern art varieties, to wit in music, to reach the rulership of public taste. To explain to ourselves this phenomenon, let us first consider how it grew possible to the Jew to become a musician.

From that turning point in our social evolution where money, with less and less disguise, was raised to the virtual patent of nobility, the Jews—to whom moneymaking without actual labor, that is, usury, had been left as their only trade— the Jews not merely could no longer be denied the diploma of a new society that needed naught but gold, but they brought it with them in their pockets. Wherefore our modern culture, accessible to no one but the well-to-do, remained the less a closed book to them, as it had sunk into a venal article of luxury. Henceforward, then, the cultured Jew appears in our society; his distinction from the uncultured, the common Jew, we now have closely to observe.

The cultured Jew has taken the most indicible pains to strip off all the obvious tokens of his lower coreligionists; in many a case he has even held it wise to make a Christian baptism wash away the traces of his origin. This zeal, however, has never got so far as to let him reap the hoped-for fruits; it has conducted only to his utter isolation, and to making him the most heartless of all human beings; to such a pitch, that we have been bound to lose even our earlier sympathy for the tragic history of his stock. His connection with the former comrades in his suffering, which he arrogantly tore asunder, it has stayed impossible for him to replace by a new connection with that society whereto he has soared up. He stands in correlation with none but those who need his money; and never yet has money thriven to the point of knitting a goodly bond 'twixt man and man. Alien and apathetic stands the educated Jew in midst of a society he does not understand, with whose tastes and aspirations he does not sympathize, whose history and evolution have always been indifferent to him. In such a situation have we seen the Jews give birth to thinkers; the thinker is the backward-looking poet; but the true poet is the foretelling prophet. For such a prophet-charge can naught equip, save the deepest, the most heartfelt sympathy with a great, a like-endeavoring community—to whose unconscious thoughts the poet gives exponent voice. Completely shut from this community, by the very nature of his situation; entirely torn from all connection with his native stock—to the genteeler Jew his learned and paid-for culture could only seem a luxury, since at bottom he knew not what to be about with it.

Now, our modern arts had likewise become a portion of this culture, and among them more particularly that art which is just the very easiest to learn—the art of music, and indeed *that* music which, severed from her sister arts, had been lifted by the force and stress of grandest geniuses to a stage in her universal faculty of expression where either, in new conjunction with the other arts, she might speak aloud the most sublime, or, in persistent separation from them, she could also speak at will the deepest bathos of the trivial. Naturally, what the cultured Jew had to speak, in his aforesaid situation, could be nothing but the trivial and indifferent, because his whole artistic bent was in sooth a mere luxurious, needless thing. Exactly as his whim inspired, or some interest lying outside art, could he utter himself now thus, and now otherwise; for never was he driven to speak out a definite, a real and necessary thing; he just merely wanted to speak, no matter what; so that, naturally, the *how* was the only "moment" left for him to care for. At present no art affords such plenteous possibility of talking in it without saying any real thing, as that of music, since the greatest geniuses have already said whatever there was to say in it as an absolute, separate art. When this had once been spoken out, there was nothing left but to babble after; and indeed with quite, distressing accuracy and deceptive likeness, just as parrots reel off human words and phrases, but also with just as little real feeling and expression as these foolish birds. Only, in the case of our Jewish music-makers this mimicked speech presents one marked peculiarity—that of the Jewish style of talk in general, which we have more minutely characterized above.

Although the peculiarities of the Jewish mode of speaking and singing come out the most glaringly in the commoner class of Jew, who has remained faithful to his fathers' stock, and though the cultured son of Jewry takes untold pains to strip them off, nevertheless they show an impertinent obstinacy in cleaving to him. Explain this mishap by physiology as we may, yet it also has its reason in the aforesaid social situation of the educated Jew. However much our luxury art may float in well-nigh nothing but the ether of our self-willed fantasy, still it keeps below one fiber of connection with its natural soil, with the genuine spirit of the folk. The true poet, no matter in what branch of art, still gains his stimulus from nothing but a faithful, loving contemplation of instinctive life, of that life which only greets his sight amid the folk. Now, where is the cultured Jew to find this folk? Not, surely, on the soil of that society in which he plays his artist role? If he has any connection at all with this society, it is merely with that offshoot of it, entirely loosened from the real, the healthy stem; but this connection is entirely loveless, and this lovelessness must ever become more obvious to him, if for sake of foodstuff for his art he clambers down to that society's foundations. Not only does he here find everything more strange and unintelligible, but the instinctive ill-will of the folk confronts him here in all its wounding nakedness, since—unlike its fellow in the richer classes—it here is neither weakened down nor broken by reckonings of advantage and regard for certain mutual interests. Thrust back with contumely from any contact with this folk, and in any case completely powerless to seize its spirit, the cultured Jew sees himself driven to the taproot of his native stem, where at least an understanding would come by all means easier to him. Willy-nilly he must draw his water from this well; yet only a *how*, and not a *what*, rewards his pains.

The Jew has never had an art of his own, hence never a life of art-enabling import: an import, a universally applicable, a human import, not even today does it offer to the searcher, but merely a peculiar method of expression—and that, the method we have characterized above. Now, the only musical expression offered to the Jew tone-setter by his native folk is the ceremonial music of their Jehova rites: the synagogue is the solitary fountain whence the Jew can draw art motives at once popular and *intelligible to himself*. However sublime and noble we may be minded to picture to ourselves this musical Service of God in its pristine purity, all the more plainly must we perceive that that purity has been most terribly sullied before it came down to us: here for thousands of years has nothing unfolded itself through an inner life-fill, but, just as with Judaism at large, everything has kept its fixity of form and substance. But a form which is never quickened through renewal of its substance must fall to pieces in the end; an expression whose content has long since ceased to be the breath of feeling grows senseless and distorted.

Who has not had occasion to convince himself of the travesty of a divine service of song, presented in a real folk synagogue? Who has not been seized with a feeling of the greatest revulsion, of horror mingled with the absurd, at hearing that sense-and-sound-confounding gurgle, yodel, and cackle, which no intentional caricature can make more repugnant than as offered here in full, in naïve seriousness? In latter days, indeed, the spirit of reform has shown its stir within this singing, too, by an attempted restoration of the older purity; but, of its very nature, what here has happened on the part of the higher, the reflective Jewish intellect is just a fruitless effort from above, which can never strike below to such a point that the cultured Jew—who precisely for his art needs seeks the genuine fount of life amid the folk—may be greeted by the mirror of his intellectual efforts in that fount itself. He seeks for the instinctive, and not the reflected, since the latter is *his* product; and all the instinctive he can light on is just that out-of-joint expression.

If this going back to the folk source is as unpurposed with the cultured Jew, as unconsciously enjoined upon him by necessity and the nature of the thing, as with every artist, with just as little conscious aim, and therefore with an insuperable domination of his whole field of view, does the hence-derived impression carry itself across into his art productions. Those rhythms and melismata of the synagogue song usurp his musical fancy in exactly the same way as the instinctive possession of the strains and rhythms of our folk song and folk dance made out the virtual shaping force of the creators of our art music, both vocal and instrumental. To the musical perceptive faculty of the cultured Jew there is therefore nothing seizable in all the ample circle of our music, either popular or artistic, but that which flatters his general sense of the intelligible: intelligible, however, and so intelligible that he may use it for his art, is merely that which in any degree approaches a resemblance to the said peculiarity of Jewish music.

In listening to either our naïve or our consciously artistic musical doings, however, were the Jew to try to probe their heart and living sinews, he would find here really not one whit of likeness to *his* musical nature; and the utter strangeness of this phenomenon must scare him back so far that he could never pluck up nerve again to mingle in our art creating. Yet his whole position in our midst never tempts the Jew to so intimate a glimpse into our essence: wherefore, either intentionally (provided he recognizes this position of his toward us) or instinctively (if he is incapable of understanding us at all), he merely listens to the barest surface of our art, but not to its life-bestowing inner organism; and through this apathetic listening alone can he trace external similarities with the only thing intelligible to his power of view, peculiar to his special nature. To him, therefore, the most external accidents on our domain of musical life and art must pass for its very essence; and therefore, when as artist he reflects them back upon us, his adaptations needs must seem to us outlandish, odd, indifferent, cold, unnatural, and awry; so that Judaic works of music often produce on us the impression as though a poem of Goethe's, for instance, were being rendered in the Jewish jargon.

Just as words and constructions are hurled together in this jargon with wondrous inexpressiveness, so does the Jew musician hurl together the diverse forms and styles of every age and every master. Packed side by side, we find the formal idiosyncrasies of all the schools, in motleyest chaos. As in these productions the sole concern is talking at all hazards, and not the object which might make that talk worth doing, so this clatter can only be made at all inciting to the ear by its offering at each instant a new summons to attention, through a change of outer expressional means. Inner agitation, genuine passion, each finds its own peculiar language at the instant when, struggling for an understanding, it girds itself for utterance: the Jew, already characterized by us in this regard, has no true passion, and least of all a passion that might thrust him on to art creation. But where this passion is not forthcoming, *there* neither is any calm: true, noble calm is nothing else than passion mollified through resignation. Where the calm has not been ushered in by passion, we perceive naught but sluggishness: the opposite of sluggishness, however, is nothing but that prickling unrest which we observe in Jewish music-works from one end to the other, saving where it makes place for that soulless, feelingless inertia. What issues from the Jews' attempts at making art must necessarily therefore bear the attributes of coldness and indifference, even to triviality and absurdity; and in the history of modern music we can but class the Judaic period as that of final unproductivity, of stability gone to ruin.

By what example will this all grow clearer to us—ay, well-nigh what other single case could make us so alive to it, as the works of a musician of Jewish birth whom Nature had endowed with specific musical gifts as very few before him? All that offered itself to our gaze, in the inquiry into our antipathy against the Jewish nature; all the contradictoriness of this nature, both in itself and as touching us; all its inability, while outside our footing, to have intercourse with us upon that footing, nay, even to form a wish to develop further the things which had sprung from out our soil: all these are intensified to a positively tragic conflict in the nature, life, and art career of the early-taken Felix Mendelssohn Bartholdy. He has shown us that a Jew may have the amplest store of specific talents, may own the finest and most varied culture, the highest and the tenderest sense of honor—yet without all these preeminences helping him, were it but one single time, to call forth in us that deep, that heart-searching effect which we await from art because we know her capable thereof, because we have felt it many a time and oft, so soon as once a hero of our art has, so to say, but opened his mouth to speak to us.

To professional critics, who haply have reached a like consciousness with ourselves hereon, it may be left to prove by specimens of Mendelssohn's art products our statement of this indubitably certain thing; by way of illustrating our general

impression, let us here be content with the fact that, in hearing
a tone-piece of this composer's, we have only been able to feel
engrossed where nothing beyond our more or less amusement-
craving fantasy was roused through the presentment, stringing
together, and entanglement of the most elegant, the smoothest
and most polished figures—as in the kaleidoscope's changeful
play of form and color—but never where those figures were
meant to take the shape of deep and stalwart feelings of the
human heart. In this latter event Mendelssohn lost even all
formal productive faculty; wherefore in particular, where he
made for drama, as in the oratorio, he was obliged quite
openly to snatch at every formal detail that had served as
characteristic token of the individuality of this or that forerunner whom he chose out for his model. It is further significant of this procedure, that he gave the preference to our old
master Bach, as special pattern for his inexpressive modern
tongue to copy. Bach's language can be mimicked, at a pinch,
by any musician who thoroughly understands his business,
though scarcely in the sense of Bach; because the formal has
still therein the upper hand, and the purely human expression
is not as yet a factor so definitely preponderant that its *what*
either can or must be uttered without conditions, for it still is
fully occupied with shaping out the *how*. The washiness and
whimsicality of our present musical style has been, if not exactly brought about, yet pushed to its utmost pitch by Mendelssohn's endeavor to speak out a vague, an almost nugatory
content as interestingly and spiritedly as possible.

I said above, the Jews had brought forth no true poet. We
here must give a moment's mention, then, to Heinrich Heine.
At the time when Goethe and Schiller sang among us, we certainly know nothing of a poetizing Jew: at the time, however,
when our poetry became a lie, when every possible thing might
flourish from the wholly unpoetic element of our life, but no
true poet—then was it the office of a highly gifted poet-Jew
to bare with fascinating taunts that lie, that bottomless aridity
and jesuitical hypocrisy of our versifying which still would
give itself the airs of true poesis. His famous musical con-
geners, too, he mercilessly lashed for their pretense to pass as
artists; no make-believe could hold its ground before him: by
the remorseless demon of denial of all that seemed worth
denying was he driven on without a rest, through all the
mirage of our modern self-deception, till he reached the point
where in turn he duped himself into a poet, and was rewarded

by his versified lies being set to music by our own composers. He was the conscience of Judaism, just as Judaism is the evil conscience of our modern civilization.

7. Christian hypocrisy

CHRISTIANITY adjusts the ills of an honorless, useless, and sorrowful existence of mankind on earth, by the miraculous love of God; who had not—as the noble Greek supposed—created man for a happy and self-conscious life upon this earth, but had here imprisoned him in a loathsome dungeon: so as, in reward for the self-contempt that poisoned him therein, to prepare him for a posthumous state of endless comfort and inactive ecstasy. Man was therefore bound to remain in this deepest and unmanliest degradation, and no activity of this present life should he exercise; for this accursed life was, in truth, the world of the devil, that is, of the senses; and by every action in it he played into the devil's hands. Therefore the poor wretch who, in the enjoyment of his natural powers, made this life his own possession must suffer after death the eternal torments of hell! Naught was required of mankind but faith—that is to say, the confession of its miserable plight, and the giving up of all spontaneous attempt to escape from out this misery; for the *undeserved Grace* of God was alone to set it free.

The historian knows not surely that this was the view of the humble son of the Galilean carpenter; who, looking on the misery of his fellow men, proclaimed that he had not come to bring peace, but a sword into the world; whom we must love for the anger with which he thundered forth against the hypocritical Pharisees who fawned upon the power of Rome, so as the better to bind and heartlessly enslave the people; and finally, who preached the reign of universal human love—a love he could never have enjoined on men whose duty it should be to despise their fellows and themselves. The inquirer more clearly discerns the hand of the miraculously converted Pharisee, Paul, and the zeal with which, in his conversion of the heathen, he followed so successfully the monition: "Be ye wise as serpents . . . ;" he may also estimate the deep and uni-

versal degradation of civilized mankind, and see in this the historical soil from which the full-grown tree of finally developed
Christian dogma drew forth the sap that fed its fruit. But thus
much the candid artist perceives at the first glance: that neither
was Christianity art, nor could it ever bring forth from itself
the true and living art.

The free Greek, who set himself upon the pinnacle of Nature, could procreate art from very joy in manhood: the Christian, who impartially cast aside both Nature and himself,
could only sacrifice to his God on the altar of renunciation; he
durst not bring his actions or his work as offering, but believed that he must seek His favor by abstinence from all self-
prompted venture. Art is the highest expression of activity of
a race that has developed its physical beauty in unison with
itself and Nature; and man must reap the highest joy from the
world of sense, before he can mold therefrom the implements
of his art; for from the world of sense alone can he derive so
much as the impulse to artistic creation. The Christian, on the
contrary, if he fain would create an artwork that should correspond to his belief, must derive his impulse from the essence
of abstract spirit, from the grace of God, and therein find his
tools. What, then, could he take for aim? Surely not physical
beauty—mirrored in his eyes as an incarnation of the devil?
And how could pure spirit, at any time, give birth to a something that could be cognized by the senses?

All pondering of this problem is fruitless; the course of history shows too unmistakably the results of these two opposite
methods. Where the Greeks, for their edification, gathered in
the amphitheatre for the space of a few short hours full of
the deepest meaning, the Christian shut himself away in the
lifelong imprisonment of a cloister. In the one case, the Popular Assembly was the judge: in the other, the Inquisition; here
the state developed to an honorable democracy: there, to a
hypocritical despotism.

Hypocrisy is the salient feature, the peculiar characteristic,
of every century of our Christian era, right down to our own
day; and indeed this vice has always stalked abroad with more
crying shamelessness, in direct proportion as mankind, in spite
of Christendom, has refreshed its vigor from its own unquenchable and inner wellspring, and ripened toward the
fulfillment of its true purpose. Nature is so strong, so inexhaustible in its regenerative resources, that no conceivable violence could weaken its creative force. Into the ebbing veins of
the Roman world, there poured the healthy blood of the fresh

Germanic nations. Despite the adoption of Christianity, a ceaseless thirst of doing, delight in bold adventure, and unbounded self-reliance remained the native element of the new masters of the world. But, as in the whole history of the Middle Ages we always light upon one prominent factor, the warfare between worldly might and the despotism of the Roman Church: so, when this new world sought for a form of utterance, it could find it only in opposition to, and strife against, the spirit of Christendom.

The art of Christian Europe could never proclaim itself, like that of ancient Greece, as the expression of a world attuned to harmony; for reason that its inmost being was incurably and irreconcilably split up between the force of conscience and the instinct of life, between the ideal and the reality. Like the order of chivalry itself, the chivalric poetry of the Middle Ages, in attempting to heal this severance, could, even amid its loftiest imagery, but bring to light the falsehood of the reconciliation; the higher and the more proudly it soared on high, so the more visibly gaped the abyss between the actual life and the idealized existence, between the raw, passionate bearing of these knights in physical life and their too delicate, etherealized behavior in romance. For the same reason did actual life, leaving the pristine, noble, and certainly not ungraceful customs of the people, become corrupt and vicious; for it durst not draw the nourishment for its art impulse from out of its own being, its joy in itself, and its own physical demeanor; but was sent for all its spiritual sustenance to Christianity, which warned it off from the first taste of life's delight, as from a thing accursed. The poetry of chivalry was thus the honorable hypocrisy of fanaticism, the parody of heroism: in place of Nature, it offered a convention.

Only when the enthusiasm of belief had smoldered down, when the Church openly proclaimed herself as naught but a worldly despotism appreciable by the senses, in alliance with the no less material worldly absolutism of the temporal rule which she had sanctified: only then commenced the so-called renaissance of art. That wherewith man had racked his brains so long he would fain now see before him clad in body, like the Church itself in all its worldly pomp. But this was only possible on condition that he opened his eyes once more, and restored his senses to their rights. Yet when man took the objects of belief and the revelations of fantasy and set them before his eyes in physical beauty, and with the artist's delight in that physical beauty—this was a complete denial of the very essence of the Christian religion; and it was the deepest humiliation to Christendom that the guidance to these art creations must be sought from the pagan art of Greece. Nevertheless, the Church appropriated to herself this newly roused art impulse, and did not blush to deck herself with the borrowed plumes of paganism; thus trumpeting her own hypocrisy.

Worldly dominion, however, had its share also in the revival of art. After centuries of combat, their power armed against all danger from below, the security of riches awoke in the ruling classes the desire for more refined enjoyment of this wealth; they took into their pay the arts whose lessons Greece had taught. *"Free"* art now served as handmaid to these exalted masters, and, looking into the matter more closely, it is difficult to decide who was the greater hypocrite: Louis XIV, when he sat and heard the Grecian hate of tyrants, declaimed in polished verses from the boards of his court theatre; or Corneille and Racine, when, to win the favor of their lord, they set in the mouths of their stage heroes the warm words of freedom and political virtue, of ancient Greece and Rome.

8. Contrast between the present-day theatre and the Greek

I HAD received the most urgent personal provocation to seek an explanation of the modern theatre's unalterable character in its social situation. 'Twere a mad attempt, undoubtedly, to take an institute whose public function was almost exclusively directed to the distraction and amusement of people bored to death by pleasure—and further, to earning money to cover the cost of exhibitions reckoned for that end—and employ it for a diametrically opposite object, namely, the snatching of a populace from out its vulgar interests of everyday, to attune it to a reverent reception of the highest and sincerest things the human mind can grasp. I had time enough to think out the reasons for that attitude of our theatre toward the Public, and on the other hand to ponder the bases of those social relations which themselves should form the conditions for the appearance of the theatre I had in mind, with the same necessity as that theatre of ours had issued from our modern relations.

Just as I had won a solid anchorage for the character of my dramatico-musical ideal in the rare and isolated doings of bril-

liant artists, so history supplied me with a typical model for
that ideal relation, dreamed by me, of theatre and public. I
found it in the theatre of ancient Athens, where its walls were
thrown open on none but special, sacred feast days, where the
taste of art was coupled with the celebration of a religious rite
in which the most illustrious members of the state themselves
took part as poets and performers, to appear like priests before the assembled populace of field and city; a populace filled
with such high awaitings from the sublimeness of the artwork
to be set before it, that a Sophocles, an Æschylus could set
before the folk the deepest-meaning of all poems, assured of
their understanding.

With the Greeks the perfect work of art, the drama, was the
abstract and epitome of all that was expressible in the Grecian
nature. It was the nation itself—in intimate connection with its
own history—that stood mirrored in its artwork, that com-
muned with itself and, within the span of a few hours, feasted
its eyes with its own noblest essence. All division of this enjoyment, all scattering of the forces concentered on *one* point, all
diversion of the elements into separate channels, must needs
have been as hurtful to this *unique* and noble artwork as to
the like-formed state itself; and thus it could only mature, but
never change its nature. Thus art was conservative, just as the
noblest sons of this epoch of the Grecian State were themselves conservative. Æschylus is the very type of this con-
servatism, and his loftiest work of conservative art is the
Oresteia, with which he stands alike opposed as poet to the
youthful Sophocles, as statesman to the revolutionary Pericles.
The victory of Sophocles, like that of Pericles, was fully in the
spirit of the advancing development of mankind; but the depo-
sition of Æschylus was the first downward step from the
height of Grecian tragedy, the first beginning of the dissolution
of Athenian polity.

9. The dissolution of the drama

WITH the subsequent downfall of tragedy, art became less and
less the expression of the public conscience. The drama separated into its component parts—rhetoric, sculpture, painting,
music, and so on, forsook the ranks in which they had moved
in unison before; each one to take its own way, and in lonely

self-sufficiency to pursue its own development. And thus it was that at the Renaissance of art we lit first upon these isolated Grecian arts, which had sprung from the wreck of tragedy. The great unitarian artwork of Greece could not at once reveal itself to our bewildered, wandering, piecemeal minds in all its fullness; for how could we have understood it? But we knew how to appropriate those dissevered handiworks of art; for as goodly handiwork, to which category they had already sunk in the Roman-Greek world, they lay not so far from our own nature and our minds. The guild and handicraft spirit of the new citizenship rose quick and lively in the towns; princes and notabilities were well pleased that their castles should be more becomingly built and decorated, their walls bedecked with more attractive paintings, than had been possible to the raw art of the Middle Ages; the priests laid hands on rhetoric for their pulpits and music for their choirs; and the new world of handicraft worked valiantly among the separate arts of Greece, so far at least as it understood them or thought them fitted to its purpose.

Each one of these dissevered arts, nursed and luxuriously tended for the entertainment of the rich, has filled the world to overflowing with its products; in each, great minds have brought forth marvels; but the one true art has not been born again, either in or since the Renaissance. The perfect artwork, the great united utterance of a free and lovely public life, the drama, tragedy—howsoever great the poets who have here and there indited tragedies—is not yet born again: for reason that it cannot be *reborn*, but must be *born anew*.

Only the great Revolution of Mankind, whose beginnings erstwhile shattered Grecian tragedy, can win for us this artwork. For only this revolution can bring forth from its hidden depths, in the new beauty of a nobler universalism, that which it once tore from the conservative spirit of a time of beautiful but narrow-meted culture—and tearing it, engulfed.

10. The necessity of revolution

BUT only revolution, not slavish restoration, can give us back that highest artwork. The task we have before us is immeasurably greater than that already accomplished in days of old.

If the Grecian artwork embraced the spirit of a fair and noble nation, the artwork of the future must embrace the spirit of a free mankind, delivered from every shackle of hampering nationality; its racial imprint must be no more than an embellishment, the individual charm of manifold diversity, and not a cramping barrier. We have thus quite other work to do than to tinker at the resuscitation of old Greece. Indeed, the foolish restoration of a sham Greek mode of art has been attempted already—for what will our artists not attempt, to order? But nothing better than an inane patchwork could ever come of it —the offspring of the same juggling endeavor which we find evinced by the whole history of our official civilization, seized as it is with a constant wish to avoid the only lawful endeavor, the striving after Nature.

No, we do not wish to revert to Greekdom; for what the Greeks knew not, and, knowing not, came by their downfall: that know we. It is their very fall, whose cause we now perceive after years of misery and deepest universal suffering, that shows us clearly what we should become; it shows us that we must love all men before we can rightly love ourselves, before we can regain true joy in our own personality. From the dishonoring slave yoke of universal journeymanhood, with its sickly money soul, we wish to soar to the free manhood of art, with the star rays of its world soul; from the weary, over-burdened day laborers of commerce, we desire to grow to fair strong men, to whom the world belongs as an eternal, inexhaustible source of the highest delights of art.

To this end we need the mightiest force of revolution; for only that revolutionary force can help us which presses forward to the goal—to that goal whose attainment alone can justify its earliest exercise upon the disintegration of Greek tragedy and the dissolution of the Athenian State.

But whence shall we derive this force, in our present state of utmost weakness? Whence the manly strength against the crushing pressure of a civilization which disowns all manhood, against the arrogance of a culture which employs the human mind as naught but steampower for its machinery? Whence the light with which to illumine the gruesome ruling heresy, that this civilization and this culture are of more value in themselves than the true living man?—that man has worth and value only as a tool of these despotic abstract powers, and not by virtue of his manhood?

When the learned physician is at the end of his resources, in despair we turn at last to Nature. Nature, then, and only

Nature, can unravel the skein of this great world fate. If Culture, starting from the Christian dogma of the worthlessness of human nature, disown humanity, she has created for herself a foe who one day must inevitably destroy her, in so far as she no longer has place for manhood; for this foe is the eternal, and only living Nature. Nature, Human Nature, will proclaim this law to the twin sisters Culture and Civilization: "So far as I am contained in you, shall ye live and flourish; so far as I am not in you, shall ye rot and die!"

In the man-destroying march of Culture, however, there looms before us this happy result: the heavy load with which she presses Nature down will one day grow so ponderous that it lends at last to downtrod, never-dying Nature the necessary impetus to hurl the whole cramping burden from her, with one sole thrust; and this heaping up of Culture will thus have taught to Nature her own gigantic force. The releasing of this force is—*revolution.*

In what way, then, does this revolutionary force exhibit itself in the present social crisis? Is it not in the mechanic's pride in the moral consciousness of his labor, as opposed to the criminal passivity or immoral activity of the rich? Does he not wish, as in revenge, to elevate the principle of labor to the rank of the one and orthodox religion of society? To force the rich, like him, to work—like him, by the sweat of their brow to gain their daily bread? Must we not fear that the exercise of this compulsion, the recognition of this principle, would raise at last the man-degrading journeymanhood to an absolute and universal might, and—to keep to our chief theme—would straightway make of art an impossibility for all time?

In truth, this is the fear of many an honest friend of art and many an upright friend of men, whose only wish is to preserve the nobler core of our present civilization. But they mistake the true nature of the great social agitation. They are led astray by the windy theories of our socialistic doctrinaires, who would fain patch up an impossible compact with the present conditions of society. They are deceived by the immediate utterance of the indignation of the most suffering portion of our social system, behind which lies a deeper, nobler, natural instinct: the instinct which demands a worthy taste of the joys of life, whose material sustenance shall no longer absorb man's whole life forces in weary service, but in which he shall rejoice as man. Viewed closer, it is thus the straining from journeymanhood to artistic manhood, to the free dignity of man.

It is for art therefore, and art above all else, to teach this social impulse its noblest meaning, and guide it toward its true direction. Only on the shoulders of this great social movement can true art lift itself from its present state of civilized barbarianism, and take its post of honor. Each has a common goal, and the twain can reach it only when they recognize it jointly. This goal is the strong fair man, to whom revolution shall give his strength, and art his beauty!

11. What is Utopia?

"UTOPIA! Utopia!" I hear the mealymouthed wiseacres of our modern state-and-art barbarianism cry; the so-called practical men, who in the manipulation of their daily practice can help themselves alone with lies and violence, or—if they be sincere and honest—with ignorance at best.

"Beautiful ideal! but, alas! like all ideals, one that can only float before us, beyond the reach of man condemned to imperfection." Thus sighs the smug adorer of the heavenly kingdom in which—at least as far as himself is concerned—God will make good the inexplicable shortcomings of this earth and its human brood.

They live and lie, they sin and suffer, in the loathliest of actual conditions, in the filthy dregs of an artificial, and therefore never realized Utopia; they toil and overbid each other in every hypocritical art, to maintain the cheat of this Utopia; from which they daily tumble headlong down to the dull, prosaic level of nakedest reality—the mutilated cripples of the meanest and most frivolous of passions. Yet they cry down the only natural release from their bewitchment, as "chimeras" or "Utopias"; just as the poor sufferers in a madhouse take their insane imaginings for truth, and truth itself for madness.

If history knows an actual Utopia, a truly unattainable ideal, it is that of Christendom; for it has clearly and plainly shown, and shows it still from day to day, that its dogmas are *not* realizable. How could those dogmas become really living, and pass over into actual life, when they were directed against life itself, and denied and cursed the principle of living? Christianity is of purely spiritual, and superspiritual contents; it preaches humility, renunciation, contempt of every earthly thing; and amid this contempt—brotherly love! How does the fulfillment work out in the modern world, which calls itself, forsooth, a Christian world, and clings to the Christian religion as its inexpugnable basis? As the arrogance of hypocrisy, as usury, as robbery of Nature's goods, and egoistic scorn of suffering fellow men.

Men cry "Utopia," when the healthy human understanding appeals from their insane experiments to the actuality of visible and tangible Nature; when it demands no more from man's godlike reason than that it should make good to us the instinct of dumb animals, and give us the means of finding for ourselves the sustenance of our life, set free from care though not from labor! And, truly, we ask from it no higher result for the community of mankind, in order that we may build upon this one foundation the noblest, fairest temple of the true art of the future!

When human fellowship has once developed its manly beauty and nobility—in such a way as we shall not attain, however, by the influence of our art alone, but as we must hope and strive for by union with the great and inevitably approaching social revolution—then will theatrical performances be the first associate undertaking from which the idea of wage or gain shall disappear entirely. For when, under the above conditions, our education more and more becomes an artistic one, then shall we be ourselves all thus far artists: that we can join together in free and common service for the one great cause of art, in its special manifestment, abandoning each sidelong glance at gain.

Art and its institutes, whose desired organization could here be only briefly touched on, would thus become the herald and the standard of all future communal institutions. The spirit that urges a body of artists to the attainment of its own true goal would be found again in every other social union which set before itself a definite and honorable aim; for if we reach the right, then all our future social bearing cannot but be of pure artistic nature, such as alone befits the noble faculties of man.

Thus would Jesus have shown us that we all alike are men and brothers; while Apollo would have stamped this mighty bond of brotherhood with the seal of strength and beauty, and led mankind from doubt of its own worth to consciousness of its highest godlike might. Let us therefore erect the altar of the future, in life as in the living art, to the two sublimest teachers of mankind: Jesus, who suffered for all men; and Apollo, who raised them to their joyous dignity!

12. The Revolution*

IF we peer across its lands and peoples, we find throughout the whole of Europe the effervescence of a mighty movement, whose first vibrations have already reached us, whose full weight threatens soon to crash upon us. Europe seems to us a huge volcano, from whose inside an ever-waxing fearsome roar resounds, from out whose crater columns of black smoke ascend to heaven big with storm, and mantle all the earth with darkness, while here and there a lava stream, a fiery harbinger, breaks through the hard-set crust and bears destruction to the vale below.

A supernatural force seems clutching at our quarter of the globe, intent on lifting it from its old rut and hurling it to pathways new.

Ay, we behold it; the old world is crumbling, a new will rise therefrom; for the lofty goddess Revolution comes rustling on the wings of storm, her stately head ringed round with lightnings, a sword in her right hand, a torch in her left, her eye so stern, so punitive, so cold; and yet what warmth of purest love, what wealth of happiness streams forth toward him who dares to look with steadfast gaze into that eye! Rustling she comes, the e'er-rejuvenating mother of mankind; destroying and fulfilling, she fares across the earth; before her soughs the storm, and shakes so fiercely at man's handiwork that vasty clouds of dust eclipse the sky, and where her mighty foot steps falls in ruins what an idle whim had built for æons, and the hem of her robe sweeps its last remains away. But in her wake there opens out a ne'er-dreamed paradise of happiness, illumed by kindly sunbeams; and where her foot had trodden down, spring fragrant flowers from the soil, and jubilant songs of freed mankind fill full the air scarce silent from the din of battle.

* Written in April 1849.—EDS.

Now turn and look below, around you. There you see one, the mightiest prince, with halting heart and catching breath, yet seeking to assume a tranquil, cool demeanor, to shut his eyes and those of others to what he clearly sees to be inevitable. There see another, his leathern face all plowed by vices, exerting all those petty sharper's arts that have brought him in so many a titlet, so many an order's crosslet; you see him with his diplomatic smile and air of mystery among the teeth-nipped lordlings, the ladylings all snatching at their smelling-salts, whom he tries to reassure by half-official information that highest personages have deigned to pay attention to this strange phenomenon, that couriers have been sent already to various parts with Cabinet orders, that the advice of that wise government-artist Metternich is even on the road from London, that the right authorities have had instructions all around, and accordingly the interesting surprise is in preparation for high-born society, at the next court ball, of taking a peep at this horrid vagrant Revolution—of course in an iron cage and fetters.

There see a third man, speculating on the approach of the apparition, running off to the Bourse, minutely reckoning the rise and fall of bondlets, higgling and haggling, alert to catch the least per-centlet, till all his plunder scatters to the winds. There, behind the dusty office desk, you see one of those warped and rusted wheels of our present state machine, scratching away with its stump of a quill, and doing its unceasing best to add fresh lumber to a paper world. Between these files of documents and contracts the hearts of live humanity are pressed like gathered leaves, and fall to powder in these modern torture rooms. Here rules a strenuous activity, for the web outspun across the continent is torn in many a corner, and the startled spiders are busy knitting up fresh threads to rectify the holes. Here not a ray of light breaks in, here reign eternal night and darkness; and into night and darkness will the whole dissolve.

But listen! from that side there sounds shrill warlike music, swords flash and bayonets, heavy guns clatter past, and serried ranks of troops unroll their length. The valiant host of heroes has set out for its brush with Revolution. The general bids march to right and left, here stations infantry, there cavalry, and wisely parcels out his bristling columns and his dread artillery; and Revolution comes apace, her head high in the clouds—they see her not, but wait for the foe; and she stands already in their midst—they see her not, still waiting for the foe; and she has seized them in her mighty whirlwind, has scattered the ranks, dispersed the force which craft had stolen —but the general he sits there, absorbed in his map, and calculating from which side the foe may be expected, and what his strength, and when he will arrive!

Stay! there you see a troubled face: an upright, thrifty burgher it belongs to. He has toiled and moiled his whole life long, has honestly cared for the weal of all, so far as lay within his power; no shame, no wrong attaches to the mite his useful diligence has earned, to keep himself in feeble age, to give his sons a footing in this joyless life. He feels indeed the advent of the storm; he knows full well that no force can withstand it; yet his heart is sad when he looks back upon his life of hardships, whose only fruit is destined to destruction. We cannot gird at him, if timidly he grapples to his hoard, if futilely he puts forth all his blindfold strength 'gainst the invader. Unhappy man! uplift thine eyes; look up to where a thousand thousands gather on the hills in joyous expectation of the dawn! Regard them; they are all thy brothers, sisters, the troops of those poor wights who hitherto knew naught of life but suffering, have been but strangers on this earth of joy; they all are waiting for that Revolution which affrights thee, their redemptrix from this world of sorrow, creatrix of a new world blessing all!

See there, there stream the legions from the factories; they've made and fashioned lordly stuffs—themselves and children, they are naked, frozen, hungry; for not to them belongs the fruit of all their labor, but to the rich and mighty one who calls men and the earth his own. See, there they troop, from fields and farmyards; they've tilled the earth and turned it to a smiling garden, and fruits in plenty, enough for all who live, have paid their pains—yet poor are they, and naked, starving; for not to them, or others who are needy, belongs earth's blessing, but solely to the rich and mighty one who calls men and the earth his own. They all, the hundred thousands, millions, are camped upon the hills and gaze into the distance, where thickening clouds proclaim the advent of emancipating Revolution; they all, to whom nothing is left to grieve for, from whom men rob the sons to train them into sturdy jailers of their fathers, whose daughters walk the city's streets with burden of their shame, an offering to the baser lusts of rich and mighty; they all, with the sallow, careworn faces, the limbs devoured by frost and hunger, they all who have never known joy encamp there on the heights and strain their eyes in blissful expectation of her coming, and listen in rapt silence to the rustle of the rising storm, which fills their ears with Revolution's greeting: I am the e'er-rejuvenating, ever-fashioning Life; where *I* am not, is Death! I am the dream, the balm, the hope of sufferers! I bring to nothing what exists, and whither I turn there wells fresh life from the dead rock. I come to you, to break all fetters that oppress you, to redeem you from the arms of death and pour young life through all your veins. Whatever stands, must fall: such is the everlasting law of Nature, such the condition of life; and I, the eternal destroyer, fulfill the law and fashion ever-youthful life. From its root up will I destroy the order of things in which ye live, for it is sprung from sin, its flower is misery and its fruit is crime; but the harvest is ripe, and *I* am the reaper. I will destroy each phantom that has rule o'er men. I will destroy the dominion of one over many, of the dead o'er the living, of matter over spirit; I will break the power of the mighty, of law, of property. Be his own will the lord of man, his own desire his only law, his strength his whole possession, *for the only Holiness is the free man, and naught higher there is than he.* Annulled be the fancy that gives One power over millions, makes millions subject to the will of one, the doctrine that One has power to bless all others. Like may not rule over like; like has no higher potence than its equal: *and as ye all are equal, I will destroy all rulership of one over other.*

Annulled be the fancy that gives death power over life, the past o'er the future. The law of the dead is their own law; it shares their lot, and dies with them; it shall not govern life. *Life is law unto itself.* And since the law is for the living, not the dead, and ye are living, with none conceivable above you, *ye yourselves are the law, your own free will the sole and highest law, and I will destroy all dominion of death over life.*

Annulled be the fancy that makes man bondslave to his handiwork, to property. Man's highest good is his fashioning force, the fount whence springs all happiness forever; and not in the created, in the act of creation itself, in the exercise of your powers lies your true highest enjoyment. Man's work is lifeless; the living shall not bind itself to what is lifeless, not make itself a thrall to that. So away with the bugbear that restrains enjoyment, that hems free force, that sets up property outside of man, and makes him thrall to his own work.

Look hence, ye wretched ones, upon those blessed fields ye now flit through as thralls, as aliens. Free shall ye wander there, free from the yoke of the living, free from the chains of the dead. What Nature made, what men have tilled and turned into a fruitful garden, belongs to men, the needy, and none shall come and say: "To me alone belongs all this; ye others are but guests I tolerate so long as I may please and they shall yield me tribute, guests I drive forth when so inclined. To me belongs what Nature made, what man has wrought, and the living needs." Away with that lie; *to need alone belongs what satisfies it,* and such is offered in abundance by Nature and your own strong arm. See there the houses in the cities, and all that gives delight to men, which ye must journey past as strangers; man's mind and strength have made it, and therefore it belongs to men, the living, and one man shall not come and say: "To me belongeth all that toiling men have made. I alone have a right to it, and the others shall enjoy but what I please and they pay toll for." Destroyed be this lie, with the others; for what the strength of men hath made, belongs to mankind for its unrestricted use, as everything besides on earth.

I will destroy the existing order of things, which parts this one mankind into hostile nations, into powerful and weak, privileged and outcast, rich and poor; for it makes unhappy men of all. I will destroy the order of things that turns millions to slaves of a few, and these few to slaves of their own might, own riches. I will destroy this order of things, that cuts enjoyment off from labor, makes labor a load, enjoyment a vice, makes one man wretched through want, another through overflow. I will destroy this order of things, which wastes man's powers in service of dead matter, which keeps the half of humankind in inactivity or useless toil, binds hundreds of thousands to devote their vigorous youth—in busy idleness as soldiers, placemen, speculators, and money-spinners—to the maintenance of these depraved conditions, whilst the other half must shore the whole disgraceful edifice at cost of overtaxing all their strength and sacrificing every taste of life. Down to its memory will I destroy each trace of this mad state of things, compact of violence, lies, care, hypocrisy, want, sorrow, suffering, tears, trickery, and crime, with seldom a breath of even impure air to quicken it, and all but never a ray of pure joy. Destroyed be all that weighs on you and makes you suffer, and from the ruins of this ancient world let rise a *new*, instinct with happiness undreamed! Nor hate, nor envy, grudge nor enmity be henceforth found among you; as brothers shall ye all who live know one another, and free, free in willing, free in doing, free in enjoying, shall ye attest the worth of life. So up, ye peoples of the earth! Up, ye mourners, ye oppressed, ye poor! And up, ye others, ye who strive in vain to cloak the inner desolation of your hearts by idle show of might and riches! Up, in miscellany follow my steps; for no distinction can I make 'twixt those who follow me. Two peoples, only, are there from henceforth: the one, that follows me, the other, that withstands me. The one I lead to happiness; over the other grinds my path: for I am Revolution, I am the ever-fashioning Life, I am the only God, to whom each creature testifies, who spans and gives both life and happiness to all that is!

And lo! the legions on the hills, voiceless they fall to their knees and listen in mute transport; and as the sunbaked soil drinks up the cooling drops of rain, so their sorrow-parching hearts drink in the accents of the rustling storm, and new life courses through their veins. Nearer and nearer rolls the storm, on its wings Revolution; wide open now the quickened hearts of those awaked to life, and victrix Revolution pours into their brains, their bones, their flesh, and fills them through and through. In godlike ecstasy they leap from the ground; the poor, the hungering, the bowed by misery, are they no longer; proudly they raise themselves erect, inspiration shines from their ennobled faces, a radiant light streams from their eyes, and with the heaven-shaking cry *I am a Man!* the millions, the embodied Revolution, the God become Man, rush down to the valleys and plains, and proclaim to all the world the new gospel of Happiness.

PART II

The Greek Ideal

1. Greek art and drama

In any serious investigation of the essence of our art of today, we cannot make one step forward without being brought face to face with its intimate connection with the art of ancient Greece. For, in point of fact, our modern art is but one link in the artistic development of the whole of Europe; and this development found its starting point with the Greeks.

After it had overcome the raw religion of its Asiatic birthplace, built upon the nature forces of the earth, and had set the fair, strong manhood of freedom upon the pinnacle of its religious convictions—the Grecian spirit, at the flowering time of its art and polity, found its fullest expression in the god Apollo, the head and national deity of the Hellenic race.

It was Apollo—he who had slain the Python, the dragon of Chaos; who had smitten down the vain sons of boastful Niobe by his death-dealing darts; who, through his priestess at Delphi, had proclaimed to questioning man the fundamental laws of the Grecian race and nation, thus holding up to those involved in passionate action the peaceful, undisturbed mirror of their inmost, unchangeable Grecian nature—it was this Apollo who was the fulfiller of the will of Zeus upon the Grecian earth; who was, in fact, the Grecian people.

Not as the soft companion of the Muses—as the later and more luxurious art of sculpture has alone preserved his likeness—must we conceive the Apollo of the springtime of the Greeks; but it was with all the traits of energetic earnestness, beautiful but strong, that the great tragedian Æschylus knew him. Thus, too, the Spartan youths learned the nature of the god, when by dance and joust they had developed their supple bodies to grace and strength; when the boy was taken from those he loved, and sent on horse to farthest lands in search of perilous adventure; when the young man was led into the circle of fellowship, his only password that of his beauty and his native worth, in which alone lay all his might and all his riches.

With such eyes also the Athenian saw the god, when all the impulses of his fair body, and of his restless soul, urged him to the new birth of his own being through the ideal expression of art; when the voices, ringing full, sounded forth the choral song, singing the deeds of the god, the while they gave to the dancers the mastering measure that meted out the rhythm of the dance—which dance itself, in graceful movements, told the story of those deeds; and when above the harmony of well-ordered columns he wove the noble roof, heaped one upon the other the broad crescents of the amphitheatre, and planned the scenic trappings of the stage. Thus, too, inspired by Dionysus, the tragic poet saw this glorious god: when, to all the rich elements of spontaneous art, the harvest of the fairest and most human life, he joined the bond of speech, and concentrating them all into one focus, brought forth the highest conceivable form of art—the drama.

The deeds of gods and men, their sufferings, their delights, as they—in all solemnity and glee, as eternal rhythm, as ever-lasting harmony of every motion and of all creation—lay disclosed in the nature of Apollo himself; here they became actual and true. For all that in them moved and lived, as it moved and lived in the beholders, here found its perfected expression; where ear and eye, as soul and heart, lifelike and actual, seized and perceived all, and saw all in spirit and in body revealed; so that the imagination need no longer vex itself with the attempt to conjure up the image. Such a tragedy-day was a feast of the God; for here the god spoke clearly and intelligibly forth, and the poet, as his high priest, stood real and embodied in his artwork, led the measures of the dance, raised the voices to a choir, and in ringing words proclaimed the utterances of godlike wisdom.

Such was the Grecian work of art; such their god Apollo, incarnated in actual, living art; such was the Grecian people in its highest truth and beauty.

2.   A fellowship of players; communion of players and audience

DRAMA is conceivable only as the fullest expression of a joint artistic longing to impart; while this longing, again, can only parley with a common receptivity. Where either of these factors lacks, the drama is no necessary, but merely an arbitrary, art product. Without these factors being at hand in actual life, the poet, in his striving for immediate presentation of the life that he had apprehended, sought to create the drama for himself alone; his creation therefore fell, perforce, a victim to all the faults of arbitrary dealing. Only in exact measure as his own proceeded from a common impulse, and could address itself to a common interest, do we find the necessary conditions of drama fulfilled—since the time of its recall to life—and the desire to answer those conditions rewarded with success.

A common impulse toward dramatic artwork can be at hand only in those who actually enact the work of art in common; these, as we take it, are the fellowships of players. At the end of the Middle Ages, we see such fellowships arising directly from the folk; while those who later overmastered them and laid down their laws from the standpoint of absolute poetic art have earned themselves the fame of destroying root-and-branch that which the man who sprang directly from such a fellowship, and made his poems for and with it, had created for the wonder of all time. From out the inmost, truest nature of the folk, Shakespeare created for his fellow players that drama which seems to us the more astounding as we see it rise by might of naked speech alone, without all help of kindred arts. One only help it had, the fantasy of his audience, which turned with active sympathy to greet the inspiration of the poet's comrades.

A genius the like of which was never heard, and a group of favoring chances ne'er repeated, in common made amends for what they lacked in common. Their joint creative force, however, was—need; and where this shows its nature-bidden might, there man can compass even the impossible to satisfy it: from poverty grows plenty, from want an overflow; the boorish figure of the homely folk's comedian takes on the bearing of a hero, the raucous clang of daily speech becomes the sounding music of the soul, the rude scaffolding of carpet-hung boards becomes a world stage with all its wealth of scene. But if we take away this artwork from its frame of fortunate conditions, if we set it down outside the realm of fertile force which bore it from the need of this one definite epoch, then do we see with sorrow that the poverty was still but poverty, the want but want; that Shakespeare was indeed the mightiest poet of all time, but his artwork was not yet the work for every age; that not his genius, but the incomplete and merely will-ing, not yet *can*-ning, spirit of his age's art had made him but the Thespis of the tragedy of the future.

In the same relation as stood the car of Thespis, in the brief time span of the flowering of Athenian art, to the stage of Æschylus and Sophocles, so stands the stage of Shakespeare, in the unmeasured spaces of the flowering time of universal human art, to the theatre of the future. The deed of the one and only Shakespeare, which made of him a universal man, a very god, is yet but the kindred deed of the solitary Beethoven, who found the language of the artist-manhood of the future: only where these twain Prometheuses—Shakespeare and Beethoven—shall reach out hands to one another; where the marble creations of Phidias shall bestir themselves in flesh and blood; where the painted counterfeit of Nature shall quit its cribbing frame on the chamber walls of the egoist, and stretch its ample breadths on the warm-life-blown framework of the future stage—there first, in the communion of all his fellow artists, will the poet also find redemption.

3. The fellowship and the community; the priest as actor

THE first and earliest association of men was the work of Nature. The purely tribal fellowship, that is, the circle of all those who claimed descent from a common ancestor and the lineal seed of his loins, is the original bond of union of every race of people that we meet in history. This tribal stem preserves in its traditional sagas, as in an ever lively memory, the instinctive knowledge of its common ancestry, while the impressions derived from the particular natural features of its surroundings exalt these legendary recollections to the rank of religious ideas. Now, in however manifold accretion these ideas and reminiscences may have heaped themselves together and crowded into novel forms, among the quickest-witted historical nations, owing to racial admixture on the one hand, and on the other to change of natural surroundings as the result of tribal migration—however broadly, in their sagas and religions, these peoples may have stretched the narrowing bands of nationality, so that the idea of their own particular origin was expanded to the theory of a universal descent and derivation of men in general from their gods, as from the gods in general—yet in every epoch and every land where myth and religion have flourished in the lively faith of any racial stem, the peculiar bond of union of this particular stem has always lain in its specific myth and its particular religion.

The Hellenic races solemnized the joint memorial celebration of their common descent in their religious feasts, that is, in the glorification and adoration of the god or hero in whose being they felt themselves included as one common whole. Finally, and with the greatest truth to life—as though from a felt need to fix with utmost definition their recollection of what was ever dropping further back into the past—they materialize their national traditions in their art, and most directly in that full-fledged work of art, the tragedy. The lyric and the dramatic artworks were each a religious act: but there was already evinced in this act, when compared with the simple primitive religious rite, a taint of artificial effort; the effort, namely, to bring forward of set purpose that common memory which had already lost its immediate living impress on the life of every day. Thus tragedy was the religious rite become a work of art, by side of which the traditional observance of the genuine religious temple rite was necessarily docked of so much of its inwardness and truth that it became indeed a mere conventional and soulless ceremony, whereas its kernel lived on in the artwork.

In the highly important matter of the externals of the religious act, the tribal fellowship shows its communal character by certain ancestral usages, by certain forms and garments. The garb of religion is, so to speak, the costume of the race by which it mutually recognizes itself, and that at the first glance. This garment, hallowed by the use of ages, this—in a manner—religio-social convention, had shifted from the religious to the artistic rite, the tragedy; in it and by it the tragic actor embodied the familiar, reverenced figure of the people's fellowship. It was by no means the mere vastness of the theatre and the distance of the audience that prescribed the heightening of the human stature by the cothurnus, or, precisely, that admitted the employment of the immobile tragic mask—but the cothurnus and the mask were necessary, religiously significant attributes which, accompanied by other symbolical tokens, first gave to the performer his weighty character of priest. Now, where a religion, commencing to fade from daily life and wholly withdrawing from its political aspect, is discernible by its outer garb alone, but this garment, as with the Athenians, can only now take on the folds of actual life when it forms the investiture of art: there must this actual life at last confess itself the core of that religion, by frankly throwing off its last disguise. But the core of the Hellenic religion, the center round which its whole system revolved, and which instinctively asserted its exclusive rule in actual life, was man. It was for Art to formulate aloud this plain confession: she did it when she cast aside the last concealing garment of religion, and showed its core in simple nakedness, the actual bodily man.

Yet this unveiling was alike the final annihilation of the collective artwork:. for its bond of union had been that very garment of religion. While the contents of the common mythical religion, the traditional subject of dramatic art, were employed to point the poet's moral, developed to fit his purpose, and finally disfigured by his self-willed fancy, the religious belief had already disappeared completely from the life of the folk fellowship, now only linked by political interests. This belief however, the honor paid to national gods, the sure assumption of the truth of primal race traditions, had formed the bond of all community. Was this now rent and hooted as a heresy, at least the core of that religion had come to light as unconditioned, actual, naked man; but this man was no longer the associate man, united by the bond of racial fellowship: only the absolute, egoistic, solitary unit—man beautiful and naked, but loosed from the beauteous bond of brotherhood.

From here on, from the shattering of the Greek religion, from the wreck of the Grecian nature state, and its resolution into the political state—from the splintering of the common tragic artwork—the manhood of world history begins with measured tread its new gigantic march of evolution, from the fallen *natural kinsmanship of national community* to the *universal fellowship of all mankind*. The band which the full-fledged man, coming to consciousness in the national Hellenian, disrupted as a cramping fetter—with this awakened consciousness—must now expand into a universal girdle embracing *all* mankind. The period from that point of time down to our own today is, therefore, the history of *absolute egoism*;

and the end of this period will be its redemption into *communism*.*

4. The folk creates art.

WHERESOEVER the folk made poetry—and only by the folk, or in the footsteps of the folk, can poetry be really made—there did the poetic purpose rise to life alone upon the shoulders of the arts of dance and tone, as the *head* of the full-fledged human being. The lyrics of Orpheus would never have been able to turn the savage beasts to silent, placid adoration if the singer had but given them forsooth some dumb and printed verse to read: their ears must be enthralled by the sonorous notes that came straight from the heart, their carrion-spying eyes be tamed by the proud and graceful movements of the body—in such a way that they should recognize instinctively in this whole man no longer a mere object for their maw, no mere objective for their feeding-, but for their hearing- and their seeing-powers—before they could be attuned duly to listen to his moral sentences.

Neither was the true folk epic by any means a mere recited poem: the songs of Homer, such as we now possess them, have issued from the critical siftings and compilings of a time in which the genuine epos had long since ceased to live. When Solon made his laws and Pisistratus introduced his political regime, men searched among the ruins of the already fallen epos of the folk and pieced the gathered heap together for reading service—much as in the Hohenstaufen times they did with the fragments of the lost *Nibelungen-lieder*. But before these epic songs became the object of such literary care, they had flourished mid the folk, eked out by voice and gesture, as a bodily enacted artwork; as it were, a fixed and crystallized blend of lyric song and dance, with predominant lingering on portrayal of the action and reproduction of the heroic dia-

---

* It is a political crime to use this word: however, there is none which will better describe the direct antithesis of *egoism*. Whosoever is ashamed today to pass current as an egoist—and indeed no one will openly confess himself as such—must allow us to take the liberty of calling him a communist.—R. WAGNER.

logue. These epic-lyrical performances form the unmistakable middle stage between the genuine older lyric and tragedy, the normal point of transition from the one to the other.

Tragedy was therefore the entry of the artwork of the folk upon the public arena of political life; and we may take its appearance as an excellent touchstone for the difference in procedure between the art-*creating* of the folk and the mere literary-historical *making* of the so-called cultured art world. At the very time when live-born epos became the object of the critical dilettantism of the court of Pisistratus, it had already shed its blossoms in the people's life—yet not because the folk had lost its true afflatus, but since it was already able to surpass the old, and from unstanchable artistic sources to build the less perfect artwork up, until it became the more perfect. For while those pedants and professors in the prince's castle were laboring at the construction of a literary Homer, pampering their own unproductivity with their marvel at their wisdom, by aid of which they yet could only understand the thing that long had passed from life—Thespis had already slid his car to Athens, had set it up beside the palace walls, dressed out his stage and, stepping from the chorus of the folk, had trodden its planks; no longer did he shadow forth the deeds of heroes, as in the epos, but in these heroes' guise enacted them.

With the folk, all is reality and deed; it *does*, and then rejoices in the thought of its own doing. Thus the blithe folk of Athens, enflamed by persecution, hunted out from court and city the melancholy sons of Pisistratus; and then bethought it how, by this its deed, it had become a free and independent people. Thus it raised the platform of its stage, and decked itself with tragic masks and raiment of some god or hero, in order itself to be a god or hero: and tragedy was born; whose fruits it tasted with the blissful sense of its own creative force, but whose metaphysical basis it handed, all regardless, to the brain-racking speculation of the dramaturgists of our modern court theatres.

Tragedy flourished for just so long as it was inspired by the spirit of the folk, and as this spirit was a veritably popular, that is, a *communal* one. When the national brotherhood of the folk was shivered into fragrants, when the common bond of its religion and primeval customs was pierced and severed by the sophist needles of the egoistic spirit of Athenian self-dissection—then the folk's artwork also ceased: then did the professors and the doctors of the literary guilds take heritage of the ruins of the fallen edifice, and delved among its beams and stones; to pry, to ponder, and to rearrange its members. With Aristophanian laughter, the folk relinquished to these learned insects the refuse of its meal, threw art upon one side for two millennia, and fashioned of its innermost necessity the history of the world; the while those scholars cobbled up their tiresome history of literature, by order of the supreme court of Alexander.

5. Definition of the folk

Who is then the folk? It is absolutely necessary that, before proceeding further, we should agree upon the answer to this weightiest of questions.

"The folk" was from of old the inclusive term for *all the units* which made up the total of a *commonality*. In the beginning, it was the family and the tribe; next, the tribes united by like speech into a nation. Practically, by the Roman world dominion which engulfed the nations, and theoretically, by the Christian religion which admitted of naught but men, that is, no racial, but only *Christian* men—the idea of "the people" has so far broadened out, or even evaporated, that we may either include in it mankind in general, or, upon the arbitrary political hypothesis, a certain, and generally the propertyless, portion of the commonwealth. But beyond a frivolous, this term has also acquired an ineradicable *moral* meaning; and on account of this it is, that in times of stir and trouble all men are eager to number themselves among the people; each one gives out that he is careful for the people's weal, and no one will permit himself to be excluded from it. Therefore in these latter days also has the question frequently been broached, in the most diverse of senses: Who then is the people? In the sum total of the body politic, can a separate party, a particular fraction of the said body claim this name for itself alone? Rather, are we not all alike "the people," from the beggar to the prince?

This question must therefore be answered according to the conclusive and world-historical sense that now lies at its root, as follows:

The "folk" is the epitome of all those men *who feel a common and collective want.* To it belong, then, all those who recognize their individual want as a collective want, or find it based thereon; ergo, all those who can hope for the stilling of their want in nothing but the stilling of a common want, and therefore spend their whole life's strength upon the stilling of their thus acknowledged common want. For only that want which urges to the uttermost is genuine want; but this want alone is the force of true need; but a common and collective need is the only true need; but only he who feels within him a true need has a right to its assuagement; but only the assuagement of a genuine need is necessity; and it is *the folk alone that acts according to necessity's behests*, and therefore irresistibly, victoriously, and right as none besides.

Who now are they who belong *not* to this people, and who are its sworn foes?

All those *who feel no want*; whose lifespring therefore consists in a need which rises not to the potence of a want, and thus is artificial, untrue, and egoistic; and not only is not embraced within a common need, but as the empty need of preserving superfluity—as which alone can one conceive of need without the force of want—is diametrically opposed to the collective need.

Where there is no want, there is no true need; where no true need, no necessary action. But where there is no necessary action, there reigns caprice; and where caprice is king, there blossoms every vice, and every criminal assault on Nature. For only by forcing back, by barring and refusing the assuagement of true need, can the false and artificial need endeavor to assuage itself.

But the satisfaction of an artificial need is *luxury*; which can only be bred and supported in opposition to, and at the cost of, the necessities of others.

Luxury is as heartless, inhuman, insatiable, and egoistic as the "need" which called it forth, but which, with all its heaping up and overreaching, it never more can still. For this need itself is no natural and therefore satisfiable one; by very reason that, being false, it has no true, essential antithesis in which it may be spent, consumed, and satisfied. Actual physical hunger has its natural antithesis, satiety, in which—by feeding—it is spent: but unwanting need, the need that craves for luxury, is in itself already luxury and superfluity. The error of it, therefore, can never go over into truth; it racks, devours, torments, and burns, without an instant's stilling; it leaves brain, heart, and sense for ever vainly yearning, and swallows up all gladness, mirth, and joy of life. For sake of one sole and yet unreachable moment of refreshment, it squanders the toil and life sweat of a thousand needy wanters; it lives upon the unstilled hunger of a thousand thousand poor, though impotent to satiate its own for but the twinkling of an eye; it holds a whole world within the iron chains of despotism, without the power momentarily to break the golden chains of that archtyrant which it is unto itself.

And this fiend, this crackbrained need-without-a-need, this need of need—this *need of luxury*, which is *luxury itself* withal—is sovereign of the world. It is the soul of that industry which deadens men, to turn them to machines; the soul of our state which swears away men's honor, the better then to take them back as lieges of its grace; the soul of our deistic science, which hurls men down before an immaterial God, the product of the sum of intellectual luxury, for his consumption. It is— alas!—the soul, the stipulation, of our—*art!*

Who then will bring to pass the rescue from this baleful state?

Want—which shall teach the world to recognize its own *true need*; that need which *by its very nature admits of satisfaction*.

Want will cut short the hell of luxury; it will teach the tortured, need-lacking spirits whom this hell embraces in its bounds the simple, homely need of sheer human physical hunger and thirst; but in fellowship will it point us to the health-giving bread, the clear sweet springs of Nature; in fellowship shall we taste their genuine joys, and grow up in communion to veritable men. In common, too, shall we close the last link in the bond of holy necessity; and the brother-kiss that seals this bond will be the *mutual artwork of the future*. But in this, also, our great redeemer and well-doer, necessity's vicegerent in the flesh—*the folk,* will no longer be a severed and peculiar class; for in this artwork we shall all be *one*— heralds and supporters of necessity, knowers of the unconscious, willers of the unwillful, betokeners of Nature—*blissful men.*

6. Myth as it relates to the folk and to art

ONLY from the Greek world view has the genuine artwork of drama been able as yet to blossom forth. But this drama's stuff was the *mythos*; and from its essence alone can we learn to comprehend the highest Grecian artwork, and its form that so ensnares us.

In the *mythos* the folk's joint poetic force seizes things exactly as the bodily eye has power to see them, and no farther; not as they in themselves really are. The vast multiplicity of surrounding phenomena, whose real association the human being cannot grasp as yet, gives him first of all an impression of unrest: in order to overcome this feeling of unrest he seeks for some connection of the phenomena among themselves, some connection which he may conceive as their First Cause. The real connection, however, is discoverable only by the understanding, which seizes the phenomena according to their reality; whereas the connection invented by the man who is able to seize the phenomena only according to their directest impression upon himself can merely be the work of fantasy—and the cause, thus subsumed for them, a mere product of his poetic imaginative force.

God and gods are the first creations of man's poetic force: in them man represents to himself the essence of natural phenomena as derived from a cause. Under the notion of this cause, however, he instinctively apprehends nothing other than his own human essence; on which alone, moreover, this imagined cause is based. If the "thrust" of the man who fain would overcome his inner disquietude at the multiplicity of phenomena, if this thrust makes toward representing as plainly as possible to himself their imagined cause—since he can regain his peace of mind only through the selfsame senses wherethrough his inner being had been disquieted—then he must also bring his God before him in a shape which not only shall the most definitely answer to his purely human manner of looking at things but shall also be outwardly the most understandable by him.

All understanding comes to us through love alone, and man is urged the most instinctively toward the essence of his own species. Just as the human form is to him the most comprehensible, so also will the essence of natural phenomena—which he does not know as yet in their reality—become comprehensible only through condensation to a human form. Thus in *mythos* all the shaping impulse of the folk makes toward realizing to its senses a broadest grouping of the most manifold phenomena, and in the most succinct of shapes. At first a mere image formed by fantasy, this shape behaves itself the more entirely according to human attributes, the plainer it is to become, notwithstanding that its content is in truth a suprahuman and supranatural one: to wit, that joint operation of multihuman or omninatural force and faculty which, conceived as merely the *concordant action* of human and natural forces in general, is certainly both natural and human, but appears superhuman and supernatural by the very fact that it is ascribed to *one* imagined individual, represented in the shape of man.

By its faculty of thus using its force of imagination to bring before itself every thinkable reality and actuality, in widest reach but plain, succinct, and plastic shaping, the folk therefore becomes in *mythos* the creator of art; for these shapes must necessarily win artistic form and content, if—which, again, is their individual mark—they have sprung from nothing but man's longing for a *seizable* portrait of things, and thus from his yearning to recognize in the object portrayed, nay *first to know* therein, himself and his own-est essence: that god-creative essence. Art, by the very meaning of the term, is nothing but the fulfillment of a longing to know oneself in the likeness of an object of one's love or adoration, to find oneself again in the things of the outer world, thus conquered by their representment. In the object he has represented, the artist says to himself: "So art thou; so feel'st and thinkest thou. And so wouldst thou do; if, freed from all the strenuous caprice of outward haps of life, thou mightest do according to thy choice." Thus did the folk portray in *mythos* to itself its *God*; thus its *hero*; and thus, at last, its *man*.

Greek tragedy is the artistic embodiment of the spirit and contents of Greek *mythos*. As in this *mythos* the widest-ranging phenomena were compressed into closer and ever closer shape, so the drama took this shape and re-presented it in the closest, most compressed of forms. The view-in-common of the essence of things, which in *mythos* had condensed itself from a view of Nature to a view of men and morals, here appeals in its distinctest, most pregnant form to the most universal receptive force of man; and thus steps, as artwork, from fantasy into reality. As in drama the shapes that had been in *mythos* merely shapes of thought, were now presented in actual bodily portrayal by living men, so the actually represented action now compressed itself, in thorough keeping with the mythic essence, into a compact, plastic whole. If a man's idea is bared to us convincingly only by his action, and if a man's character consists in the complete harmony between his idea and his action, then this action, and therefore also its underlying idea—entirely in the sense of the *mythos*—gains significance, and correspondence with a wide-reaching content, by its manifesting itself in utmost concentration. An action which consists of many parts, is either overweighted, redundant, and unintelligible—when all these parts are of equally suggestive, decisive importance; or it is petty, arbitrary, and meaningless —when these parts are nothing but odds and ends of actions. The content of an action is the idea that lies at the bottom of it: if this idea is a great one, wide of reach, and drawing upon man's whole nature in any one particular line, then it also ordains an action which shall be decisive, one and indivisible; for only in such an action does a great idea reveal itself to us.

Now, by its nature, the content of Greek *mythos* was of this wide-reaching but compact quality; and in their tragedy it likewise uttered itself, with fullest definition, as this one, necessary, and decisive action. To allow this action, in its weightiest significance, to proceed in a manner fully vindicated by the idea of its transactors—*this* was the task of the tragic poet; to bring to understanding the necessity of the action, by and in the demonstrated truth of the idea—in this consisted the solution of that task. The unitarian form of his artwork, however, lay already mapped out for him in the contours of the *mythos*; which he had only to work up into a living edifice, but in no wise to break to pieces and newly fit together in favor of an arbitrarily conceived artistic building. The tragic poet merely imparted the content and essence of the myth in the most conclusive and intelligible manner; his tragedy is nothing other than the artistic completion of the myth itself; while the myth is the poem of a life view in common.

7.   The value of myth is its eternal truth.

THE incomparable thing about the *mythos* is that it is true for all time, and its content, how close soever its compression, is inexhaustible throughout the ages. The only task of the poet was to expound it. Even the Greek tragedian did not always stand in full unconstraint before the myth he had to expound: the myth itself was mostly juster to the essence of the individuality than was the expounding poet. The tragedian had completely taken up the spirit of this *mythos* into himself, however, in so far as he made the essence of the individuality the irremovable center of his artwork, from which the latter fed and refreshed itself on every hand. So undisfigured stood before the poet's soul this all-begetting essence of the individuality, that therefrom a Sophoclean Ajax and Philoctetes could spring forth—heroes whom no side glance at the prudent world's opinion could lure from their nature's self-annihilating necessity and truth, to drift into the shallow waters of politics, on which the weatherwise Ulysses understood so masterly to ship him to and fro.

To-day we need only to expound faithfully the myth of Œdipus according to its inmost essence, and we in it win an intelligible picture of the whole history of mankind, from the beginnings of society to the inevitable downfall of the state. The necessity of this downfall was foreboded in the *mythos*: it is the part of actual history to accomplish it.

The *mythos* is the poet's ideal stuff—that native, nameless poem of the folk, which throughout the ages we ever meet new-handled by the great poets of periods of consummate culture; for in it there almost vanishes the conventional form of man's relations, merely explicable to abstract reason, to show instead the eternally intelligible, the purely human, but in just that inimitable concrete form which lends to every sterling myth an individual shape so swiftly cognizable.

8. Feeling is the basis of understanding.

TONE speech is the beginning and end of word speech; as the feeling is beginning and end of the understanding, as *mythos* is beginning and end of history, the lyric beginning and end of poetry. The mediator between beginning and middle, as between the latter and the point of exit, is the fantasy.

The march of this evolution is such, however, that it is no retrogression, but a progress to the winning of the highest human faculty; and it is traveled, not merely by mankind in general, but substantially by every social individual.

Just as in the unconscious feeling lie all the germs for evolution of the understanding, while this latter holds within it a necessitation to vindicate the unconscious feeling, and the man

who from out his understanding vindicates this feeling is first
the man of intellect; just as in *mythos* justified by history,
which alike grew out of *it*, is first won a really intelligible
image of life: so does the lyric also hold within itself each
germ of the intrinsic art of poetry, which necessarily can but
end with speaking out the vindication of the lyric; and this
work of vindication is precisely the highest human artwork,
the *entire drama.*

PART III

*The Origins of Modern Opera,
Drama, and Music*

1. *Development of the aria; Gluck's contribution*

ALONG two lines has Music developed in that art genre which she dominates, the opera: along an *earnest*—with all the tone poets who felt lying on their shoulders the burden of responsibility that fell to Music when she took upon herself alone the aim of drama; along a *frivolous*—with all the musicians who, as though driven by an instinctive feeling of the impossibility of achieving an unnatural task, have turned their backs upon it and, heedful only of the profit which opera had won from an uncommonly widespread popularity, have given themselves over to an unmixed musical empiricism. It is necessary that we should commence by fixing our gaze upon the first, the *earnest* line.

The musical basis of opera was—as we know—nothing other than the *aria*; this aria, again, was merely the folk song as rendered by the art singer before the world of rank and quality, but with its word poem left out and replaced by the product of the art poet to that end commissioned. The conversion of the folk tune into the operatic aria was primarily the work of that art singer, whose concern was no longer for the right delivery of the tune, but for the exhibition of his throat dexterity. It was he who parceled out the resting points he needed, the alternation of more lively with more placid phrasing, the passages where, free from any rhythmic or melodic curb, he might bring his skill to bearing as it pleased him best. The composer merely furnished the singer, the poet in his turn the composer, with the material for their virtuosity.

The natural relation of the artistic factors of drama was thus, at bottom, as yet not quite upheaved: it was merely distorted, inasmuch as the performer, the most necessary condition for drama's possibility, represented but one solitary talent—that of absolute song dexterity—and nowise all the conjoint faculties of artist-man. This one distortion of the character of the performer, however, sufficed to bring about the ultimate perversion of the natural relation of those factors: to wit, the absolute preferment of the musician before the poet. Had that singer been a true, sound, and whole dramatic

95

performer, then had the composer come necessarily into his proper position toward the poet; since the latter would then have firmly spoken out of the dramatic aim, the measure for all else, and ruled its realizing. But the poet who stood nighest that singer was the composer—the composer who merely helped the singer to attain his aim; while this aim, cut loose from every vestige of dramatic, nay, even poetic bearing, was nothing other, through and through, than to show off his own specific song dexterity.

This original relation of the artistic factors of opera to one another we have to stamp sharply on our minds, in order to recognize clearly, in the sequel, how this distorted relation became only all the more entangled through every attempt to set it straight.

Into the dramatic cantata, to satisfy the luxurious craving of these eminent sirs for change in their amusements, there was dovetailed next the ballet. Dance and dance tune, borrowed just as waywardly from the folk dance and its tune as was the operatic aria from the folk song, joined forces with the singer, in all the sterile immiscibility of unnatural things; while it naturally became the poet's task, midst such a heaping up of inwardly incongruous matter, to bind the samples of the diverse art dexterities, now laid before him, into some kind of patchwork harmony. Thus, with the poet's aid, an ever more obviously imperative dramatic cohesion was thrust on that which, in its actual self, was crying for no cohesion whatever; so that the aim of drama—forced on by outward want—was merely lodged, by no means housed. Song tune and dance tune stood side by side in fullest, chillest loneliness, for exhibition of the agility of singer or of dancer; and only in that which was to make shift to bind them, to wit, the musically recited dialogue, did the poet ply his lowly calling, did the drama peep out here and there.

Neither was recitative itself, by any means, some new invention proceeding from a genuine urgence of opera toward the drama. Long before this mode of intoning was introduced into opera, the Christian Church had used it in her services, for the recitation of biblical passages. The banal singsong of these recitals, with its more listlessly melodic than rhetorically expressive incidence of tone, had been early fixed by ritualistic prescript into an arid semblance, without the reality, of speech; and this it was that, merely molded and varied by musical caprice, passed over into the opera. So that, what with aria, dance tune, and recitative, the whole apparatus of musical drama—unchanged in essence down to our very latest opera—was settled once for all. Further, the dramatic ground plans laid beneath this apparatus soon won a kindred stereotyped persistence. Mostly taken from an entirely misconstrued Greek mythology, they formed a theatric scaffolding from which all capability of rousing warmth of human interest was altogether absent, but which, on the other hand, possessed the merit of lending itself to the good pleasure of every composer in his turn; in effect, the majority of these texts were composed over and over again by the most diverse of musicians.

The so famous revolution of Gluck, which has come to the ears of many ignoramuses as a complete reversal of the views previously current as to opera's essence, in truth consisted merely in this: that the musical composer revolted against the willfulness of the singer. The composer, who, next to the singer, had drawn the special notice of the public to himself—since it was he who provided the singer with fresh supplies of stuff for his dexterity—felt his province encroached upon by the operations of the latter, in exact measure as he himself was busied to shape that stuff according to his own inventive fancy, and thus secure that his work also, and perchance at last only his work, might catch the ear of the audience. For the reaching of his ambitious goal there stood two ways open to the composer: either, by use of all the musical aids already at his disposal, or yet to be discovered, to unfold the purely sensuous contents of the aria to their highest, rankest pitch; or—and this is the more earnest path, with which we are concerned at present—to put shackles on caprice's execution of that aria, by himself endeavoring to give the tune, before its execution, an expression answering to the underlying word text.

As, by the nature of these texts, they were to figure as the feeling discourse of the dramatis personae, so had it already occurred, quite of itself, to feeling singers and composers to furnish forth their virtuosity with an impress of the needful warmth; and Gluck was surely not the first who indited feeling airs, nor his singers the first who delivered them with fit expression. But that he *spoke out with consciousness and firm conviction* the fitness and necessity of an expression answering to the text substratum, in aria and recitative, this it is that makes him the departure point of an at any rate thorough change in the quondam situation of the artistic factors of opera toward one another. Henceforth the scepter of opera

passes definitely over to the composer: the singer becomes
the *organ of the composer's aim,* and this aim is consciously
declared to be the matching of the dramatic contents of the
text substratum with a true and suitable expression. Thus, at
bottom, a halt was cried only to the unbecoming and heartless
vanity of the singing virtuoso; but with all the rest of opera's
unnatural organism things remained on their old footing.
Aria, recitative, and dance piece, fenced off each from each,
stand side by side as unaccommodated in the operas of Gluck
as they did before him, and as, with scarcely an exception,
they still stand today.

In the situation of the poet toward the composer not one
jot was altered; rather had the composer grown more dicta-
torial, since, with his declared consciousness of a higher mission—made good against the virtuoso singer—he set to work
with more deliberate zeal at the arrangement of the opera's
framework. To the poet it never occurred to meddle with
these arrangements; he could not so much as dream of music,
to which the opera had owed its origin, in any form other
than those narrow, close-ruled forms he found set down before
him—as binding even upon the musician himself. To tamper
with these forms by advancing claims of dramatic necessity,
to such an extent that they should cease to be intrinsic
shackles on the free development of dramatic truth, would
have seemed to him unthinkable; since it was precisely in
these forms alone—inviolable even by the musician—that he
could conceive of music's essence. Wherefore, once engaged
in the penning of an opera text, he must needs pay even more
painful heed than the musician himself to the observance of
those forms; at utmost leave it to that musician, in his own
familiar field, to carry out enlargements and developments,
in which he could lend a helping hand but never take the
initiative. Thus the poet, who looked up to the composer with
a certain holy awe, rather confirmed the latter's dictatorship in
opera than set up rival claims thereto; for he was witness to
the earnest zeal the musician brought to his task.

2. *Mozart and Rossini; the death of opera*

WHOSOEVER insists on seeing in Mozart an experimenting
musician who turns, forsooth, from one attempt to solve the
operatic problem to the next can only counterpoise this error

by placing alongside it another, and, for instance, ascribing naïveté to Mendelssohn when, mistrustful of his own powers, he took his cautious, hesitating steps along that endless stretch of road which lay between himself and opera. The naïve, truly inspired artist casts himself with reckless enthusiasm into his artwork; and only when this is finished, when it shows itself in all its actuality, does he win from practical experience that genuine force of reflection which preserves him in general from illusions, yet in the specific case of his feeling driven again to artwork by his inspiration, loses once more its power over him completely. There is nothing more characteristic of Mozart, in his career of opera composer, than the unconcernedness wherewith he went to work: it was so far from occurring to him to weigh the pros and cons of the aesthetic problem involved in opera, that he the rather engaged with utmost unconstraint in setting any and every operatic textbook offered him, almost heedless whether it were a thankful or a thankless task for him as pure musician. If we piece together all his aesthetic hints and sayings, culled from here and there, we shall find that the sum of his reflection mounts no higher than his famous definition of his "nose." He was so utterly and entirely a musician, and nothing but musician, that through him we may also gain the clearest and most convincing view of the true and proper position of the musician toward the poet. Indisputably his weightiest and most decisive stroke for music he dealt precisely in opera—in opera, over whose conformation it never for a moment struck him to usurp the poet's right, and where he attempted nothing but what he could achieve by purely musical means. In return, however, through the very faithfulness and singleness of his adoption of the poet's aim—wherever and howsoever present—he stretched these purely musical means of his to such a compass that in none of his absolute-musical compositions, and particularly his instrumental works, do we see the art of music so broadly and so richly furthered as in his operas. The noble, straightforward simplicity of his purely musical instinct, that is, his intuitive penetration into the arcana of his art, made it wellnigh impossible to him *there* to bring forth magical effects, as composer, where the poem was flat and meaningless. How little did this richest-gifted of all musicians understand our modern music-makers' trick of building gaudy towers of music upon a hollow, valueless foundation, and playing the rapt and the inspired where all the poetaster's botch is void and flimsy, the better to show that the musician is the jack in

office and can go any length he pleases, even to making something out of nothing—the same as the good God! Oh, how
doubly dear and above all honor is Mozart to me, that it was
not possible to him to invent music for *Tito* like that of *Don
Giovanni,* for *Cosi fan tutte* like that of *Figaro!* How shamefully would it have desecrated music!

Music Mozart always made, but *beautiful* music he could
never write excepting when inspired. Though this inspiration
must ever come from within, from his own possessions, yet
it could only leap forth bright and radiant when kindled
from without, when to the spirit of divinest love within him
was shown the object worthy love, the object that in ardent
heedlessness of self it could embrace. And thus would it have
been precisely the most absolute of all musicians, Mozart
himself, who would have long since solved the operatic problem past all doubt, who would have helped to pen the truest,
fairest, and completest drama, if only he had met the poet
whom he would only have had to help. But he never met that
poet: at times it was a pedantically wearisome, at times a friv-
olously sprightly maker of opera texts, that reached him
arias, duets, and ensemble pieces to compose; and these he
took and so turned them into music, according to the warmth
they each were able to awake in him, that in every instance
they received the most answering expression of which their
last particle of sense was capable.

Thus did Mozart only prove the exhaustless power of music
to answer with undreamed fullness each demand of the poet
upon her faculty of expression; for all his unreflective method,
the glorious musician revealed this power, even in the truthfulness of dramatic expression, the endless multiplicity of its
motivation, in far richer measure than Gluck and all his followers. But so little was a fundamental principle laid down
in his creations, that the pinions of his genius left the *formal*
skeleton of opera quite unstirred: he had merely poured his
music's lava stream into the molds of opera. Themselves,
however, they were too frail to hold this stream within them;
and forth it flowed to where, in ever freer and less cramping
channels, it might spread itself according to its natural bent,
until in the symphonies of Beethoven we find it swollen to
a mighty sea. Whereas in instrumental music the innate capabilities of music developed into boundless power, those
operatic forms, like burned-out bricks and mortar, stayed
chill and naked in their pristine shape, a carcass waiting for
the coming guest to pitch his fleeting tent within.

Only for the history of music in general is Mozart of so strikingly weighty moment; in no wise for the history of opera in particular, as a specific genre of art. Opera, whose unnatural being was bound to life by no laws of genuine necessity, was free to fall a ready booty to the first musical adventurer who came its way.

The unedifying spectacle presented by the art doings of so-called followers of Mozart we here may reasonably pass by. A tolerably long string of composers figured to themselves that Mozart's opera was a something whose form might be imitated; wherewith they naturally overlooked the fact that this form was nothing in itself, and Mozart's musical spirit everything. But to reconstruct the creations of spirit by a pedantic setting of two and two together has not as yet succeeded in the hands of any one.

One thing alone remained to utter in those forms. Albeit Mozart, in unclouded naïveté, had evolved their purely musical-artistic content to its highest pitch, yet the real secret of the whole opera embroglio, in keeping with its source of origin, was still to be laid bare to nakedest publicity in those same forms. The world was yet to be plainly told, and without reserve, what longing and what claim on art it was that opera owed its origin and existence to: that this longing was by no means for the genuine drama, but had gone forth toward a pleasure merely seasoned with the sauces of the stage; in no sense moving or inwardly arousing, but merely intoxicating and outwardly diverting. In Italy, where this—as yet unconscious—longing had given birth to opera, it was at last to be fulfilled with open eyes.

This brings us back to a closer dealing with the essence of the aria.

So long as arias shall be composed, the root character of that art form will always betray itself as an absolute-musical one. The folk song issued from an immediate double growth, a consentaneous action of the arts of poetry and tone. This art—as opposed to that almost only one we can now conceive, the deliberate art of culture—we ought perhaps scarcely to style as art; but rather to call it an instinctive manifestment of the spirit of the folk through the organ of artistic faculty. Here the word poem and the tone poem are one. It never happens to the folk to sing its songs without a "text"; without the words the folk would brook no tune. If the tune varies in the course of time, and with the divers offshoots of the folk stem, so vary too the words. No severing of these twain can the folk imagine; for *it* they make as firmly knit a whole as man and wife.

The man of luxury heard this folk song merely from afar; in his lordly palace he listened to the reapers passing by; what staves surged up into his sumptuous chambers were but the staves of tone, whereas the staves of poetry died out before they reached him. Now, if this tone stave may be likened to the delicate fragrance of the flower, and the word stave to its very chalice, with all its tender stamens: the man of luxury, solely bent on tasting with his nerves of smell, and not alike with those of sight, squeezed out this fragrance from the flower and distilled therefrom an extract, which he decanted into phials to bear about him at his lief, to sprinkle on his splendid chattels and himself whene'er he listed. To gladden his eyes with the flower itself, he must necessarily have sought it closer, have stepped down from his palace to the woodland glades, have forced his way past branches, trunks, and bracken; whereto the eminent and leisured sir had not one spark of longing. With this sweet-smelling residue he drenched the weary desert of his life, the aching void of his emotions; and the artificial growth that sprang from this unnatural fertilizing was nothing other than the operatic aria. Into whatsoever wayward intermarriages it might be forced, it stayed still ever fruitless, forever but itself, but what it was and could not else be: a sheer musical substratum.

The whole cloud body of the aria evaporated into melody; and this was sung, was fiddled, and at last was whistled, without its ever recollecting that it ought by rights to have a word stave, or at the least a word sense under it. Yet the more this extract, to give it some manner of stuff for physically clinging to, must yield itself to every kind of experiment— among which the most pompous was the serious pretext of the drama—the more folk felt that it was suffering by mixture with the threadbare foreign matter, nay, was actually losing its own pungency and pleasantness.

Now, the man from whom this perfume, unnatural as it was, acquired again a corpse which, concocted though it was, at least imitated as cleverly as possible that natural body which had once breathed forth its very soul in fragrance; the uncommonly handy modeler of *artificial* flowers, which he shaped from silk and satin and drenched their arid cups with that distilled substratum, till they began to smell like veritable blooms—this great artist was Joachimo Rossini.

In the glorious, healthy, single-hearted artist nature of Mozart that melòdic scent had found so fostering a soil, that it eke put forth again the bloom of noble art which holds our inmost souls as captives still. Yet even with Mozart it found this food only when the akin, the sound, the purely human offered itself as poetry, for wedding with his wholly musical nature; and it was well-nigh a stroke of luck that this repeatedly occurred for him. Where Mozart was left unheeded by this fecund god, there, too, the artificial essence of that scent could only toilsomely uphold its false, unnecessary life by artificial measures. Melody, however costly were its nurture, fell sick of chill and lifeless formalism, the only heritage the early sped could leave his heirs; for in his death he took away with him—his life.

What Rossini saw around him, in the first flower of his teeming youth, was but the harvesting of Death. When he looked upon the serious, so-called dramatic opera of France, he saw with the keen insight of young joy-in-life a garish corpse; which even Spontini, as he stalked along in gorgeous loneliness, could no longer stir to life, since—as though for some solemn sacrament of self—he had already embalmed himself alive. Driven by his prickling sense of life, Rossini tore the pompous cerecloths from this corpse, as one intent on spying out the secret of its former being. Beneath the jeweled and embroidered trappings he disclosed the true life-giver of even this majestic mummy: and that was—*melody*. When he looked upon the native Opera of Italy and the work of Mozart's heirs, he saw nothing but death again; death in empty forms whose only life showed out to him as melody—melody downright, when stripped of that pretense of character which must seem to him a hollow sham if he turned to what of scamped, of forced and incomplete had sprung therefrom.

To live, however, was what Rossini meant; to do this, he saw well enough that he must live with those who had ears to hear him. The only living thing he had come upon in opera was absolute melody; so he merely needed to pay heed to the *kind* of melody he must strike in order to be heard. He turned his back on the pedantic lumber of heavy scores, and listened where the people sang without a written note. What he there heard was what, out of all the operatic box of tricks, had stayed the most unbidden in the ear: the *naked, ear-delighting, absolute-melodic melody;* that is, melody that was just melody and nothing else; that glides into the ear—one knows not why; that one picks up—one knows not why; that one exchanges today with that of yesterday, and forgets again tomorrow—also, one knows not why; that sounds sad when we are merry, and merry when we are out of sorts; and that still we hum to ourselves—we haven't a ghost of knowledge why.

This melody Rossini struck; and behold!—the mystery of opera was laid bare. What reflection and aesthetic speculation had build up, Rossini's opera melodies pulled down and blew it into nothing, like a baseless dream. The "dramatic" opera met the fate of learning with her problems: those problems whose foundation had really been mistaken insight, and which the deepest pondering could only make but more mistaken and insoluble; until at last the sword of Alexander sets to work, and hews the leathern knot asunder, strewing its thousand thongs on every side. This Alexander-sword is just the naked deed; and such a deed Rossini did, when he made the opera public of the world a witness to the very definite truth that people were merely wanting to hear "delicious melodies" where mistaken artists had earlier fancied to make musical expression do duty for the aim and contents of a drama.

The whole world hurrahed Rossini for his melodies: Rossini, who so admirably knew how to make the employment of these melodies a special art. All organizing of form he left upon one side; the simplest, barrenest, and most transparent that came to hand he filled with all the logical contents it had ever needed—with narcotizing melody. Entirely unconcerned for form, just because he left it altogether undisturbed, he turned his whole genius to the invention of the most amusing hocus-pocus for execution within those forms. To the singers, erstwhile forced to study the dramatic expression of a wearisome and nothing-saying "text," he said: "Do whatever you please with the words; only, before all don't forget to get yourselves liberally applauded for risky runs and melodic *entrechats*." Who so glad to take him at his word as the singers?—To the instrumentists, erstwhile trained to accompany pathetic snatches of song as intelligently as possible in a smooth ensemble, he said: "Take it easy; only, before all don't forget to get yourselves sufficiently clapped for your individual skill, wherever I give you each his opportunity." Who more lavish of their thanks than the instrumentists?—To the opera librettist, who had erstwhile sweated blood beneath the self-willed orderings of the dramatic composer, he said: "Friend, you may put your nightcap on; I have really no more use for you." Who so obliged for such release from sour, thankless toil, as the opera poet?

But who more idolized Rossini, for all these deeds of good, than the whole civilized world—so far as the opera house could hold it? And who had better reason than it had? Who, with so much talent, had shown it such profound consideration as Rossini?—Did he learn that the public of one city had a particular fancy for prima donna's runs, while another preferred a sentimental song, straightway he gave his prima donnas nothing but runs, for the first city; for the second, only sentimental songs. Did he discover that *here* folk liked to hear the drum in the band, at once he made the overture to a rustic opera begin with a rolling of the drum. Was he told that people *there* were passionately fond of a crescendo, in ensemble pieces, he sat down and wrote an opera in the form of a continuously recurring crescendo. Only once had he cause to rue his complaisance. For Naples he was advised to be more careful with his construction; his more solidly built-up opera did not take; and Rossini resolved never in his life again to think of carefulness, even if advised to.

Not the smallest charge of vanity or overweening self-conceit can we bring against Rossini, if, looking at the vast success of his treatment of opera, he laughed people in the face and told them he had found the true secret for which his predecessors had groped in vain. When he maintained that it would be easy for him to consign to oblivion the operas of his greatest forerunners, not excepting Mozart's *Don Giovanni,* by the simple expedient of composing the same subject over again in *his own* fashion, it was by no means arrogance that spoke out here, but the certain instinct of what the public really asked from opera. In very deed, our musical pietists would have only had to see their own complete confusion, in the appearance of a Rossinian "Don Giovanni"; for it may be taken for granted that, with the genuine, verdict-giving theatrical public, Mozart's *Don Giovanni* must have had to yield—if not for ever, still for long enough—to that of Rossini. For this is the real turn that Rossini gave the opera question: down to their last rag, his operas appealed to the public; he made this public, with all its whims and wishes, the determinative factor in the opera.

If the opera public had at all possessed the character and significance of the folk, in the proper sense of the word,

Rossini must have seemed to us the most thorough-paced revolutionary in the whole domain of art. In face of one section of our society, however, a section only to be regarded as an unnatural outgrowth from the folk, and which in its social superfluity, nay, harmfulness, can be looked on only as the knot of caterpillars that erodes the healthy, nourishing leaves of the natural folk tree, and thence at most derives the vital force to flutter through a day's luxurious existence as a giddy swarm of butterflies; in face of such a folk's scum, which, gathering above a sediment of sordid filth, can rise to vicious elegance but never into sterling human culture; in short—to give the thing its fittest name—in face of our opera public, Rossini was no more than reactionary: whereas we have to view Gluck and his followers as methodic revolutionaries on principle, though powerless for radical results. Under the banner of the luxurious but only genuine content of the opera and its logical development, Joachimo Rossini reacted just as successfully against the doctrinaire maxims of the revolutionary Gluck as Prince Metternich, his great protector, under the banner of the inhuman but only veritable content of European statecraft and its logical enforcement, reacted againsct the doctrinaire maxims of the liberal revolutionaries who, *within* this system of the state and without a total upheaval of its unnatural content, desired to install the human and the reasonable in the selfsame forms which breathed that content out of every pore. As Metternich,* with perfect logic on his side, could not conceive the *state* under any form but that of *absolute monarchy*, so Rossini, with no less force of argument, could conceive the *opera* under no other form than that of *absolute melody*. Both men said: "Do you ask for opera and state? Here you have them—there are no others!"

With Rossini the real *life history of opera* comes to end. It was at end, when the unconscious seedling of its being had evolved to nakedness and conscious bloom; when the musician had been avowed the absolute factor of this artwork, invested with despotic power; when the taste of the theatre public had been recognized as the only standard for his demeanor. It was at end, when all pretense of drama had been scrupulously swept away; when the performers had been allotted the showiest virtuosity of song as their only

---

* It should not be forgotten that Metternich, only two years before the writing of this sentence, had played an important part in suppressing the Austro-German revolutionary movement.—Tr.

task, and their hence-sprung claims on the composer had been acknowledged as their most inalienable of rights. It was at end, when the great musical public had come to take quite characterless melody for music's only content, a band-box of operatic "numbers" for the only joinery of musical form, the intoxication of an opera night's narcotic fumes for the sole effect of music's essence. It was at end—that day the deified of Europe, Rossini lolling in the rankest lap of luxury, deemed it becoming to pay the world-shy anchorite, the moody Beethoven, already held for half-insane, a ceremonial visit—which the latter did not return. What thing may it have been, the wanton, roving eye of Italy's voluptuous son beheld, when it plunged unwitting in the eerie glance, the sorrow-broken, faint with yearning—and yet death-daring look of its unfathomable opposite? Did there toss before it the locks of that wild shock of hair, of the Medusa head that none might look upon and live? Thus much is certain: with Rossini died the opera.

The history of opera, since Rossini, is at bottom nothing elst but the history of operatic melody; of its application from an art-speculative, its execution from an effect-hunting stand-point.

3. Weber's contribution

WEBER'S objection to Rossini was directed only against his melody's shallowness and want of character; by no means against the unnatural position of the musician toward the drama. On the contrary, Weber only added to this unnatural-ness, in that he assigned himself a still more heightened posi-tion, as against the poet, by a characteristic ennobling of his melody; a position loftier in exact degree as his melody out-topped Rossini's in just that point of nobility of character. To Rossini the poet hung on like a jolly trencherman, whom the composer—distinguished, but affable person that he was —treated to his heart's content with oysters and champagne; so that, in the whole wide world, the poet found himself nowhere better off than with the famous maestro. Weber, on the other hand, from unbending faith in the characteristic pureness of his one and indivisible melody, tyrannized over the poet with dogmatic cruelty, and forced him to erect the very stake on which the wretch was to let himself be burned to ashes for the kindling of the fire of Weber's melody. The poet of *Der Freischütz*, entirely without his own knowledge, had committed this act of suicide: from out his very ashes he protested, while the flames of Weber's fire were already filling all the air; he called to the world that these flames were really leaping forth from *him*. But he made a radical mistake; his wooden logs gave forth no flame until they were consumed— destroyed: their ashes alone, the prosaic dialogue, could he claim as his property after the fire.

After *Der Freischütz* Weber sought him out a more ac- commodating poet; for a new opera he took into his pay a lady, from whose more unconditional subservience he even demanded that, after the burning of the funeral pile, she should not leave behind so much as the last ashes of her prose: she should allow herself to be consumed flesh and bone in the furnace of his melody. From Weber's correspondence with Frau von Chezy, during the preparation of the text of *Euryanthe*, we learn with what painstaking care he felt again compelled to rack the last drop of blood from the poetic helper; how he rejects and prescribes, and once more pre- scribes and rejects; here cuts, there asks for more; insists on lengthenings here and shortenings there—nay extends his orders even to the characters themselves, their motives and their actions. Was he in this, mayhap, a peevish malcontent, or a boastful parvenu who, inflated by the success of his *Freischütz*, desired to play the despot where by rights he should have obeyed? No, no! Out of his mouth there spake alone the honorable artist-care of the musician, who tempted by stress of circumstance, had undertaken to construct the drama itself from absolute melody.

Weber here was led into a serious error, but into an error which was necessarily bound to take him. He had lifted melody to its fairest, most feeling height of nobleness; he wanted now to crown it as the Muse of Drama herself, and by her strenuous hand to chase away the whole ribald pack of profaners of the stage. As in the *Freischütz* he had led each lyric fiber of the opera poem into this melody, so now he wished to shower down the drama from the beams of his melodic planet. One might almost say that the melody for his *Euryanthe* was ready before a line of its poem; to provide the latter, he wanted only someone who should take his melody completely into ear and heart, and merely poetize upon it. Since this was not practicable, however, he and his poetress fell into a fretful theoretical quarrel, in which a clear agreement was possible from neither the one side nor the other—so that in this case of all others, when calmly tested, we may plainly see into what painful insecurity men of Weber's gifts and artistic love of truth may be misled, by holding fast to a fundamental artistic error.

After all was done, the impossible was bound to stay impossible for Weber too. Despite all his suggestions and instructions to the poet, he could not procure a dramatic groundwork which he might entirely dissolve into his melody; because he wished to call into being a genuine drama, and not merely a play filled out with lyric moments, where—as in *Der Freischütz*—he would need to employ his music for nothing but those lyric moments. In the text of *Euryanthe,* besides the dramatic-lyric elements—for which, as I have expressed myself, the melody was ready in advance—there was still so much of additional matter quite foreign to absolute music, that Weber was unable to get command of it by his melody proper. If this text had been the work of a veritable poet, who should only have called upon the musician for aid, in the same manner as the musician had now called upon the poet: then this musician, in his affection for the proffered drama, would never have had a moment's hesitancy. Where he recognized no fitting stuff to feed or vindicate his broader musical expression, he would have deployed only his lesser powers, to wit, of furnishing an accompaniment subordinate but ever helpful to the whole; and only where the fullest musical expression was necessarily conditioned by the stuff itself would he have entered with his fullest powers.

The text of *Euryanthe,* however, had sprung from the converse relationship between poet and musician, and wherever the composer—the virtual author of that opera—should by rights have stood aside or withdrawn into the background, there he now could see only a doubled task, namely, that of imprinting on a musically quite sterile stuff a stamp which should be musical throughout. In this Weber could have succeeded only if he had turned to music's frivolous line; if, looking quite aside from truth, he had given rein to the epicurean element, and set death and the devil to amusing melodies *à la* Rossini. But this was the very thing against which Weber lodged his strongest artistic protest: *his* melody should be everywhere *characteristic*, that is, true and answering to each emotion of his subject. Thus he was forced to betake himself to some other expedient.

Wherever his broad-breathed melody—mostly ready in advance, and spread above the text like a glittering garment—would have done that text too manifest a violence, there Weber broke this melody itself in pieces. He then took up the separate portions of his melodic building, and, always according to the declamatory requirements of the words, re-joined them together into a skillful mosaic; which latter he coated with a film of fine melodic varnish, in order thus to preserve for the whole construction an outward show of absolute melody, detachable as much as possible from the text words. The desired illusion, however, he did not succeed in effecting.

Not only Rossini, but Weber himself had made absolute melody so decidedly the main content of opera, that, wrested from its dramatic framework and even stripped of its text words, it had passed over to the public *in its barest nakedness*. A melody must be able to be fiddled and blown, or hammered out upon the pianoforte, *without* thereby losing the smallest particle of its individual essence, if it was ever to become a real melody for the public. To Weber's operas, too, the public merely went to hear as many of such melodies as possible, and the musician was terribly mistaken when he flattered himself that he would see that lacquered declamatory mosaic accepted as melody by this public: for, to tell the truth, that was what the composer really made for. Though in the eyes of Weber himself that mosaic could be justified only by the words of the text, yet on the one side the public was entirely indifferent—and that with perfect justice—to those words; while on the other side it transpired that this text itself had not been quite suitably reproduced in the music. For it was just this immature half-melody that turned the attention of the hearer away from the words, and made him look out anxiously for the formation of a whole melody that never came to light—so that any longing for the presentment of a poetic thought was throttled in advance, while the enjoyment of a melody was all the more painfully curtailed as the longing for it was roused indeed, but never satisfied. Beyond the passages in *Euryanthe* where the composer's artistic judgment could hold his own broad natural melody completely justified, we see in that work his higher artistic efforts crowned with true and beautiful success only where, for love of truth, he quite renounces absolute melody, and—as in the opening scene of the first act—gives the noblest, most faithful musical expression to the emotional dramatic declamation as such; where he therefore sets the aim of his own artistic labors no longer in the music but in the poem, and merely employs his music for the furthering of that aim: which, again, could be attained by nothing but music with such fullness and so convincing truth.

Criticism has never dealt with *Euryanthe* in the measure that its uncommonly instructive content deserves. The public gave an undecided voice, half stirred, half chagrined. Criticism, which at bottom always waits upon the public voice, in order—according to its own intention of the moment—either from that and the outward success to take its cue, or else doggedly to oppose it: this criticism has never been able to take proper stock of the utterly contradictory elements that cross each other in this work, to sift them carefully, and from the composer's endeavor to unite them into one harmonious whole to find a warrant for its ill-success. Yet never, so long as opera has existed, has there been composed a work in which the inner contradictions of the whole genre have been more consistently worked out, more openly exhibited, by a gifted, deeply feeling and truth-loving composer, for all his high endeavor to attain the best. These contradictions are: *absolute, self-sufficing melody, and—unflinchingly true dramatic expression.* Here one or the other must necessarily be sacrificed—either melody or drama. Rossini sacrificed the drama; the noble Weber wished to reinstate it by force of his more judicious melody. He had to learn that this was an impossibility. Weary and exhausted by the troubles of his *Euryanthe*, he sank back upon the yielding pillow of an Oriental fairy dream: through the wonder-horn of Oberon he breathed away his last life's breath.

4. Nadir of opera: music by Meyerbeer, libretto by Scribe

WHAT this noble, lovable Weber, aglow with a pious faith in the omnipotence of his pure melody, vouchsafed him by the fairest spirit of the folk—what *he* had striven for, in vain, was undertaken by a friend of Weber's youth, by Jacob Meyerbeer; but from the standpoint of Rossinian melody.

Meyerbeer passed through all the phases of this melody's development; not from an abstract distance, but in a very concrete nearness, always on the spot. As a Jew, he owned no mother tongue, no speech inextricably entwined among the sinews of his inmost being: he spoke with precisely the same interest in any modern tongue you chose, and set it to music with no further sympathy for its idiosyncrasies than just the question as to how far it showed a readiness to become a pliant servitor to absolute music. This attribute of Meyerbeer's has given occasion to a comparison of him with Gluck; for the latter, too, although a German, wrote operas to French and Italian texts. As a fact, Gluck did not create his music from the instinct of speech (which in such a case must always be the *mother* speech): what he, as musician, was concerned with in his attitude toward speech was its rhetoric, that utterance of the speech organism which merely floats upon the surface of this myriad of organs. Not from the generative force of these organs, did his productive powers mount through the rhetoric into the musical expression; but from the sloughed-off musical expression he harked back to the rhetoric, merely so as to give that baseless expression some ground of vindication. Thus every tongue might well come equally to Gluck, since he was busied only with his rhetoric: if music, in this transcendental line, had been able to pierce through the rhetoric into the very organism of speech, it must then have surely had to transform itself entirely.—In order not to interrupt the course of my argument, I must reserve this extremely weighty topic for thorough investigation in a more appropriate place; for the present I content myself with commending to notice, that Gluck's concern was with an animated rhetoric in general— no matter in what tongue—since in that alone did he find a vindication for his melody; whereas since Rossini this rhetoric has been completely swallowed up in absolute melody, leaving only its materialest of frameworks, its vowels and its consonants, as a scaffolding for musical tone.

Meyerbeer, through his indifference to the spirit of any tongue, and his hence-gained power to make with little pains its outer side his own (a faculty our modern education has brought within the reach of all the well-to-do), was quite cut out for dealing with absolute music divorced from any lingual ties. Moreover, he thus was able to witness on the spot the salient features in the aforesaid march of opera music's evolution: everywhere and everywhen he followed on its footsteps. Above all is it noteworthy that he merely *followed* on this march, and never kept *abreast* of, to say nothing of outstripping it. He was like the starling who follows the plowshare down the field, and merrily picks up the earthworm just uncovered in the furrow. Not one departure is his own, but each he has eavesdropped from his forerunner, exploiting it with monstrous ostentation; and so swiftly that the man in front has scarcely spoken a word, than *he* has bawled out the entire phrase, quite unconcerned as to whether he has caught the meaning of that word; whence it has generally arisen that he has actually said something slightly different from what the man in front intended. But the noise of the Meyerbeerian phrase was so deafening that the man in front could no longer arrive at bringing out his own real meaning: willy-nilly, if only to get a word in edgeways, he was forced at last to chime into that phrase.

In Germany alone was Meyerbeer unsuccessful, in his search for a new-fledged phrase to fit anyhow the word of Weber: what Weber uttered from the fill of his melodic life could not be echoed in the lessoned, arid formalism of Meyerbeer. At last, disgusted with the fruitless toil, he betrayed his friend by listening to Rossini's siren strains, and departed for the land where grew those raisins. Thus he became the weathercock of European opera music, the vane that always veers at first uncertain with the shift of wind, and comes to a standstill only when the wind itself has settled on its quarter. Thus Meyerbeer in Italy composed operas *à la* Rossini, precisely till the larger wind of Paris commenced to chop, and Auber and Rossini with their *Muette** and their *Tell* blew the new gale into a storm! With one bound was Meyerbeer in Paris! There he found, however, in the Frenchified Weber (need I recall *Robin des bois?*) and the be-Berliozed Beethoven, certain moments to which neither Auber nor Rossini had paid attention, as lying too far out of their way, but which Meyerbeer in virtue of his cosmopolitan capacity knew very well to valuate. He summed up all his overhearings in one monstrous hybrid phrase, whose strident outcry put Rossini and Auber to sudden silence: "Robert," the grim "Devil," set his clutches on them all.

In the survey of our operatic history, there is something most painful about being *able to speak good only of the dead*,

---

* *La Muette de Portici*, better known as *Masaniello*.—EDS.

and being forced to pursue the living with remorseless bitterness! But if we want to be candid, since we *must*, we have to recognize that the departed masters of this art deserve alone the martyr's crown; if they were victims to an illusion, yet that illusion showed in them so high and beautiful, and they themselves believed so earnestly its sacred truth, that they offered up their whole artistic lives in sorrowful, yet joyful, sacrifice thereto. No living and still active tone-setter any longer strives from inner stress for such a martyrdom; the illusion now is laid so bare, that no more can anyone repose implicit trust in it. Bereft of faith, nay, robbed of joy, operatic art has fallen, at the hand of its modern masters, to a mere commercial article. Even the Rossinian wanton smile is now no more to be perceived; all round us nothing but the yawn of ennui, or the grin of madness! Almost we feel most drawn toward the aspect of the madness; in it we find the last remaining breath of that illusion from which there blossomed once such noble sacrifice.

The juggling side of the odious exploitation of our modern opera affairs we shall therefore here forget, now that we must call before us the work of the last surviving and still active hero of operatic composition: that aspect could fill us only with indignation, whereby we might perhaps be betrayed into inhuman harshness toward a personage, did we lay on it alone the burden of the foul corruption of those affairs which surely hold this personage the more a captive as to us it seems set upon their dizziest peak, adorned with crown and scepter. Do we not know that kings and princes, precisely in their most arbitrary dealings, are now the greatest slaves of all?—No, in this king of operatic music let us look only upon the traits of madness, by which he appears to us an object of regret and warning, not of scorn! For the sake of everlasting art, we must learn to read the symptoms of this madness; because by its contortions shall we plainest recognize the illusion that gave birth to an artistic genre, as to whose erroneous basis we must thoroughly clear up our minds before ever we can gain the healthy, youthful courage to set rejuvenating hands to art itself.

To this inquiry we may now press on with rapid step, as we have already shown the essence of that madness, and have only to observe a few of its most salient features in order to be quite sure about it.

We have seen the frivolous opera melody—that is, robbed of any real connection with the poem's text—grow big with taking up the tune of national song, and seen it swell into the pretense of Historic Characteristique. We have further noticed how, with an ever-dwindling individualization of the chief roles in the musical drama, the character of the action was more and more allotted to the—"emancipated"—masses, from whom this character was then to fall as a mere reflex on the main transactors. We have remarked that only by a historic costume could the surrounding mass be stamped with any distinctive, at all cognizable character; and have seen the composer, so as to maintain his supremacy against the scene painter and stage tailor—to whom had virtually fallen the merit of establishing the Historic Characteristique—compelled to outdo them by the most unwonted application of his purely musical nostrums. Finally, we have seen how the most desperate departure in instrumental music brought the composer an extraordinary sort of mosaic melody, whose waywardest of combinations offered the means of appearing strange and outlandish, whenever he had a fancy that way—and how, by a miraculous employment of the orchestra, calculated solely for material surprise, he believed he could imprint on such a method the stamp of a quite special Characteristique.

Now, we must not leave out of sight that, after all, this whole conjuncture could never have arisen without the poet's confederacy; wherefore we shall turn, for a moment, to an examination of the most modern relationship of the musician to the poet.

Through Rossini the new operatic tendency started decidedly from Italy: *there* the poet had degenerated into an utter nonentity. But with the transshipment of Rossini's tendency to Paris, the position of the poet also altered. We have already denoted the peculiarities of French opera, and found that its kernel was the entertaining conversation of the couplet. In French comic opera the poet had erstwhile relinquished to the composer but a limited field, which he was to cultivate for himself while the poet abode in undisputed possession of the ground estate. Now although, in the nature of the thing, that musical terrain had gradually so encroached upon the rest that it took up in time the whole estate, yet the poet still held the title deeds, and the musician remained a mere feoffee, who certainly regarded the entire fief as his hereditary property, but notwithstanding—as in the whilom Romo-German Empire —owed allegiance to the emperor as his feudal lord. The poet enfeoffed, and the musician enjoyed. In this situation alone have there ever come to light the healthiest of opera's progeny, when viewed as a dramatic genre. The poet honestly bestirred himself to invent characters and situations, to provide an entertaining and enthralling piece, which only in its final elaboration did he trim for the musician and the latter's forms; so that the actual weakness of these French opera poems lay more in the fact that, by their very content, they mostly called for no music at all, than in that they were swamped by music in advance. On the stage of the Opéra Comique this entertaining, often delightfully witty genre was in its native element; and in it the best work was always done when the music could enter with unforced naturalness into the poetry.

This genre was now translated by Scribe and Auber into the pompous phraseology of so-called "grand opera." In *La Muette de Portici* we still can plainly recognize a well-planned theatric piece, in which the dramatic interest is nowhere as yet subordinated with manifest intention to a purely musical one: only, in this poem the dramatic action is already essentially transferred to the operations of the surrounding mass, so that the main transactors behave more as talking representatives of the mass than as real persons who act from individual necessity. So slack already, arrived before the imposing chaos of grand opera, did the poet hold the reins of the opera carriage; those reins he was soon to drop upon the horses' backs! But whereas in *La Muette*, and in *Tell*, the poet still kept the reins within his hand, since it occurred to neither Auber nor Rossini to do anything else but just take their musical ease and melodious comfort in the stately opera coach—unworried as to how and whither the well-drilled coachman steered its wheels—now Meyerbeer, to whom that rank melodic ease did not come so in the grain, felt impelled to seize the coachman's reins, and by the zigzag of his route arouse the needful notice, which he could not succeed in attracting to himself so long as he quietly sat in the coach, with no company other than his own musical personality.

Merely in scattered anecdotes has it come to our ears, what painful torments Meyerbeer inflicted on his poet, Scribe, during the sketching of his opera subjects. But if we paid no heed to any of these anecdotes, and knew absolutely nothing of the mysteries of those opera confabulations between Scribe and Meyerbeer, we should still see clearly by the resultant poems themselves what a pothersome, bewildering incubus must have weighed on the else so rapid, so easy-working and quick-witted Scribe, when he had to cobble up those bombastical, rococo texts for Meyerbeer. While Scribe continued to write fluent, often interestingly planned dramatic poems for other composers; texts in any case worked out with considerable natural skill, and at least based always on a definite plot, with easily intelligible situations to suit that plot—yet this uncommonly expert poet turned out for Meyerbeer the veriest fustian, the lamest galimatias; actions without a plot, situations of the most insane confusion, characters of the most ridiculous buffoonery. This could never have come about by natural means: so easily does no sober judgment, like that of Scribe, submit to the experiments of craziness. Scribe must first have had his brain unhinged for him, before he conjured up a *Robert the Devil*; he must have first been robbed of all sound sense for dramatic action, before he lent himself in *The Huguenots* to the mere compilation of scene-shifters' nuances and contrasts; he must have been violently initiated into the mysteries of historical hanky-panky, before he consented to paint a *Prophet* of the sharpers.

We here perceive a determinant influence of the composer on the poet, akin to that which Weber exerted on the poetess of *Euryanthe*: but from what diametrically opposite motives! Weber wanted a drama that could pass with all its members, with every scenic nuance, into his noble, soulful melody. Meyerbeer, on the contrary, wanted a monstrous piebald, historico-romantic, diabolico-religious, fanatico-libidinous, sacro-frivolous, mysterio-criminal, autolyco-sentimental dramatic hotchpotch, therein to find material for a curious chimeric music—a want which, owing to the indomitable buckram of his musical temperament, could never be quite suitably supplied. He felt that, with all his garnered store of musical effects, there was still a something wanting, a something hitherto nonexistent, but which he could bring to bearing were he only to collect the whole thing from every farthest cranny, heap it together in one mass of crude confusion, dose it well with stage gunpowder and lycopodium, and spring it crashing through the air.

What he wanted therefore from his librettist was, so to speak, an inscenation of the Berliozian orchestra; only—mark this well!—with the most humiliating degradation of it to the sickly basis of Rossini's vocal trills and *fermate*—for sake of "dramatic" opera. To bring the whole stock of elements of musical effect into some sort of harmonious concord through the drama would have necessarily appeared to him a sorry way of setting about his business; for Meyerbeer was no idealistic dreamer, but, with a keen practical eye to the modern opera public, he saw that by a harmonious concord he would have gained no one to his side, whereas by a rambling hotch-potch he must certainly catch the moods of all, that is, of each man in his line. So that nothing was more important for him, than a maze of mad cross-purposes, and the merry Scribe must sweat blood to concoct a dramatic medley to his taste. In cold-blooded care the musician stood before it, calmly meditating as to which piece of the monstrosity he could fit out with some particular tatter from his musical storeroom, so strikingly and cryingly that it should appear quite out of the ordinary, and therefore—"characteristic."

Thus, in the eyes of our art criticism, he developed the powers of music into Historical Characteristique, and brought matters so far that he was told, as the most delicate compliment, that the texts of his operas were terribly poor stuff *but what wonders his music knew how to make out of this wretched rubbish!*—So the utmost triumph of music was reached: the composer had razed the poet to the ground, and upon the ruins of operatic poetry the musician was crowned the only *authentic poet!*

The secret of Meyerbeer's operatic music is—*effect*. If we wish to gain a notion of what we are to understand by this "effect," it is important to observe that in this connection we do not as a rule employ the more homely word *Wirkung* [lit. "a working"]. Our natural feeling can only conceive of *Wirkung* as bound up with an antecedent *cause*: but here, where we are instinctively in doubt as to whether such a correlation subsists, or are even as good as told that it does not subsist at all, we look perplexedly around us for a word to denote anyhow the impression which we think we have received from, for example, the music pieces of Meyerbeer; and so we fall upon a foreign word, not directly appealing to our natural feeling, such as just this word "effect." If, then, we wish to define what we understand by this word, we may translate "effect" by "a working, without a cause."

As a fact, the Meyerbeerian music produces, on those who are able to edify themselves thereby, a working-without-a-cause. This miracle was possible only to the extremest music, that is, to an expressional power which—in opera—had from the first sought to make itself more and more independent of anything worth expressing, and had finally proclaimed its attainment of complete independence by reducing to a moral and artistic nullity the object of expression, which alone should have given to this expression its being, warranty, and measure; by reducing it to such a degree that this *object* now could gain its being, warranty, and measure only from a mere act of grace on the part of music—an act which had thus itself become devoid of any real expression. This act of grace, however, could be made possible only in conjunction with other coefficients of absolute working. In the extremest instrumental music appeal had been made to the vindicating force of fantasy, to which a program, or mayhap a mere title, had given an extramusical leverage: in opera this leverage was to be materialized, that is, the imagination was to be absolved from any painful toil. What had there been programmatically adduced from moments of the phenomenal life of man or nature was here to be presented in the most material reality, so as to produce a fantastic working without the smallest fellow working of the fantasy. This material leverage the composer borrowed from the scenic apparatus, inasmuch as he took also purely for their own sake the workings it was able to produce, that is, absolved them from the only object that, lying beyond the realm of mechanism and on the soil of life-portraying poetry, could have given them conditionment and vindication. Let us explain our meaning clearly by one example, which will at the same time characterize the most exhaustively the whole of Meyerbeerian art.

Let us suppose that a poet has been inspired with the idea of a hero, a champion of light and freedom, in whose breast there flames an all-consuming love for his downtrod brother men, afflicted in their holiest rights. The poet wishes to depict this hero at the zenith of his career, in the full radiance of his deeds of glory, and chooses for his picture the following supreme moment. With thousands of the folk—who have left house and home, left wife and children, to follow his inspiring call, to conquer or to die in fight against their powerful oppressors—the hero has arrived before a fortressed city, which must be stormed by his unpracticed mob if the work of freedom is to come to a victorious issue. Through earlier hardships and mishaps, disheartenment has spread apace; evil passions, discord, and confusion are raging in his hosts: all is lost if all shall not be won today. This is a plight in which heroes wax to their fullest grandeur. In the solitude of the night just past the hero has taken counsel of the god within him, of the spirit of the purest love for fellow men, and with its breath has sanctified himself; and now the poet takes him in the gray of dawn, and leads him forth among those hosts, who are already wavering as to whether they should prove coward beasts or godlike heroes.

At his mighty voice, the folk assemble. That voice drives home into the inmost marrow of these men, who now alike grow conscious of the god within them; they feel their hearts uplifted and ennobled, and their inspiration in its turn uplifts the hero to still loftier heights; from inspiration he presses on to deed. He seizes the standard and waves it high toward those fearful walls, the embattled city of the foe, who, so long as they lie secure behind their trenches, make impossible a better future for mankind. "On, then, comrades! To die or conquer! This city *must* be ours!"

The poet now has reached his utmost confines: upon the boards he wills to show the one instant when this high-strung mood steps suddenly before us with all the plainness of a great reality; the scene must now become for us the stage of all the world; Nature must now declare herself a sharer in this exaltation; no longer can she stay a chilling, chance bystander. Lo! sacred Want compels the poet: he parts the cloudy curtains of the morn, and at his .word the streaming sun mounts high above the city, that city henceforth hallowed to the victory of the inspired.

Here is the flower of all-puissant art, and this wonder blossoms only from the art of drama.

Only, the opera composer has no longing for wonders such as blossom merely from the dramatic poet's inspiration and may be effectuated by a picture taken lovingly from life itself: he .wishes for the *effect* but not the *cause*, since the latter lies outside his sway. In a leading scene of Meyerbeer's *Le Prophète*, where the *externals* resemble those just described, we obtain for the ear the purely physical effect of a hymnlike melody, derived from the folk song and swelled into a sound like thunder: for the eye, that of a sunrise in which there is positively nothing for us to see but a masterstroke of mechanism. The object that should be fired by that melody should be shone on by this sun, *the inspired hero* who from very ecstasy must pour his soul into that melody, who at the stressful climax of necessity called forth the dawning of this sun—the warranty, the kernel of the whole luxuriant dramatic fruit— *is absolutely not to hand*. In his place there functions a characteristically costumed tenor, whom Meyerbeer has commissioned through his private-secretary-poet, Scribe, to sing as charmingly as possible and at the same time behave a wee bit communistically, in order that the gentry might have an extra dash of piquancy to think into the thing. The hero of whom we spoke before is some poor devil who out of sheer weakness has taken on the role of trickster, and finally bewails in the most pitiful fashion—by no means any error, any fanatical hallucination, which might at a pinch have called for a sun to shine on it—but solely his weakness and mendacity.

What considerations may have joined forces to call into the world such an unworthy object under the title of a "Prophet" we shall here leave unexplored; let it suffice us to observe the resultant, which is instructive enough in all conscience. First, we see in this example the complete moral and artistic dishonorment of the poet, in whose work even those who are most favorably disposed to the composer can find no single hair'sbreadth of merit: so!—the poetic aim is no longer to attract us in the slightest; on the contrary, it is to revolt us. The performer is now to interest us as nothing but a costumed singer; in the above-named scene, he can do this only by his singing of that aforesaid melody, which makes its effect entirely for itself—as melody. Wherefore the sun is likewise to work entirely for itself, namely, as a successful theatrical copy of the authentic sun: so that the ground of its "working" comes not at all into the province of drama, but into that of sheer mechanics—the only thing left for us to think about when it puts in its appearance; for how alarmed the composer would be, if one chose to take this appearance as an intentional transfiguration of the hero, in his capacity of champion of mankind! No, no: for him and his public, everything must be done to turn such thoughts away, and guide attention solely to that masterstroke of mechanism. And thus in this unique scene, so heaped with honors by the public, the whole of art is resolved into its mechanical integers: the externals of art are turned into its essence; and this essence we find to be—*effect*, the absolute effect, that is, the stimulus of an artificial love titillation, without the potence of an actual taste of love.

5. Opera affirms the separation of the arts.

As man by love sinks his whole nature in that of woman, in order to pass over through her into a third being, the child—and yet finds but himself again in all the loving trinity, though

in this self a widened, filled, and finished whole: so may each
of the individual arts find its own self again in the perfect,
throughly liberated artwork—nay, look upon itself as broadened to this artwork—so soon as, on the path of genuine love
and by sinking of itself within the kindred arts, it returns upon
itself and finds the guerdon of its love in the perfect work of
art to which it knows itself expanded. Only that art variety,
however, which wills the common artwork, reaches therewith
the highest fill of its own particular nature; whereas that art
which merely wills *itself*, its own exclusive fill of self, stays
empty and unfree—for all the luxury that it may heap upon
its solitary semblance. But the *will* to form the common artwork arises in each branch of art by instinct and unconsciously, so soon as e'er it touches on its own confines and
gives itself to the answering art, not merely strives to take
from it. It stays *throughout itself* only when it *throughly gives
itself away*: whereas it must fall to its very opposite, if it at
last must feed only upon the other: "Whose bread I eat, his
song I'll sing." But when it gives itself *entirely* to the second,
and stays *entirely* enwrapped therein, it then may pass from
that *entirely* into the third; and thus become once more *entirely itself*, in highest fullness, in the associate artwork.

Of all these arts not one so sorely needed an espousal with
another, as that of *Tone*; for her peculiar character is that of
a fluid nature element poured out betwixt the more defined
and individualized substances of the two other arts. Only
through the rhythm of dance, or as bearer of the word, could
she brace her deliquescent being to definite and characteristic
corporeality. But neither of the other arts could bring herself
to plunge, in love without reserve, into the element of Tone:
each drew from it so many bucketsful as seemed expedient for
her own precise and egoistic aims; each took from Tone, but
gave not in return; so that poor Tone, who of her life-need
stretched out her hands in all directions, was forced at last
herself to *take* for very means of maintenance. Thus she engulfed the word at first, to make of it what suited best her
pleasure: but while she disposed of this word as her willful
feeling listed, in Catholic music, she lost its bony framework
—so to say—of which, in her desire to become a human
being, she stood in need to bear the liquid volume of her
blood, and round which she might have crystallized a sinewy
flesh. A new and energetic handling of the word, in order to
gain shape therefrom, was shown by Protestant church music;
which, in the "Passion music," pressed on toward an ecclesi-

astical drama, wherein the word was no longer a mere shifting vehicle for the expression of feeling, but girt itself to thoughts depicting action. In this church drama, Music, while still retaining her predominance and building everything else into her own pedestal, almost compelled Poetry to behave in earnest and like a man toward her. But coward Poetry appeared to dread this challenge; she deemed it as well to cast a few neglected morsels to swell the meal of this mightily waxing monster, Music, and thus to pacify it; only, however, to regain the liberty of staying undisturbed within her own peculiar province, the egoistic sphere of literature. It is to this selfish, cowardly bearing of Poetry toward Tone that we stand indebted for that unnatural abortion the oratorio, which finally transplanted itself from the church into the concert hall. The oratorio would give itself the airs of drama; but only precisely in so far as it might still preserve to Music the unquestioned right of being the chief concern, the only leader of the drama's "tone."

Where Poetry fain would reign in solitude, as in the spoken play, she took Music into her menial service, for her own convenience; as, for instance, for the entertainment of the audience between the acts, or even for the enhancement of the effect of certain dumb transactions, such as the irruption of a cautious burglar, and matters of that sort! Dance did the selfsame thing, when she leaped proudly onto saddle, and graciously condescended to allow Music to hold the stirrup. Exactly so did Tone behave to Poetry in the oratorio: she merely let her pile the heap of stones, from which she might erect her building as she fancied.

But Music at last capped all this ever-swelling arrogance by her shameless insolence in the opera. Here she claimed tribute of the art of Poetry down to its utmost farthing: it was no longer merely to make her verses, no longer merely to suggest dramatic characters and sequences, as in the oratorio, in order to give her a handle for her own distention—but it was to lay down its whole being and all its powers at her feet, to offer up complete dramatic characters and complex situations, in short, the entire ingredients of drama; in order that she might take this gift of homage and make of it whatever her fancy listed.

The Opera, as the seeming point of reunion of all the three related arts, has become the meeting place of these sisters' most self-seeking efforts. Undoubtedly Tone claims for herself the supreme right of legislation therein; nay, it is solely to her struggle—though led by egoism—toward the genuine artwork

of the drama that we owe the opera at all. But in degree as
Poetry and Dance were bid to be her simple slaves, there rose
amid *their* egoistic ranks a growing spirit of rebellion against
their domineering sister. The arts of Dance and Poetry had
taken a personal lease of drama *in their own way*: the spec-
tacular play and the pantomimic ballet were the two territories
between which Opera now deployed her troops, taking from
each whatever she deemed indispensable for the self-glorification of music. Play and Ballet, however, were well aware of
her aggressive self-sufficiency: they only lent themselves to
their sister against their will, and in any case with the mental
reservation that on the first favorable opportunity they each
would clear themselves an exclusive field. So Poetry leaves
behind her feeling and her pathos, the only fitting wear for
Opera, and throws her net of modern intrigue around her
sister Music; who, without being able to get a proper hold of
it, must willy-nilly twist and turn the empty cobweb, which
none but the nimble play-sempstress herself can plait into a
tissue: and there she chirps and twitters, as in the French con-
fectionary operas, until at last her peevish breath gives out,
and sister Prose steps in to fill the stage. Dance, on the other
hand, has only to espy some breach in the breath-taking of the
tyrannizing songstress, some chilling of the lava stream of musical emotion—and in an instant she flings her legs astride the
boards; trounces sister Music off the scene, down to the solitary confinement of the orchestra; and spins and whirls and
runs around, until the public can no longer see the wood for
wealth of leaves, that is, the opera for the crowd of legs.

Thus opera becomes the mutual compact of the egoism of
the three related arts.

6. *Origin of modern drama: the romance and Greek drama*

THE modern drama has a twofold origin: the one a natural,
and peculiar to our historic evolution, namely, the *romance*—
the other an alien, and grafted on our evolution by reflection,
namely, the *Greek drama* as looked at through the misunderstood rules of Aristotle.

The real kernel of all our poesy may be found in the romance. In their endeavor to make this kernel as tasty as possible, our poets have repeatedly had recourse to a closer or more distant imitation of the Greek drama.

The topmost flower of that drama which sprang directly from romance we have in the plays of Shakespeare; in the farthest removal from this drama, we find its diametrical opposite in the *tragédie* of Racine. Between these two extremes our whole remaining dramatic literature sways undecided to and fro. In order to apprehend the exact character of this wavering, we must look a little closer into the natural origin of our drama.

Searching the history of the world, since the decay of Grecian art, for an artistic period of which we may justly feel proud, we find that period in the so-called Renaissance, a name we give to the termination of the Middle Ages and the commencement of a new era. Here the inner man is struggling, with a veritable giant's force, to utter himself. The whole ferment of that wondrous mixture, of Germanic individual herodom with the spirit of Roman-Catholicizing Christendom, is thrusting from within outward, as though in the externalizing of its essence to rid itself of indissoluble inner scruples. Everywhere this thrust evinced itself as a passion for delineation of surface, and nothing more; for no man can give himself implicitly and wholly, unless he be at one within. But this the artist of the Renaissance was not; he seized only the outer surface, to flee from his inner discord. Though this bent proclaimed itself most palpably in the direction of the plastic arts, yet it is no less visible in poetry. Only, we must bear in mind that, whereas painting had addressed itself to a faithful delineation of the living man, poetry was already turning from this mere delineation to his *representment* and that by stepping forward from romance to drama.

The poetry of the Middle Ages had already brought forth the narrative poem and developed it to its highest pitch. This poem described men's doings and undergoings, and their sum of moving incident, in much the same way as the painter bestirred himself to present the characteristic moments of such actions. But the field of the poet who waived all living, direct portrayal of his action by real men was as unbounded as his reader's or hearer's force of imagination, to which alone he appealed. In this field he felt the more tempted into extravagant combinations of incidents and localities, as his vision em-

braced an ever wider horizon of outward actions going on
around him, of actions born from the very spirit of that adven-
turous age. Man, at variance with himself, and seeking in art
production a refuge from his inward strife—just as he had
earlier sought in vain to heal this strife itself by means of art*
—felt no urgence to speak out a definite *something* of his
inner being, but rather to go a-hunting for this something in
the world outside. In a sense he dissipated his inner thoughts
by an altogether wayward dealing with everything brought
him from the outer world; and the more motley he could
make his mixture of these diverse shows, the surer might he
hope to reach his instinctive goal, of inward dissipation. The
master of this charming art, but reft of any inwardness, of any
hold on soul—was Ariosto.

But the less these shimmering pictures of fantasy were able,
after many a monstrous divagation, to distract in turn the
inner man; and the more this man, beneath the weight of
political and religious deeds of violence, found himself driven
by his inner nature to an energetic counterthrust: so much the
plainer, in the class of poetry now under notice, do we see his
struggle to become master of the multifarious stuff from within
outward, to give his fashionings a firm-set center, and to take
this center, this axis of his artwork, from his own beholdings,
from his firm-set will-ing of something in which his inner
being may speak out. This something is the matrix of the
newer age, the condensing of the individual essence to a definite artistic will. From the vast mass of outward matters,
which theretofore could never show themselves diversified
enough to please the poet, the component parts are sorted into
groups akin; the multiple points of action are condensed into
a definite character drawing of the transactors. Of what unspeakable weight it is, for any inquiry into the nature of art,
that this inner urgence of the poet, such as we may see before
our very eyes, could at last content itself with nothing but
reaching the plainest utterance through direct portrayal to the
senses: in one word, *that the romance became a drama!* This
mastery of the outward stuff, so as to show the inner view of
the essence of that stuff, could be brought to a successful issue
only by setting the subject itself before the senses in all the
persuasiveness of actuality; and this was to be achieved in
drama and nothing else.

* We need only recall the genuine Christian poetry.—R. WAG-
NER.

With fullest necessity did Shakespeare's drama spring from life and our historic evolution: his creation was just as much conditioned by the nature of our poetic art as the drama of the future, in strict keeping with its nature, will be born from the satisfaction of a need which Shakespearian drama has aroused but not yet stilled.

Shakespeare—of whom we here must always think as in company with his forerunners, and only as their chief—condensed the narrative romance into the drama, inasmuch as he translated it, so to say, for performance on the stage. Human actions, erewhile merely figured by the narrative talk of poesy, he now gave to actual talking men to bring before both eye and ear—to men who, so long as the performance lasted, identified themselves in look and bearing with the to-be-represented persons of the romance. For this he found a stage and actors, who till then had hidden from the poet's eye—like a subterranean stream of genuine folk's artwork, flowing secretly, yet flowing ever—but, now that want compelled him to their finding, were discovered swiftly by his yearning gaze. The characteristic of this folk stage, however, lay in that the *mummers* addressed themselves *to the eye*, and intentionally, almost solely to the eye; whence their distinctive name. Their performances, being given in open places before a wide-stretched throng, could produce effect by almost nothing but gesture; and by gesture only actions can be rendered plainly, but not—if speech is lacking—the inner motives of such actions: so that the play of these performers, by its very nature, bristled with just as grotesque and wholesale odds and ends of action as the romance whose scrappy plethora of stuff the poet was laboring to compress. The poet, who looked toward this folk's play, could not but see that for want of an intelligible speech it was driven into a monstrous plethora of action; precisely as the narrative romancist was driven thither by his inability actually to display his talked-of persons and their haps. He needs must cry to these mummers: "Give me your stage; I give you my speech; and so we both are suited!"

In favor of drama, we see the poet narrowing down the folk stage to the theatre. Exactly as the action itself, through a clear exposition of the motives that called it forth, must be compressed into its weightiest definite moments, so did the necessity become evident, to compress the showplace also; and chiefly out of regard for the spectators, who now were not merely to see, but alike plainly to hear. Together with its effect upon the space, this curtailment had also to extend to the time duration, of the dramatic play. The mystery stage of the Middle Ages, set up in spreading fields, in streets or open places of the towns, offered the assembled populace an entertainment lasting all day long, nay—as we even still may see—for several days on end: whole histories, the complete adventures of a lifetime, were represented; from these the constant ebb and flow of lookers-on might choose, according to their fancy, what most they cared to see. Such a performance formed a fitting pendant to the monstrously discursive histories of the Middle Ages themselves: just as masklike in their dearth of character, in their lack of any individual stir of life, just as wooden and rough-hewn were the much-doing persons of these histories *be-read*, as were the players of those *beheld*.

For the same reasons that moved the poet to narrow down the action and the showplace, he had therefore to curtail the time length of performance also, since he wanted to bring to his spectators, no longer fragments, but a self-included whole; so that he took his spectator's power of giving continuous and undivided attention to a fascinating subject, when set before him, as the measure for the length of that performance. An artwork which merely appeals to fantasy, like the be-read romance, may lightly break the current of its message; since fantasy is of so wayward a nature that it hearkens to no laws other than those of whimsy chance. But that which steps before the senses, and would address them with persuasive, unmistakable distinctness, has not only to trim itself according to the quality, faculty, and naturally bounded vigor of those senses, but to show itself complete from top to toe, from beginning to end: if it would not, through sudden break or incompleteness of its exposition, appeal once more for needful supplementing to the fantasy, to the very factor it had quitted for the senses.

Upon this narrowed stage one thing alone remained still left entirely to fantasy—*the demonstration of the scene* itself, wherein to frame the performers conformably with the local requirements of the action. Carpets hung the stage around; an easily shifted writing on a notice board informed the spectator what place, whether palace or street, forest or field, was to be *thought of* as the scene. Through this one compulsory appeal to fantasy, unavoidable by the stagecraft of those days, a door in the drama remained open to the motley-stuffed romance and the much-doing history. As the poet, hitherto busied only with a speaking, bodily representation of the romance, did not yet feel the necessity of a naturalistic representment of the surrounding scene as well, neither could he experience the necessity of compressing the action, to be represented, into a still more definite circumscription of its leading moments. We here see plain as day how it is necessity alone that drives the artist toward a perfect shaping of the artwork; the artistic necessity that determines him to turn from fantasy to sense, to assist the indefinite force of fancy to a sure, intelligent operation through the senses. This necessity which shapes all art, which alone can satisfy the artist's strivings, comes to us solely from the definiteness of a universally sentient intuition: if we render complete justice to all its claims, then it drives us withal to the completest art creation.

Shakespeare, who did not yet experience this one necessity, of a naturalistic representment of the scenic surroundings, and therefore only so far sifted and compressed the redundance of his dramatized romance as he was bidden to by the necessity he did experience—to wit, of narrowing the showplace, and curtailing the time length, of an action represented by men of flesh and blood—Shakespeare, who within these limits quickened history and romance into so persuasive, so characteristic a truth, that he showed us human beings with individualities so manifold and drastic as never a poet before—this Shakespeare nevertheless, through his dramas being not yet shaped by that single aforesaid necessity, has been the cause and starting point of an unparalleled confusion in dramatic art for over two centuries, and down to the present day.

In the Shakespearian drama the romance and the loose-joined history had been left a door, as I have expressed it, by which they might go in and out at pleasure: this open door was the relinquishing to fantasy the representment of the scene. We shall see that the consequent confusion increased in exact degree as that door was relentlessly shut from the other side, and as the felt deficiency of scene, in turn, drove people into arbitrary deeds of violence against the living drama.

Among the so-called Romanic nations of Europe, with whom the adventure hunting of the romance—which tumbled every Germanic and Romanic element into one mass of wild confusion—had raged the maddest, this romance had also become the most ill-suited for dramatizing. The stress to seize the motley utterances of earlier fantastic whim, and shape them by the strenuous inwardness of human nature into plain and definite show, was exhibited in any marked degree only by the Germanic nations, who made into their deed of Protestance the inward war of conscience against tormenting outward prescripts. The Romanic nations, who outwardly remained beneath the Catholic yoke, clove steadfastly to the line along which they had fled before the irreconcilable inward strife, in order to distract from without—as I have above expressed myself—their inward thoughts. Plastic art, and an art of poetry which—as descriptive—was kindred to the plastic, if not in utterance, yet in essence: these are the arts, externally distracting, diverting, and engaging, peculiar to these nations.

The educated Frenchman and Italian turned his back upon his native folk's play;* in its raw simplicity and formlessness it recalled to him the whole chaos of the Middle Ages, which he had just been laboring to shake off him, like some heavy, troublous dream. No, he harked back to the historic feeders of his language, and chiefly from Roman poets, the literary copiers of the Greeks, he chose his pattern for that drama which he set before the well-bred world of gentlemen, in lieu of the Folk's play that now could entertain alone the rabble. Painting and architecture, the principal arts of the Romanic Renaissance, had made the eye of this well-bred world so full of taste, so exacting in its demands, that the rough carpet-hung platform of the British Shakespeare could not content it. For a showplace, the players in the princes' palaces were given the sumptuous hall, in which, with a few minor modifications, they had to erect their scene. Stability of scene was set fast as the criterion for the whole drama; and in this the accepted line of taste of the well-bred world concurred with the modern origin of the drama placed before it, with the rules of Aristotle. The princely spectator, whose eye had been trained by plastic art into his best-bred organ of positive sensuous pleasure, had no lief that *this* sense of all others should be bandaged, to submit itself to sightless fantasy; and that the less, as

---

* As I am writing no history of the modern drama, but, agreeably to my object, have only to point out in its twofold development the chief lines along which the root difference between those two evolutionary paths is plainest visible, I have passed over the Spanish theatre, since in it alone those diverse paths are characteristically crossed with one another. This makes it indeed of the highest significance in itself, but to us it affords no antitheses so marked as the two we find, with determinant influence upon all newer evolution of the drama, in Shakespeare and the French *tragédie.*—R. WAGNER.

he shrank on principle from any excitation of the indefinite, medieval-shaping fantasy. At the drama's each demand for change of scene, he must have been given the opportunity of seeing that scene displayed with strict fidelity to form and color of its subject, to allow a change at all. But what was made possible in the later mixing of the two dramatic genres, it was by no means needful to ask for here, since from the other side the rules of Aristotle, by which alone this fictive drama was constructed, made unity of scene its weightiest condition. So that the very thing the Briton, with his organic creation of the drama from within, had left disregarded as an outer moment, became an outward-shaping "norm" for the French drama; which thus sought to construct itself from without inward, from mechanism into life.

Now, it is important to observe closely, how this outward unity of scene determined the whole attitude of the French drama, almost entirely excluding from this scene any representment of the action, and replacing it by the mere delivery of speeches. Thus the root poetic element of medieval and more recent life, the action-packed romance, must also be shut out on principle from any representment on this scene, since the introduction of its multifarious stuff would have been downright impossible without a constant shifting. So that not only the outward form, but the whole cut of the plot, and finally its subject too, must be taken from those models which had guided the French playwright in planning out his form. He was forced to choose plots which did not need to be first condensed into a compact measure of dramatic representability, but such as lay before him already thus condensed.

From their native sagas the Greek tragedians had condensed such stuffs, as the highest artistic outcome of those sagas: the modern dramatist, starting with outward rules abstracted from these poems, and faced with the poetic element of his own era's life, which was only to be mastered in an exactly opposite fashion, namely, that of Shakespeare, could never compress it to such a density as should answer to the standard outwardly imposed; therefore nothing remained for him but—naturally disfiguring—imitation and repetition of those already finished dramas. Thus in Racine's *tragédie* we have talk upon the scene, and behind the scene the action; grounds of movement, with the movement cut adrift and turned outside; willing without can-ning. All art was therefore focused on *the mere outside of talk*, and quite logically in Italy—whence the new art genre had started—this soon lost itself in that musical delivery which we have already learned to recognize as the specific content of opera-ware. The French *tragédie*, also, of necessity passed over into opera: *Gluck* spoke aloud the actual content of this tragedy-ware. Opera was thus the premature bloom on an unripe fruit, grown from an unnatural, artificial soil. With what the Italian and French drama began, to wit, the outer form, to that must the newer drama first attain by organic evolution from within, upon the path of Shakespeare's drama; then first will ripen, also, the natural fruit of musical drama.

Between these two extremes, however, between the Shakespearian and the Racinian drama, did modern drama grow into its unnatural, mongrel shape; and Germany was the soil on which this fruit was reared.

Here Roman Catholicism continued side by side, in equal strength, with German Protestantism: only, each was so hotly engaged in combat with the other, that, undecided as the battle stayed, no natural art flower came to light. The inward stress, which with the Briton threw itself into dramatic representment of history and romance, remained with the German Protestant an obstinate endeavor inwardly to appease that inward strife itself. We have indeed a Luther, whose art soared up to the religious lyric; but we have no Shakespeare. On the other hand, the Roman-Catholic south could never swing itself into that genial, light-minded oblivion of the inward conflict, wherewith the Romanic nations took up plastic art: with gloomy earnestness it guarded its religious dream. While the whole of Europe threw itself on art, still Germany abode a meditant barbarian. Only what had already outlived itself outside took flight to Germany, upon its soil to blossom through an aftersummer. English comedians, whom the performers of Shakespearian dramas had robbed of their bread at home, came over to Germany to play their grotesquely pantomimic antics before the folk: not till long after, when *it* had likewise faded out of England, followed Shakespeare's drama itself; German players, fleeing from the ferule of their wearisome dramatic tutors, laid hands on it and trimmed it for their use.

From the south, again, the opera had forced its way in— that outcome of Romanic drama. Its distinguished origin, in the palaces of princes, commended it to German princes in their turn; so that these princes introduced the opera into

Germany, whereas—mark well!—the Shakespearian play was brought in by the folk. In opera the scenic penury of Shakespeare's stage was contrasted by its utmost opposite, the richest and most farfetched mounting of the scene. The musical drama became in truth a peepshow, whereas the Play remained a *hear*-play. We need not here go far for reasons for the scenic and decorative extravagance of the opera genre: this loose-limbed drama was constructed from without; and only from without, by luxury and pomp, could it be kept alive at all. One thing, however, it is important to observe: namely, that this scenic ostentation, with its unheard-of complexity and farfetched change of exhibition to the eye, proceeded from the same dramatic tendency which had originally set up unity of scene as its "norm." Not the poet, who, when compressing the romance into the drama, had left its plethora of stuff thus far unhedged, as in that stuff's behoof he could change the scene as often and as swiftly as he chose, by mere appeal to fantasy—not the poet, from any wish to turn from that appeal to fantasy to a positive confirmation by the senses —not *he* invented this elaborate mechanism for shifting actually presented scenes: but a longing for outward entertainment and constant change thereof, a sheer lust of the eye, had called it forth. Had the poet devised this apparatus, we should have had further to suppose that he felt the necessity of a frequent change of scene as a need inherent in the drama's plethora of stuff itself; and since the poet, as we have seen, was constructing organically from within outward, this supposition would have as good as proved that the historic and romantic plethora of stuff was a necessary postulate of the drama: for only the unbending necessity of such a postulate could have driven him to invent a scenic apparatus whereby to enable that plethora of stuff also to utter itself as a panoramic plethora of scene. But the very reverse was the case.

Shakespeare felt a necessity impelling him to represent history and romance dramatically; in the freshness of his ardor to content this impulse, there came to him no feeling of the necessity for a naturalistic representation of the scene as well —had he experienced this further necessity, toward a completely convincing representation of the dramatic action, he would have sought to answer it by a still more careful sifting, a still more strenuous compression of the romance's plethora of stuff: and that in exactly the same way as he had contracted the showplace, abridged the time length of performance, and for their sakes had already curtailed this plethora of stuff itself. The impossibility of still further condensing the romance—an insight which he certainly would have arrived at —must then have enlightened him as to the true nature of this romance: namely, that its nature does not really correspond with that of drama; a discovery which *we* could never make, till the undramatic plethora of history's stuff was brought to our feeling *by the actualization* of the scene, whereas the circumstance that this scene *need only be suggested* had alone made possible to Shakespeare the dramatized romance.

Now, the necessity of a representment of the scene, in keeping with the place of action, could not for long remain unfelt; the medieval stage was bound to vanish, and make room for the modern. In Germany this was governed by the character of the folk's mimetic art, which likewise, since the dying-out of mystery and Passion plays, took its dramatic basis from the history and the romance. At the time when German mimic art first took an upward swing—about the middle of the past century—this basis was formed by the burgher-romance, in its keeping with the then folk spirit. It was by far more manageable, and especially less cumbered with material, than the historic or legendary romance that lay to Shakespeare's hand: a suitable representment of its local scenes could therefore be effected with far less outlay than would have been required for Shakespeare's dramatizations.

The Shakespearian pieces taken up by these players had to submit to the most hampering adaptation on every side, in order to become performable by them at all. I here pass over every other ground and measure of this adaptation, and lay my finger on that of the purely scenic requirements, since it is the weightiest for the object of my present inquiry. These players, the first importers of Shakespeare to the German stage, were so honest to the spirit of their art, that it never occurred to them to make his pieces representable by either accompanying his constant change of scene with a kaleidoscopic shifting of their own theatric scenery, or even for his sake renouncing any actual exhibition whatsoever of the scene, and returning to the sceneless medieval stage. No, they maintained the standpoint of their art, once taken up, and to it subordinated Shakespeare's plethora of scene; inasmuch as they downright left out those scenes which seemed to them of little weight, while the weightier ones they tacked together.

It was from the standpoint of Literature, that people first perceived what Shakespeare's artwork had lost hereby, and urged a restoration of the original form of these pieces for their performance too. For this, two opposite plans were broached. The first proposal, and the one not carried out, is Tieck's. Fully recognizing the essence of Shakespearian drama, Tieck demanded the restoration of Shakespeare's stage, with its scene referred to an appeal to fantasy. This demand was thoroughly logical, and aimed at the very spirit of Shakespearian drama. But, though a half-attempt at restoration has time out of mind remained unfruitful, on the other hand a radical one has always proved impossible. Tieck was a radical restorer, to be honored as such, but bare of influence. The second proposal was directed to employing the gigantic apparatus of operatic scenery for the representation of Shakespearian drama too, by a faithful exhibition of the constant change of scene that had originally been only hinted at by him. Upon the newer English stage, people translated Shakespeare's scene into the most realistic actuality; wonders of mechanism were invented, for the rapid change of the most elaborate stage mountings: marches of troops and mimic battles were presented with astonishing exactitude. In the larger German theatres this course was copied.

In face of this spectacle, the modern poet stood brooding and bewildered. As literature, Shakespearian drama had given him the exalting impression of the most perfect poetic unity; so long as it had only addressed his fantasy, that fantasy had been competent to form therefrom a harmoniously rounded image: but now, with the fulfillment of his necessarily wakened longing to see this image embodied in a thorough representment to the senses, he saw it vanish suddenly before his very eyes. The embodiment of his fancy-picture had merely shown him an unsurveyable mass of realisms and actualisms, out of which his puzzled eye absolutely could not reconstruct it. This phenomenon produced two main effects upon him, both of which resulted in a disillusionment as to Shakespeare's tragedy. Henceforth the poet either renounced all wish to see his dramas acted on the stage, so as to be at peace again to model according to his intellectual aim the fancy-picture he had borrowed from Shakespearian Drama—that is, he wrote literary dramas for dumb reading—or else, so as practically to realize his fancy-picture on the stage, he instinctively turned more or less toward the reflective type of drama, whose modern origin we have traced to the pseudo-antique drama, constructed according to Aristotle's rules of unity.

Both these effects and tendencies are the guiding motives in the works of the two most important dramatic poets of modern times—Goethe and Schiller.

7. *Essence of the romance*

LET us now try to make plain to ourselves what is the life view of the modern world which has found its artistic expression in the romance.

So soon as the reflective understanding looked aside from the image, to inquire into the actuality of the things summed up in it, the first thing it saw was an ever-waxing multitude of units, where the poetic view had seen a whole. Anatomical Science began her work, and followed a diametrically opposite path to that of the folk's poem. Where the latter instinctively united, she separated purposely; where it fain would represent the grouping, she made for an exactest knowledge of the parts: and thus must every intuition of the folk be exterminated step by step, be overcome as heresy, be laughed away as childish. The nature view of the folk has dissolved into physics and chemistry, its religion into theology and philosophy, its commonwealth into politics and diplomacy, its art into science and aesthetics—and its myth into the historic chronicle.

Even the new world won from the myth its fashioning force. From the meeting and mingling of two chief mythic rounds, which could never entirely permeate each other, never lift themselves into a plastic unity, there issued the medieval romance.

In the Christian *mythos* we find that That to which the Greek referred all outer things, what he had therefore made the sure-shaped meeting place of all his views of nature and the world—the *human being*—had become the à priori Incomprehensible, become a stranger to itself. The Greek, by a comparison of outward things with man, had reached the human being from without: returning from his rovings through the breadth of nature, he found in man's stature, in his instinctive ethical notions, both quieting and measure. But this measure was a fancied one, and realized in art alone.

With his attempt to deliberately realize it in the state, the contradiction between that fancy standard, and the reality of actual human self-will, revealed itself: insofar as state and individual could seek to uphold themselves only by the openest overstepping of that fancy standard. When the natural custom had become an arbitrarily enacted law, the racial commonwealth an arbitrarily constructed political state, then the instinctive life bent of the human being in turn resisted law and state with all the appearance of egoistic caprice. In the strife between that which man had recognized as good and right, such as law and state, and that toward which his bent-to-happiness was thrusting him—the freedom of the individual— the human being must at last become incomprehensible to himself; and this confusion as to himself, was the starting point of the Christian *mythos*. In this latter the *individual* man, athirst for reconcilement with himself, strode on toward a longed-for, but yet a faith-vouchsafed redemption into an extramundane being, in whom both law and state were so far done away with, as they were conceived included in his unfathomable will. Nature, from whom the Greek had reached a plain conception of the human being, the Christian had to overlook altogether: as he took for her highest pinnacle redemption-needing man, at discord with himself, she could but seem to him the more discordant and accursed. Science, which dissected Nature into fragments, without ever finding the real bond between those fragments, could only fortify the Christian view of Nature.

The Christian myth, however, won bodily shape in the person of a man who suffered martyr's death for the withstanding of law and state; who, in his submission to judgment, vindicated law and state as outward necessities; but through his voluntary death, withal, annulled them both in favor of an inner necessity, the liberation of the individual through redemption into God. The enthralling power of the Christian myth consists in its portrayal of a *transfiguration through death*. The broken, death-rapt look of an expiring dear one, who, already past all consciousness, for the last time sends to us the lightning of his glance, exerts on us an impression of the most poignant grief. But this glance is followed with a smile on the wan cheeks and blanching lips; a smile which, sprung in itself from the joyful feeling of triumph over death's last agony, at onset of the final dissolution, yet makes on us the impression of a forebodal of overearthly bliss, such as could only be won by extinction of the bodily man.

And just as we have seen him in his passing, so does the departed one stay pictured in our memory: it removes from his image all sense of willfulness or uncertainty in his physical life utterance; our spiritual eye, the gaze of loving recollection, sees the henceforth but remembered one in the soft glamor of unsuffering, reposeful bliss. Thus the moment of death appears to us as the moment of actual redemption into God; for, through his dying, we think alone of the beloved as parted from all feeling of a life whose joys we soon forget amid the yearning for imagined greater joys, but whose griefs, above all in our longing after the transfigured one, our minds hold fast as the essence of the sensation of life itself.

This *dying*, with the yearning after it, is the sole true content of the art which issued from the Christian myth; it utters itself as dread and loathing of actual life, as flight before it—as longing for death. For the Greek, death counted not merely as a natural, but also as an ethical, necessity; yet *only as the counterpart of life,* which *in itself* was the real object of all his viewings, including those of art. The very actuality and instinctive necessity of life determined of themselves the tragic death; which in itself was nothing else but the rounding of a life fulfilled by evolution of the fullest individuality, of a life expended on making tell this individuality. To the Christian, however, death was *in itself* the object. For him, life had its only sacredness and warranty as the preparation for death, in the longing for its laying down. The conscious stripping off the physical body, achieved with the whole force of will, the purposed demolition of actual being, was the object of all Christian art; which therefore could only be limned, described, but never *represented*, and least of all in drama. The distinctive element of drama is its artistic realizing of the movement of a sharply outlined content. A movement, however, can chain our interest only when it *increases*; a diminishing movement weakens and dissipates our interest—excepting where a necessary lull is given expression to in passing.

In a Greek drama the movement waxes from the beginning, with constantly accelerated speed, to the mighty storm of the catastrophe; whereas the genuine, unmixed Christian drama must perforce begin with the storm of life, to weaken down its movement to the final swoon of dying out. The Passion plays of the Middle Ages represented the sufferings of Jesus in the form of a series of living pictures: the chief and most affecting of these pictures showed Jesus hanging on the cross;

hymns and psalms were sung during the performance. The legend, that Christian form of the romance, could alone give charm to a portrayal of the Christian stuff, because it appealed only to the fantasy—as alone was possible with this stuff—and not to physical vision. To music alone was it reserved to represent this stuff to the senses also, namely, by an outwardly perceptible motion; albeit merely in this wise, that she resolved it altogether into moments of feeling, into blends of color without drawing, expiring in the tinted waves of harmony in like fashion as the dying one dissolves from out of the actuality of life.

8. Myth diluted by Christianity

THROUGH the adoption of Christianity the folk had lost all true understanding of the original, vital relations of this *mythos*, and when the life of its single body had been resolved by death into the myriad lives of a swarm of fables, the Christian religious view was fitted under it, as though for its fresh quickening. By its intrinsic property, this view could do absolutely nothing more than light up *that corpse* of *mythos* and deck it with a mystic apotheosis. In a sense it justified the death of myth, inasmuch as it set before itself those clumsy actions, that tangle of cross-purposes—in themselves no longer explicable or vindicable by any intelligible idea still proper to the folk—in all their whimsical caprice, and, finding it impossible to assign an adequate motive to them, conveyed them to the Christian death as their redeeming issue. The Christian chivalric romance gives a faithful expression to the life of the Middle Ages, by beginning with the myriad leavings of the corpse of the ancient hero *mythos*, with a swarm of actions whose true idea appears to us unfathomable and capricious, because their motives, resting on a view of life quite alien to the Christian's, had been lost to the poet: to expose the utter lack of rhyme or reason in these actions, and out of their own mouths to vindicate to the instinctive feeling the necessity of their transactors' downfall—be it by a sincere adoption of the Christian rules, which inculcated a life of contemplation and inaction, or be it by the uttermost effectuation of the Christian view, the martyr's death itself—this was the natural bent and purpose of the spiritual poem of chivalry.

The original stuff of the pagan *mythos*, however, had already swelled into the most extravagant complexity of "actions," by admixture of the sagas of every nation—of sagas cut adrift, like the Germanic, from their vital root. By Christianity every folk, which adopted that confession, was torn from the soil of its natural mode of viewing, and the poems that had sprung therefrom were turned into playthings for the unchained fantasy. In the multifarious intercourse of the Crusades, the Orient and the Occident had interchanged these stuffs, and stretched their manysidedness to a monstrosity. Whereas in earlier days the folk included nothing but the *homelike* in its myths, now that its understanding of the homelike had been lost, it sought for recompense in a constant novelty of the *outlandish*. In its burning hunger, it gulped down everything foreign and unwonted: its voracious fantasy exhausted all the possibilities of human imagination—to digest them into the wildest medley of adventures.

This bent at last the Christian view could no more guide, albeit itself, at bottom, had been its generator; for this bent was primarily nothing but the stress to flee from an un-understood reality, to gain contentment in a world of fancy. But this fancied world, however great the divagations of fantasy, still must take its archetype from the actual world and nothing else: the imagination finally could do over again only what it had done in *mythos*; it pressed together all the realities of the actual world—all that it could comprehend—into close-packed images, in which it individualized the essence of totalities and thus furbished them into marvels of monstrosity. In truth this newer thrust of fantasy, just as with the *mythos*, made again toward finding the reality; and that, the reality of a vastly extended outer world. Its effectuation, in this sense, did not go long a-begging. The passion for adventures, in which men yearned to realize the pictures of their fancy, condensed itself at last to a passion for undertakings whose goal—after the thousand-times proved fruitlessness of mere adventures—should be the knowledge of the outer world, a tasting of the fruit of actual experiences reaped on a definite path of earnest, keen endeavor. Daring voyages of discovery undertaken with a conscious aim, and profound scientific researches grounded on their results, at last uncloaked to us the world as it really is. By this knowledge was the romance of the Middle Ages destroyed, and the delineation of *fancied* shows was followed by the delineation of their reality.

This reality, however, had stayed untroubled, undisfigured by our errors, in the phenomena of *Nature alone*, unreachable by our activity. On the reality of *human* life our errors had lain the most distorting hand of violence. To vanquish these as well, to know the life of man in the necessity of its individual and social nature; and finally, since that stands within our might, *to shape it*—this is the trend of humankind since ever it wrested to itself the outward faculty of knowing the phenomena of Nature in their genuine essence; for from this knowledge have we won the measure for the knowledge, also, of the essence of mankind.

9. *The romance versus drama. Romance turned to politics eventually.*

MAN can only be comprehended in conjunction with men in general, with his surrounding: man divorced from this, above all *the modern man*, must appear of all things the most incomprehensible. The restless inner discord of this man, who between "will" and "can" had created for himself a chaos of tormenting notions, driving him to war against himself, to self-laceration and bodiless abandonment to the Christian death—this discord was not so much to be explained, as Christianity had sought to do, from the nature of the individual man himself, as from the confusion wrought on this nature by an unintelligent view of the essence of society. Those torturing notions, which disturbed this view, must needs be referred back to the reality that lay at bottom of them; and, as this reality, the investigator had to recognize the true condition of human society. Yet neither could this condition, in which a thousandfold authority was fed upon a millionfold injustice and man was hedged from man by infranchisable barriers, first imagined and then realized—neither could *this* be comprehended out of its mere self; out of historical traditions converted into rights, out of the heart of facts and finally of the spirit of historical events, out of the ideas which had called them forth, must it be unriddled.

Before the gaze of the investigator, in his search for the human being, these historic facts upheaped themselves to so huge a mass of recorded incidents and actions that the medieval romance's plethora of stuff seemed naked penury compared therewith. And yet this mass, whose closer regardal showed it stretching into ever more intricate ramifications, was to be pierced to its core by the searcher after the reality of man's affairs, in order to unearth from amid its crushing waste the one thing that might reward such toil, the genuine undisfigured man in all his nature's verity. Faced with an expanse of matters of fact beyond what his two eyes could grasp, the historical investigator must perforce set bounds to his avidity of research. From a broader conjunction, which he could only have suggested, he must tear off fragments: by them to show with greater exactitude a closer coherence, without which no historical representment can ever be intelligible. But even within the narrowest bounds, this coherence, through which alone a historic action is understandable, is only to be made possible by the most circumstantial setting forth of a surrounding; in which, again, we can never take any sort of interest, until it is brought to view by the liveliest description. Through the felt necessity of such description, the investigator must needs become a poet again: but his method could only be one opposed outright to that of the dramatic poet. The dramatic poet compresses the surrounding of his personages into proportions easy to take in, in order to allow their action—which again he compresses, both in utterance and content, into comprehensive main action—to issue from the essential "idea" of the individual, to allow this individuality to come to a head therein, and by it to display man's common essence along one of its definite lines.

The romance writer, on the other hand, has to explain the action of a historic chief personage by the outer necessity of the surrounding: in order to give us the impression of historic truth, he has above all to bring to our understanding the character of this surrounding, since therein lie grounded all the calls which determine the individual to act *thus* and not otherwise. In the historical romance we try to make comprehensible to ourselves the man whom we positively cannot understand from a purely human standpoint. If we attempt to image to ourselves the action of a historic man as downright and purely human, it cannot but appear to us highly capricious, without rhyme or reason, and in any case unnatural, just because we are unable to vindicate the "idea" of that action on grounds of purely human nature. The idea of a historic personage is the idea of an individual only in so far as he acquires it from a generally accepted view of the essence of things; this generally accepted view, however—*not* being a purely human one, nor therefore valid for every place and time—finds its only explanation in a purely historic relation, which changes with the lapse of time and is never the same at two epochs. This relation, again, and its mutation we can clear up to ourselves only by following the whole chain of historic events, whose many-membered series has so worked upon a simpler historic relation that it has taken *this* particular shape, and that precisely *this* idea has enounced itself therein as a commonly current view. Wherefore the individual, in whose action this idea is to express itself, must be degraded to an infinitesimal measure of individual freedom, to make his action and idea at all comprehensible to us: his idea, to be in any way cleared up, is to be vindicated only through the idea of his surrounding; while this latter, again, can make itself plain only in a number of actions, which have to encroach the more upon the space of the artistic portrait, as only in its intricate branching and extension can the surrounding, also, become understood of us.

Thus the romance writer has to occupy himself almost solely with a description of the surrounding, and to become understandable he must be circumstantial. On what the dramatist *pre*supposes, for an understanding of the surrounding, the romance writer has to employ his whole powers of portrayal; the current view, on which the dramatist takes his footing from the first, the romance writer has to develop cunningly and fix in the course of his portrayal. The drama, therefore, goes from within outward, the romance from without inward. From a simple, universally intelligible surrounding, the dramatist rises to an ever richer development of the individuality; from a complex, toilsomely explained surrounding, the romance writer sinks exhausted to a delineation of the individual, which, poverty-stricken in itself, could be tricked out with individuality by that surrounding alone. In the drama, a sinewy and fully self-developed individuality enriches its surrounding; in the romance, the surrounding feeds the ravenings of an empty individuality. Thus the drama lays bare to us the organism of mankind, inasmuch as it shows the individuality as the essence of the species; whereas the romance shows us the mechanism of history, according to which the species becomes the essence of the individuality. And thus also, the art procedure in drama is an *organic* one, in romance a *mechanical*: for the drama gives us the *man*, the romance explains to us the *citizen*; the one shows us the fullness of human nature, the other apologizes for its penury on plea of the state. The drama, then, shapes from innermost necessity, the romance from outermost constraint.

Yet the romance was no arbitrary but a necessary product of our modern march of evolution: it gave honest artistic expression to life affairs which were to be portrayed only by it, and not by drama. The romance made for representing actuality; and its endeavor was so sincere, that at last it demolished itself, as artwork, in favor of this actuality. Its highest pitch, as an art form, was reached by the romance when, from the standpoint of purely artistic necessity, it made its own the *mythos'* plan of molding types. Just as the medieval romance had welded into wondrous shapes the motley shows of foreign peoples, lands, and climates, so the newer historical romance sought to display the motleyest utterances of the spirit of whole historic periods as issuing from the essence of one particular historic individual. In this procedure, the customary method of looking at history could but countenance the romance writer. In order to arrange the excess of historical facts for easy survey by our eye, we are accustomed to regarding the most prominent personalities alone, and in them to consider as embodied the spirit of a period. As such personalities, the wisdom of the chronicler has mostly bequeathed us the rulers; those from whose will and ordering the historic undertakings and state economy were supposed to have issued. The unclear "idea" and contradictory manner of action of these chiefs, but above all the circumstance that they never really reached their aimed-for goal, allowed us in the first place so far to misunderstand the spirit of history that we deemed it necessary to explain the caprice in these rulers' actions by higher, inscrutable influences, guiding and foreordering the course and scope of history. Those factors of history seemed to us willless tools—or if willful, yet self-contradictory—in the hands of an extrahuman, heavenly power. The end results of history we posited as the cause of its movement, or as the goal toward which a higher, conscious spirit had therein striven from the beginning. Led by this view, the expounders or setters-forth of history believed themselves justified in deriving the seemingly arbitrary actions of its ruling personages from "ideas" in which was mirrored back the imputed consciousness of a governing world spirit: wherefore they destroyed the unconscious necessity of these rulers' motives of action, and, so soon as they deemed they had sufficiently accounted for those actions, they displayed them as arbitrary out-and-out.

Through this procedure alone, whereby historic actions could be disfigured and combined at will, did the romance succeed in inventing types, and in lifting itself to a certain height of artwork, whereon it might seem qualified anew for dramatization. Our latter days have presented us with many such an historical drama, and the zest of making history in behoof of the dramatic form is nowadays so great, that our skilled historical stage conjurors fancy the secret of history itself has been revealed for the sole benefit of the playmaker. They believe themselves all the more justified in their procedure, as they have even made it possible to invest history's dramatic installation with the completest unity of place and time: they have thrust into the inmost recesses of the whole historic mechanism, and have discovered its heart to be the antechamber of the prince, where man and the state make their mutual arrangements between breakfast and supper. That this artistic unity and this history, however, are equal forgeries, and that a falsehood can have only a forged effect— *this* has established itself plainly enough in the course of our present-day historic drama. But that true history itself is no stuff for Drama—this we now know also; since this historical drama has made it clear to us, that even the romance could reach its appointed height, as art form, only by sinning against the truth of history.

From this height the romance stepped down again, in order, while giving up its aimed-for purity as art work, to engage in truthful portraiture of historic life.

The seeming caprice in the actions of historical chief personages could be explained, to the honor of mankind, only through discovering the soil from which those actions sprang of instinct and necessity. As one had earlier thought it incumbent to place this necessity *above,* soaring over the historic personages and using them as tools of its transcendent wisdom; and as one at last had grown convinced of both the artistic and the scientific barrenness of this view: so thinkers and poets now sought for this explanatory necessity *below,* among the foundations of all history. The soil of history is *man's social nature*: from the individual's need to unite

himself with the essence of his species, in order in society
to bring his faculties into highest play, arises the whole
movement of history. The historic phenomena are the outward
manifestations of an inner movement, whose core is the social
nature of man. But the prime motor of this nature is the
individual, who only in the satisfaction of his instinctive
longing for love can appease his bent to happiness. Now, to
argue from this nature's manifestations to its core—from the
dead body of the completed fact to go back upon the inner
life of man's social bent, from which that fact had issued as
a ready, ripe, and dying fruit—in *this* was evinced the
evolutionary march of modern times.

What the thinker grasps by its essence, the poet seeks to
show in its phenomena: the phenomena of human society,
which *he*, too, had recognized as the soil of history, the poet
strove to set before him in a conjunction through which he
might be able to explain them. As the most seizable conjunction of social phenomena he took the wonted surroundings
of burgher life, in order by their description to explain to
himself the man who, remote from any participation in the
outward facts of history, yet seemed to him to condition them.
However, this burgher society, as I have before expressed
myself, was nothing but a precipitate from that history which
weighed upon it from above—at least in its outward form.
Without a doubt, since the consolidation of the modern state,
the world's new life-stir begins to center in the burgher class:
the living energy of historic phenomena weakens down in
direct ratio as the burgher class endeavors to bring its claims
to tell upon the state. But precisely through its inner lack of
interest in the events of history, through its dull, indifferent
looking-on, it bares to us the burden wherewith they weigh
it down, and under which it shrugs its shoulders in resigned
ill-will. Our burgher society is in so far no living organism,
as its shaping is effected from above, by the reaction of
historic agencies. The physiognomy of burgher society is the
flattened, disfigured physiognomy of history, with all its expression washed out: what the latter expresses through living
motion in the breath of time, the former gives us in the
dull expanse of space. But this physiognomy is the mask of
burgher society, under which it still hides from the human-
seeking eye the man himself: the artistic delineators of this
society could describe only the features of that mask, not those
of the veritable human being; the more faithful was their

description, the more must the artwork lose in living force of expression.

If, then, this mask was lifted, to peer beneath it into the unvarnished features of human society, it was inevitable that a chaos of unloveliness and formlessness should be the first to greet the eye. Only in the garment of history had the human being—bred by this history, and by it crippled and degraded from his true sound nature—preserved an aspect at all tolerable to the artist. This garment once removed, we were horrified to see nothing but a shriveled, loathly shape, which bore no trace of resemblance to the true man, such as our thoughts had pictured in the fullness of his natural essence; no trace beyond the sad and suffering glance of the stricken unto death—that glance whence Christianity had derived the transports of its inspiration. The yearner for art turned away from this sight: like Schiller, to dream him dreams of beauty in the realm of thought; or, like Goethe, to shroud the shape itself in a cloak of artistic beauty—so well as it could be got to hang thereon. His romance of *Wilhelm Meister* was such a cloak, wherewith Goethe tried to make bearable to himself the sight of the reality: it answered to the naked reality of modern man for just so far as he was conceived and exhibited as struggling for an artistically beautiful form.

Up to then the human shape had been veiled, no less for the eye of the historical student than for that of the artist, in the costume of history or the uniform of the state: this costume left free play to fancy, this form to disputations. Poet and thinker had before them a vast assortment of discretionary shapes, among which they might choose at their artistic pleasure or arbitrary assumption a garment for the human being, whom they still conceived alone in that which was wrapped about him from without. Even Philosophy had allowed this garment to lead her astray, in respect of man's true nature; while the writer of historical romances was—in a certain sense—a mere costume drawer. With the baring of the actual shape of modern society, the romance now took a more practical stand: the poet could no longer extemporize artistic fancies, now that he had the naked truth unveiled before him, the actuality that filled the looker-on with horror, pity, and indignation. His business was only to display this actuality, without allowing himself to belie it— he needed only to feel pity, and at once his passion became a vital force. He still could poetize, when he was bent alone on portraying the fearful immorality of our society: but the deep gloom, into which his own portrayings cast him, drove away all pleasure of poetic contemplation, in which he now could less and less delude himself; it drove him out into the actuality itself, there to strive for human society's now recognized real need. On its path to practical reality the romance poem, too, stripped off yet more and more its artistic garment: its possible unity, as art form, must part itself—to operate through the intelligence—into the practical plurality of everyday occurrences. An artistic bond was no longer possible, where everything was struggling to dissolve, where the strenuous bond of the historic state was to be torn asunder. The romance poem turned to Journalism; its contents flew asunder, into political articles; its art became the rhetoric of the *Tribune*, the breath of its discourse a summons to the people.

Thus the poet's art has turned to politics: no one now can poetize, without politizing. Yet the politician will never become a poet, precisely until he ceases to be a politician: but in a purely political world to be *not* a politician is as good as to say one does not exist at all; whosoever at this instant steals away from politics, he only belies his own being. The poet cannot come to light again until we have no more politics.

Politics, however, are the secret of our history, and of the state of things therefrom arising. Napoleon put this clearly. He told Goethe that the role of fate in the ancient world is filled, since the empire of the Romans, by politics. Let us lay to heart this saying of him who smarted in St. Helena! In it is briefly summed the whole truth of what we have to comprehend before we can come to an understanding, also, about the content and the form of drama.

10. The state versus the individual; understanding versus feeling

THE poet, then, who had to portray the battle of the individuality against the state could *portray* the state alone; but the free individuality he could merely *suggest to thought*. The state was the actual extant thing, in all its pomp of form and color; whereas the individuality was but the thing imagined, shapeless, colorless, and nonextant. All the features, contours, and colors, which lend the individuality its set, its definite and knowable artistic shape, the poet had to borrow from a society politically divided up and compressed into a state; not to take them from the rightful individuality, which gains its own drawing and color from contact with other individualities. The individuality, thus merely thought out but not portrayed, could therefore be exhibited to nothing but the thought, and not to the directly seizing feeling. Our drama has therefore been an appeal to the understanding—not to the feeling. It thus has taken the place of the didactic poem, which exhibits a subject from the life only as far as it suits the conscious aim, of imparting a thought to the understanding. But to impart a thought to the understanding the poet has to proceed just as circumspectly as, on the contrary, he must go to work with the greatest simplicity and straightforwardness when he addresses himself to the directly receptive feeling. The feeling seizes nothing but the actual, the physically enacted, the perceivable by the senses: to *it* one can only impart the fulfilled, the rounded off, the thing that is just wholly what it is, just what at this instant it *can* be. To the feeling the at-one-with-itself alone is understandable; whatsoever is at variance with itself, what has not reached an actual and definite manifestation, confounds the feeling and drives it into thinking—drives it into an act of combination which does away with it as feeling.

In order to convince it, the poet who turns toward the feeling must be already so at one with himself that he can dispense with any aid from the mechanism of logic and address himself with full consciousness to the infallible receptive powers of the unconscious, purely human feeling. With this message of his he has therefore to proceed as straightforwardly and (in view of physical perception) as unconditionally, as the feeling is addressed by the actual phenomenon itself—such as warmth, the wind, the flower, the animal, the man. But in order to impart the highest thing impartable, and alike the most convincingly intelligible—the purely human individuality—the *modern* dramatic poet, as I have pointed out, has to move along a directly opposite path. From out the enormous mass of its actual surroundings—in the visible measure-, form-, and color-giving state, and in history petrified into a state—he has first with infinite toil to reconstruct this individuality; in order at last, as we have seen, to do nothing more than exhibit it to the thought.* The thing that our feeling involuntarily seizes in advance is solely the form and color of the state. From the earliest impressions of our youth, we see man only in the shape and character given him by the state; the individuality drilled into him by the state our involuntary feeling takes for his real essence; we cannot seize him otherwise than by those distinctive qualities which in truth are not his very own, but merely lent him by the state. Today the folk cannot conceive the human being otherwise than in the uniform of his "class," the uniform in which, from youth up, it sees his body clad; and the "folk's playwright," also, can address himself understandably to the folk only when not for a single instant does he tear it from this state-burgherly illusion—which holds its unconscious feeling captive to such a degree, that it would be placed in the greatest bewilderment if one attempted to reconstruct before it the actual human being beneath this visible semblance.† Wherefore, to exhibit the purely human individuality, the modern poet has to turn, not to the *feeling,* but to the *understanding;* since even to himself it is only a thought-out thing. For this, his method of procedure must be a hugely circumstantial one: all that the modern sentiment takes as the most comprehensible, he has, so to say, slowly and circumspectly to divest of its form and color, *under the very eyes* of this sentiment, and, throughout this systematic stripping

---

* In *Egmont* Goethe had employed the whole course of the piece in loosening this purely human individuality, with toilsome wealth of detail, from the conditions of its state-historical surrounding; in the solitude of the dungeon, and immediately before its death, he now wished to show it to the feeling as coming into oneness with itself: for this, he must reach out hands to Marvel and to Music. How characteristic it is, that it was the idealizing Schiller, of all others, who could not understand this uncommonly significant feature of Goethe's highest artistic truthfulness! But how mistaken, also, was it of Beethoven not to reserve his music for this appearance of the Wondrous; instead of introducing it— at the wrong time—in the middle of the politico-prosaic exposition. —RICHARD WAGNER.

† The folk must be something like that pair of children who were standing before a picture of Adam and Eve, and could not make out which was the man and which the woman, because they were unclothed. How characteristic of all our views is it not, again, that commonly our eye is pained and embarrassed by the sight of an undraped human figure, and we generally find it quite disgusting: our own body first becomes intelligible to us, by our pondering on it!—RICHARD WAGNER.

process, gradually to bring the feeling round to thinking; since, after all, the individuality he makes for is nothing but a thing of thought. Thus the modern poet must turn aside from the feeling, to address the understanding: to him, feeling is the obstacle; only when he has overcome it with the utmost caution does he come to his main purpose, the demonstration of a thought to the understanding.

The *understanding* is thus, from first to last, the human faculty which the modern poet wishes to address; and with it he can parley only through the *organ* of the combining, dispersing, severing and repiecing understanding; through abstract and conditioned word speech, which merely describes and filters down the impressions and acquirements of the feeling. Were our state itself a worthy object of feeling, the poet, to reach his purpose, would have in a certain measure to pass over, in his drama, from tone speech to word speech; in Greek tragedy such was very near the case, but from opposite reasons. This tragedy's basis was the lyric, from which it advanced to word speech in the same way as society advanced from the natural, ethicoreligious ties of feeling, to the political state. The return from understanding to feeling will be the march of the drama of the future, in so far as we shall advance from the *thought-out* individuality to the genuine one. But, from the very beginning of his work, the modern poet has to exhibit a surrounding—the state—which is void of any purely human sentiment, and therefore is uncommunicable through the feeling's highest utterance. So that he can reach his purpose, at all, only through the organ of the "combining" understanding, through unemotional modern speech; and rightly does the playwright of nowadays deem it unfitting, bewildering and disturbing, to employ music for an object which can at best be intelligibly conveyed as thought to the understanding, but never to the feeling as emotion.

11. Poetry impossible in modern speech

THE understanding, condensed from feeling through the fantasy, acquired in prosaic word speech an organ through which it could make itself intelligible *alone,* and in direct ratio as it became unintelligible to feeling. In modern prose we speak a language we do not understand with the feeling, since its connection with the objects, whose impression on our faculties first ruled the molding of the speech roots, has become incognizable to us; a language which we speak as it was taught us in our youth—not as, with waxing self-dependence of our feeling, we haply seize, form, and feed it from ourselves and the objects we behold; a language whose usages and claims, based on the logic of the understanding, we must unconditionally obey when we want to impart our thoughts. This language, in our feeling's eyes, rests therefore on a convention which has a definite scope—namely, to make ourselves thus far intelligible according to a given norm, in which we are to think and to *dominate* our feelings, that we may demonstrate to the understanding an aim of the understanding. Our feeling—which quite of itself found unconscious expression in the primitive speech—we can only *describe* in this language; and describe in a far more circuitous way than an object of the understanding, because we are obliged to screw ourselves *down* from our intellectual language to its real stock, in the same way as we screwed ourselves *up* from that stock to *it*.

Our language accordingly rests upon a state historico-religious convention, which in France, under the rule of Convention personified, under Louis XIV, was also very logically fixed into a settled "norm," by an Academy under orders. Upon no living and ever-present, no really felt *conviction* does it rest, for it is the tutored opposite of any such conviction. In a sense, we cannot discourse in this language according to our innermost emotion, for it is impossible to *invent* in it according to that emotion; in *it,* we can only impart our emotions to the understanding, but not to the implicitly understanding feeling; and therefore in our modern evolution it was altogether consequent, that the feeling should have sought a refuge from absolute intellectual speech by fleeing to absolute tone speech, our music of today.

In modern speech no *poesis* is possible—that is to say, a poetic aim cannot be *realized* therein, but only spoken out *as such*.

12. While language declines, music, a new language of feeling, develops, until poetry becomes either philosophy or blends with music.

IF we look closer at the evolutionary history of the modern European languages, even today we meet in their so-called word roots a rudiment that plainly shows us how at the first beginning the formation of the mental concept of an object ran almost completely parallel with the subjective feeling of it; and the supposition that the earliest speech of man must have borne a great analogy with song, might not perhaps seem quite ridiculous. Starting with a physical meaning for his words, in any case quite subjectively felt, the speech of man evolved along a more and more abstract line; so that at last there remained nothing but a conventional meaning, depriving the feeling of any share in understanding the words, just as their syntax was made entirely dependent on rules to be acquired by learning. In necessary agreement with the moral evolution of mankind, there grew up equally in speech and manners a convention, whose laws were no longer intelligible to natural feeling, but were drilled into youth by maxims comprehensible to nothing but reflection.

Now, ever since the modern European languages—divided into different stocks, to boot—have followed their conventional drift with a more and more obvious tendency, music, on the other hand, has been developing a power of expression unknown to the world before. 'Tis as though the purely human feeling, intensified by the pressure of a conventional civilization, had been seeking an outlet for the operation of its own peculiar laws of speech; an outlet through which, unfettered by the laws of logical thought, it might express itself intelligibly to itself. The uncommon popularity of music in our times; the constantly increasing interest, spreading through every stratum of society, in the products of the deepest-meaning class of music; the ever-growing eagerness to make musical training an integral part of education: all this, so manifest and undeniable in itself, at like time proves the correctness of the postulate that music's modern evolution has answered to a profoundly inward need of mankind's, and that, however unintelligible her tongue when judged by the laws of logic, she must possess a more persuasive title to our comprehension than anything contained within those laws.

In face of this irrefutable conclusion, there would henceforth stand only two ways open to poetry. Either a complete removal into the field of abstraction, a sheer combining of mental concepts and portrayal of the world by expounding the logical laws of thought. And this office she fulfills as philosophy. Or an inner blending with music, with that music whose infinite faculty has been disclosed to us by the symphony of Haydn, of Mozart, and Beethoven.

13. Haydn and Mozart develop dance music into the modern symphony and make use of folk song and speaking melody.

THE harmonized dance is the basis of the modern symphony. In the symphony of Haydn the rhythmic dance melody moves with all the blithesome freshness of youth: its entwinements, disseverings, and reunitings, though carried out with highest contrapuntal ingenuity, yet hardly show a trace of the results of such ingenious treatment; but rather take the character peculiar to a dance ordained by laws of freest fantasy—so redolent are they of the warm and actual breath of joyous human life. To the more tempered motion of the middle section of the symphony we see assigned by Haydn a broad expansion of the simple song tune of the folk; in this it spreads by laws of melos peculiar to the character of song, through soaring graduations and "repeats" enlivened by most manifold expression. This form of melody became the very element of the symphony of song-abundant and song-glad Mozart. He breathed into his instruments the passionate breath of human voice, that voice toward which his genius bent with overmastering love. In effect it was from the realm of dramatic music, already widened by himself to undreamed capability of expression, that Mozart first entered on the symphony; for those few symphonic works of his whose peculiar worth has kept them living to this day, we owe to the creative period when he had fully unfolded his genius as opera composer. He lifted up the "singing" power of instrumental music to such a height that it was now enabled not only to embrace the mirth and inward still content which it had learned from Haydn, but the whole depth of endless heart's desire.

14.   Yet they fail to achieve dramatic pathos or continuity of action—their works are characterized by a "lofty glee."

YET to the composer of *Figaro* and *Don Giovanni* the framework of the symphonic movement offered a curb on that mobile love of figure painting which had found such congenial scope in the passionately changeful situations of those dramatic drafts. For in the symphony of Haydn and Mozart, dramatic pathos is completely excluded, so that the most intricate involvements of the thematic motives in a movement could never be explained on the analogy of a dramatic action, but solely by the mazes of an ideal dance, without a suspicion of rhetorical dialectics. Here there is no "conclusion," no problem, no solution. Wherefore also these symphonies bear one and all the character of lofty glee. Never are two themes of diametrically opposite character confronted here; diverse as they may seem, they always supplement each other as the manly and the womanly element of one whole character.

15.   Beethoven makes music express storm and stress. But absolute music can express only mirth or endless yearning; it lacks the deed, the moral will. The Ninth Symphony is the redemption of music into drama.

IT was Beethoven who opened up the boundless faculty of instrumental music for expressing elemental storm and stress. His power it was, that took the basic essence of the Christian's harmony, that bottomless sea of unhedged fullness and unceasing motion, and clove in twain the fetters of its freedom. Harmonic melody—for so must we designate this melody divorced from speech, in the distinction from the rhythmic melody of dance—was capable, though merely borne by instruments, of the most limitless expression together with the most unfettered treatment. In long, connected tracts of sound, as in larger, smaller, or even smallest fragments, it turned beneath the Master's poet hand to vowels, syllables, and words and phrases of a speech in which a message hitherto unheard, and never spoken yet, could promulgate itself. Each letter of this speech was an infinitely soul-full element; and the measure of the joinery of these elements was utmost free commensuration, such as could be exercised by none but a tone poet who longed for the unmeasured utterance of this unfathomed yearning.

Glad in this unspeakable expressive language, but suffering beneath the weight of longing of his artist soul—a longing which, in its infinity, could be only an "object" to itself, not satisfy itself outside—the happy-wretched, sea-glad and sea-weary mariner sought for a surer haven wherein to anchor from the blissful storms of passionate tumult. Was his faculty of speech unending—so also was the yearning which inspired that speech with its eternal breath. How then proclaim the end, the satisfaction, of this yearning, in the selfsame tongue that was naught but its expression? If the utterance of im-measurable heart-yearning be vented in this elemental speech of absolute tone, then the *endlessness* of such utterance, like that of the yearning itself, is its only true necessity; the yearn-ing cannot find contentment in any finite *shutting off* of sound —for that could only be caprice.

Now, by the definite expression which it borrows from the rhythmic dance melody, instrumental music may well portray and bring to close a placid and self-bounded mood; for reason that it takes its measure from an originally outward-lying object, namely, the motion of the body. If a tone piece yield itself *ab initio* to this expression, which must always be conceived as that of mirth, in greater or in less degree—then, even mid the richest, most luxuriant unfolding of the faculty of tonal speech, it holds within itself the necessary grounds of every phase of "satisfaction"; while equally inevitably must this "satisfaction" be a matter of caprice, and therefore in truth unsatisfying, when that sure and sharp-cut mode of utterance endeavors merely *thus* to terminate the storms of endless yearning.

The transition from the endless agitation of desire to a mood of joyous satisfaction can necessarily take place no otherwise than by the ascension of desire into an *object*. But, in keeping with the character of infinite yearning, this "object" can be none other than such an one as shows itself with finite, physical and ethical exactitude. Absolute Music, however, finds well-marked bounds dividing her from such an object; without indulging in the most arbitrary of assumptions, she can now and never, of her own unaided powers, bring the physical and ethical man to distinct and plainly recognizable presentment. Even in her most infinite enhancement, she still is but *emotion;* she enters *in the train* of the ethical deed, but not as that *deed itself;* she can set moods and feelings side by side, but not evolve one mood from out another by any dictate of her own necessity—she lacks the *moral will*.

What inimitable art did Beethoven employ in his "C-minor Symphony," in order to steer his ship from the ocean of infinite yearning to the haven of fulfillment! He was able to raise the utterance of his music *almost* to a moral resolve, but not to speak aloud that final word; and after every onset of the will, without a moral handhold, we feel tormented by the equal possibility of falling back again to suffering, as of being led to lasting victory. Nay, this falling-back must almost seem to us more "necessary" than the morally ungrounded triumph, which therefore—not being a necessary consummation, but a mere arbitrary gift of grace—has not the power to lift us up and yield to us that *ethical* satisfaction which we demand as outcome of the yearning of the heart.

Who felt more uncontented with this victory than Beethoven himself? Was he lief to win a second of the sort? 'Twas well enough for the brainless herd of imitators, who from glorious "major"-jubilation, after vanquished "minor"-tribulation, prepared themselves unceasing triumphs—but not for the Master, who was called to write upon his works the *world history of music*.

With reverent awe, he shunned to cast himself afresh into that sea of boundless and insatiate yearning. He turned his steps toward the blithesome, life-glad men he spied encamped on breezy meads, along the outskirt of some fragrant wood beneath the sunny heaven; kissing, dancing, frolicking. There in shadow of the trees, amid the rustling of the leaves, beside the tender gossip of the brook, he made a happy pact with Nature; there he felt that he was man, felt all his yearning thrust back deep into his breast before the sovereignty of sweet and blissful *manifestation*. So thankful was he toward this manifestation that, faithfully and in frank humility, he superscribed the separate portions of the tone work, which he built from this idyllic mood, with the names of those life pictures whose contemplation had aroused it in him: "Reminiscences of Country Life" he called the whole.

But in very deed they were only "Reminiscences"— pictures, and not the direct and physical actuality. Toward this actuality he was impelled with all the force of the artist's inexpugnable yearning. To give his tone shapes that same compactness, that directly cognizable and physically sure stability, which he had witnessed with such blessed solace in Nature's own phenomena—this was the soul of the joyous impulse which created for us that glorious work the "Symphony in A-major." All tumult, all yearning and storming of the heart become here the blissful insolence of joy, which snatches us away with bacchanalian might and bears us through the roomy space of Nature, through all the streams and seas of life, shouting in glad self-consciousness as we tread throughout the universe the daring measures of this human sphere-dance. This symphony is the *Apotheosis of Dance* herself: it is Dance in her highest aspect, as it were the loftiest deed of bodily motion incorporated in an ideal mold of tone. Melody and Harmony unite around the sturdy bones of Rhythm to firm and fleshy human shapes, which now with giant limbs' agility, and now with soft, elastic pliance, *almost before our very eyes,* close up the supple, teeming ranks; the while now gently, now with daring, now serious,* now wanton, now pensive, and again exulting, the deathless strain sounds forth and forth; until, in the last whirl of delight, a kiss of triumph seals the last embrace.

And yet these happy dancers were merely shadowed forth

---

* Amid the solemn-striding rhythm of the second section, a secondary theme uplifts its wailing, yearning song; to that rhythm, which shows its firm-set tread throughout the entire piece, without a pause, this longing melody clings like the ivy to the oak, which without its clasping of the mighty bole would trail its crumpled, straggling wreaths upon the soil, in forlorn rankness; but now, while weaving a rich trapping for the rough oak rind, it gains for itself a sure and undisheveled outline from the stalwart figure of the tree. How brainlessly has this deeply significant device of Beethoven been exploited by our modern instrumental composers, with their eternal "subsidiary themes!"—R. WAGNER.

in tones, mere sounds that imitated men! Like a second Prometheus who fashioned men of clay (*"thon"*), Beethoven had sought to fashion them of *tone*. Yet not from *"thon"* or tone, but from both substances together, must man, the image of live-giving Zeus, be made. Were Prometheus' moldings only offered to the *eye,* so were those of Beethoven only offered to the *ear*. But only *where eye and ear confirm each other's sentience of him, is the whole artistic man at hand.*

But where could Beethoven find *those* men, to whom to stretch out hands across the element of his music? Those men with hearts so broad that he could pour into them the mighty torrent of his harmonic tones? With frames so stoutly fair that his melodic rhythms should *bear* them and not *crush* them? —Alas, from nowhere came to him the brotherly Prometheus who could show to him these men! He needs must gird his loins about, and start *to find out for himself the country of the manhood of the future.*

From the shore of dance he cast himself once more upon that endless sea, from which he had erstwhile found a refuge on this shore; the sea of unallayable heart-yearning. But 'twas in a stoutly built and giant-bolted ship that he embarked upon the stormy voyage; with firm-clenched fist he grasped the mighty helm: he *knew* the journey's goal, and was determined to attain it. No imaginary triumphs would he prepare himself, nor after boldly overcome privations tack back once more to the lazy haven of his home; for he desired to measure out the ocean's bounds, and find the land which needs must lie beyond the waste of waters.

Thus did the Master urge his course through unheard-of possibilities of absolute tone speech—not by fleetly slipping past them, but by speaking out their utmost syllable from the deepest chambers of his heart—forward to where the mariner begins to sound the sea depth with his plumb; where, above the broadly stretched-forth shingles of the new continent, he touches on the heightening crests of solid ground; where he has now to decide him whether he shall face about toward the bottomless ocean, or cast his anchor on the new-found shore. But it was no madcap love of sea adventure, that had spurred the Master to so far a journey; which might and main he willed to land on this new world, for toward *it* alone had he set sail. Staunchly he threw his anchor out; and this anchor was *the word*. Yet this word was not that arbitrary and senseless cud which the modish singer chews from side to side, as the gristle of his vocal tone; but the necessary, all-powerful, and all-uniting word into which the full torrent of the heart's emotions may pour its stream; the steadfast haven for the restless wanderer; the light that lightens up the night of endless yearning: the word that the redeemed world-man cries out aloud from the fullness of the world-heart. This was the word which Beethoven set as crown upon the forehead of his tone creation; and this word was —"*Freude!*" (Rejoice!) With this word he cries to men: "*Breast to breast, ye mortal millions! This one kiss to all the world!*"—And *this word* will be the language of the *artwork of the future.*

The last symphony of Beethoven is the redemption of Music from out her own peculiar element into the realm of *universal art*. It is the human evangel of the art of the future. Beyond it no forward step is possible; for upon it the perfect artwork of the future alone can follow, the *universal drama* to which Beethoven has forged for us the key.

16. Three descriptive and analytic programs; the importance of identifying the poetic subjects of Beethoven's works

THE characteristic of the great compositions of Beethoven is that they are veritable poems, in which it is sought to bring a real subject to representation. The obstacle to their comprehension lies in the difficulty of finding with certainty the subject that is represented. Beethoven was completely possessed by a subject: his most significant tone pictures are indebted almost solely to the individuality of the subject that filled him; the consciousness of this made it seem to him superfluous to indicate his subject otherwise than in the tone picture itself. Just as our literary poets really address themselves only to other literary poets, so Beethoven, in these works, involuntarily addressed himself only to tone poets. The absolute musician, that is to say, the manipulator of absolute music, could not understand Beethoven, because this absolute musician fastens only on the "how" and not the "what." The layman, on the other hand, could but be completely confused by these tone pictures, and at best receive pleasure only from that which to the tone poet was merely the material means of expression.

If no special poetic subject is expressed in the tone speech, it may undoubtedly pass as easily understandable; for there can here be no question of *real* understanding. If, however, the expression of the tone speech is conditioned by a poetic subject, this speech at once becomes the most incomprehensible of all, unless the poetic subject be at the same time defined by some means of expression other than those of absolute music.

The poetic subject of a tone piece by Beethoven is thus only to be divined by a tone poet; for, as I remarked before, Beethoven involuntarily appealed only to such, to those who were of like feelings, like culture, aye, well-nigh like capability with himself. Only a man like this can make these compositions intelligible to the laity, and above all by making the subject of the tone poem clear both to the executants and to the audience, and thus making good an involuntary error in the technique of the tone poet, who omitted this indication.

a. The "Eroica" Symphony

THIS highly significant tone poem—the Master's Third Symphony, and the first work with which he struck his own peculiar path—is in many respects not so easy to understand as its name might allow one to suppose; and that precisely since the title "Heroic" ("Eroica") Symphony instinctively misleads one into trying to see therein a series of heroic episodes, presented in a certain historicodramatic sense by means of pictures in tone. Whoever approaches this work with such a notion, and expects to understand it, will find himself at first bewildered and lastly undeceived, without having arrived at any true enjoyment. If therefore I here permit myself to communicate as tersely as possible the view I have gained of the poetic contents of this tone creation, it is in the sincere belief that to many a hearer of the forthcoming performance of the "Heroic" Symphony I may facilitate an understanding, which he otherwise could acquire only through frequent attendance at particularly lifelike renderings of the work.

In the first place, the designation "heroic" is to be taken in its widest sense, and in nowise to be conceived as relating merely to a military hero. If we broadly connote by "hero" the whole, the full-fledged man, in whom are present all the purely human feelings—of love, of grief, of force—in their highest fill and strength, then we shall rightly grasp the subject which the artist lets appeal to us in the speaking accents of his tone work. The artistic space of this work is filled with all the varied, intercrossing feelings of a strong, a consummate individuality, to which nothing human is a stranger, but which includes within itself all truly human, and utters it in such a fashion that—after frankly manifesting every noble passion— it reaches a final rounding of its nature, wherein the most feeling softness is wedded with the most energetic force. The heroic tendence of this artwork is the progress toward that rounding off.

The First Movement embraces, as in a glowing furnace, all the emotions of a richly gifted nature in the heyday of unresting youth. Weal and woe, lief and lack, sweetness and sadness, living and longing, riot and revel, daring, defiance, and an ungovernable sense of self make place for one another so directly, and interlace so closely that, however much we mate each feeling with our own, we can single none of them from out the rest, but our whole interest is given merely to this one, this human being who shows himself brimful of every feeling. Yet all these feelings spring from one main faculty—and that is *force*. This force, immeasurably enhanced by each emotional impression and driven to vent its overfill, is the mainspring of the tone piece: it clinches—toward the middle of the movement—to the violence of the destroyer, and in its braggart strength we think we see a wrecker of the world before us, a titan wrestling with the gods.

This shattering force, that filled us half with ecstasy and half with horror, was rushing toward a tragic crisis, whose serious import is set before our feeling in the Second Movement. The tone poet clothes its proclamation in the musical apparel of a funeral march. Emotion tamed by deep grief, moving in solemn sorrow, tells us its tale in stirring tones: an earnest, manly sadness goes from lamentation to thrills of softness, to memories, to tears of love, to searchings of the heart, to cries of transport. Out of grief there springs new force, that fills us with a warmth sublime; instinctively we

seek again this force's fountainhead in grief; we give ourselves to it, till sighing we swoon away; but here we rouse
ourselves once more to fullest force: we will not succumb, but
endure. We battle no more against mourning, but bear it now
ourselves on the mighty billows of a man's courageous heart.
To whom were it possible to paint in words the endless play of
quite unspeakable emotions, passing from grief to highest
exaltation, and thence again to softest melancholy, till they
mount at last to endless recollection? The tone poet alone
could do it, in this wondrous piece.

Force robbed of its destructive arrogance—by the chasten-
ing of its own deep sorrow—the Third Movement shows in
all its buoyant gaiety. Its wild unruliness has shaped itself to
fresh, to blithe activity; we have before us now the lovable
glad man, who paces hale and hearty through the fields of
Nature, looks laughingly across the meadows, and winds his
merry hunting horn from woodland heights; and what he
feels amid it all, the master tells us in the vigorous, healthy
tints of his tone painting; he gives it lastly to the horns themselves to say—those horns which musically express the
radiant, frolicsome, yet tenderhearted exultation of the man.
In this Third Movement the tone poet shows us the man of
feeling from the side directly opposite to that from which he
showed him in its immediate predecessor: there the deeply,
stoutly suffering—here the gladly, blithely doing man.

These two sides the Master now combines in the Fourth—
the last—Movement, to show us finally the man entire,
harmoniously at one with self, in those emotions where the
memory of sorrow becomes itself the shaping force of noble
deeds. This closing section is the harvest, the lucid counterpart and commentary, of the first. Just as there we saw all
human feelings in infinitely varied utterance, now permeating
one another, now each in haste repelling each: so here this
manifold variety unites to one harmonious close, embracing
all these feelings in itself and taking on a grateful plasticity
of shape. This shape the Master binds at first within one
utmost simple theme, which sets itself before us in sure
distinctness, and yet is capable of infinite development, from
gentlest delicacy to grandest strength. Around this theme,
which we may regard as the firm-set manly individuality, there
wind and cling all tenderer and softer feelings, from the very
onset of the movement, evolving to a proclamation of the
purely womanly element; and to the manlike principal theme

—striding sturdily through all the tone piece—this womanly at last reveals itself in ever more intense, more many-sided sympathy, as the overwhelming power of *love*. At the close of the movement this power breaks itself a highway straight into the heart. The restless motion pauses, and in noble, feeling calm this love speaks out; beginning tenderly and softly, then waxing to the rapture of elation, it takes at last the inmost fortress of the man's whole heart. Here it is that once again this heart recalls the memory of its life pang: high swells the breast filled full by love—that breast which harbors woe within its weal; for woe and weal, as purely human feeling, are one thing and the same. Once more the heartstrings quiver, and tears of pure humanity well forth; yet from out the very quick of sadness there bursts the jubilant cry of force—that force which lately wed itself to love, and nerved wherewith *the whole, the total man* now shouts to us the avowal of his godhood.

But only in the master's tone speech was the unspeakable to be proclaimed—the thing that words could here but darkly hint at.

b. The "Coriolan" Overture

THIS comparatively little-known work of the great tone poet is certainly one of his most significant creations, and nobody, who has a close acquaintance with the subject of portrayal, can hear a good performance of it without being profoundly moved. I therefore permit myself to sketch that subject as I have found it expressed in the tone poet's own presentment of it, so as to prepare, for those who feel like me, the same sublime enjoyment as I myself have reaped.

Coriolanus, the man of force untamable, unfitted for a hypocrite's humility, banished therefore from his father city and, with its foes for allies, combating that city to extermination; Coriolanus, moved by mother, wife, and child, at last abandoning vengeance, and condemned to death by his confederates for this treason wrought against them—this Coriolanus I may presuppose as known to most men.

From all this great political canvas, so rich in bearings and "relations" whose setting forth, how allowable soever to the poet, was quite forbidden the musician—since *he* can express moods, feelings, passions and their opposites, but no sort or manner of political relations—Beethoven seized for his presentment one unique scene, the most decisive of them all, as though to snatch at its very focus the true, the purely human emotional content of the whole wide-stretching stuff, and transmit it in the most enthralling fashion to the likewise purely human feeling. This is the scene between Coriolanus, his mother, and wife, in the enemy's camp before the gates of his native city. If, without fear of any error, we may conceive the plastic subject of all the Master's symphonic works as representing scenes between man and woman, and if we may find the archetype of all such scenes in genuine dance itself, whence the symphony in truth derived its musical form: then we here have such a scene before us in utmost possible sublimity and thrillingness of content. The whole tone piece might well be taken for the musical accompaniment of a pantomimic show—only in the sense that, whereas we must imagine the subject itself as set before the eye in pantomime, this accompaniment makes known to us the *entire* language seizable by the ear.

The first few bars present us with the figure of the *man* himself: gigantic force, indomitable sense-of-self, and passionate defiance express themselves as fury, hate, revenge, determination to destroy. It needs only the name of "Coriolanus" to conjure up his form before us at one stroke, to make us feel instinctively the feelings of his clamorous heart. Close beside him stands the *woman:* mother, wife, and child. Grace, gentleness and manners mild confront the headstrong male with childlike pleas, with wifely prayers and mother's admonition, to turn the stubborn heart from its fell purpose.

Coriolanus knows the danger menacing his scorn:* his birthplace has sent out to him the most insidious of advocates. Upon all the sleek and crafty politicians, there at home, he had felt the power to turn his back in cold contempt; their embassies addressed his political understanding, his civic prudence: a scathing word anent their baseness had kept them at his arm's length. But here the fatherland addressed his heart, his involuntary, his purely human Feeling; for this assault he had no other armor—than to ward his eyes, his ears, against the irresistible. Thus at the pleaders' earliest plaint he hastily averts his gaze, his hearing; we see the turbulent gesture with which he breaks the woman's prayer

* *Trotz* = "scorn" in the sense of proud, unbending *defiance,* inspired by a feeling of the justice of one's own cause.—TR.

and shuts his eyes—yet cannot hush the sorrowful lament that echoes after him.

In the inmost chamber of his heart the worm of ruth begins to gnaw the giant's scorn. But terribly this scorn defends itself; stung by the worm's first bite, it breaks out in fuming anguish; his storm of rage, his dreadful throes, lay bare the foaming grandeur of this vengeful scorn itself, and alike the burning violence of the pain inflicted by remorse's tooth. Deep-moved by this appalling spectacle, we see the woman falter and break down in sobs; scarce dares her plea now issue longer from her breast, racked as it is with fellow feeling for the man's tempestuous grief. Fearsomely the war of feeling wages to and fro: where the woman looked for naught but rugged arrogance, she now must see in the very force of scorn its cruelest of sufferings.

But this scorn has now become the only life force of the man: Coriolanus without his vengeance, without his annihilating anger, is no more Coriolanus, and he must cease to live if he give up his scorn. This is the bond that holds his power of life together; the outlawed rebel, the ally of his country's foes, cannot become again what once he was: to let go his vengeance means to cast away his being—to forego the annihilation of his birthplace, to annihilate himself. He faces the woman with the announcement of this awful choice, this only choice now left him. He cries to her: *"Rome* or *I!* For one must fall!"

Here once again he shows himself in the full sublimeness of his shattering ire. And here again the woman wins the power to plead: Mercy! Reconciliation! Peace!—she prays him. Ah! she little understands him, she cannot see that Peace with Rome means his undoing! Yet the woman's wailing tears his heart asunder; once more he turns away, to fight the fearful fight between his scorn and his necessity of self-destruction. Then with a sudden effort he pauses in the torturing strife, and seeks himself the gaze of the beloved woman, to read with agony of bliss his own death warrant in her pleading mien. His bosom heaves in presence of this sight; all inward storms and struggles rush together to one great resolution; the offering of self is sealed—Peace and Reconcilement!

The whole force the hero heretofore had turned on the destruction of his fatherland, the thousand swords and arrows of his hate and unslaked vengeance, with violent hand he girds them to *one* point, and—plunges it into his heart. Felled by his own death thrust, the colossus crashes down: at foot of the woman who besought for peace, he breathes out his dying breath.

c. The Ninth Symphony (with parallel passages from the poems of Goethe)

THOUGH it must be admitted that the essence of higher instrumental music consists in its uttering in tones a thing unspeakable in words, we believe we may distantly approach the solution of an unachievable task by calling certain lines of our great poet Goethe to our aid; words that, albeit standing in no manner of direct connection with Beethoven's work, and in nowise exhausting the meaning of his purely musical creation, yet so sublimely express the higher human moods at bottom of it.

FIRST MOVEMENT

The First Movement appears to be founded on a titanic struggle of the soul, athirst for Joy, against the veto of that hostile power which rears itself 'twixt us and earthly happiness. The great chief theme, which steps before us at one stride as if disrobing from a spectral shroud, might perhaps be translated, without violence to the spirit of the whole tone poem, by Goethe's words:

| *Entbehren sollst du! Sollst ent-* *behren!* | Go wanting, shalt thou! Shalt go wanting! |

Against this mighty foe we find a noble forwardness, a manly energy of defiance, advancing in the middle of the piece to an open fight with its opponent, a fight in which we think we see two giant wrestlers; each of whom desists once more, invincible. In passing gleams of light we recognize the sad-sweet smile of a happiness that seems to seek for us, for whose possession we strive, but whose attainment that archfiend withholds, overshadowing us with its pitch-black wings; so even our distant glimpse of bliss is troubled, and back we sink to gloomy brooding that can only lift itself again to stern resistance, new war against the joy-devouring demon. Thus force, revolt, defiance, yearning, hope, midway-attainment, fresh loss, new quest, repeated struggle make out the elements of ceaseless motion in this wondrous piece; which yet falls ever and anon to that abiding state of utter joylessness which Goethe pictures in the words:

Nur mit Entsetzen'wach' ich Morgensauf,	Grim terror greets me as I wake at morn,
Ich möchte bittre Thränen weinen,	With bitter tears the light I shun
Den Tag zu sehn, der mir in seinem Lauf	Of yet another day whose course forlorn
Nicht Einen Wunsch erfüllen wird, nicht Einen,	Shall not fulfill one wish, not one;
Der selbst die Ahnung jeder Lust	A day that e'en the budding thought
Mit eigensinn'gem Krittel mindert,	Of gladness with its carping strangles,
Die Schöpfung meiner regen Brust	Before whate'er my heart hath wrought
Mit tausend Lebensfratzen hindert.	Life's thousand mocking figures dangles.
Auch muss ich, wenn die Nacht sich niedersenkt,	And when at last the night descends,
Mich ängstlich auf das Lager strecken;	I lay me on my bed in sorrow.
Auch da wird keine Rast geschenkt,	E'en then the day all rest forfends:
Mich werden wilde Träume schrecken.	In hideous dreams it paints the morrow.

At the movement's close this gloomy, joyless mood, expanding to colossal form, appears to span the all, in awful majesty to take possession of a world that God had made for —*Joy.*

SECOND MOVEMENT

With the very first rhythms of this Second Movement a wild excitement seizes us: a new world we enter, wherein we are swept on to frenzied orgy. 'Tis as if, in our flight from despair, we rushed in breathless haste to snatch a new and unknown happiness; for the older, that erewhile lit us with its distant smiles, now seems to have vanished clean away. Goethe depicts a stress not unlike this, as follows:

Von Freude sei nicht mehr die Rede,	Nay! speak to me no more of joy,
Dem Taumel weih' ich mich, dem schmerzlichsten Genuss!	To riot will I plunge, to raging pleasures.
Lass in den Tiefen der Sinnlichkeit	Let us in surfeit of the senses slake

Uns glühende Leidenschaften stillen!	The fever of passions all too tragic;
In undurchdrungenen Zauber-hüllen	Unquestioning its threadbare magic,
Sei jedes Wunder gleich bereit!	Each kill-care for a wonder take.
Stürzen wir uns in das Rau-schen der Zeit,	Come, dive into the whirling hour,
In's Rollen der Begebenheit!	The rushing stream of sweet and sour!
Da mag denn Schmerz und Genuss,	No matter if pleasure and pain,
Gelingen und Verdruss,	If fleeting loss and gain,
Mit einander wechseln, wie es kann,	Change places in a moment's span:
Nur rastlos bethätigt sich der Mann!	Unrest alone proves man is man.

With the abrupt entry of the middle section there suddenly opens out to us a scene of earthly jollity: a certain boisterous bluntness seems expressed in the simple oft-repeated theme, a naïve, self-contented mirth; and we are tempted to think of Goethe's painting of such lowly pleasures:

Dem Volke hier wird jeder Tag ein Fest.	The folk here makes each day a feast.
Mit wenig Witz und viel Be-hagen	With little wit and much con-tentment
Dreht jeder sich im engen Zir-keltanz.	Each spins his narrow round of dance.

But we are not disposed to view this banal gaiety as the goal of our restless quest of happiness and noble Joy; our gaze clouds over, and we turn from the scene to trust our-selves anew to that untiring force which spurs us on without a pause to light upon that bliss which, ah! we never *thus* shall light on; for once again, at the movement's close, we are driven to that earlier scene of jollity, and now we thrust it with impatience from us so soon as recognized.

THIRD MOVEMENT

How differently these tones address our heart! How pure, how heavenly the strain wherewith they calm our wrath, allay the soul's despairing anguish, and turn its turbulence to gentle melancholy! It is as if a memory were awakened, the memory of purest happiness from early days:

Sonst stürzte sich der Him-
melsliebe Kuss
Aufmich herab, in ernster Sab-
bathstille,
Da klang so ahnungsvoll des
Glockentones Fülle,
Und ein Gebet war brünstiger
Genuss.

In days long gone, e'er rained
on me the kiss
Of Heaven's love in Sabbath's
solemn quiet;
The pealing church bells rang
aloud the sweetest fiat,
And prayer to me was ecstasy
of bliss.

With this memory we reach again that tender yearning so beautifully expressed in this movement's second theme, to which we might appropriately apply these other lines of Goethe's:

Ein unbegreiflich holdes Seh-
nen
Trieb mich durch Wald und
Wiesen hinzugeh'n,
Und unter tausend heissen
Thränen
Fühlt' ich mir eine Welt ent-
steh'n.

A fathomless enraptured yearning
Drove me through woods afar
from mortal eyes,
And midst a flood of teardrops
burning
I felt a world around me rise.

It appears as the yearning of love, and in turn is answered by that hope-inspiring, soothing first theme—this time in a somewhat livelier dress; so that with the second theme's return it seems to us that Love and Hope came arm-in-arm to wield their whole persuasive force upon our troubled spirit:

Was sucht ihr, mächtig und
gelind,
Ihr Himmelstöne, mich am
Staube?
Klingt dort umher, wo weiche
Menschen sind.

Why seek me out, ye tones
from Heaven,
Why shower your potent blessings on the dust?
Go sound where men are made
of softer metal.

Thus the still-quivering heart appears to waive aside their solace: but their gentle might is stronger than our already yielding pride; conquered, we throw ourselves into the arms of these sweet messengers of purest happiness:

O tönet fort, ihr süssen Him-
melslieder,
Die Thräne quillt, die Erde hat
mich wieder.

Sound on, thou soothing-sweet
angelic strain:
My tears find vent, earth welcomes me again.

Ay, the wounded heart is healing; it plucks up strength, and mans itself to high resolve—as we gather from the well-nigh triumphal passage toward the movement's close. This exaltation is not yet free from all reaction of the outlived storm; but each recurrence of our former grief is met at once by fresh exertion of that gracious spell, till finally the lightning ceases, the routed tempest rolls away.

FOURTH MOVEMENT

The transition from the Third to the Fourth Movement—which begins as with a shriek of horror—we again may fairly characterize by Goethe's words:

Aber ach! schon fühl' ich bei dem besten Willen
Befriedigung noch nicht aus dem Busen quillen!
Welch' holder Wahn,—doch ach, ein Wähnen nur!
Wo fass' ich dich, unendliche Natur?
Euch Brüste, wo? Ihr Quellen alles Lebens,
An denen Himmel sowie Erde hängt,
Dahin die welke Brust sich drängt.—
Ihr quellt, ihr tränkt, und schmacht' ich so vergebens?

Ah me! howe'er I hold my spirit willing,
I feel no balm from out my bosom rilling.
A beauteous dream—but, ah, the cheat of sight!
Where seize I thee, O Nature infinite?
Ye milky paps, ye founts of all life's main,
To you both earth and heaven cling
To cool their parching at your spring.
Ye well, ye drench, and I must thirst in vain?

With this opening of the last movement Beethoven's music takes on a more definitely *speaking* character: it quits the mold of purely instrumental music, observed in all the three preceding movements, the mode of infinite, indefinite expression; the musical poem is urging toward a crisis, a crisis to be voiced only in human speech. It is wonderful how the Master makes the arrival of man's voice and tongue a positive necessity, by this awe-inspiring recitative of the bass strings; almost breaking the bounds of absolute music already, it stems the tumult of the other instruments with its virile eloquence, insisting on decision, and passes at last into a songlike theme whose simple, stately flow bears with it, one by one, the other instruments, until it swells into a mighty flood. This seems to be the ultimate attempt to phrase by instrumental means alone a stable, sure, unruffled joy: but the rebel rout appears incapable of that restriction; like a raging sea it heaps its waves, sinks back, and once again, yet louder than before, the wild chaotic yell of unslaked passion storms our ear. Then a human voice, with the clear, sure utterance of articulate words, confronts the din of instruments; and we know not at which to wonder most, the boldness of the inspiration, or the naïveté of the Master who lets that voice address the instruments as follows:

Ihr Freunde, nicht diese Töne! Sondern lasst uns angenehmere anstimmen und freudenvollere!	No, friends, not tones like these! But let us sing a strain more cheerful and agreeable!*

With these words light breaks on chaos; a sure and definite mode of utterance is won, in which, supported by the conquered element of instrumental music, we now may hear expressed with clearness what boon it is the agonizing quest of Joy shall find as highest, lasting happiness:

Freude, schöner Götterfunken, Tochter aus Elysium, Wir betreten Feuertrunken,	Joy, thou fairest of immortals, Daughter of Elysium, Fired by thee we pass the portals Leading to thy halidom.
Himmlische, dein Heiligthum. Deine Zauber binden wieder, Was die Mode streng getheilt,	Thy dear spell rebinds together What the mode had dared divide;
Alle Menschen werden Brüder, Wo dein sanfter Flügel weilt.	Man in man regains his brother Where thy fost'ring wings abide.
Wem der grosse Wurf gelungen, Eines Freundes Freund zu sein, Wer ein holdes Weib errungen,	Who the joy hath learned to gain him Friend of his to be his friend; Who a loving wife hath ta'en him,

---

* It is not the meaning of the word that really takes us with this entry of the human voice, but the human character of that voice. Neither is it the thought expressed in Schiller's verses that occupies our minds thereafter, but the familiar sound of the choral chant; in which we ourselves feel bidden to join and thus take part in an ideal divine service, as the congregation really did at entry of the chorale in Johann Sebastian Bach's great passions. In fact, it is obvious, especially with the chief-melody proper, that Schiller's words have been built in perforce and with no great skill; for this melody had first unrolled its breadth before us as an entity *per se,* entrusted to the instruments alone, and there had thrilled us with the nameless joy of a paradise regained.—R. WAGNER.

Mische seinen Jubel ein!

Ja,—wer auch nur Eine Seele

Sein nennt auf dem Erden-rund!
Und wer's nie gekonnt', der stehle
Weinend sich aus diesem Bund!

Freude trinken alle Wesen
An den Brüsten der Natur;

Alle Guten, alle Bösen
Folgen ihrer Rosenspur!
Küsse gab sie uns und Reben,
Einen Freund, geprüft im Tod!
Wollust ward dem Wurm ge-geben,
Und der Cherub steht vor Gott!—

Gladsome cry to ours shall lend!
Yea—who but can claim one being
For his own on all earth's strand.
He who dares not, let him flee-ing
Slink with sobs from out our band.

Joy is dew'd on all creation
From great Nature's mother-breast,
Good and bad in ev'ry nation
Cull her roses, east and west.
Wine and kisses hath she given,
One prov'd friend where death erst trod;
E'en the worm to joy is thriven,

And the Cherub stands 'fore God.

Warlike sounds draw nigh: we believe we see a troop of striplings marching past, their blithe heroic mood expressed in the words:

Froh, wie seine Sonnen fliegen

Durch des Himmels präch-t'gen Plan,
Laufet, Brüder, eure Bahn,

Freudig, wie ein Held zum Sie-gen.

Glad as there his suns are lead-ing
Swift their course through fields of blue,
Onward brothers stout and true,
Hero-like to vict'ry speeding.

This leads to a brilliant contest, expressed by instruments alone: we see the youths rush valiantly into the fight, whose victor's spoil is Joy; and once again we feel impelled to quote from Goethe:

Nur der verdient sich Freiheit wie das Leben,
Der täglich sie erobern muss.

But he may claim his due in life and freedom,
Who battles for it day by day.

The battle, whose issue we never had doubted, is now fought out; the labors of the day are crowned with the smile

of Joy, of Joy that shouts in consciousness of happiness
achieved anew:

Freude, schöner Götterfunken, *Tochter aus Elysium,* *Wir betreten Feuertrunken,*	Joy, thou fairest of immortals, Daughter of Elysium, Fired by thee we pass the portals
Himmlische, dein Heilig- *thum.*	Leading to thy halidom.
Deine Zauber binden wieder *Was die Mode streng getheilt,*	Thy blest magic binds together What the mode had dared divide;
Alle Menschen werden Brüder, *Wo dein sanfter Flügel weilt.*	Man in man regains his brother Where thy fost'ring wings abide.

In the transport of Joy a vow of *universal brotherhood*
leaps from the overflowing breast; uplifted in spirit, we turn
from embracing the whole human race to the great Creator
of nature, whose beatific Being we consciously attest—ay,
in a moment of sublimest ecstasy, we dream we see between
the cloven skies:

Seid umschlungen, Millionen!	Hand to hand, earth's happy millions!
Diesen Kuss der ganzen Welt!	To the world this kiss be sent!
Brüder, über'm Sternenzelt	Brothers, o'er heav'n's starry tent
Muss ein lieber Vater wohnen!	Sure our Father dwells 'mid billions.
Ihr stürzt nieder, Millionen?	To your knees, ye countless billions
Ahnest due den Schöpfer, *Welt?*	Knowest thy Creator, world?
Such' ihn über'm Sternenzelt!	Seek him where heav'n's tent is furl'd,
Über Sternen muss er wohnen!	Throned among his starry bil- lions.

And now it is as if a revelation had confirmed us in the
blest belief that *every human soul is made for Joy.* With all
the force of strong conviction we cry to one another:

Seid umschlungen, Millionen!	Hand to hand, earth's happy millions!
Diesen Kuss der ganzen Welt!	This fond kiss to all the world!

and:

Freude, schöner Götterfunken,	Joy, thou fairest of immortals,
Tochter aus Elysium,	Daughter of Elysium,
Wir betreten feuertrunken,	Fired by thee we pass the portals
Himmlische, dein Heiligthum.	Leading to thy halidom.

With God to consecrate our universal love, we now dare taste the purest joy. Not merely in the throes of awe, but gladdened by a blissful truth revealed to us, we now may answer the question:

Ihr stürzt nieder, Millionen?	To your knees, ye favor'd millions?
Ahnest du den Schöpfer, Welt?	Knowest thy Creator, world?

with:

Such' ihn über'm Sternenzelt!	Seek him where the stars are strewn!
Brüder, über'm Sternenzelt	Brothers, o'er the starry dome
Muss ein lieber Vater wohnen!	Surely dwells a loving Father!

In intimate possession of our granted happiness, of childhood's buoyancy regained, we give ourselves henceforth to its enjoyment. Ah! we have been regiven innocence of heart, and softly outspreads its wings of blessing o'er our heads:

Freude, Tochter aus Elysium,	Joy, thou daughter of Elysium!
Deine Zauber binden wieder	Thy sweet spell rebinds together
Was die Mode streng getheilt,	What the Mode had dared divide;
Alle Menschen werden Brüder,	Man in man regains his brother
Wo dein sanfter Flügel weilt.	Where thy fost'ring wings abide.

To the gentle happiness of Joy succeeds its jubilation—we clasp the whole world to our breast; shouts and laughter fill the air, like thunder from the clouds, the roaring of the sea; whose everlasting tides and healing shocks lends life to earth, and keep life sweet for the *joy* of man to whom God gave the earth as home of happiness:

Seid umschlungen, Millionen!

Diesen Kuss der ganzen Welt!

Brüder, über'm Sternenzelt
Muss ein lieber Vater wohnen!

Freude! Freude, schöner Göt-
terfunken!

Hand to hand, ye countless millions!
To the world this kiss be sent!
Brothers, o'er the starry tent
Our Father dwells 'mid joyful billions.
Joy, blest joy! thou brightest spark of godhood!

PART IV

The Artwork of the Future

1. Music and reality, Schopenhauer's theory extended by Wagner

IT was Schopenhauer who first defined the position of music among the fine arts with philosophic clearness, ascribing to it a totally different nature from that of either plastic or poetic art. He starts from wonder at music's speaking a language immediately intelligible by everyone, since it needs no whit of intermediation through abstract concepts; which completely distinguishes it from poetry, in the first place, whose sole material consists of concepts, employed by it to visualize the *idea*. For according to this philosopher's so luminous definition, it is the ideas of the world and of its essential phenomena, in the sense of Plato, that constitute the "object" of the fine arts; whereas, however, the poet interprets these ideas to the visual consciousness through an employment of strictly rationalistic concepts in a manner quite peculiar to his art, Schopenhauer believes he must recognize *in music itself an idea of the world*, since he who could entirely translate it into abstract concepts would have found withal a philosophy to explain the world itself.

Though Schopenhauer propounds this theory of music as a paradox, since it cannot strictly be set forth in logical terms, he also furnishes us with the only serviceable material for a further demonstration of the justice of his profound hypothesis; a demonstration which he himself did not pursue more closely, perhaps for simple reason that as layman he was not conversant enough with music, and moreover was unable to base his knowledge thereof sufficiently definitely on an understanding of the very musician whose works have first laid open to the world that deepest mystery of music: Beethoven.

In making use of this material supplied us by the philosopher, I fancy I shall do best to begin with a remark in which Schopenhauer declines to accept the idea derived from a knowledge of "relations" as the essence of the thing-in-itself, but regards it merely as expressing the objective character of things, and therefore as still concerned with their phenomenal appearance. "And we should not understand this character

itself"—so Schopenhauer goes on to say—"were not the inner
essence of things confessed to us elsewise, dimly at least and
in our feeling. For that essence cannot be gathered from the
ideas, nor understood through any mere *objective* knowledge;
wherefore it would ever remain a mystery, had we not access
to it from quite another side. Only inasmuch as every observer
[literally, knower, or perceiver] is an individual withal, and
thereby part of nature, stands there open to him in his own
self-consciousness the adit to nature's innermost; and there
forthwith, and most immediately, it makes itself known to
him as *will*."

If we couple with this what Schopenhauer postulates as
the condition for entry of an idea into our consciousness,
namely, "a temporary preponderance of intellect over will,
or to put it physiologically, a strong excitation of the sensory
faculty of the brain without the smallest excitation of the
passions or desires," we have only further to pay close heed
to the elucidation which directly follows it, namely, that our
consciousness has two sides: in part it is a consciousness of
one's own self, which is the will; in part a consciousness of
other things, and chiefly then a *visual* knowledge of the
outer world, the apprehension of objects. "The more the
one side of the aggregate consciousness comes to the front,
the more does the other retreat."

After well weighing these extracts from Schopenhauer's
principal work, it must be obvious to us that musical conception, as it has nothing in common with the seizure of an
idea (for the latter is absolutely bound to physical perception
of the world), can have its origin nowhere but upon that side
of consciousness which Schopenhauer defines as facing inward. Though this side may temporarily retire completely,
to make way for entry of the purely apprehending "subject"
on its function (that is, the seizure of ideas), on the other
hand it transpires that only from this inward-facing side of
consciousness can the intellect derive its ability to seize the
character of things. If this consciousness, however, is the
consciousness of one's own self, that is, of the will, we must
take it that its repression is indispensable indeed for purity
of the outward-facing consciousness, but that the nature of
the thing-in-itself—inconceivable by that physical [or "visual"]
mode of knowledge—would be revealed to this inward-facing
consciousness only when it had attained the faculty of seeing
within as clearly as that other side of consciousness is able
in its seizure of ideas to see without.

For a further pursuit of this path, Schopenhauer has also given us the best of guides, through his profound hypothesis concerning the physiologic phenomenon of clairvoyance, and the dream theory he has based thereon. For as in that phenomenon the inward-facing consciousness attains the actual power of sight where our waking daylight consciousness feels nothing but a vague impression of the midnight background of our will's emotions, so from out this night *tone* bursts upon the world of waking, a direct utterance of the will. As dreams must have brought to everyone's experience, beside the world envisaged by the functions of the waking brain there dwells a second, distinct as is itself, no less a world displayed to vision; since this second world can in no case be an object lying outside us, it therefore must be brought to our cognizance by an *inward* function of the brain; and this form of the brain's perception Schopenhauer here calls the dream organ.

Now, a no less positive experience is this: besides the world that presents itself to sight, in waking as in dreams, we are conscious of the existence of a second world, perceptible only through the ear, manifesting itself through sound; literally a *sound world* beside the *light world*, a world of which we may say that it bears the same relation to the visible world as dreaming to waking: for it is quite as plain to us as is the other, though we must recognize it as being entirely different. As the world of dreams can come to vision only through a special operation of the brain, so music enters our consciousness through a kindred operation; only, the latter differs exactly as much from the operation consequent on *sight*, as that dream organ from the function of the waking brain under the stimulus of outer impressions.

As the dream organ cannot be roused into action by outer impressions, against which the brain is now fast locked, this must take place through happenings in the inner organism that our waking consciousness merely feels as vague sensations. But it is this inner life through which we are directly allied with the whole of nature, and thus are brought into a relation with the essence of things that eludes the forms of outer knowledge, time and space; whereby Schopenhauer so convincingly explains the genesis of prophetic or telepathic, fatidical dreams, ay, in rare and extreme cases the occurrence of somnambulistic clairvoyance. From the most terrifying of such dreams we wake with a scream, the immediate expression of the anguished will, which thus makes definite entrance into the sound world first of all, to manifest itself without. Now, if we take the scream in all the diminutions of its vehemence, down to the gentler cry of longing, as the root element of every human message to the ear; and if we cannot but find in it the most immediate utterance of the will, through which the latter turns the swiftest and the surest toward without, then we have less cause to wonder at its immediate intelligibility than at an *art* arising from this element: for it is evident, upon the other hand, that neither artistic beholding nor artistic fashioning can result from aught but a diversion of the consciousness from the agitations of the will.

To explain this wonder, let us first recall our philosopher's profound remark, adduced above, that we should never understand even the ideas that by their very nature are only seizable through will-freed, that is, objective contemplation, had we not another approach to the essence-of-things which lies beneath them, namely, our direct consciousness of our own self. By this consciousness alone are we enabled to understand withal the inner nature of things outside us, inasmuch as we recognize in them the selfsame basic essence that our self-consciousness declares to be our very own. Our each illusion hereanent had sprung from the mere *sight* of a world around us, a world that in the show of daylight we took for something quite apart from us:* first through (intellectual) perception of the ideas, and thus upon a circuitous path, do we reach an initial stage of undeception, in which we no longer see things parceled off in time and space, but apprehend their generic character; and this character speaks out the plainest to us from the works of plastic art, whose true province it therefore is to take the illusive surface of the light-shown world and, in virtue of a most ingenious playing with that semblance, lay bare the idea concealed beneath.

In daily life the mere sight of an object leaves us cold and unconcerned, and only when we become aware of that object's bearings on our will does it call forth an emotion; in harmony wherewith it very properly ranks as the first aesthetic principle of plastic art, that its imagings shall entirely avoid such references to our individual will, and prepare for our sight that calm which alone makes possible a pure beholding of the object according to its own character. Yet the effector

---

* Cf. "In lichten Tages Schein, wie war Isolde mein?" and in fact the whole love scene in *Tristan und Isolde,* Act II.—Tr.

of this aesthetic, will-freed contemplation, into which we momentarily plunge, here remains nothing but the *show* of things. And it is this principle of tranquilization by sheer pleasure in the semblance, that has been extended from plastic art to all the arts, and made a postulate for every manner of aesthetic pleasing. Whence, too, has come our term for *beauty* (*Schönheit*); the root of which word in our German language is plainly connected with show (*Schein*) as object, with seeing (*Schauen*) as subject.

But that consciousness which alone enabled us to grasp the idea transmitted by the show we looked on must feel compelled at last to cry with Faust: "A spectacle superb! But still, alas! a spectacle. Where seize I thee, O Nature infinite?"

This cry is answered in the most positive manner by *music*. Here the world outside us speaks to us in terms intelligible beyond compare, since its sounding message to our ear is of the selfsame nature as the cry sent forth to it from the depths of our own inner heart. The object of the tone perceived is brought into immediate rapport with the subject of the tone emitted: without any reasoning go-between we understand the cry for help, the wail, the shout of joy, and straightway answer it in its own tongue. If the scream, the moan, the murmured happiness in our own mouth is the most direct utterance of the will's emotion, so when brought us by our ear we understand it past denial as utterance of the same emotion; no illusion is possible here, as in the daylight show, to make us deem the essence of the world outside us not wholly identical with our own; and thus that gulf which seems to sight is closed forthwith.

Now, if we see an art arise from this immediate consciousness of the oneness of our inner essence with that of the outer world, our most obvious inference is that this art must be subject to aesthetic laws quite distinct from those of every other. All aesthetes hitherto have rebelled against the notion of deducing a veritable art from what appears to them a purely pathologic element, and have consequently refused to music any recognition until its products show themselves in a light as cold as that peculiar to the fashionings of plastic art. Yet that its very rudiment is felt, not seen, by our deepest consciousness as a world's idea, we have learned to recognize forthwith through Schopenhauer's eventful aid, and we understand that idea as a direct revelation of the oneness of the will; starting with the oneness of all human being, our consciousness is thereby shown beyond dispute our unity with nature, whom equally we recognize through sound.

Difficult as is the task of eliciting music's nature as an art, we believe we may best accomplish it by considering the inspired musician's *modus operandi*. In many respects this must radically differ from that of other artists. As to the latter, we have had to acknowledge that it must be preceded by a will-freed, pure beholding of the object, an act of like nature with the effect to be produced by the artwork itself in the mind of the spectator. Such an object, however, to be raised to an idea by means of pure beholding, does not present itself to the musician at all; for his music is itself a world's-idea, an idea in which the world immediately displays its essence, whereas in those other arts this essence has to pass through the medium of the understanding before it can *become* displayed. We can but take it that the *individual will*, silenced in the plastic artist through pure beholding, awakes in the musician as the *universal will*, and—above and beyond all power of vision—now recognizes itself as such in full self-consciousness. Hence the great difference in the mental state of the concipient musician and the designing artist; hence the radically diverse effects of music and of painting: here profoundest stilling, there utmost excitation of the will. In other words we here have the will in the individual as such, the will imprisoned by the fancy of its difference from the essence of things outside, and unable to lift itself above its barriers save in the purely disinterested beholding of objects; whilst there, in the musician's case, the will feels *one* forthwith, above all bounds of individuality: for hearing has opened it the gate through which the world thrusts home to it, it to the world.

This prodigious breaking down the floodgates of appearance must necessarily call forth in the inspired musician a state of ecstasy wherewith no other can compare: in it the will perceives itself the almighty will of all things: it has not mutely to yield place to contemplation, but proclaims itself aloud as conscious world idea. One state surpasses his, and one alone—the saint's, and chiefly through its permanence and imperturbability; whereas the clairvoyant ecstasy of the musician has to alternate with a perpetually recurrent state of individual consciousness, which we must account the more distressful, the higher has his inspiration carried him above all bounds of individuality. And this suffering again, allotted him as penalty for the state of inspiration in which he so unutterably entrances us, might make us hold the musician in higher reverence than other artists, ay, well-nigh give him claim to rank as holy. For his art, in truth, compares with the communion of all the other arts as *religion* with the *Church*.

We have seen that in the other arts the will is longing to become pure knowledge, but that this is possible only in so far as it stays stock-still in its deepest inner chamber: 'tis as if it were awaiting tidings of redemption from there outside; content they it not, it sets itself in that state of clairvoyance; and here, beyond the bounds of time and space, it knows itself the world's both one and all. What it here has seen, no tongue can impart: as the dream of deepest sleep can be conveyed to the waking consciousness only through translation into the language of a second, an allegoric dream which immediately precedes our wakening, so for the direct vision of its self the will creates a second organ of transmission— an organ whose one side faces toward that inner vision whilst the other thrusts into the reappearing outer world with the sole direct and sympathetic message, that of tone. The will cries out; and in the countercry it knows itself once more: thus cry and countercry become for it a comforting, at last an entrancing play with its own self.

Sleepless one night in Venice, I stepped upon the balcony of my window overlooking the Grand Canal: like a deep dream the fairy city of lagoons lay stretched in shade before me. From out of the breathless silence rose the strident cry of a gondolier just woken on his bark; again and again his voice went forth into the night, till from the remotest distance its fellow cry came answering down the midnight length of the Canal: I recognized the drear melodic phrase to which the well-known lines of Tasso were also wedded in his day, but which in itself is certainly as old as Venice's canals and people. After many a solemn pause the ringing dialogue took quicker life, and seemed at last to melt in unison; till finally the sounds from far and near died softly back to new-won slumber. Whate'er could sun-steeped, color-swarming Venice of the daylight tell me of itself, that that sounding dream of night had not brought infinitely deeper, closer, to my consciousness?

Another time I wandered through the lofty solitude of an upland vale in Uri. In broad daylight from a hanging pasture land came shouting the shrill yodel of a cowherd, sent forth across the broadening valley; from the other side anon there answered it, athwart the monstrous silence, a like exultant herd call: the echo of the towering mountain walls here mingled in; the brooding valley leaped into the merry lists of sound. So wakes the child from the night of the mother womb, and answer it the mother's crooning kisses; so understands the yearning youth the woodbird's mate call, so speaks to the musing man the moan of beasts, the whistling wind, the howling hurricane, till over him there comes that dreamlike state in which the ear reveals to him the inmost essence of all his eye had held suspended in the cheat of scattered show, and tells him that his inmost being is one therewith, that only in *this* wise can the essence of things without be learned in truth.

The dreamlike nature of the state into which we thus are plunged through sympathetic hearing—and wherein there dawns on us that other world, that world from whence the musician speaks to us—we recognize at once from an experience at the door of every man: namely, that our eyesight is paralyzed to such a degree by the effect of music upon us, that with eyes wide open we no longer intensively see. We experience this in every concert room while listening to any tone piece that really touches us, where the most hideous and distracting things are passing before our eye, things that assuredly would quite divert us from the music, and even move us to laughter, if we actively saw them; I mean, besides the highly trivial aspect of the audience itself, the mechanical movements of the band, the whole peculiar working apparatus of an orchestral production. That this spectacle—which preoccupies the man untouched by the music—at last ceases to disturb the spellbound listener, plainly shows us that we no longer are really conscious of it, but, for all our open eyes, have fallen into a state essentially akin to that of hypnotic clairvoyance. And in truth it is in this state alone that we immediately belong to the musician's world. From out that world, which nothing else can picture, the musician casts the meshwork of his tones to net us, so to speak; or, with his wonder-drops of sound he dews our brain as if by magic, and robs it of the power of seeing aught save our own inner world.

2. Beethoven's symphonies reveal another world, whose logic is the logic of feeling.

In Beethoven's symphonies instruments speak a language whereof the world at no previous time had any knowledge: for here, with a hitherto unknown persistence, the purely musical expression enchains the hearer in an inconceivably varied mesh of nuances; rouses his inmost being to a degree unreachable by any other art; and in all its changefulness reveals an ordering principle so free and bold that we can but deem it more forcible than any logic, yet without the laws of logic entering into it in the slightest—nay, rather, the reasoning march of thought, with its track of causes and effects, here finds no sort of foothold. So that this symphony must positively appear to us a revelation from another world; and in truth it opens out a scheme of the world's phenomena quite different from the ordinary logical scheme, and whereof one foremost thing is undeniable—that it thrusts home with the most overwhelming conviction, and guides our feeling with such a sureness that the logic-mongering reason is completely routed and disarmed thereby.

3. Poetry will combine with music in drama which also obeys the logic of feeling.

Poetry will lightly find the path hereto, and perceive her final ascension into music to be her own, her inmost longing, so soon as she grows aware of a need in music, herself, which poetry alone can still. To explain this need, let us first attest that ineradicable attribute of all human apperception which spurs it to find out the laws of causality, and in presence of every impressive phenomenon to ask itself instinctively the question "Why?" Even the hearing of a symphonic tone piece does not entirely silence this question; rather, since it cannot give the answer, it brings the hearer's inductive faculty into a confusion which not only is liable to disquiet him, but also becomes the ground of a totally false judgment. To answer this disturbing, and yet so irremissible question, so that in a manner of speaking it is circumvented from the first, can only be the poet's work. But it can succeed in the hands of none but that poet who is fully alive to music's tendence and exhaustible faculty of expression, and therefore drafts his poem in such a fashion that it may penetrate the finest fibers of the musical tissue, and the spoken *thought* entirely dissolve into the *feeling*. Obviously, no other form of poetry can help us here, save that in which the poet no longer describes, but brings his subject into actual and convincing representment to the senses; and this sole form is drama. Drama, at the moment of its actual scenic representation, arouses in the beholder such an intimate and instant interest in an action borrowed faithfully from life itself, at least in its possibilities, that man's sympathetic feeling already passes into that ecstatic state where it clean forgets the fateful question "Why?" and willingly yields itself, in utmost excitation, to the guidance of those new laws whereby music makes herself so wondrously intelligible and—in a profounder sense —supplies withal the only fitting answer to that "Why?"

4. Essence of drama is knowing through feeling.

ONLY in the most perfect artwork therefore, in *the drama*, can the insight of the experienced one impart itself with full success; and for the very reason that, through employment of every artistic expressional faculty of man, the poet's aim is in drama the most completely carried from the understanding to the feeling—to wit, is artistically imparted to the feeling's most directly receptive organs, the senses. The drama, as the most perfect artwork, differs from all other forms of poetry in just this—that in it the aim is lifted into utmost imperceptibility by its *entire realization*. In drama, wherever the aim, that is, the intellectual will, stays still observable, there the impression is also a chilling one; for where we see the poet still *will*-ing, we feel that as yet he *can* not. The poet's can-ning, however, is the complete ascension of the aim into the artwork, the *emotionalizing of the intellect*. His aim he can reach only by physically presenting to our eyes the things of life in their fullest spontaneity; and thus, by vindicating life itself out of the mouth of its own necessity; for the feeling, to which he addresses himself, can understand this necessity alone.

In presence of the dramatic artwork, nothing should remain for the combining intellect to search for. Everything in it must come to an issue sufficient to set our feeling at rest thereon; for in the setting at rest of this feeling resides the repose itself, which brings us an instinctive understanding of life. In the drama we must become *knowers* through *the feeling*. The understanding tells us, *"So is it,"* only when the feeling has told us, *"So must it be."* Only through *itself*, however, does this feeling become intelligible to itself: it understands no language other than its own. Things which can be explained to us only by the infinite accommodations of the understanding embarrass and confound the feeling. In drama, therefore, an action can be explained only when it is completely vindicated by the feeling; and it thus is the dramatic poet's task, not to invent actions, but to make an action so intelligible through its emotional necessity that we may altogether dispense with the intellect's assistance in its vindication. The poet therefore has to make his main scope the *choice of the action*—which he must so choose that, alike in its character as in its compass, it makes possible to him its entire vindication from out the feeling; for in this vindication alone, resides the reaching of his aim.

An action which can be explained only on grounds of historic relations, unbased upon the present; an action which can be vindicated only from the standpoint of the state, or understood alone by taking count of religious dogmas stamped upon it from without—not sprung from common views within—such an action, as we have seen, is representable only to the understanding, not to the feeling. At its most successful, this was to be effected through narration and description, through appeal to the intellect's imaginative force; not through direct presentment to the feeling and its definitely seizing organs, the senses: for we saw that those senses were positively unable to take in the full extent of such an action, that in it there lay a mass of relations beyond all possibility of bringing to physical view and bound to be relegated, for their comprehension, to the combining organ of thought. In a politicohistorical drama, therefore, it became the poet's business eventually to give out

his aim quite nakedly—as such: the whole drama stayed unintelligible and unimpressive, if this aim, in the form of a human "moral," did not at laśt quite visibly emerge from amid
the desert waste of pragmatic motives, employed for sheer
description's sake. In the course of such a piece, one asked
oneself instinctively: "What is the poet trying to tell us?"

Now, an action which is to justify itself before and through
the feeling, busies itself with no *moral*; its whole moral consists precisely in its justification by the instinctive human feeling. It is a goal to itself, in so far as it has to be vindicated
only and precisely by the feeling out of which it springs.
Wherefore this action can be such a one only as proceeds
from relations the truest, that is, the most seizable by the feeling, the nighest to human emotions, and thus the simplest—
from relations such as can spring only from a human society
intrinsically at one with itself, uninfluenced by inessential notions and nonpresent grounds of right: a society belonging to
itself alone, and not to any past.

However, no action of life stands solitary and apart: it has
always some sort of correlation with the actions of other men;
through which it is conditioned alike as by the individual feelings of its transactor himself. The weakest correlation is that
of mere petty, insignificant actions; which require for their explanation less the strength of a necessary feeling than the way-
wardness of whim. But the greater and more decisive an action
is, and the more it can be explained only from the strength of
a necessary *feeling*: in so much the more definite and wider a
connection does it also stand with the actions of others. A
great action, one which the most demonstratively and exhaustively displays the nature of man along any one particular line,
issues only from the shock of manifold and mighty opposites.
But for us to be able rightly to judge these opposites themselves, and to fathom their actions by the individual feelings of
the transactors, a great action must be represented in a wide
circle of relations; for only in such a circle is it to be understood. The poet's chief and especial task will thus consist in
this: that at the very outset he shall fix his eye on such a
circle, shall completely gauge its compass, shall scrutinize each
detail of the relations contained therein, with heed both to its
own measure and to its bearing on the main action; this done,
that he then shall make the measure of his understanding of
these things the measure of their understandableness as a work
of art, by drawing in this ample circle toward its central point,
and thus condensing it into the periphery which gives an un-

derstanding of the central hero. This *condensation* is the work proper to the poetizing intellect; and this intellect is the center and the summit of the whole man, who from thence divides himself into the receiver and the imparter.

As an object is seized in the first place by the outward-turned instinctive feeling, and next is brought to the imagination, as the earliest function of the brain: so the understanding, which is nothing else but the imaginative force as regulated by the actual measure of the object, has to advance in turn through the imagination to the instinctive feeling—in order to impart what it now has recognized. In the understanding objects mirror themselves as what they actually are; but this mirrored actuality is, after all, a mere thing of thought: to impart this *thought-out* actuality, the understanding must display it to the feeling in an image akin to what the feeling had originally brought to *it*; and this image is the work of fantasy. Only through the fantasy can the understanding have commerce with the feeling. The understanding can grasp the full actuality of an object only when it breaks the image in which the object is brought it by the fantasy, and parcels it into its singlest parts; when it fain would bring these parts before itself again in combination, it has at once to cast for itself an image, which no longer answers strictly to the actuality of the thing, but merely in the measure wherein man has power to recognize it. Thus even the simplest action confounds and bewilders the understanding, which would fain regard it through the anatomical microscope, by the immensity of its ramifications: would it comprehend that action, it can do so only by discarding the microscope and fetching forth the image which alone its human eye can grasp; and this comprehension is ultimately enabled by the instinctive feeling—as vindicated by the understanding. This image of the phenomena, in which alone the feeling can comprehend them, and which the understanding, to make itself intelligible to the feeling, must model on that image which the latter originally brought it through the fantasy—this image, for the aim of the poet, who must likewise take the phenomena of life and compress them from their viewless many-memberedness into a compact, easily surveyable shape—this image is nothing else but *the wonder*.

5. Need to concentrate motives in drama

In the interest of intelligibility, therefore, the poet has so to limit the number of his action's moments, that he may win the needful space for the motivation of those retained. All those motives which lay hidden in the moments excised, he must fit into the motives of his main action in such a way that they shall not appear detached; because in detachment they would also demand their own specific moments of action, the very ones excised. On the contrary, they must be so included in the chief motive, that they do not shatter, but *strengthen* it as a whole. But the strengthening of a motive makes also necessary a strengthening of the moment of action itself, which is nothing but the fitting utterance of that motive. A strong motive cannot utter itself through a weak moment of action; both action and motive must thereby become un-understandable.

In order, then, to enounce intelligibly a chief motive thus strengthened by taking into it a number of motives which in ordinary life would only utter themselves through numerous moments of action, the action thereby conditioned must also be a strengthened, a powerful one, and in its unity more ample than any that ordinary life brings forth; seeing that in ordinary life the selfsame action would only have come to pass in company with many lesser actions, in a widespread space, and within a greater stretch of time. The poet who, in favor of the perspicuity of the thing, would draw together not only these actions but this expanse of space and time as well, must not merely cut off parts, but condense the whole intrinsic contents. A condensement of the shape of actual life, however, can be comprehended by the latter only when—as compared with itself—it appears magnified, strengthened, unaccustomed. It is just in his busy scattering through time and space, that man cannot understand his own life energy: but the image of this energy, as brought within the compass of his understanding, is what the poet's shapings offer him for view; an image wherein this energy is condensed into an utmost-strengthened "moment," which, taken apart, most certainly seems wondrous and unwonted, yet shuts within itself its own unwontedness and wondrousness, and is in nowise taken by the beholder for a wonder but apprehended as the most intelligible representment of reality.

In virtue of this wonder, the poet is able to display the most measureless conjunctures in an all-intelligible unity. The greater, the farther-reaching the conjuncture he desires to make conceivable, the stronger has he to intensify the attributes of his shapings. Time and space, to let them appear in keeping with the movement of these figures, he will alike condense from their amplest stretch, to shapings of his wonder; the attributes of infinitely scattered moments of time and space will he just as much collect into one intensified attribute, as he had assembled the scattered motives into one chief motive; and the utterance of this attribute he will enhance as much, as he had strengthened the action issuing from that motive. Even the most unwonted shapes, which the poet has to evoke in this procedure, will never truly be un-natural; because in them Nature's essence is not distorted, but merely her utterances are gathered into one lucid image, such as is alone intelligible to artist-man. The poetic daring, which gathers Nature's utterances into such an image, can *first for us* be crowned with due success, precisely because *through experience we have gained a clear insight into Nature's essence.*

6. *Myth represents a concentration of motives; summary of relations of myth, drama, feeling, and motives.*

IF, then, we wish to define the Poet's work according to its highest power thinkable, we must call it *the—vindicated by the clearest human consciousness, the new-devised to answer the beholdings of an ever-present life, the brought in drama to a show the most intelligible—the mythos.*

We now have only to ask ourselves, through *what expressional means* this *mythos* is the most intelligibly to be displayed in drama. For this, we must go back to that "moment" of the whole artwork which conditions its very essence; and this is the necessary *vindication of the action through its mo-*

tives, for which the poetizing understanding turns to face the instinctive *feeling*, upon the latter's unforced fellow feeling to ground an understanding of them. We have seen that the condensation—so necessary for a practical understanding—of the manifold moments of action, immeasurably ramified in actual reality, was conditioned by the poet's longing to display a great conjucture of human life's phenomena, through which alone can the necessity of these phenomena be grasped. This condensation he could bring about, in keeping with his main scope, only by taking up into the motives of the moments chosen for actual representment all those motives which lay at bottom of the moments of action that he had discarded; and by vindicating their adoption, before the judgment seat of feeling, in that he let them appear as a strengthening of the chief motives; which latter, in turn, conditioned of themselves a strengthening of their corresponding moments of action. Finally we saw that this strengthening of a moment of action could be achieved only by lifting it above the ordinary human measure, through the poetic figment of the wonder—in strict correspondence with human nature, albeit exalting and enhancing its faculties to a potency unreachable in ordinary life —of the wonder, which was not to stand beyond the bounds of life, but to loom so large from out its very midst that the shows of ordinary life should pale before it. And now we have only to come to definite terms, as to *wherein should consist the strengthening of the motives* which are to condition from out themselves that strengthening of the moments of action.

What is the meaning, in the sense indicated above, of a "Strengthening of the Motives"?

It is impossible—as we have already seen—that a heaping up of motives can be the thing we mean; because motives thus crowded together, without any possible utterance as action, must remain unintelligible to the feeling; and even to the understanding—if explicable—they would still be reft of any vindication. Many motives to a scanty action could only appear petty, whimsical, and irrelevant, and could not possibly be employed for a great action, excepting in a caricature. The strengthening of a motive cannot therefore consist in a mere addition of lesser motives, but in the complete absorption of *many motives* into this *one*. An interest common to divers men at divers times and under divers circumstances, and ever shaping itself afresh according to these diversities: such an interest

—once that these men, these times and circumstances are typi-
cally alike at bottom, and in themselves make plain an essential trait of human nature—is to be made the interest of one
man, at one given time and under given circumstances. In the
interest of this man all outward differences are to be raised
into one definite thing; in which, however, the interest must
reveal itself according to its greatest, most exhaustive compass. But this is as good as saying that from the interest all
which savors of the particularistic and accidental must be
taken away, and it must be given in its full truth as a necessary, purely human *utterance of feeling*. Of such an emotional
utterance *that* man is incapable who is not as yet at one with
himself about his necessary interest: the man whose feelings
have not yet found the object strong enough to drive them to
a definite, a necessary enunciation; but who, faced with powerless, accidental, unsympathetic outward things, still splits himself into two halves. But should this mighty object front him
from the outer world, and either so move him by its strange
hostility that he girds up his whole individuality to thrust it
from him, or attract him so irresistibly that he longs to ascend
into it with his whole individuality—then will his interest also,
for all its definiteness, be so wide-embracing that it takes into
it all his former split-up, forceless interests, and entirely con-
sumes them.

7. Word speech must be strengthened to suit mythic drama.

THE moment *of this consumption* is the act which the poet has
to prepare for, by strengthening a motive in such sort, that a
powerful moment of action may issue from it; and this preparation is the last work of his enhanced activity. Up to this
point his organ of the poetizing intellect, word, speech, can do
his bidding; for up to here he has had to set forth interests in
whose interpreting and shaping a necessary feeling took no
share as yet—interests variously influenced by given circumstances from without, without there being any definite working on within in such a way as to drive the inner feeling to a
necessary, choiceless activity, in its turn determining the outer

course of things. Here still reigned the combining understanding, with its parceling of parts and piecing together of
this or that detail in this or that fashion; here it had not directly to *display*, but merely to shadow forth to draw com-
parisons, to make like intelligible by like—and for *this*, not
only did its organ of word speech quite suffice, but it was the
only one through which the intellect could make itself intelligible.—But where the thing prepared for is to become a
reality, where the poet has no longer to separate and compare,
where he wants to let the thing that gainsays all choice and
definitely gives itself without conditions, the determinant motive strengthened to a determinative force—to let this proclaim
itself in the very utterance of a necessary, all-dominating feeling—there he can no longer work with the merely shadowing,
explounding word speech, *except he so enhance it* as he has
already enhanced the motive: and this he can do only by
pouring it into tone speech.

8.   *From ordinary speech a new art speech must be created, a concise and vigorous style.*

IF we want to keep on reasonable terms with life, we have to
win from the prose of our ordinary speech the heightened
expression in which the poetic aim shall manifest itself in all
its potence to the feeling. A verbal expression which tears
asunder the bond of connection with ordinary speech, by basing its physical manifestment on imported "moments" foreign
to the nature of our ordinary speech—such as that prosodic
rhythm above denoted—can only bewilder the feeling.

In modern speech no intonations are employed other than
those of the prosaic speaking accent, which has no fixed
dwelling in the natural stress of the root syllables, but in each
fresh phrase is lodged wherever needful for the purpose of an
understanding of one particular aim, in keeping with that
phrase's sense. The speech of modern daily life differs from
the older, poetic speech in this: that, for sake of an understanding, it needs a far more copious use of words and clauses
than did the other. In our language of daily life we discuss
matters having no more touch with the meaning of our own

roots of speech than they have with nature at large; it therefore has to take the most complicated turns and twists, in order to paraphrase the meanings of primitive or imported speech roots—which have become altered or newly accommodated to our social relations and views, and in any case estranged from our feeling—and thus to bring them to a conventional understanding. As our sentences are diffuse and endlessly expanded, to admit this apparatus of accommodation, they would be made completely unintelligible if the speaking accent gave prominence to the root syllables by a frequent emphasis. A comprehension of these phrases must have its path smoothed for it, by the accent being employed but very sparingly, and only for their weightiest moments; whereas all the remaining moments, however weighty the significance of their roots, must naturally be left entirely unemphasized, for very reason of their frequency.

If now we give a little thought to what we have to understand by the compression and concentration of the moments of action and their motives, as necessary to a realization of the poetic aim; and if we recognize that these operations, again, can only be effected through a similarly compressed and concentrated expression: then we shall be driven at once to see *how* we have to deal with our language. Just as we cut away from these "moments" of action, and for their sakes from their conditioning motives, all that was accidental, petty, and indefinite; just as we had to remove from their content all that disfigured it from outside, all that savored of the state, of pragmatically historical and dogmatically religious—in order to display that content as a purely human one and dictated by the feeling: so also have we to cut away from the verbal expression all that springs from, and answers to, these disfigurements of the purely human and feeling-bidden; and to remove it in such a way that this purely human core shall alone remain.

But the very thing which marred the purely human content of a verbal utterance is the same which so stretched out the phrase that its speaking accent had to be most sparingly distributed, while a disproportionate number of the words must necessarily be left unemphasized. So that the poet, who wanted to assign a prosodic weight to these unemphasizable words, gave himself up to a complete illusion; as to which a conscientious scanning of his verse, out loud, must have in so far enlightened him as he saw the phrase's sense disfigured and made unintelligible by such a method of delivery. Certainly,

the beauty of a verse has hitherto consisted in the poet's having cut away from his phrase, as much as possible, whatever
auxiliary words too cumbrously hedged in its main accent: he
has sought for the simplest expressions, needing the fewest go-
betweens, in order to bring his accents closer together; and for
this purpose he has also freed his subject matter, as much as
he could, from a burdensome surrounding of historicosocial
and state-religious relations and conditionings. But the poet
has never heretofore been able to bring this to such a point
that he could impart his subject unconditionally to the feeling
and nothing else—any more than he has brought his vehicle
of expression to a like enhancement; for this enhancement to
the highest pitch of emotional utterance could only have been
reached precisely in an ascension of the verse into the melody
—an ascension which, as we have seen because we *must* see,
has not as yet been rendered feasible. Where the poet, however, has believed that he had condensed the speaking verse
itself into a pure moment of feeling, without this ascension of
his verse into actual melody, *there* neither he nor the object of
his portrayal has been comprehended either any longer by the
understanding or by the feeling. We all know verses of this
sort, the attempts of our greatest poets to tune words, without
music, into tones.

Only that poetic aim whose nature we have already explained above, and in its necessary thrust toward realization,
can succeed in so freeing the prose phrase of modern speech
from all its mechanical apparatus of qualifying words that the
genuine accents may be drawn together into a swiftly seizable
message. A faithful observance of the mode of expression we
employ when our feeling is highly wrought, even in ordinary
life, will supply the poet with an unfailing measure for the
number of accents in a natural phrase. In frank emotion,
when we let go all conventional consideration for the spun-out
modern phrase, we try to express ourselves briefly and to the
point, and if possible, *in one breath*. But in this succinct expression we emphasize far more strongly than usual—through
the force of feeling—and also shift our accents closer together; while, to make these accents *im*press the hearer's feeling as forcibly as we want to *ex*press in them our own feelings,
we dwell on them with sharply lifted voice. These accents
round themselves instinctively into a phrase, or a main section
of a phrase, during the outflow of the breath, and their number will always stand in direct ratio to the excitement; so that,
for instance, an ireful, an *active* emotion will allow a greater

number of accents to be emitted in one breath, whereas a deep, a *suffering* one will consume the wholè breath force in fewer, more long-drawn tones.

The accents being governed by the breath, and shaping themselves to either a whole phrase or a substantial section of a phrase according to the subject of expression, the poet will therefore regulate their number by the particular emotion to which he gives his immediate sympathy; and he will see to it that his coil of words is rid of that excess of auxiliary and explanatory lesser words peculiar to the complicated phrase of literature: at least so far that their numerical bulk—despite the slurring of their intonation—shall not consume the breath in vain. The harm of our complex modern phrase, as regards the expression of feeling, has consisted in its being overstocked with unemphatic side words, which have taken up the speaker's breath to such an extent that, already exhausted, or for sake of "saving" himself, he could dwell only briefly on the main accent; and thus an understanding of the hastily accented main word could be imparted only to the understanding, but not to the feeling: since it needs the *fullness* of a sensuous expression to rouse the feeling's interest.

9. Rhythm determined not by artificial metrics but by the natural liftings and lowerings of the speaking accent

WE thus arrive at the natural basis of rhythm, in the spoken verse, as displayed in the *liftings and lowerings* of the accent; while this accent's utmost definiteness and endless variety can only come to light through its intensifying into musical rhythm.

Whatever number of liftings of the voice we may decide on for one breath, and thus for one phrase or segment of a phrase, in keeping with the mood to be expressed, yet they will never be of equal strength among themselves. In the first place a *completely equal strength* of accents is not permitted by the sense of a clause, which always contains both *con-*

ditioning and *conditioned* "moments," and, according to its character, either lifts the cónditioner above the condition*ee*, or the other way about. But neither does the feeling permit an equal strength of accents; since the feeling, of all others, can be roused to interest only by an easily grasped and physically marked *distinction* between the moments of expression. Though we shall have to learn that this interest is finally to be determined the most surely through a modulation of the musical tone, for the present we shall neglect that means of enhancement, and merely bring home to ourselves the influence which an unequal strength of accents must necessarily exert upon the rhythm of the phrase.

Now that we have drawn the accents together and freed them from their surrounding load of side words, and mean to show their differentiation into weaker and stronger ones, we can do it only in a way that shall completely answer to the *good and bad halves of the musical bar*, or—which is the same thing at bottom—to the "good and bad" bars of a musical period. But these good and bad bars, or half-bars, make themselves known to the feeling, as such, only through their standing in a mutual relation whose path, again, is paved and lighted by the smaller, intermediate fractions of the bar. Were the good and bad half-bars to stand entirely naked side by side—as in the chorales of the Church—they could make themselves known to feeling only as the merest ridge and hollow of the accent, whereby the "bad" bar-halves of a period must entirely lose their own accent, and in fact would cease to count at all as such: only by the intervening fractions of the bar acquiring rhythmic life, and being brought to a share in the accent of the bar-halves, can the weaker accent of the "bad" half-bars be also made to tell.

Now, the accented word phrase governs of itself the characteristic relation of those bar-fractions to the bar-halves, and that through the *hollows* of the accent and the ratio of these "hollows" to the "ridges." In ordinary pronunciation the unemphatic words and syllables, which we place on the slope of the wave, mount upward to the main accent through a swelling of the emphasis, and fall away again through a slacking of the emphasis. The point to which they fall, and from which they mount to a fresh main accent, is the weaker, minor accent, which—in keeping with both the sense and the expression of the phrase—is governed by the main accent as much as is the planet by the fixed star. The number of preparatory or aftersyllables depends solely on the sense of the poetic diction; of which, however, we presuppose that it shall express itself in utmost succinctness. But the more necessary it may seem to the poet, to increase the number of his preparatory or aftersyllables, so much the more characteristically is he thus enabled to liven the rhythm and give the accent itself a special importance—just as, on the other hand, he may specialize the character of an accent by placing it close beside the following one, *without* any preparation or afterthought.

His power here is boundless in variety: but he cannot become fully conscious of it until he intensifies the rhythm of the speaking accent into the rhythm of music, in its endless livening by dance's varied motion. The purely musical beat affords the poet possibilities of speech expression which he was forced to forego, from the outset, for his merely spoken word verse. In merely spoken verse the poet had to restrict the number of syllables in a "hollow" to two at the utmost, since with three he could not have avoided an emphasis being placed on one of them, which naturally would have thrown his verse awry at once. This false accentuation he would never have had to fear, if genuine prosodic longs and shorts had stood at his behest; but since he could allot his emphasis only to the speaking accent, and since its incidence must be assumed as possible on every root syllable, for sake of the verse —it passed his wit to find a means of indicating the proper accent so unmistakably that it should not be given to root syllables on which he wished *no* emphasis to be placed.

We are here speaking, of course, of verses communicated by means of writing, and read as written: the living verse, un-belonging to literature, we have in nowise to understand as without its rhythmic-musical melody; and if we take a good look at the monuments of Grecian lyric which have come down to us, we shall find that a merely recited Greek verse presents us with the embarrassment—whenever we deliver it in accordance with the instinctive accentuation of speech—of placing the accent on syllables which were left unemphasized in the original rhythmic melody, *as being included in the upstroke.* In merely spoken verse we can never employ more than two syllables in the "hollow," because more than two syllables would at once displace the correct accent, and the resulting dissolution of the verse would force us into the necessity of speaking it out as nothing but a washy prose.

The truth is, that in spoken, or to-be-spoken, verse we lack the "moment" that might fix the duration of the crest of the wave in such a way that by it we could accurately measure out the hollows. According to our sheer pronouncing powers, we cannot stretch the duration of an accented syllable beyond the length of two unaccented syllables, without falling into the fault of drawling, or—as in fact we call it—"singsong." In ordinary speech this "singsong," where it does not really become an actual singing and thus completely do away with ordinary speech, is rightly held for a fault; for, as a mere toneless drawling of the vowel, or even of a consonant, it is rightdown ugly. Yet at the bottom of this tend to drawling—where it is not a sheer habit of dialect, but shows itself involuntarily, in an access of emotion—there lies a something which our prosodists and metricists would have done well to regard, when they set themselves the task of explaining Grecian meters. They had nothing in ear but our hurried speaking accent, cut loose from the melody of feeling, when they invented the measure by which two "shorts" must always go to one "long"; the explanation of Greek meters, in which six or more "shorts" are matched at times by two or even a single "long," must have readily occurred to them if they had had in ear for that so-called "long" the *long-held note of a musical bar,* such as those lyrists still had at least in *their* ear when they varied the setting of words to known folk melodies. This sustained and rhythmically measured tone, however, is a thing the poet of our speaking verse had no longer in his ear, whereas he now knew only the brief-lived accent of speech. But if we hold fast by this tone, whose duration we not only can accurately determine in the musical bar but also divide into its rhythmic fractions in the most varied manner, then we shall obtain in those fractions the rhythmically vindicated, the meaningly distributed, melodic moments of expression for the syllables of the "hollow"; while their number will have solely to be regulated by the sense of the phrase and the intended effect of the expression, since we have found in the musical beat the certain measure in accordance with which they cannot fail of coming to an understanding.

This beat, however, the poet has to regulate solely by the expression he intends; he himself must make it into a knowable measure, and not have it haply thrust on him as such. This he does by distributing the accents, whether stronger or weaker, in such sort that they shall form a phrase- or breathing-segment to which a following one may correspond, and that this following one may appear necessarily conditioned by the first; for only in a necessary, an enforcing, or assuaging repetition can a weighty moment of expression display itself intelligibly to feeling. The arrangement of the stronger and weaker accents is therefore what sets the measure for the particular kind of beat, and for the rhythmic structure of the "period." Let us now gain an idea of such a measure-setting arrangement, as issuing from the poet's aim.

We shall take the case of an expression which is of such a character as to allow the emphasizing of three accents in one breath, whereof the first is the strongest, the second the weakest (as is almost always to be assumed in such a case), and the third again a lifted one: here the poet would instinctively arrange a phrase of two even bars, whereof the first would have the strongest accent on its "good" half, and on its "bad" half the weaker one, while the second bar would have the third, the other lifted accent on its downbeat. The "bad" half of the second bar would serve for taking breath, and for the upstroke toward the first bar of the second rhythmic phrase, which must suitably reiterate its predecessor. In this phrase the "hollows" would mount as an upstroke for the downbeat of the first bar, and fall away as a downstroke to its "bad half"; from which, again, they would mount to the "good half" of the second bar. Any strengthening of the *second* accent, as called for by the sense of the phrase, would be easily effected rhythmically (apart from a melodic rise of pitch) by allowing either the depression between it and the first accent, or the upstroke toward the third, to drop out completely—which must necessarily draw increased attention to just this intermediate accent.

10. Alliteration unifies expression; Stabreim defined and illustrated.

UNTIL we are able, so to say, to "feel back" our sensations—made utterly unintelligible to ourselves by state politics or religious dogmas—and thus to reach their original truth, we shall never be in a position to grasp the sensuous substance of our *roots of speech.*

The *sense* of a root is "objective" sensation embodied therein; but first by its *embodiment* does a sensation become *understandable,* and this body itself is alike a *sensuous* one, and one that can be determinately apprehended by nothing but the answering sense of hearing. The poet's utterance will therefore be a swiftly understandable one, if he concentrates the to-be-expressed sensation to its inmost essence; and this inmost essence will necessarily be a *unitarian* one, in the kinship of its conditioning and its conditioned moments. But a unitarian sensation instinctively utters itself in a uniform mode of expression; and this uniform expression wins its fullest enablement from that *oneness* of the speech root which reveals itself in a kinship of the conditioning and conditioned chief moments of the phrase.

In Stabreim the kindred speech roots are fitted to one another in such a way that, just as they sound alike to the physical ear, they also knit like objects into one collective image in which the feeling may utter its conclusions about them. Their sensuously cognizable resemblance they win either from a kinship of the vowel sounds, especially when these stand open in front, without any initial consonant;* or from the sameness of this initial consonant itself, which characterizes the likeness as one belonging peculiarly to the object;† or again, from the sameness of the terminal consonant that closes up the root behind (as an assonance), provided the individualizing force of the word lies in that terminal.‡

11. Poetic value of Stabreim

A SENSATION [or "emotion"] such as can vindicate its own expression through the Stabreim of root words which call instinctively for emphasis is comprehensible to us beyond all doubt—provided the kinship of the roots is not deliberately disfigured and made unknowable through the sense of the phrase, as in our modern speech; and only when this sensation, so expressed, has brought our feeling instinctively to grasp it as *one thing,* does that feeling warrant any mixing of it with another. In the Stabreim, again, poetic speech has an

* "Erb' und eigen." "Immer und ewig."
† "Ross und Reiter." "Froh und frei."
‡ "Hand und Mund." "Recht und Pflicht."

infinitely potent means of making a *mixed* sensation swiftly understandable by the already biased feeling; and this means we may likewise call a *sensuous* one—in the significance that it, too, is grounded on a comprehensive, and withal a definite *sense* in the speech root. In the first place, the purely sensuous aspect of the Stabreim is able to unite the physical expression of one sensation with that of another, in such a way that the union shall be keenly perceptible to the ear, and caress it by its naturalness. But further—through this innate power of the similar "clang"—the *sense* of the Stabreim-ed root word which introduces the fresh sensation already dawns upon the ear as one *essentially akin,* that is, as an antithesis included in the genus of the main sensation; and now, in all its general affinity with the first-expressed sensation, it is transmitted through the captivated hearing to the feeling, and onward through this, at last, to the understanding itself.*

12. Use of rhyme; passing over of word speech into tone speech

To impart a feeling with utmost plainness, the poet has already ranged his row of words into a musical bar, according to their spoken accents, and has sought by the consonantal Stabreim to bring them to the feeling's understanding in an easier and more sensuous form; he will still more completely facilitate this understanding, if he takes the vowels of the accented root words, as earlier their consonants, and knits them also into such a rhyme as will most definitely open up their understanding to the feeling. An understanding of the vowel, however, is not based upon its superficial analogy with a rhyming vowel of another root; but, since *all the vowels are primally akin to one another,* it is based on the *disclosing of this ur-kinship* through giving full value to the vowel's *emotional content, by means of musical tone.* The vowel itself is nothing but *a tone condensed:* its specific manifestation is determined through its turning toward the outer surface of the

* "Die Liebe bringt Lust und—Leid," [Love brings delight and —Load].—R. WAGNER.

feeling's "body"; which latter—as we have said—displays to the "eye" of hearing the mirrored image of the outward object that has acted on it. The object's effect on the body of feeling itself is manifested by the vowel through a direct utterance of feeling along the nearest path, thus expanding the individuality it has acquired from without into the universality of pure emotion; and this takes place in the musical tone. To that which bore the vowel, and bade it outwardly condense itself into the consonant—to that the vowel returns as a specific entity, enriched by the world outside, in order to dissolve itself in *it,* now equally enriched. This enriched, this individually established tone expanded to the universality of feeling is the redeeming "moment" of the poet's thought; and thought, in this redemption, becomes an immediate *outpour of the feeling.*

By the poet's resolving the vowel of his accentuated and Stabreim-ed root word into its mother element, the musical tone, he now enters definitely upon the realm of tone speech. From this instant he has to attempt no further regulation of his accents according to a measure of kinship which shall be cognizable by that "eye" of hearing; but now that the vowels have become musical tones, their kinship, as needful for their swift adoption by the feeling, is regulated by a measure which is cognizable solely to the "ear" of hearing, and surely and imperiously grounded on that "ear's" receptive idiosyncrasy.

Already in word speech the prime affinity of all vowels is shown so definitely that when root syllables lack an initial consonant we recognize their aptitude for Stabreim by the very fact of the vowel's standing open in front, and we are by no means governed by a strict outward likeness of the vowel; we rhyme, for instance, "eye and ear" (*Aug' und Ohr*).* This Ur-kinship, which has preserved itself in word speech as an unconscious moment of feeling, brings the full [power of] tone speech quite unmistakably to feeling's consciousness. Inasmuch as it widens the specific vowel into a musical tone, it tells our feeling that this vowel's particularity

* How admirably our language characterizes in this rhyme the two most open-lying organs of reception, through the vowels likewise lying open toward without; it is as though these organs herein proclaimed themselves as turned, with the whole fill of their universal receptive force, directly and nakedly from within outward. —R. WAGNER.

is included in an ur-akin relationship, and born from out this kinship; and it bids us acknowledge as the mother of the ample vowel family the purely human feeling, in its immediate facing outward—the feeling, which only faces outward so as to address itself, in turn, to our own purely human feeling.

13. Different functions of the word poet and tone poet

THE characteristic distinction between the word poet and the tone poet consists in this: the word poet has concentrated an infinitude of scattered moments of action, sensation, and expression—only cognizable by the understanding—to a point the most accessible to the feeling; now comes the tone poet, and has to expand this concentrated, compact point to the utmost fullness of its emotional content. In its thrust toward an impartal to the feeling, the procedure of the poetizing understanding was directed to assembling itself from farthest distances into the closest cognizability by the sensory faculty; from here, from the point of immediate contact with the sensory faculty, the poem has now to broaden itself out, exactly as the recipient sensory organ—likewise concentrated upon an outward-facing point, for sake of taking in the poem —now broadens itself to wider and yet wider circles, under the immediate influence of the acquisition, until it rouses at last the whole inner emotional faculty.

14. Melody and feeling

To the word poet the disclosure of a kinship of his lifted accents—such as should be obvious to the feeling, and through this at last to the understanding itself—was only possible through the consonantal Stabreim of the root words. What determined this kinship, however, was merely the particularity of their common consonant; no other consonant could rhyme with it, and therefore the kinship was restricted to one specific family, which was cognizable to the feeling precisely and only through its making itself known as a completely shut-off family. The tone poet, on the contrary, has at his disposal a clan whose kindred reaches to infinity; and whereas the word poet had to content himself with presenting to the feeling merely the specially accented root words of his phrase, as allied in sense and sound through the complete alikeness of their initial consonants, the musician, on the other hand, has before all to display the kinship of his tones in such an extension that, starting with the accents, he pours it over *all* —even the least emphasized—vowels of the phrase; so that not alone the vowels of the accents, but all the vowels in general display themselves to the feeling as akin to one another.

Just as the accents in the phrase did not first of all acquire their special light through its sense alone, but through their being thrown into physical relief by the unemphasized words and syllables that lay in the "hollow," so have the chief tones to win their special light from the lesser tones, which must bear precisely the same relation to them as the up- and down-strokes bear to the "ridges." The choice and significance of those minor words and syllables, as well as their bearing on the accentuated words, were governed in the first place by the intellectual content of the phrase; only in degree as this intellectual content, through a condensation of its bulk, was intensified into a compact utterance conspicuous to the sense of hearing did it transform itself into an emotional content. Now, the choice and significance of the lesser tones, as also their bearing on the chief tones, are in so far independent of the intellectual content of the phrase as the latter has already condensed itself to an emotional content, in the rhythmic verse and by the Stabreim; while the full realization of this emotional content, through its most direct communication to the senses, is further to be accomplished solely in that quarter where the pure language of feeling has already been recognized as the only efficacious one, in that the vowel has been resolved into the singing tone. From the instant of the musical intonation of the vowel in word speech, the feeling has become the appointed orderer of all further announcements to the senses, and henceforward musical feeling alone prescribes the choice and significance both of lesser tones and chief tones; and that, according to the nature of the tone clan whose particular member has been chosen to give the necessary emotional expression to the phrase.

This kinship of the tones, however, is musical *harmony;* and we here have first to take it according to its superficial extension, in which the unit families of the broad-branched clan of *tone varieties* display themselves [in open rank]. If we keep in eye at present its aforesaid *horizontal* extension, we expressly reserve the all-determining attribute of harmony, in its *vertical* extension toward its primal base, for the decisive moment of our exposition. But that horizontal extension, being the surface of harmony, is its physiognomy as still discernible by the poet's eye: it is the water mirror which still reflects upon the poet his own image, while at the same time it presents this image to the view of him whom the poet wanted to address. This image, however, is in truth the poet's realized aim—a realization which can only fall to the lot of the musician, in his turn, when he mounts from the depths, to the surface of the sea of harmony; and on that surface will be celebrated the glorious marriage of poetry's begetting thought with music's endless power of birth.

That wave-borne mirror image is *melody.* In it the poet's thought becomes an instinctively enthralling moment of feeling; just as music's emotional power therein acquires the faculty of definite and convincing utterance, of manifesting itself as a sharp-cut human shape, a plastic individuality. Melody is the redemption of the poet's endlessly conditioned thought into a deep-felt consciousness of emotion's highest freedom: it is the willed and achieved unwillful, the conscious and proclaimed unconscious, the vindicated necessity of an endless-reaching content, condensed from its farthest branchings into an utmost definite utterance of feeling.

15. *Tonality and expression; setting* Stabreim

THE bond of kinship of those tones whose rhythmic-moving chain, with its links of "ridge and hollow," makes out the verse melody, is first of all made plain to feeling *in the key;* for it is this which prescribes the particular tone ladder [or *scale*] in which the tones of that melodic chain are contained as separate rungs. Hitherto, in the necessary endeavor to impart his poem to the feeling, we have seen the poet engaged in drawing together the organic units of his diction—assembled from circles wide apart—and removing from them all that was heterogeneous, so as to lead them before the feeling, especially through the [Stab-]rhyme, in the utmost displayable kinship. At bottom of this thrust of his there lay an instinctive knowledge of feeling's nature, which takes in alone the homogeneous, alone the thing that in its oneness includes alike the conditioned and the conditioner; of feeling, which seizes the imparted feeling according to its generic essence, so that it refuses to heed the opposite contained therein, qua opposites, but is guided by the nature of the *genus* in which those opposites are reconciled. The understanding loosens, the feeling binds; that is, the understanding loosens the genus into the antitheses which lie within it, whereas the feeling binds them up again into one harmonious whole. This unitarian expression the poet most completely won, at last, in the ascension of his word verse into the melody of song; and the latter wins its unitarian expression, its unfailing operation on the feeling, through instinctively displaying to the senses the inner kinship of its tones.

16. Modulation and action

FOR the sentient ear, as we have seen, the Stabreim already coupled speech roots of the opposite emotional expression (as *Lust und Leid, Wohl und Weh*), and thus presented them to the feeling as generically akin. Now, in a far higher measure can musical modulation make such a union perceptible to the feeling. If we take, for instance, a Stabreim-ed verse of completely like emotional content, such as: *Liebe giebt Lust zum Leben,** then, as a like emotion is physically disclosed in the accents' Stabreim-ed roots, the musician would here receive no natural incitement to step outside the once selected key, but would completely satisfy the feeling by

* "Love gives delight to living."

keeping the various inflections of the musical tone to that one key alone. On the contrary, if we take a verse of mixed emotion, such as: *die Liebe bringt Lust und Leid,* then here, where the Stabreim combines two opposite emotions, the musician would feel incited to pass across from the key first struck in keeping with the first emotion, to another key in keeping with the second emotion, and determined by the latter's relation to the emotional rendered in the earlier key. The word *Lust* (delight)—which, as the climax of the first emotion, appears to thrust onward to the second—would have in this phrase to obtain an emphasis quite other than in that: *die Liebe giebt Lust zum Leben;* the note sung to it would instinctively become the determinant leading tone, and necessarily thrust onward to the other key, in which the word *Leid* (sorrow) should be delivered. In this attitude toward one another, *Lust und Leid* would become the manifestment of a specific emotion, whose idiosyncrasy would lie precisely in the point where two opposite emotions displayed themselves as conditioning one the other, and thus as necessarily belonging together, as actually akin; and this manifestment is possible alone to music, in her faculty of harmonic modulation, because in virtue thereof she exerts a binding sway upon the "sensuous" feeling such as no other art has force for.

Let us next see how musical modulation, hand in hand with the verse's content, is able to lead back again to the first emotion. Let us follow up the verse *die Liebe bringt Lust und Leid* with a second: *doch in ihr Weh auch webt sie Wonnen**—then *webt,* again, would become a tone leading into the first key, as from *here* the second emotion returns to the first, but now enriched, emotion. To the feeling's sensory organ the poet, in virtue of his Stabreim, could only display this return as an advance from the feeling of *Weh* to that of *Wonnen,* but not as a rounding off of the generic feeling *Liebe;* whereas the musician becomes completely understandable by the very fact that he quite markedly goes back to the first tone variety, and therefore definitely denotes the genus of the two emotions as one and the same—a thing impossible to the poet, who was obliged to change the root initial for the Stabreim. Only, by the *sense* of both verses the poet indicated the generic bond uniting the emotions; he thus desired its realization to the feeling, and determined the realizing process of the musician.

---

* "But with her woe she weaves things winsome."—Tr.

For his procedure, which, if unconditioned, would seem arbitrary and unintelligible, the musician thus obtains his vindication from the poet's aim—from an aim which the latter could only suggest, or at utmost, merely approximately realize for fractions of his message (precisely in the Stabreim), but whose full realization is possible precisely to the musician; and that, through his power of employing the ur-kinship of the tones harmoniously to display to feeling the primal unity of the emotions.

We may easiest gain a notion of how immeasurably great this power is if we imagine the sense of the above-cited pair of verses as still more definitely laid down: in such sort that, between the advance from the one emotion and the return thereto in the second verse, a longer sequence of verses shall express the most manifold gradation and blend of inter-mediate emotions—in part corroborating, in part reconciling —until the final return of the chief emotion. Here, to realize the poetic aim, the musical modulation would have to be led across to, and back from, the most diverse keys; but all the adventitious keys would appear in an exact affinitive relation to the primary key, which itself will govern the particular light they throw upon the expression, and, in a manner, will lend them first their very capability of giving that light. The chief key, as the ground tone of the emotion first struck, would reveal its own ur-kinship with all the other keys, and thus, in virtue of the intensified expression, would display the dominant emotion in such a height and breadth, that only emotions *kindred to it* could dominate our feeling, so long as its utterance lasted; that this one emotion, in virtue of its intensity and its extension, would usurp our whole emotional faculty; and thus this unique emotion would be raised to an all-embracing one, an omnihuman, an unfailingly intelligible.

The Art of Transmutation. Letter to Mathilde Wesendonck, October 29, 1858

OF one attribute that I have acquired in my art I am now becoming more and more distinctly conscious, since it influences me in life as well. It is inborn in my nature to swing from one extreme of temper to another; the uttermost rebounds, moreover, can hardly help but touch; in fact, life's safeguard often lies therein. At bottom, too, true art has no subject other than the display of these extremes of mood in their ultimate relations to each other: that which alone is

worth aiming at here, the weighty crisis, can really be won
from nothing but these uttermost antithesises. For art, however, from a material use of these extremes there may easily
arise a vicious mannerism, which may degenerate into snatching at outward effect. In this snare have I seen caught, in
particular, the modern French school, with Victor Hugo at
its head. . . . Now, I recognize that the peculiar tissue of my
music (naturally in exactest agreement with the poetic
structure)—what my friends now consider so new and significant—owes its texture in especial to that intensely delicate
feeling which prompts me to mediate and knit together all the
nodes of transition between extremes of mood. My subtlest
and deepest art I now might call the art of Transmutation; the
whole consists of such transitions: I have taken a dislike to
the abrupt and harsh; often it is unavoidable and needful,
but even then it should not enter without the mood being so
definitely prepared for a sudden change, as of itself to summon
it. My greatest masterpiece in this art of subtlest and most
gradual transition is assuredly the big scene in the second act
of *Tristan and Isolde*. The commencement of this scene offers
the most overbrimming life in its most passionate emotions—
its close the devoutest, most consecrate desire of death. Those
are the piers: now see, child, how I've spanned them, how it
all leads over from the one abutment to the other! And that's
the whole secret of my musical form, as to which I make
bold to assert that it has never been so much as dreamed before in such clear and extended coherence and such en-
compassing of every detail.

17.   Harmony imparts feeling tone to melody.

UP to the present, we have shown the condition for a melodic
advance from one tone variety to another as lying in the
poetic aim, in so far as the latter itself had already revealed
its emotional content; and by this showing we have proved
that the instigating ground for melodic motion, to be justified even in the eyes of feeling, can be supplied by nothing
but that aim. Yet what *enables* this advance, so necessary
to the Poet, naturally does not lie in the domain of word

speech, but quite definitely in that of music alone. This own-est element of music, *harmony* to wit, is merely in *so* far still governed by the poetic aim, as it is the other, the womanly element into which this aim pours itself for its own realization, for its redemption. For this is the *bearing* element, which takes up the poetic aim solely as a begetting seed, to shape it into finished semblance by the prescripts of its own, its womanly organism. This organism is a specific, an individual one, and no begetter, but a bearer: it has received from the poet the fertilizing seed, but the fruit it forms and ripens by its own individual powers.

That melody which we have seen appearing on the surface of harmony, is conditioned as to its distinctive, its purely musical expression by harmony's upward-working depths alone: as it manifests itself as a horizontal chain, so is it connected by a plumbline with those depths. This plumbline is the harmonic chord, a vertical chain of tones in closest kinship, mounting from the ground tone to the surface. The chiming of this chord first gives to the melodic note the peculiar significance wherein it, and it alone, has been employed to mark a distinctive moment of the expression. Now, just as the ground tone, with the chord determined by it, first gives to the melody's unit note a particular expression—seeing that the selfsame tone upon another of its kindred ground tones acquires a quite other significance—so each melodic progress from one key to another is likewise governed by the changing ground tone, which of itself prescribes the harmony's leading tone, as such. The presence of that ground tone, and of the harmonic chord thereby determined, is indispensable in the eyes of feeling, if this latter is to seize the melody in all its characteristic expression. But the presence of the ground harmony means its *concurrent sounding out*. The sounding out of the harmony to a melody is the first thing that fully persuades the feeling as to the emotional content of that melody, which otherwise would leave to it something undetermined. But only amid the fullest determination of every "moment" of expression is the feeling itself determined to a swift, direct, and instinctive interest; and a full determination of the expression, again, can only mean *the completest impartal to the senses of all its necessary moments.*

18. *Poet and musician unite in the orchestra.*

THE harmony, however, only the musician can invent, and not the poet. Wherefore the melody which we have seen the poet inventing from out of the word verse was more a *discovered* one—as being conditioned by harmony—than one *invented* by him. The conditions for this musical melody must first have been to hand, before the poet could find it as already validly conditioned. Before the poet could find this melody, to his redemption, the musician had already conditioned it by his own-est powers: he now brings it to the poet as a melody warranted by its harmony; *and only melody such as has been made possible by the very essence of our modern music is the melody that can redeem the poet—that can alike arouse and satisfy his stress.*

Poet and musician herein are like two travelers who have started from one departure point, from thence to journey straight ahead in the opposite directions. Arrived at the opposite point of the earth, they meet again; each has wandered round one half the planet. They fall a-questioning one another, and each tells each what he has seen and found. The poet describes the plains, the mountains, valleys, fields, the men and beasts which he has met upon his distant journey through the mainland. The musician has voyaged across the seas, and recounts the wonders of the ocean: on its breast he has often been nigh to sinking, and its deeps and strange-shaped monsters have filled him half with terror, half with joy.

Roused by each other's stories, and irresistibly impelled to learn for themselves the other which each has not yet seen —so as to make into an actual experience impressions merely taken up in fancy—they part again, each to complete his journey round the earth. At their first starting point they meet at last once more; the poet now has battled through the seas, the musician has stridden through the continents. Now they part no more, for both now *know* the earth: what they earlier had imagined in their boding dreams, as fashioned thus and thus, has now been witnessed by them in its actuality. They are one; for each knows and feels what the other feels and knows. The poet has become musician, the musician poet: now they are both an entire artistic man.

At the point where their roads first met, after wandering round the first half of the earth, the mutual discourse of the poet and musician was *that melody* which we now have in eye—the melody whose utterance the poet had shaped from out his inmost longing, but whose manifestation the musician conditioned from amid his own experiences. When they pressed their hands in fresh farewell, each had in mind what he himself had not as yet experienced, and to gain this crowning experience they quitted each other anew.

Let us take the Poet first, in his mastering the experiences of the musician. These he now reaps for himself, albeit guided by the counsel of the musician, who had already sailed the open seas upon his sturdy ship, had found the course to firm-set land, and now has accurately mapped out for him the chart. On this new voyage we shall see the poet become the selfsame man as the musician upon his own new journey across the other earth-half, as traced out for him by the poet; so that we now may look on both these journeyings as one and the same thing.

When the poet now commits himself to the vast expanse of harmony, as it were to prove the truth of that [other] melody the musician had "told of," he no longer finds the wayless tone wastes which the musician had first encountered on his earlier voyage; to his delight he meets with the wondrous bold, the passing new, the infinitely delicate, yet giant-bolted framework of the ship that first sea wanderer had built; the poet mounts on board it, safely to make the passage of the waves. The musician had taught him the handling of the helm, the trimming of the sails, and all the cunningly devised expedients for breasting storms and tempests. Sailing the wide seas at the helm of this glorious ship, the poet, who before had toiled to measure hill and valley step by step, now rejoices at his consciousness of man's all-conquering might; let the billows rear them never so proudly, from *its* high deck they seem to him the willing, faithful bearers of his lofty fortune, that fortune of the poetic aim. This ship is the strong, enabling implement of his widest and his mightiest will; with fervent love his thanks go forth to the musician, who invented it in direst stress of weather, and now has made it over to his hands: for this trusty ship is the conqueror of the endless floods of harmony—*the orchestra.*

19. Orchestra's power of speech; analogy with gesture

THE orchestra indisputably possesses a *faculty of speech*, and the creations of modern instrumental music have disclosed it to us. In the symphonies of Beethoven we have seen this faculty develop to a height whence it felt thrust on to speak out that which, by its very nature, it can not speak out. Now that in the word-verse melody we have brought it that which it could not speak out, and have assigned to it, as carrier of this kindred melody, the office in which—completely eased in mind—it is to speak out nothing but what its nature fits it alone to speak: now, we have plainly to denote this speaking faculty of the orchestra as the faculty of uttering the unspeakable.

This definition, however, is not to convey the idea of a merely imaginary thing, but of a thing quite real and palpable.

The orchestra is no mere compost of washy tone ingredients, but consists of a rich association of instruments—with unbounded power of adding to its numbers; whilst each of these is a definite individuality, and invests the tone produced by it with an equally individual garment. A tone mass without some such individual distinction between its members is nowhere to be found, and can at best be thought, but never realized. But what determines the individuality, in the present case, is—as we have seen—the particular idiosyncrasy of the unit instrument, whose consonant-like timbre converts into a thing apart, as it were, the vowel of the tone produced. Whereas, however, this consonantal timbre can never lift itself to the suggestiveness of the word-speech-consonant's appeal to feeling's understanding, nor is it capable of that consonant's change and consequent play of influence upon the vowel, so neither can the tone speech of an instrument ever condense itself to an expression such as that attainable solely by the organ of the understanding, namely, word speech; yet, as pure organ of the feeling, it speaks out the very thing which word speech in itself can not speak out—without further ado, then: that which, looked at from the standpoint of our human intellect, is *the unspeakable*. That this unspeak-

217

able is not a thing unutterable per se, but merely unutterable through the organ of our understanding; thus, not a mere fancy, but a reality—this is shown plainly enough by the instruments of the orchestra themselves, whereof each for itself, and infinitely more richly in its changeful union with other instruments, speaks out quite clearly and intelligibly.*

Let us first take into view that unspeakable which the orchestra can express with greatest definition, and indeed, in union with another thing unspeakable—*with gesture.*

The bodily gesture, as determined by an inner emotion which proclaims itself in the significant movements of certain members most capable of expression, and finally in the features of the face—this bodily gesture is in so far a thing unutterable, as speech can only hint at or describe it, whereas those members of those features were the only channels for its actual utterance. Something that word speech can fully impart, that is, an object communicable *by* the understanding *to* the understanding, has no need at all of accompaniment or rein- forcement by gesture; nay, unneedful gestures could only mar the message. With such a message, however, as we have seen above, neither is the sensory organ of the recipient hearing roused, but merely serves as an uninterested go-between. But a message which word speech cannot fully and convincingly convey to feeling—which here has also to be roused—thus an expression which borders on passion, imperatively needs strengthening through a concomitant gesture. We thus see that where the hearing is to be roused to greater "sensuous" interest, the messenger involuntarily has to address the eye as well: eye and ear must mutually assure each other of a higher-pitched message, before they can transmit it convinc- ingly to the feeling.

Now, the gesture, in its needful message to the eye, delivered precisely That which word speech was incompetent to express—had the latter been able to do so, the gesture would have been superfluous and disturbing. The eye was thus aroused by the gesture in a way which still lacked its fitting counterpart, of a message to the ear; but this counter- part is needful, for rounding the expression into one com-

---

* This easy explanation of the "unspeakable" one might extend, perhaps not altogether wrongly, to the whole matter of religious philosophy; for although that matter is given out as absolutely unutterable, from the standpoint of the *speaker,* yet mayhap it is utterable enough if only the fitting organ be employed.—R. WAGNER.

pletely understandable by feeling. True that the word verse, roused into melody, at last dissolves the intellectual content of the original verbal message into an emotional content: but in this melody there is not as yet contained that "moment" of the message to the ear which shall completely answer to the gesture; for precisely in this [verse] melody, as the *most highly roused* expression of the words, lay the first *incitement* to intensify the gesture—namely, to supply the corroborative "moment" which the melody still needed, and needed just because it could not as yet bring anything of its own exactly to correspond thereto.

The verse melody, then, has contained only the antecedent condition for the gesture. That, however, which is to vindicate the gesture before the judgment seat of feeling, in the same way as the speaking verse was to be vindicated through the melody, or the melody to be vindicated—or better, *elucidated* —through the harmony—that lies beyond the power of *this* melody which arose from out the *speaking* verse, and which with one essential aspect of its body remains strictly conditioned by word speech; for it was word speech that could not deliver the particular tale of gesture, and therefore called the latter to its aid; and now, it positively cannot find a completely fitting vehicle for conveying it to the longing ear. But now there comes the language of the orchestra, completely sundered from this word speech; and that tale of gesture's, which was unutterable in word-tone speech, the orchestra is just as able to impart to the ear as the gesture itself imparts it to the eye.

This faculty the orchestra has won from its accompaniment of the most physical of all gestures, the *dance gesture,* to which such an accompaniment was a necessity dictated by its very essence, to make its message understandable; since the gestures of dance, like gesture in general, bear much the same relation to the orchestral melody as the word verse bears to the vocal melody thereby conditioned. So that gesture and orchestra melody, together, first form such a whole, a thing so intelligible in itself, as word-tone melody forms for *its* part. Their most physical point of contact, that is, the point where both—the one in space, the other in time: the one to the eye, the other to the ear—displayed themselves as altogether like and mutually conditioned—dance gesture and orchestra had this common point in *rhythm*; and after each departure from it, to this point they must perforce return in order to stay or to become intelligible, for it is *it* that lays bare their prime affinity. But from this point both gesture and orchestra expand, in equal measure, to their respective idiosyncrasies of speaking power. Just as gesture reveals to the eye a thing which gesture can utter, so the orchestra conveys to the ear a something exactly answering to that revelation, precisely in the same way as musical rhythm, at the starting point of their kinship, explained to the ear the thing revealed to the eye in the most palpable moments of the dance. The setting down of the uplifted foot was the same thing to the eye, as to the ear was the accentuated downbeat of the bar; and thus also the mobile instrumental tone figure, melodically uniting the downbeats of the bar, is altogether the same thing to the ear, as to the eye is the movement of the feet, or other expressive members of the body, in the intervals between their exchange.

Now, the further gesture departs from its definite, but at like time most straitened basis—that of the dance, the more sparingly gesture distributes its sharpest accents, in the most manifold and delicate expressional nuances to attain an endless apitude for speech: so much the more manifold and delicate become the tone figures of instrumental speech, which, convincingly to impart the unspeakable of gesture, now wins a melodic expression immeasurable in its wealth of idiom. Nor can either its content or its form be characterized in word speech, for very reason that they are already completely made known to the ear through the orchestral melody, and only further wait adoption by the eye; and that, as the content and form of the gesture answering to this melody.

That this idiomatic language of the orchestra is a long way from having evolved in opera to the fullness of which it is capable is to be explained by the fact—already mentioned in its proper place—that, with its utter lack of a genuine dramatic basis, the opera has always drawn its byplay directly from the pantomimic dance. These ballet mimetics had the very narrowest range of movement and gesture, and at last were stereotyped into settled make-believes, because they altogether lacked the necessary conditions that might have prescribed, and alike explained, a greater multiplicity. Such conditions are contained in word speech; and indeed, no word speech *dragged on* to help, but one that *summons* gesture to lend its help. As though instinctively aware of its potentiality, the orchestra sought in absolute instrumental music, set loose from pantomine, for that heightened power of speech which it thus could not gain in pantomine or opera; and we have seen that this effort, when put forth in its highest force and sincerity, must lead to the longing for a justification through the word, and through gesture prompted by the word. We now have only to learn, from the other side, how the complete realization of the poetic aim is in turn to be effected by nothing but the highest, the most lucid vindication of the word-verse melody through the perfected language of the orchestra, in its alliance with gesture.

In its will to realize itself in drama, the poetic aim stipulates for the highest and most manifold expression that gesture owns: yes, it demands from it a force, diversity, a finesse and mobility, such as nowhere but in drama can come to "necessary" show, and which are therefore to be *invented* of a quite specific character; for the dramatic action, with all its motives, is an action lifted high above life, and intensified to the point of wonder. The compact moments and motives of action were to be made intelligible to feeling only by means of an equally concise expression, which was to rise from the word verse to a melody immediately determining the feeling. Now, just as this utterance intensifies itself to melody, so it necessarily requires an intensifying of the gestures which it prompts, a lifting of them above the measure of those of ordinary talk. Moreover this gesture, in keeping with the character of drama, is no mere monologue of a solitary individual, but intensifies itself to utmost manifoldness —so to say, to a "many-voiced" gesture—through the characteristic reaction of the mutual encounter of *many* individuals. The dramatic aim not only draws within its sphere the inner emotion per se, but, for sake of its own realizing, it specifically demands that this emotion shall be proclaimed in the outer, bodily appearance of the performers. Pantomine contented itself with typical masks, for the stature, bearing, and dress of the performers: the all-enabled drama tears away these typical masks—since it possesses the warranty therefor, in its faculty of speech—and shows the performers as specific individualities, proclaiming themselves precisely thus and not otherwise. Wherefore the dramatic aim prescribes the stature, mien, bearing, motion, and dress of the performer, down to their tiniest detail, so that at every instant he may appear as this one, this swiftly and definitely knowable individuality, in full distinction from its fellows. This drastic distinction of the one individuality is to be achieved, however, *only* when all its fellows, when all the individualities in touch with it, display themselves with an equally sure and drastic definition.

20. *Foreboding and remembrance*

MUSIC cannot think: but she can materialize thoughts, that is, she can give forth their emotional-contents as no longer merely recollected, but made present. This she can do, however, only when her own manifestment is conditioned by a poetic aim, and when this latter, again, reveals itself as no mere thing of thought, but a thing expounded in the first place by the organ of the understanding, namely, word speech. A musical motive (*Motiv*)* can produce a definite impression on the feeling, inciting it to a function akin to thought, only when the emotion uttered in that motive has been definitely conditioned by a definite object, and proclaimed by a definite individual before our very eyes. The omission of these conditionings sets a musical motive before the feeling in a most indefinite light; and an indefinite thing may return in the same garment as often as one pleases, yet it will remain a mere recurrence of the indefinite, and we shall neither be in a position to justify it by any felt necessity of its appearance, nor, therefore, to associate it with anything else.

But a musical motive into which the thought-filled word verse of a dramatic performer has poured itself—so to say, before our eyes—is a thing conditioned by necessity: with its return a *definite* emotion is discernibly conveyed to us, and conveyed to us through the physical agency of the orchestra, albeit now unspoken by the performer; for the latter now feels driven to give voice to a fresh emotion, derived in turn from that earlier one. Wherefore the concurrent sounding of such

* In his critical writings and correspondence Wagner never employs the term *Leitmotiv*. But in a letter of 1867 to Heinrich Porges he uses the word *Hauptmotiv* (principal motive) to mean the same thing. The closing bars of Act II of *Tristan*, he informs Porges, are "formed melodically out of King Mark's *Hauptmotiv* (of good will); consequently they contain the *Motiv* of self-reproach, which appears to overcome Tristan."—EDS.

a motive unites for us the conditioning, the nonpresent emotion with the emotion conditioned thereby and coming at
this instant into voice; and inasmuch as we thus make our
feeling a living witness to the organic growth of one definite
emotion from out another, we give to it the faculty of thinking: nay, we here give it a faculty of higher rank than thinking, to wit, the instinctive *knowledge* of a thought made real
in emotion.

Before we proceed to a discussion of the results which follow from the orchestra's above-suggested faculty of speech,
for the shaping of the drama, we must determine another
of its salient capabilities, so as to take that faculty's full
compass. The capability to which we here refer, comes to the
orchestra from a union of those aptitudes which have accrued
to it from its alliance with gesture, on the one hand, and its
remembrance of the verse melody on the other. Just as
gesture, originating in the most physical of dance's postures,
has evolved to the most intellectual *mimik*; just as verse
melody, from a mere thinking of an emotion, has advanced
to the most "present" enouncement of an emotion: so the
speaking faculty of the orchestra—which has won from both
its shaping force, and fed and flourished on their utmost
ripening—so does it grow from out this double source to a
highest special capability, wherein we see the two divided
arms of the orchestral river, now richly tinged by tributary
brooks and streams, as though united again into one common
flow. To wit: where gesture lapses into rest, and the melodic
discourse of the actor hushes—thus where the drama prepares
its future course in inner moods as yet unuttered—there may
these still unspoken moods be spoken by the orchestra in such
a way that their utterance shall bear the character of a
foreboding necessitated by the poet's aim.

A foreboding is the herald of an emotion as yet unspoken
—because as yet unspeakable, in the sense of our customary
word speech. Unspeakable is any emotion which is not as yet
defined; and it is undefined so long as it has not been yet
determined through a fitting *object*. The first thrill of this
emotion, the foreboding, is thus its instinctive longing for
definement through an object; through an object which it
predetermines, in its turn, by the force of its own need; moreover, an object which must answer to it, and for which it
therefore waits. In its manifestment as a foreboding, I might
compare the emotional fund to a well-tuned harp, whose

strings are sounding to the touch of passing winds, and wait the player who shall grasp them into shapely chords.

Such a presentiment as this has the poet to wake within us, *in order, through its longing, to make us necessary sharers in the creation of his artwork.* By calling forth this longing, he provides himself with the conditioning force, in our aroused receptiveness which alone can make it possible for him to shape the creatures of his fancy in accordance with his settled aim. In the evocation of moods such as the poet needs must wake in us, if he is to procure our indispensable assistance, absolute instrumental speech has already proved itself all-powerful; since precisely the arousing of indefinite, of presaging, emotions has been its most characteristic effect; but this aptitude could become a weakness, wherever it wanted to give a definite shape, withal, to the emotions it had aroused. Now, if we apply to the "moments" of the drama this extraordinary, this unique enabling aptitude of instrumental speech; if we entrust it to the poet, to be set in motion for the furtherance of a definite aim, then we must come to terms as to *whence* this language has to take the sensuous moments of expression in which it is to clothe itself, to accord with the poetic aim.

We have already seen that our absolute instrumental music was obliged to borrow the sensuous "moments" for its expression, either from a dance rhythm familiar to our ear of yore, and from the thence-sprung tune—or from the melos of the folk song, to which our ear had been equally brought up. The absolute instrumental composer endeavored to raise the everlasting indefiniteness of these "moments" into a definite expression by fitting them together according to their kinship or contrast; by increasing or diminishing the strength, and hastening or slackening the speed, of their delivery; and finally by an idiomatic characterization, which he sought among the manifold individualities of the tone instruments themselves. In virtue of all this, he presented an image to the fantasy; and eventually he could but feel compelled to explain the object of his description by giving it an exact, an extra-musical label. So-called "tone painting" has been the manifest last stage of our absolute instrumental music's evolution; in it this art has sensibly chilled down its own expression, no longer addressing itself to the feeling, but to the fantasy: an experience which anyone may make for himself, by hearing a Mendelssohnian, or still more a Berliozian, orchestral composition, on top of a tone piece by Beethoven. Nevertheless, it is not to be denied that this evolutionary course was a "necessary" one, and the definite veering off into tone painting was prompted by more upright motives than, for instance, the return to the fugal style of Bach. Above all must it not be forgotten that the sensuous power of instrumental speech has been uncommonly enriched and heightened through this same tone painting.

We have now to recognize that not only can this power be heightened beyond all measure, but its expression be at the same time rid of its chillingness, if the tone painter may but address himself again to feeling, in place of fantasy. This opportunity is offered him when the subject of his mere describings to thought is revealed in actual presence to the senses; and indeed, as no mere help toward an understanding of his tone picture, but as conditioned by a highest poetic aim, for whose realization the tone picture is itself to be the helper. The subject of the tone picture could be nothing but a moment from the life of nature, or of man himself. But it is precisely such moments from natural or human life, to whose delineation the musician has hitherto felt drawn, that the poet now needs in preparation for weighty dramatic crises, and it has been to the utmost detriment of his intended artwork that the whilom absolute playwright must abjure these moments in advance—because, the more completely were they to impress the eye, yet without the supplementary aid of an emotion-guiding music their stage effect was bound to be held unjustified, disturbing, and detractive, not furthersome and helping.

Those indefinite presentiments, which the poet must necessarily arouse in us, will always have to be allied with some sort of show that presents itself to the eye. This will be a "moment" of the natural surrounding, or, in fact, of the human centerpiece of that surrounding: in any case, a "moment" whose motion is not as yet determined by any *definitely* revealed emotion; for the latter can be expressed only by word speech, in its aforesaid alliance with gesture and music—by that very word speech whose definite announcement we have here to pave the way for, through its evocation by our longing. No language is capable of so *movingly* expressing a preparatory repose, as that of the orchestra: to develop this repose into an impatient longing is its most peculiar office.

What is offered our eye by a scene of nature or a still and silent human figure, and through that eye attunes our feelings into placid contemplation, this same thing Music can present to our emotions in such a way that, starting from the "moment" of repose, she moves them to a state of strained expectancy, and thus awakes the longing which the poet needs on our part to assist him in the revelation of his aim. Nay, for this stirring of our feeling toward a definite object, the poet needs to prepare our eye for the determinant show itself—to wit, he must not even present us with the scene from nature, nor with his human characters, until our roused expectancy demands their presence and sanctions their behavior, as fulfilling the necessities prefigured by it.

In the exercise of this uttermost faculty, musical expression will remain quite vague and nondeterminant, till it takes into it the poetic aim above denoted. For the physical "moments" of the preparatory tone piece, however, this aim is able so to draw upon the definite phenomenon about to be realized, that they shall answer just as closely to that phenomenon as its eventual appearance answers to the expectations awakened in us by the premonitory music. Thus heralded, the actual phenomenon steps before us as a fulfilled longing, a justified foreboding; and, bearing in mind that the poet must lead his drama's shows before the feeling as towering over those of wonted life—in fact, as wondrous—we now have to admit that these shows would not display themselves as such, or would appear outrageous and unintelligible, if their eventual naked revelation could not be so conditioned by our preparatory feeling of their necessity as to make us downright demand them in fulfillment of an expectation. But only to an orchestral language thus inspired by the poet is it possible to rouse in us this necessary expectancy; wherefore without the orchestra's artistic aid the drama of wonders can neither be planned nor carried out.

21. *Example from* Lohengrin

CONSIDER an instance* where the gesture explained by the orchestra is of downright decisory importance. A situation has just been rounded off; obstacles have been set aside; and the

* The illustration refers to the close of Act II of *Lohengrin*.— TR.

mood is one of satisfaction. The poet wishes, however, to deduce from this situation its "necessary" successor, and this aim of his can be realized only by letting us feel that that mood is *not* completely satisfied, in truth, those obstacles are *not* entirely set aside. He is concerned to make us recognize that the seeming quietude of his dramatis personae is merely a self-illusion, on their part; and thus to so attune our feeling that we ourselves may frame the necessity of a further, an altered, development of the situation, through our co-creative sympathy: to this end he brings before us the gesture of a mysterious personage whose motives, as hitherto divulged, have inspired us with anxiety as to a final satisfactory solution; and he makes this gesture *threaten* the chief character. This threat is meant to fill us with foreboding, while the orchestra is to elucidate the character of that foreboding—and this it can do only by knitting it with a *remembrance*; wherefore he prescribes for this weighty moment the emphatic repetition of a melodic phrase which we have already heard as the musical expression of words referring to the threat, and which has the characteristic property of recalling to us the image of an earlier situation; and now, in union with the threatening gesture, this phrase becomes for us a prophecy, engrossing and instinctively determining our feeling.

22. The new musicodramatic unity

Now let us take a hasty glance at the form of our supposed drama, so as to assure ourselves that—for all its necessary and fundamental, its ever newly shaping change—it is a form essentially, nay, uniquely *one*. But let us also consider *what* it is, that makes this unity possible.

Just as the joinery of my individual scenes excluded every alien and unnecessary detail, and led all interest to the dominant chief mood, so did the whole building of my drama join itself into one organic unity, whose easily surveyed members were made out by those fewer scenes and situations which set the passing mood: no mood could be permitted to be struck in any one of these scenes that did not stand in a weighty relation to the moods of all the other scenes, so that the development of the moods of all the other scenes, the constant obviousness of this development, should establish the unity of the drama in its very mode of expression. Each of these chief moods, in keeping with the nature of the stuff, must also gain a definite musical expression, which should display itself to the sense of hearing as a definite musical theme. Just as, in the progress of the drama, the intended climax of a decisory chief mood was to be reached only through a development, continuously present to the feeling, of the individual moods already roused: so must the musical expression, which directly influences the physical feeling, necessarily take a decisive share in this development to a climax.

The orchestra is the organ for preserving the unity of expression. Wherever, for a plainer definement of the dramatic situation, the word-tone language of the dramatis personae abates itself in such a way as to expose its close kinship with the language of daily life—with the organ of the understanding—there the orchestra makes good this sunk expression, through its power of musically conveying a foreboding or remembrance; so that the awakened feeling remains in its uplifed mood, and never has to follow on that downward path by transforming itself into a purely intellectual function. Between the foreboding and remembrance, there stands the verse melody as the borne and bearing individuality, conditioned by an emotional surrounding consisting of moments of utterance drawn alike from its own promptings and from those of others, already experienced or yet to be experienced. These referential moments for rounding off the emotional expression withdraw into the background so soon as ever the individual comes to oneness with himself, and thus advances to the fullest expression of the verse melody; *then* the orchestra will merely support this melody in its elucidatory function; but when the full colors of the verse melody fade down again to a merely tonal word speech, then the orchestra resumes its function of making good the joint emotional expression through prophetic reminiscences, and of basing necessary transitions of feeling, as it were, upon our own, our ever-vigilant, sympathy.

Let us not forget, however, that the orchestra's equalizing moments of expression are never to be determined *by the caprice of the musician*, as a random tricking out of sound, but *only by the poet's aim*. Should these "moments" utter anything not connected with the situation of the dramatis personae, anything superfluous thereto, then the unity of expression is itself disturbed by this departure from the content. A mere absolute-musical embellishment or drooping or inchoate situation—a favorite operatic device for the self-glorification of music, in so-called "ritornels" and interludes, and even in the song accompaniments—such a trick upheaves at once the unity of expression, and casts the interest of the ear on music no longer as an expression, but, in a manner, as herself the thing expressed.

In opera, hitherto, the musician has not so much as attempted to devise a unitarian form for the whole artwork: each several vocal piece was a form filled out for itself, and merely hung together with the other tone pieces of the opera through a similarity of outward structure—by no means through any true conditionment by an inner content. The disconnected was so peculiarly the character of operatic music. Only the separate tone piece had a form coherent in itself; and this was derived from absolute-musical good pleasure, maintained by custom, and imposed upon the poet as an iron yoke. The connecting principle, within these forms, consisted in a ready-made theme making place for a second, a middle theme, and repeating itself according to the dictates of musical caprice. In the larger work of absolute instrumental music—the symphony—alternation, repetition, augmentation and diminution of the themes made out the movement of each ʼseparate section, which strove to vindicate itself before the feeling by establishing the utmost possible unity of form, through the coordination and recurrence of its themes. The vindication of their recurrence, however, rested on a merely imagined, but never realized, assumption; and nothing but the poetic aim can really bring about this vindication, because it downright demands the latter as a necessary condition for its being understood.

In their suggestive, their ever-warranted return, analogous to that of the Stabreim, the chief motives of the dramatic action—having become distinguishable melodic moments which fully materialize their content—now mold themselves into a continuous artistic form. The new form of dramatic music will have the unity of the symphonic movement; and this it will attain by spreading itself over the whole drama, in the most intimate cohesion therewith, not merely over single smaller, arbitrarily selected parts. So that this unity consists in a tissue of root themes pervading all the drama, themes which contrast, complete, reshape, divorce, and inter-

twine with one another as in the symphonic movement; only
that here the needs of the dramatic action dictate the laws
of parting and combining, which were there originally borrowed from the motions of the dance.

In this unity of the *expression*, ever making present, and
ever embracing the full compass of the content, there is at like
time solved, and solved in the only decisive way, the whilom
problem of the *unity* of *time and space*.

Time and space, as abstractions from the real living attributes of the action, could only chain the attention of our
drama-constructing poets because a single, a completely realizing expression did not stand at their service for the poetic
content planned by them. Time and space are thought-out
attributes of actual physical phenomena; and so soon as the
latter are thought about, they have in truth already lost their
force of manifestment: the body of these abstractions is the
real, the sense-appealing, of an action which displays itself in
a definite spacial surrounding, and in a period of motion conditioned thereby. To set the unity of the drama in the unity of
space and time means to set it at naught; for time and space
are nothing in themselves, and only become some-thing
through their being *annulled* by something *real*, by a human
action and its natural surrounding. This human action must be
the thing united in itself, that is, the thing that hangs together;
by the possibility of making its connection a surveyable one is
conditioned the assumption of its time length, and by the possibility of a completely adequate representment of the scene is
conditioned its extension in space; for it wills but one thing—
to make itself intelligible to feeling.

In the singlest space and the most compact time one may
spread out an action as completely discordant and disconnected as you please—as we may see to our heart's content in
our unity pieces. On the contrary, the unity of an action consists in its intelligible connection; and only through *one* thing
can this reveal itself intelligibly—which thing is neither time
nor space, but the *expression*. If in the preceding pages we
have ascertained *what* is this unitarian, that is, this continuous
expression, which at all times keeps the continuity in presence;
and if we have shown it as a thing by all means possible: then
in this expression we have also won back the severed by the
necessity of space and time as a thing once more united, and
a thing made ever present where needful for an understanding;
for its "necessary" presence lies not in time or space, but in
the *impression* which is made on us within them. The limita-

tions of space and time, which arose from lack of this expression, are upheaved at once by its acquirement; both time and space are annihilated, through the actuality of the drama.

23. Relation of the poet to the musician

It remains for me to denote only *the relation between poet and musician* which follows from the argument above. To do this briefly, let us first ask ourselves the question: "Has the poet to *restrict* himself in presence of the musician, and the musician in presence of the poet?"

Freedom of the individual has hitherto seemed possible through nothing but a—wise—restriction from without: moderation of his impulses, and thus of the force of his abilities, was the first thing required of the unit by the state community. The full effectuation of an individuality had to be looked on as synonymous with an infringement of the individuality of others, whereas the individual's self-restraint was reckoned as his highest wisdom and virtue. Taken strictly, this virtue, preached by sages, besung by didactists, and finally claimed by the state as the duty of subservience, by religion as the duty of humility—this virtue was a virtue never coming forth; willed, but not practiced; imagined, but not realized: and so long as a virtue is demanded, it will never in truth be exercised. Either the exercise of this virtue was an act despotically imposed— and thus without that merit of virtue imagined for it; or it was a necessary, an unreflective act of free will, and then its enabling force was not the self-restricting will—but *love*.

Those same sages and lawgivers who claimed the practice of self-restraint through reflection never reflected for an instant that they had thralls and slaves beneath them, from whom they cut off every possibility of practicing that virtue; and yet these latter were in fact the only ones who really restrained themselves for another's sake—because they were compelled to. Among that ruling and "reflecting" aristocracy the self-restraint of its members, toward one another, consisted in nothing but the prudence of egoism, which counseled them to segregate themselves, to take no thought for others; and this policy of *laisser aller*—clever enough at giving itself a quite agreeable outward show, in forms it borrowed from those of reverence and friendship—yet was only possible to these gentry on condition that other men, mere slaves and chattels, should stand ready to maintain the hedged-off self-dependence of their masters. In the terrible demoralization of our present social system, revolting to the heart of every veritable man, we may see the necessary consequence of asking for an impossible virtue, and a virtue which eventually is held in currency by a barbarous police. Only the total vanishing of this demand, and of the grounds on which it has been based—only the upheaval of the most unhuman inequality of men, in their stationings toward life, can bring about the *fancied* issue of that claim of self-restriction: and that, by making possible *free love*. But love will bring about that fancied issue in a measurelessly heightened measure, for it is not at all a *self-restraint*, but something infinitely greater—to wit, *the highest evolution of our individual powers—together with the most necessitated thrust toward our own self-offering for sake of a beloved object.*

Now, if we apply this criterion to the case above, we shall see that self-*restriction* of either the poet or the musician, in its ultimate consequences would only bring about the drama's death, or rather, would withstand its ever being brought to life. So soon as poet and musician restricted each other, they could have no end in view other than each to let his own particular talent shine out for itself; and seeing that the object, on which they were bringing these lights of theirs to shine was just the drama, the latter would naturally fare like the sick man betwixt two doctors, each endeavoring to display his special scientific skill in an opposite direction: with the strongest constitution in the world, the invalid would go to the ground. If poet and musician, however, do not restrict each other, but rouse each other's powers into highest might, by love; if in this love they are all that ever they can be; if they *mutually go under* in the offering that each brings each—the offering of his very highest potence—then the drama in its highest plenitude is born.

If the *poet's aim*—as such—is still at hand and visible, then it has not as yet gone under into the musical expression; but if the *musician's expression*—as such—is still apparent, then it, in turn, has not yet been inspired by the poetic aim. Only when the expression, as a marked and special thing, goes under in the realization of this aim, only *then* is neither aim nor expression any longer at hand, but the reality which each had *willed* is *can*-ned. And this reality is the drama; in whose presentment we must be reminded no more of aim or expression, but its content must instinctively engross us, as a human action vindicated "necessarily" before our feeling.

Let us tell the musician, then, that every, even the tiniest, moment of his expression *in which the poetic aim is not contained*, and which is not conditioned "necessarily" by that aim and its realization—that every such moment is superfluous, disturbing, bad; that each utterance of his is unimpressive if it stays unintelligible, and that it becomes intelligible only by taking into it the poet's aim; that he himself, however, as realizer of the poetic aim, stands infinitely higher than in his arbitrary dealings without that aim—for, as a conditioned, a "satisfying" message, his own is an even higher one than that of the conditioning, the "needy" aim in itself, albeit the latter is the highest aim man has; that, finally, in the conditioning of his message by this aim, he will be incited to a far richer exhibition of his powers than ever he was while at his lonely post, where—for sake of utmost understandableness—he was obliged to *restrain himself,* that is, to hold himself to a function not belonging to him as musician: whereas he now is necessarily challenged to the most unrestrained unfoldment of his powers, precisely because he needs and must be *nothing but musician.*

To the *poet* let us say that if his aim—in so far as it is to be displayed to the ear—*cannot be entirely realized in the expression of his musician ally,* then neither is it a highest poetic aim at all; that wherever his aim is still discernible he has not completely poetized it; and therefore, that he can measure *the height of poetry* to which his aim has reached only by *the completeness* wherewith it is realizable in the *musical expression.*

So, let us finally denote the measure of poetic worth as follows: as Voltaire said of the opera: "What is too silly to be said, one gets it sung," so let us reverse that maxim for the drama which we have in view, and say: *What is not worth the being sung, neither is it worth the poet's pains of telling.*

After what has been said above, it might seem almost superfluous to ask the further question: Ought we to think of the poet and musician as *two persons* or as *one*?

The poet and musician, whom we mean, are very well

thinkable as two persons. In fact the musician, in his practical intermediation between the poetic aim and its final bodily realization through an actual scenic representation, might necessarily be conditioned by the poet as a separate person.

24. One artist or two?

YET if we consider the present attitude assumed by poet and musician toward each other, and if we find it ordered by the same maxims of self-restriction and egoistic severance as those which govern all the factors of our modern social state, then we cannot but feel that, in an unworthy public system where every man is bent on shining for himself alone, *there* none but the individual unit can take into himself the spirit of community, and cherish and develop it according to his powers—how inadequate soe'er they be. Not to *two*, at the hour that is, can come the thought of jointly making possible the perfected drama; for, in parleying on this thought, the two must necessarily and candidly avow the impossibility of its realization in face of public life, and that avowal would nip their undertaking in the bud. Only the lonely one, in the thick of his endeavor, can transmute the bitterness of such a self-avowal into an intoxicating joy which drives him on, with all the courage of a drunkard, to undertake the making possible the impossible; for he *alone* is thrust forward by *two* artistic forces which he cannot withstand—by forces which he willingly lets drive him to self-offering.

25. Conclusion

WE have seen the poet driven onward by his yearning for a perfect emotional expression, and seen him reach the point where he found his verse reflected on the mirror of the sea of harmony, as musical melody: unto this sea was he compelled to thrust; only the mirror of this sea could show him the image of his yearning; and this sea he could not create from his own will, but it was the other of his being, that wherewith he needs must wed himself, but which he could not prescribe from out himself, nor summon into being. So neither can the artist prescribe from his own will, nor summon into being, that life of the future which once shall redeem him: for it is the other, the antithesis of himself, for which he yearns, toward which he is thrust; that which, when brought him from an opposite pole, is for the first time present for him, first takes his semblance up into it, and knowably reflects it back. Yet again, this living ocean of the future cannot beget that mirror image by its unaided self: it is a mother element, which can bear alone what it has first received. This fecundating seed, which in *it* alone can thrive, is brought it by the poet, that is, the artist of the present; and this seed is the quintessence of all rarest life sap, which the past has gathered up therein, to bring it to the future as its necessary, its fertilizing germ: *for this future is not thinkable, except as stipulated by the past.*

Now, the *melody* which appears at last upon the water mirror of the harmonic ocean of the future is the clear-seeing eye wherewith this life gazes upward from the depth of its sea abyss to the radiant light of day. But the *verse*, whose mere mirror image it is, is the own-est poem of the artist of the present, begotten by his most peculiar faculty, engendered by the fullness of his yearning. *And just as this verse, will the prophetic artwork of the yearning artist of the present once wed itself with the ocean of the life of the future.* In that life of the future will this artwork be what today it yearns for but cannot actually be as yet: for that life of the future will be entirely what it *can* be, only through its taking up into its womb this artwork.

The begetter of the artwork of the future is none other than the artist of the present, who presages that life of the future, and yearns to be contained therein. He who cherishes this longing within the inmost chamber of his powers, he lives already in a better life—but only one can do this thing:
the artist.

PART V

Wagner's Development

1. Autobiographical sketch

MY name is Wilhelm Richard Wagner, and I was born at Leipzig on May the 22nd, 1813. My father was a police actuary, and died six months after I was born. My stepfather, Ludwig Geyer, was a comedian and painter; he was also the author of a few stage plays, of which one, *Der Bethlehemitische Kindermord* (The Slaughter of the Innocents), had a certain success. My whole family migrated with him to Dresden. He wished me to become a painter, but I showed a very poor talent for drawing.

My stepfather also died ere long—I was only seven years old. Shortly before his death I had learned to play "Ub' immer Treu und Redlichkeit" and the then newly published "Jungfernkranz" upon the pianoforte; the day before his death, I was bid to play him both these pieces in the adjoining room; I heard him then, with feeble voice, say to my mother, "Has he perchance a talent for music?" On the early morrow, as he lay dead, my mother came into the children's sleeping room, and said to each of us some loving word. To me she said, "He hoped to make *something* of thee." I remember, too, that for a long time I imagined that something indeed would come of me.

In my ninth year I went to the Dresden Kreuzschule: I wished to study, and music was not thought of. Two of my sisters learned to play the piano passably; I listened to them, but had no piano lessons myself. Nothing pleased me so much as *Der Freischütz*; I often saw Weber pass before our house, as he came from rehearsals; I always watched him with a reverent awe. A tutor who explained to me Cornelius Nepos was at last engaged to give me pianoforte instructions; hardly had I got past the earliest finger exercises, when I furtively practiced, at first by ear, the Overture to *Der Freischütz*; my teacher heard this once, and said nothing would come of me. He was right; in my whole life I have never learned to play the piano properly. Thenceforward I played only for my own amusement, nothing but overtures, and with the most fearful "fingering." It was impossible for me to play a passage clearly, and I therefore conceived a just dread of all scales and runs.

Of Mozart, I cared only for *The Magic Flute*; *Don Giovanni* was distasteful to me, because of the Italian text beneath it: it seemed to me such rubbish.

But this music strumming was quite a secondary matter: Greek, Latin, mythology, and ancient history were my principal studies. I wrote verses too. Once there died one of my schoolfellows, and our teacher set us the task of writing a poem upon his death; the best lines were then to be printed: my own were printed, but only after I had cleared them of a heap of bombast. I was then eleven years old. I promptly determined to become a poet; and sketched out tragedies on the model of the Greeks, urged by my acquaintance with Apel's works: *Polyidos, Die Atolier*, and so on, and so on. Moreover, I passed in my school for a good head "in litteris"; even in the "third form" I had translated the first twelve books of the Odyssey. For a while I learned English also, merely so as to gain an accurate knowledge of Shakespeare; and I made a metrical translation of Romeo's monologue. Though I soon left English on one side, yet Shakespeare remained my exemplar, and I projected a great tragedy which was almost nothing but a medley of *Hamlet* and *King Lear*. The plan was gigantic in the extreme; two-and-forty human beings died in the course of this piece, and I saw myself compelled, in its working out, to call the greater number back as ghosts, since otherwise I should have been short of characters for my last acts. This play occupied my leisure for two whole years.

Meanwhile, I left Dresden and its Kreuzschule, and went to Leipzig. In the Nikolaischule of that city I was relegated to the "third form," after having already attained to the "second" in Dresden. This circumstance embittered me so much that thenceforward I lost all liking for philological study. I became lazy and slovenly, and my grand tragedy was the only thing left me to care about. Whilst I was finishing this I made my first acquaintance with Beethoven's music, in the Leipzig Gewandhaus concerts; its impression upon me was overpowering. I also became intimate with Mozart's works, chiefly through his *Requiem*. Beethoven's music to *Egmont* so much inspired me, that I determined—for all the world—not to allow my now completed tragedy to leave the stocks until provided with suchlike music. Without the slightest diffidence, I believed that I could myself write this needful music, but thought it better first to clear up a few of the general principles of thorough bass. To get through this as swiftly as possible, I borrowed for a week Logier's *Method of Thorough Bass*, and studied it in hot haste. But this study did not bear such rapid fruit as I had expected: its difficulties both provoked and fascinated me; I resolved to become a musician.

During this time my great tragedy was unearthed by my family: they were much disturbed thereat, for it was clear as day that I had woefully neglected my school lessons in favor of it, and I was forthwith admonished to continue them more diligently. Under such circumstances, I breathed no word of my secret discovery of a calling for music; but, notwithstanding, I composed in silence a sonata, a quartet, and an aria. When I felt myself sufficiently matured in my private musical studies, I ventured forth at last with their announcement. Naturally, I now had many a hard battle to wage, for my relations could consider my penchant for music only as a fleeting passion—all the more as it was unsupported by any proofs of preliminary study, and especially by any already won dexterity in handling a musical instrument.

I was then in my sixteenth year, and, chiefly from a perusal of E. A. Hoffmann's works, on fire with the maddest mysticism: I had visions by day in semislumber, in which the "keynote," "third," and "dominant" seemed to take on living form and reveal to me their mighty meaning: the notes that I wrote down were stark with folly. At last a capable musician was engaged to instruct me: the poor man had a sorry office in explaining to me that what I took for wondrous shapes and powers were really chords and intervals. What could be more disturbing to my family than to find that I proved myself negligent and refractory in this study also? My teacher shook his head, and it appeared that here too no good thing could be brought from me.

My liking for study dwindled more and more, and I chose instead to write overtures for full orchestra—one of which was once performed in the Leipzig theatre. This overture was the culminating point of my foolishness. For its better understanding by such as might care to study the score, I elected to employ for its notation three separate tints of ink: red for the "strings," green for the "woodwind," and black for the "brass." Beethoven's Ninth Symphony was a mere Pleyel sonata by the side of this marvelously concocted overture. Its performance was mainly prejudiced by a fortissimo thud on the big drum, that recurred throughout the whole overture at regular intervals of four bars; with the result that the audience gradually passed from its initial amazement at the obstinacy of the drum beater to undisguised displeasure, and finally to a mirthful mood that much disquieted me. This first performance of a composition of mine left on me a deep impression.

But now the July Revolution took place; with one bound I became a revolutionist, and acquired the conviction that every decently active being ought to occupy himself with politics exclusively. I was happy only in the company of political writers, and I commenced an overture upon a political theme. Thus was I minded, when I left school and went to the university: not, indeed, to devote myself to study for any profession—for my musical career was now resolved on—but to attend lectures on philosophy and aesthetics. By this opportunity of improving my mind I profited as good as nothing, but gave myself up to all the excesses of student life; and that with such reckless levity that they very soon revolted me. My relations were now sorely troubled about me, for I had almost entirely abandoned my music. Yet I speedily came to my senses; I felt the need of a completely new beginning of strict and methodical study of music, and Providence led me to the very man best qualified to inspire me with fresh love for the thing, and to purge my notions by the most thorough instruction. This man was Theodor Weinlig, the cantor of the Leipzig Thomasschule. Although I had previously made my own attempts at fugue, it was with him that I first commenced a thorough study of counterpoint, which he possessed the happy knack of teaching his pupils while playing.

At this epoch I first acquired an intimate love and knowledge of Mozart. I composed a sonata, in which I freed myself from all buckram, and strove for a natural, unforced style of composition. This extremely simple and modest work was published by Breitkopf und Härtel. My studies under Weinlig were ended in less than half a year, and he dismissed me himself from his tuition as soon as he had brought me so far forward that I was in a position to solve with ease the hardest problems of counterpoint. "What you have made your own by this dry study," he said, "we call self-dependence." In that same half-year I also composed an overture on the model of Beethoven; a model which I now understood somewhat better. This overture was played in one of the Leipzig Gewandhaus concerts, to most encouraging applause. After several other works, I then engaged in a symphony: to my head exemplar, Beethoven, I allied Mozart, especially as shown in his great C-major Symphony. Lucidity and force—albeit with many a strange aberration—were my end and aim.

My symphony completed, I set out in the summer of 1832

on a journey to Vienna, with no object other than to get a hasty glimpse of this renowned music city. What I saw and heard there edified me little; wherever I went I heard *Zampa.* and Straussian potpourris on *Zampa.* Both—and especially at that time—were to me an abomination. On my homeward journey I tarried a while in Prague, where I made the acquaintance of Dionys Weber and Tomaschek; the former had several of my compositions performed in the conservatoire, and among them my symphony. In that city I also composed an opera book of tragic contents: *Die Hochzeit.* I know not whence I had come by the medieval subject matter —a frantic lover climbs to the window of the sleeping chamber of his friend's bride, wherein she is awaiting the advent of the bridegroom; the bride struggles with the madman and hurls him into the courtyard below, where his mangled body gives up the ghost. During the funeral ceremony, the bride, uttering one cry, sinks lifeless on the corpse.

Returned to Leipzig, I set to work at once on the composition of this opera's first "number," which contained a grand sextet that much pleased Weinlig. The textbook found no favor with my sister; I destroyed its every trace.

In January of 1833 my symphony was performed at a Gewandhaus concert, and met with highly inspiriting applause. At about this time I came to know Heinrich Laube.

To visit one of my brothers, I traveled to Würzburg in the spring of the same year, and remained there till its close; my brother's intimacy was of great importance to me, for he was an accomplished singer. During my stay in Würzburg I composed a romantic opera in three acts, *Die Feen,* for which I wrote my own text, after Gozzi's *Die Frau als Schlange.* Beethoven and Weber were my models; in the ensembles of this opera there was much that fell out very well, and the finale of the second act, especially, promised a good effect. The "numbers" from this work which I brought to a hearing at concerts in Würzburg, were favorably received. Full of hopes for my now finished opera, I returned to Leipzig at the beginning of 1834, and offered it for performance to the director of that theatre. However, in spite of his at first declared readiness to comply with my wish, I was soon forced to the same experience that every German opera composer has nowadays to win: we are discredited upon our own native stage by the success of Frenchmen and Italians, and the production of our operas is a favor to be cringed for. The performance of my *Feen* was set upon the shelf.

Meanwhile I heard Wilhelmine Schröder-Devrient sing in Bellini's *Romeo and Juliet*. I was astounded to witness so extraordinary a rendering of such utterly meaningless music. I grew doubtful as to the choice of the proper means to bring about a great success; far though I was from attaching to Bellini a signal merit, yet the subject to which his music was set seemed to me to be more propitious and better calculated to spread the warm glow of life than the painstaking pedantry with which we Germans, as a rule, brought naught but laborious make-believe to market. The flabby lack of character of our modern Italians, equally with the frivolous levity of the latest Frenchmen, appeared to me to challenge the earnest, conscientious German to master the happily chosen and happily exploited means of his rivals, in order then to outstrip them in the production of genuine works of art.

I was then twenty-one years of age, inclined to take life and the world on their pleasant side. *Ardinghello* (by Heinse) and *Das Junge Europa* (by H. Laube) tingled through my every limb; while Germany appeared in my eyes a very tiny portion of the earth. I had emerged from abstract mysticism, and I learned a love for matter. Beauty of material and brilliancy of wit were lordly things to me: as regards my beloved music, I found them both among the Frenchmen and Italians. I foreswore my model, Beethoven; his last symphony I deemed the keystone of a whole great epoch of art, beyond whose limits no man could hope to press, and within which no man could attain to independence. Mendelssohn also seemed to have felt with me, when he stepped forth with his smaller orchestral compositions, leaving untouched the great and fenced-off form of the symphony of Beethoven; it seemed to me that, beginning with a lesser, completely unshackled form, he fain would create for himself therefrom a greater.

Everything around me appeared fermenting: to abandon myself to the general fermentation I deemed the most natural course. Upon a lovely summer's journey among the Bohemian watering places, I sketched the plan of a new opera, *Das Liebesverbot*, taking my subject from Shakespeare's *Measure for Measure*—only with this difference, that I robbed it of its prevailing earnestness, and thus remolded it after the pattern of *Das Junge Europa;* free and frank physicalism gained, of its own sheer strength, the victory over puritanical hyprocisy.

In the summer of this same year, 1834, I further took the post of music director at the Magdeburg theatre. The practical application of my musical knowledge to the functions of a conductor bore early fruit; for the vicissitudes of intercourse with singers and singeresses, behind the scenes and in front of the footlights, completely matched my bend toward many-hued distraction. The composition of my *Liebesverbot* was now begun. I produced the Overture to *Die Feen* at a concert; it had a marked success. This notwithstanding, I lost all liking for this opera, and, since I was no longer able personally to attend to my affairs at Leipzig, I soon resolved to trouble myself no more about this work, which is as much as to say that I gave it up.

For a festival play for New Year's day, 1835, I hastily threw together some music which aroused a general interest. Such lightly won success much fortified my views that in order to please, one must not too scrupulously choose one's means. In this sense I continued the composition of my *Liebesverbot,* and took no care whatever to avoid the echoes of the French and Italian stages. Interrupted in this work for a while, I resumed it in the winter of 1835–6, and completed it shortly before the dispersal of the Magdeburg opera troupe. I had now only twelve days before the departure of the principal singers; therefore my opera must be rehearsed in this short space of time, if I still wished them to perform it. With greater levity than deliberation, I permitted this opera—which contained some arduous roles—to be set on the stage after ten days' study. I placed my trust in the prompter and in my conductor's baton. But, spite of all my efforts, I could not remove the obstacle that the singers scarcely half knew their parts. The representation was like a dream to us all: no human being could possibly get so much as an idea what it was all about; yet there was some consola-tion in the fact that applause was plentiful. For various reasons, a second performance could not be given.

In the midst of all this, the "earnestness of life" had knocked at my door; my outward independence, so rashly grasped at, had led me into follies of every kind, on all sides I was plagued by penury and debts. It occurred to me to venture upon something out of the ordinary, in order not to slide into the common rut of need. Without any sort of prospect, I went to Berlin and offered the director to produce my *Liebesverbot* at the theatre of that capital. I was received at first with the fairest promises; but, after long suspense, I had to learn that not one of them was sincerely meant. In the sorriest plight I left Berlin, and applied for the post of

musical director at the Königsberg theatre, in Prussia—a post
which I subsequently obtained. In that city I got married in
the autumn of 1836, amid the most dubious outward circumstances. The year which I spent in Königsberg was completely lost to my art, by reason of the pressure of petty
cares. I wrote one solitary overture: "Rule Britannia."

In the summer of 1837 I visited Dresden for a short time.
There I was led back by the reading of Bulwer's *Rienzi* to
an already cherished idea, namely, of turning the last of
Rome's tribunes into the hero of a grand tragic opera.
Hindered by outward discomforts, however, I busied myself
no further with dramatic sketches. In the autumn of this
year I went to Riga, to take up the position of first musical
director at the theatre recently opened there by Holtei. I
found there an assemblage of excellent material for opera,
and went to its employment with the greatest liking. Many
interpolated passages for individual singers in various operas
were composed by me during this period. I also wrote the
libretto for a comic opera in two acts: *Die Glückliche Bären-
familie,* the matter for which I took from one of the stories in
the *Thousand and One Nights.* I had composed only two
"numbers" for this, when I was disgusted to find that I was
again on the high road to music-making à la Adam. My
spirit, my deeper feelings, were wounded by this discovery,
and I laid aside the work in horror. The daily studying
and conducting of Auber's, Adam's, and Bellini's music
contributed its share to a speedy undoing of my frivolous
delight in such an enterprise.

The utter childishness of our provincial public's verdict
upon any art manifestation that may chance to make its
first appearance in their own theatre—for they are accustomed
only to witnessing performances of works already judged and
accredited by the greater world outside—brought me to the
decision, at no price to produce for the first time a largish
work at a minor theatre. When, therefore, I felt again the
instinctive need of undertaking a major work, I renounced
all idea of obtaining a speedy representation of it in my
immediate neighborhood: I fixed my mind upon some
theatre of first rank that would some day produce it, and
troubled myself but little as to where and when that theatre
would be found. In this wise did I conceive the sketch of a
grand tragic opera in five acts: *Rienzi, the Last of the
Tribunes;* and I laid my plans on so important a scale, that
it would be impossible to produce this opera—at any rate

for the first time—at any lesser theatre. Moreover, the wealth and force of the material left me no other course, and my procedure was governed more by necessity than by set purpose. In the summer of 1838 I completed the poem; at the same time, I was engaged in rehearsing our opera troupe, with much enthusiasm and affection, in Méhul's *Jacob and His Sons*.

When, in the autumn, I began the composition of my *Rienzi*, I allowed naught to influence me except the single purpose to answer to my subject. I set myself no model, but gave myself entirely to the feeling which now consumed me, the feeling that I had already so far progressed that I might claim something significant from the development of my artistic powers, and expect some not insignificant result. The very notion of being consciously weak or trivial—even in a single bar—was appalling to me.

During the winter I was in the full swing of composition, so that by the spring of 1839 I had finished the long first two acts. About this time my contract with the director of the theatre terminated, and various circumstances made it inconvenient to me to stay longer at Riga. For two years I had nursed the plan of going to Paris, and with this in view, I had, even while at Königsberg, sent to Scribe the sketch of an opera plot, with the proposal that he should elaborate it for his own benefit and procure me, in reward, the commission to compose the opera for Paris. Scribe naturally left this suggestion as good as unregarded. Nevertheless, I did not give up my scheme; on the contrary, I returned to it with renewed keenness in the summer of 1839; and the long and the short of it was that I induced my wife to embark with me upon a sailing vessel bound for London.

This voyage I never shall forget as long as I live; it lasted three and a half weeks, and was rich in mishaps. Thrice did we endure the most violent of storms, and once the captain found himself compelled to put into a Norwegian haven. The passage among the crags of Norway made a wonderful impression on my fancy; the legends of the Flying Dutchman, as I heard them from the seamen's mouths, were clothed for me in a distinct and individual color, borrowed from the adventures of the ocean through which I then was passing.

Resting from the severe exhaustion of the transit, we remained a week in London; nothing interested me so much as the city itself and the Houses of Parliament—of the theatres, I visited not one. At Boulogne-sur-Mer I stayed four weeks, and there made the acquaintance of Meyerbeer. I brought under his notice the two finished acts of my *Rienzi*; he promised me, in the friendliest fashion, his support in Paris. With very little money, but the best of hopes, I now set foot in Paris. Entirely without any personal references, I could rely on no one but Meyerbeer. He seemed prepared, with the most signal attentiveness, to set in train whatever might further my aims; and it certainly seemed to me that I should soon attain a wished-for goal—had it not unfortunately so turned out that, during the very period of my stay in Paris, Meyerbeer was generally, nay, almost the whole time, absent from that city. It is true that he wished to serve me even from a distance; but, according to his own announcement, epistolary efforts could avail nothing where only the most assiduous personal mediation is of any efficacy.

First of all, I entered upon negotiations with the Théâtre de la Renaissance, where both comedy and opera were then being given. The score of my *Liebesverbot* seemed best fitted for this theatre, and the somewhat frivolous subject appeared easily adaptable to the French stage. I was so warmly recommended by Meyerbeer to the director of the theatre that he could not help receiving me with the best of promises. Thereupon, one of the most prolific of Parisian dramatists, Dumersan, offered to undertake the poetical setting of the subject. He translated three "numbers," destined for a trial hearing, with so great felicity that my music looked much better in its new French dress than in its original German; in fact, it was music such as Frenchmen most readily comprehend, and everything promised me the best success—when the Théâtre de la Renaissance immediately became bankrupt. All my labors, all my hopes, were thus in vain.

In the same winter, 1839–40, I composed—besides an overture to the first part of Goethe's *Faust*—several French ballads; among others, a French translation made for me of H. Heine's "The Two Grenadiers." I never dreamed of any possibility of getting my *Rienzi* produced in Paris, for I clearly foresaw that I should have had to wait five or six years, even under the most favorable conditions, before such a plan could be carried out; moreover, the translation of the text of the already half-finished composition would have thrown insuperable obstacles in the way.

Thus I began the summer of 1840 completely bereft of immediate prospects. My acquaintance with Habeneck,

Halévy, Berlioz, and so on, led to no closer relations with these men: in Paris no artist has time to form a friendship with another, for each is in a red-hot hurry for his own advantage. Halévy, like all the composers of our day, was aflame with enthusiasm for his art only so long as it was a question of winning a great success: so soon as he had carried off this prize, and was enthroned among the privileged ranks of artistic "lions," he had no thought for anything but making operas and pocketing their pay. Renown is everything in Paris: the happiness and ruin of the artist. Despite his standoff manners, Berlioz attracted me in a far higher degree. He differs by the whole breadth of heaven from his Parisian colleagues, for he makes no music for gold. But he cannot write for the sake of purest art; he lacks all sense of beauty. He stands, completely isolated, upon his own position; by his side he has nothing but a troupe of devotees who, shallow and without the smallest spark of judgment, greet in him the creator of a brand-new musical system and completely turn his head—the rest of the world avoids him as a madman.

My earlier easygoing views of the means and ends of music received their final shock—from the Italians. These idolized heroes of song, with Rubini at their head, finished by utterly disgusting me with their music. The public to whom they sang added their quota to this effect upon me. The Paris Grand Opera left me entirely unsatisfied, by the want of all genius in its representations: I found the whole thing commonplace and middling. I openly confess that the *mise en scène* and the decorations are the most to my liking of anything at the Académie Royale de Musique.

The Opéra Comique would have had much more chance of pleasing me—it possesses the best talents, and its performances offer an ensemble and an individuality such as we know nothing of in Germany—but the stuff that is nowadays written for this theatre belongs to the very worst productions of a period of degraded art. Whither have flown the grace of Méhul, Isouard, Boieldieu, and the young Auber, scared by the contemptible quadrille rhythms which rattle through this theatre today? The only thing worthy the regard of a musician that Paris now contains, is the Conservatoire with its orchestral concerts. The renderings of German instrumental compositions at these concerts produced on me a deep impression, and inducted me afresh into the mysteries of noble art. He who would fully learn the Ninth Symphony of Beethoven

must hear it executed by the orchestra of the Paris Conservatoire. But these concerts stand alone in utter solitude; there
is naught that answers to them.

I hardly mixed at all with musicians: scholars, painters,
and so on, formed my entourage, and I gained many a rare
experience of friendship in Paris. Since I was so completely
bare of present Paris prospects, I took up once more the
composition of my *Rienzi*. I now destined it for Dresden: in
the first place, because I knew that this theatre possessed the
very best material—Devrient, Tichatschek, and so on;
secondly, because I could more reasonably hope for an
entrée there, relying upon the support of my earliest acquaintances. My *Liebesverbot* I now gave up almost completely; I
felt that I could no longer regard myself as its composer.
With all the greater freedom, I followed now my true artistic
creed, in the prosecution of the music to my *Rienzi*. Manifold
worries and bitter need besieged my life. On a sudden, Meyerbeer appeared again for a short space in Paris. With the most
amiable sympathy he ascertained the position of my affairs,
and desired to help. He therefore placed me in communication with Léon Pillet, the director of the Grand Opera, with a
view to my being entrusted with the composition of a two-
or three-act opera for that stage. I had already provided
myself for this emergency with an outline plot.

The Flying Dutchman, whose intimate acquaintance I had
made upon the ocean, had never ceased to fascinate my
fantasy; I had also made the acquaintance of H. Heine's
remarkable version of this legend, in a number of his *Salon;*
and it was especially his treatment of the redemption of this
Ahasuerus of the seas—borrowed from a Dutch play under
the same title—that placed within my hands all the material
for turning the legend into an opera subject. I obtained the
consent of Heine himself; I wrote my sketch, and handed it
to M. Léon Pillet, with the proposal that he should get me a
French textbook made after my model. Thus far was everything set on foot when Meyerbeer again left Paris, and the
fulfillment of my wish had to be relinquished to destiny.

I was very soon astounded by hearing from Pillet that the
sketch I had tendered him pleased him so much that he
should be glad if I would cede it to him. He explained: that
he was pledged by a previous promise to supply another
composer with a libretto as soon as possible; that my sketch
appeared to be the very thing for such a purpose, and I should
probably not regret consenting to the surrender he begged,

when I reflected that I could not possibly hope to obtain a direct commission for an opera before the lapse of four years, seeing that he had in the interval to keep faith with several candidates for grand opera; that such a period would naturally be loo long for myself to be brooding over this subject; and that I should certainly discover a fresh one, and console myself for the sacrifice. I struggled obstinately against this suggestion, without being able, however, to effect anything further than a provisional postponement of the question. I counted upon the speedy return of Meyerbeer, and held my peace.

During this time I was prompted by Schlesinger to write for his *Gazette Musicale*. I contributed several longish articles on "German Music," and so on, and so on, among which the one which found the liveliest welcome was a little romance entitled "A Pilgrimage to Beethoven." These works assisted not a little to make me known and noticed in Paris. In November of this year I put the last touches to my score of *Rienzi,* and sent it posthaste to Dresden. This period was the culminating point of the utter misery of my existence. I wrote for the *Gazette Musicale* a short story, "The Life's End of a German Musician in Paris," wherein I made the wretched hero die with these words upon his lips: "I believe in God, Mozart, and Beethoven."

It was well that my opera was finished, for I saw myself now compelled to bid a long farewell to any practice of my art. I was forced to undertake, for Schlesinger, arrangements of airs for all the instruments under heaven, even the *cornet à piston;* thus only was a slight amelioration of my lot to be found. In this way did I pass the winter of 1840–1, in the most inglorious fashion. In the spring I went into the country, to Meudon; and with the warm approach of summer I began to long again for brainwork. The stimulus thereto was to touch me quicker than I had thought for; I learned, forsooth, that my sketch of the text of *The Flying Dutchman* had already been handed to a poet, Paul Fouché, and that if I did not declare my willingness to part therewith, I should be clean robbed of it on some pretext or other. I therefore consented at last to make over my sketch for a moderate sum.

I had now to work posthaste to clothe my own subject with German verses. In order to set about its composition, I required to hire a pianoforte; for, after nine months' interruption of all musical production, I had to try to surround myself with the needful preliminary of a musical atmosphere. As soon as the piano had arrived, my heart beat fast for very fear; I dreaded to discover that I had ceased to be a musician. I began first with the "Sailors' Chorus" and the "Spinning Song"; everything sped along as though on wings, and I shouted for joy as I felt within me that I still was a musician. In seven weeks the whole opera was composed; but at the end of that period I was overwhelmed again by the commonest cares of life, and two full months elapsed before I could get to writing the overture to the already finished opera—although I bore it almost full-fledged in my brain. Naturally, nothing now lay so much at my heart as. the desire to bring it to a speedy production in Germany; from Munich and Leipzig I had the disheartening answer: the opera was not at all fitted for Germany. Fool that I was! I had fancied it was fitted for Germany alone, since it struck on chords that can vibrate only in the German breast.

At last I sent my new work to Meyerbeer, in Berlin, with the petition that he would get it taken up for the theatre of that city. This was effected with tolerable rapidity. As my *Rienzi* had already been accepted for the Dresden court theatre, I therefore now looked forward to the production of two of my works upon the foremost German stages; and involuntarily I reflected on the strangeness of the fact that Paris had been to me of the greatest service for Germany. As regards Paris itself, I was completely without prospects for several years: I therefore left it in the spring of 1842. For the first time I saw the Rhine—with hot tears in my eyes, I, poor artist, swore eternal fidelity to my German fatherland.

2. Rienzi

To do something grand, to write an opera for whose production only the most exceptional means should suffice—a work, therefore, which I should never feel tempted to bring before the public amid such cramping relations as those which then oppressed me, and the hope of whose eventual production should thus incite me to make every sacrifice in order to extricate myself from those relations—this is what resolved me to resume and carry out with all my might my former plan for *Rienzi*. In the preparation of this text, also, I took no thought for anything but the writing of an effective operatic libretto. The "grand opera" with all its scenic and musical display, its sensationalism and massive vehemence, loomed large before me; and not merely to copy it, but with reckless extravagance to outbid it in its every detail, became the object of my artistic ambition.

However, I should be unjust to myself, did I represent this ambition as my only motive for the conception and execution of my *Rienzi*. The stuff really aroused my enthusiasm, and I put nothing into my sketch which had not a direct bearing on the grounds of this enthusiasm. My chief concern was my Rienzi himself; and only when I felt quite contented with him, did I give rein to the notion of a "grand opera." Nevertheless, from a purely artistic point of view, this "grand opera" was the pair of spectacles through which I unconsciously regarded my Rienzi stuff; nothing in that stuff did I find enthrall me but what could be looked at through these spectacles. True, that I always fixed my gaze upon the stuff itself, and did not keep one eye open for certain ready-made musical effects which I might wish to father on it by hook or crook; only, I saw it in no light other than that of a "five-act opera," with five brilliant "finales," and filled with hymns, processions, and musical clash of arms. Thus I bestowed no greater care upon the verse and diction than seemed needful for turning out a good, and not a trivial, opera text.

I did not set out with the object of writing duets, trios, and so on; but they found their own way in, here and there, because I looked upon my subject exclusively through the medium of "opera." For instance, I by no means hunted about in my stuff for a pretext for a ballet; but with the eyes of the opera composer. I perceived in it a self-evident festival that Rienzi must give to the people, and at which he would have to exhibit to them, in dumbshow, a drastic scene from their ancient history: this scene being the story of Lucretia and the consequent expulsion of the Tarquins from Rome.* Thus in every department of my plan I was certainly ruled by the stuff alone; but on the other hand, I ruled this stuff according to my only chosen pattern, the form of the grand opera. My

---

* That this pantomime has had to be omitted from the stage performances of *Rienzi* has been a serious drawback to me; for the ballet that replaced it has obscured my nobler intentions, and turned this scene into nothing more nor less than ordinary operatic spectacle.—R. WAGNER.

artistic individuality, in its dealings with the impressions of life, was still entirely under the influence of purely artistic, or rather art-formalistic, mechanically operating impressions.

3. The Flying Dutchman: use of myth

THE mood in which I adopted the legend of the Flying Dutchman I have already stated in general terms: the adoption was exactly as old as the mood itself, which, at first merely brooding within me and battling against more seductive impressions, at last attained the power of outwardly expressing itself in a cognate work of art. The figure of the Flying Dutchman is a mythical creation of the folk: a primal trait of human nature speaks out from it with heart-enthralling force. This trait, in its most universal meaning, is the longing after rest from amid the storms of life. In the blithe world of Greece we meet with it in the wanderings of Ulysses and his longing after home, house, hearth, and wife: the attainable, and at last attained, reward of the city-loving son of ancient Hellas. The Christian, without a home on earth, embodied this trait in the figure of the Wandering Jew: for that wanderer, forever doomed to a long-since outlived life, without an aim, without a joy, there bloomed no earthly ransom; death was the sole remaining goal of all his strivings; his only hope, the laying down of being.

At the close of the Middle Ages a new, more active impulse led the nations to fresh life: in the world-historical direction its most important result was the bent to voyages of discovery. The sea, in its turn, became the soil of life; yet no longer the narrow landlocked sea of the Grecian world, but the great ocean that engirdles all the earth. The fetters of the older world were broken; the longing of Ulysses, back to home and hearth and wedded wife, after feeding on the sufferings of the "never-dying Jew" until it became a yearning for death, had mounted to the craving for a new, an unknown home, invisible as yet, but dimly boded. This vast-spread feature fronts us in the *mythos* of the Flying Dutchman—that seaman's poem from the world-historical age of journeys of discovery. Here we light upon a remarkable mixture, a blend, effected by the spirit of the folk, of the character of Ulysses with that of the Wandering Jew. The

Hollandic mariner, in punishment for his temerity, is condemned by the Devil (here, obviously, the element of flood and storm*) to do battle with the unresting waves, to all eternity. Like Ahasuerus, he yearns for his sufferings to be ended by death; the Dutchman, however, may gain this redemption, denied to the undying Jew, at the hands of—*a woman* who, of very love, shall sacrifice herself for him. The yearning for death thus spurs him on to seek this woman; but she is no longer the home-tending Penelope of Ulysses, as courted in the days of old, but the quintessence of womankind; and yet the still unmanifest, the longed-for, the dreamed-of, the infinitely womanly woman—let me out with it in one phrase: *the woman of the future.*

This was that Flying Dutchman who arose so often from the swamps and billows of my life, and drew me to him with such resistless might; this was the first *folk poem* that forced its way into my heart, and called on me as man and artist to point its meaning, and mold it is a work of art.

From here begins my career as *poet,* and my farewell to the mere concoctor of opera texts. And yet I took no sudden leap. In no wise was I influenced by reflection; for reflection comes only from the mental combination of existing models: whereas I nowhere found the specimens which might have served as beacons on my road. My course was new; it was bidden me by my inner mood, and forced upon me by the pressing need to impart this mood to others. In order to enfranchise myself from within outward, that is, to address myself to the understanding of like-feeling men, I was driven to strike out for myself, as artist, a path as yet not pointed me by any outward experience; and that which drives a man hereto is necessity, deeply felt, incognizable by the practical reason, but overmastering necessity.

4. Tannhäuser. *The conception of higher love*

THE German folk's-book of *Tannhäuser* fell into my hands. This wonderful creation of the folk at once usurped my liveliest emotions: indeed it was now that it first *could* do so.

---

* Note to the original edition: "A critic recently considered this Devil and this Flying Dutchman as an orthdox (*dogmatischer*) Devil and an orthodox ghost."

Tannhäuser, however, was by no means a figure completely new to me: I had early made his acquaintance through Tieck's narration. He had then aroused my interest in the same fantastically mystic manner in which Hoffmann's stories had worked upon my young imagination; but this domain of romance had never exercised any influence upon my art-productive powers. I now read through again the utterly modern poem of Tieck, and understood at once why his coquettish mysticism and catholic frivolity had not appealed in any definite way to my sympathy; the folk's-book and the homely *Tannhäuserlied* explained this point to me, as they showed me the simple genuine inspiration of the Tannhäuser legend in such swiftly seizable and undisfigured traits.

But what most irresistibly attracted me was the connection, however loose, between Tannhäuser and the "Singers' Tourney in the Wartburg," which I found established in that folk's-book. With this second poetic subject also I had already made an earlier acquaintance, in a tale of Hoffmann's; but, as with Tieck's Tannhäuser, it had left me without the slightest incitation to dramatic treatment. I now decided to trace this Singers' Tourney, whose whole entourage breathed on me the air of home, to its simplest and most genuine source; this led me to the study of the middle-high-German poem of the *Sängerkrieg*, into which one of my friends, a German philologist who happened to possess a copy, was fortunately able to induct me. This poem, as is well known, is set in direct connection with a larger epos, that of *Lohengrin*. That also I studied, and thus with one blow a whole new world of poetic stuff was opened out to me; a world of which in my previous search, mostly for ready-made material adapted to the genre of opera, I had not had the slightest conception.

I have said that my yearning for home had nothing of the character of political patriotism in it; yet I should be untruthful did I not admit that a political interpretation of the German home was among the objects of my indefinite longing. This I naturally could not find in the present, and any justification of the wish for such a rendering I—like our whole historical school—could only seek out in the past. In order to assure myself of what it was, in particular, that I held dear in the German home for which I was yearning, I recalled the image of the impressions of my youth, and, to conjure up a clearer vision, I turned the pages of the book of history. I also took advantage of this opportunity to seek again for an operatic subject: but nowhere in the ample outlines of the old German Kaiser world could I find one; and, although without distinctly realizing it, I felt that the features of this epoch were unfitted for a faithful and intelligible dramatization in exact measure as they presented a dearth of seizable motive to my musical conception.

At last I fastened on *one* episode, since it seemed to offer me the chance of giving a freer rein to my poetic fancy. This was a moment from the last days of the Hohenstaufen era. Manfred, the son of Friedrich II, tears himself from his lethargy and abandonment to lyric luxury, and, pressed by hot need, throws himself upon Luceria; which city, in the heart of the realms of Holy Church, had been assigned by his father to the Saracens, after their dislodgement from Sicily. Chiefly by aid of these warlike and lightly kindled Sons of Araby, he wins back from the Pope and ruling Guelphs the whole of the disputed realm of Sicily and Apuleia; the dramatic sketch concluding with his coronation.

Into this purely historical plot I wove an imaginary female figure: I now recall the fact that her form had taken shape in my mind from the memory of an engraving which I had seen long previously; this picture represented Friedrich II surrounded by his almost exclusively Arabian court, among which my fancy was principally attracted by the Oriental forms of singing and dancing women. The spirit of this Friedrich, my favorite hero, I now embodied in the person of a Saracen maiden, the fruit of the embraces of Friedrich and a daughter of Araby, during the Kaiser's peaceful sojourn in Palestine.

Tidings of the downfall of the Ghibelline house had come to the girl in her native home; fired with that same Arabian enthusiasm which not long since gave the East its songs of ardent love for Bonaparte, she made her way to Apuleia. There, in the court of the dispirited Manfred, she appears as a prophetess, inspires him with fresh courage, and spurs him on to action; she kindles the hearts of the Arabs in Luceria, and, instilling enthusiasm whithersoever she goes, she leads the emperor's son through victory on victory to throne. Her descent she has kept enwrapt in mystery, the better to work on Manfred's mind, by the riddle of her apparition; he loves her passionately, and fain would break the secret's seal: she waves him back with an oracular saying. His life being attempted, she receives the death thrust in her own breast: dying, she confesses herself as Manfred's sister, and unveils the fullness of her love to him. Manfred, crowned, takes leave of happiness for ever.

This picture which my homesick fantasy had painted, not without some warmth of color, in the departing light of a historical sunset, completely faded from my sight so soon as ever the figure of Tannhäuser revealed itself to my inner eye. That picture was conjured from outside: this figure sprang from my inmost heart. In its infinitely simple traits, it was to me more wide-embracing, and alike more definite and plain, than the richly colored, shimmering tissue—half historical and half poetic—which like a showy cloak of many folds concealed the true, the supple human form my inner wish desired to look on, and which stepped at once before me in the new-found Tannhäuser. Here was the very essence of the *folk's* poem, that ever seizes on the *kernel* of the matter, and brings it again to show in simple plastic outlines; whilst there, in the history—that is, the event not such as it was, but such alone as it comes within *our* ken—this matter shows itself in endless trickery of outer facings, and never attains that fine plasticity of form until the eye of the folk has plunged into its inner soul, and given it the artistic mold of myth.

If at last I turned impatiently away, and owed the strength of my repugnance to the independence already developed in my nature, both as artist and as man: so did that double revolt, of man and artist, inevitably take on the form of a yearning for appeasement in a higher, nobler element; an element which in its contrast to the only pleasures that the material present spreads in modern life and modern art, could but appear to me in the guise of a pure, chaste, virginal, unseizable, and unapproachable ideal of love. What, in fine, could this love yearning, the noblest thing my heart could feel—what other could it be than a longing for release from the present, for absorption into an element of endless love, a love denied to earth and reachable through the gates of death alone? And what, again, at bottom, could such a longing be, but the yearning of love; aye, of a real love seeded in the soil of fullest sentience—yet a love that could never come to fruitage on the loathsome soil of modern sentience? How absurd, then, must those critics seem to me, who, drawing all their wit from modern wantonness, insist on reading into my *Tannhäuser* a specifically Christian and impotently pietistic drift! They recognize nothing but the fable of their own incompetence, in the story of a man whom they are utterly unable to comprehend.

The above is an exact account of the mood in which I was when the unlaid ghost of Tannhäuser returned again, and urged me to complete his poem. When I reached the sketch and working out of the *Tannhäuser* music, it was in a state of burning exaltation that held my blood and every nerve in fevered throbbing. My true nature—which, in my loathing of the modern world and ardor to discover something nobler and beyond-all noblest, had quite returned to me—now seized, as in a passionate embrace, the opposing channels of my being, and disembouched them both into one stream: a longing for the highest form of love. With this work I penned my death warrant: before the world of modern art, I now could hope no more for life. This I *felt*; but as yet I *knew* it not with full distinctness: that knowledge I was not to gain till later.

Overture to *Tannhäuser*

To begin with, the orchestra leads before us the Pilgrims' Chant alone; it draws near, then swells into a mighty outpour, and finally passes away. Evenfall: last echo of the chant. As night breaks, magic sights and sounds appear: a rosy mist floats up, exultant shouts assail our ear; the whirlings of a fearsomely voluptuous dance are seen. These are the Venusberg's seductive spells, that show themselves at dead of night to those whose breast is fired by daring of the senses.

Attracted by the tempting show, a shapely human form draws nigh: 'tis Tannhäuser, Love's minstrel. He sounds his jubilant Song of Love in joyous challenge, as though to force the wanton witchery to do his bidding. Wild cries of riot answer him: the rosy cloud grows denser round him, entrancing perfumes hem him in and steal away his senses. In the most seductive of half-lights, his wonder-seeing eye beholds a female form indicible; he hears a voice that sweetly murmurs out the siren call, which promises contentment of the darer's wildest wishes. Venus herself it is, this woman who appears to him. Then heart and senses burn within him; a fierce, devouring passion fires the blood in all his veins: with irresistible constraint it thrusts him nearer; before the Goddess' self he steps with that canticle of love triumphant, and now he sings it in ecstatic praise of her.

As though at wizard spell of his, the wonders of the Venus-

berg unroll their brightest fill before him: tumultuous shouts
and savage cries of joy mount up on every hand; in drunken
glee Bacchantes drive their raging dance and drag Tannhäuser
to the warm caresses of Love's Goddess, who throws her
glowing arms around the mortal drowned with bliss, and
bears him where no step dare tread, to the realm of Being-
no-more. A scurry, like the sound of the Wild Hunt, and
speedily the storm is laid. Merely a wanton whir still pulses in
the breeze, a wave of weird voluptuousness, like the sensuous
breath of unblest love, still soughs above the spot where
impious charms had shed their raptures, and over which the
night now broods once more.

But dawn begins to break already: from afar is heard again
the Pilgrims' Chant. As this chant draws closer yet and closer,
as the day drives farther back the night, that whir and sough-
ing of the air—which had erewhile sounded like the eerie cries
of souls condemned—now rises, too, to ever gladder waves;
so that when the sun ascends at last in splendor, and the
Pilgrims' Chant proclaims in ecstasy to all the world, to all
that lives and moves thereon, Salvation won, this wave itself
swells out the tidings of sublimest joy. 'Tis the carol of the
Venusberg itself, redeemed from curse of impiousness, this
cry we hear amid the hymn of God. So wells and leaps each
pulse of life in chorus of redemption; and both dissevered
elements, both soul and senses, God and Nature, unite in the
atoning kiss of hallowed love.

5. Lohengrin. *Its novelty. Elsa and Lohengrin as antithesis, representing the unconscious and the conscious*

I MUST here attest that at the time when I first learned the
story of Lohengrin, in connection with that of Tannhäuser,
the tale indeed affected me, but in no wise prompted me to
store the "stuff" for future working up. Not only because I
was then completely saturated with Tannhäuser, but also because the form in which Lohengrin first stepped before me
made an almost disagreeable impression upon my feeling, did

I not at that time keep a sharper eye upon him. The medieval poem presented Lohengrin in a mystic twilight that filled me with suspicion and that haunting feeling of repugnance with which we look upon the carved and painted saints and martyrs on the highways, or in the churches, of Catholic lands. Only when the immediate impression of this reading had faded, did the shape of Lohengrin rise repeatedly, and with growing power of attraction, before my soul; and this power gathered fresh force to itself from outside, chiefly by reason that I learned to know the myth of Lohengrin in its simpler traits, and alike its deeper meaning, as the genuine poem of the folk, such as it has been laid bare to us by the discoveries of the newer searchers into saga lore. After I had thus seen it as a noble poem of man's yearning and his longing—by no means merely seeded from the Christian's bent toward supernaturalism, but from the truest depths of universal human nature—this figure became ever more endeared to me, and ever stronger grew the urgence to adopt it and thus give utterance to my own internal longing; so that, at the time of completing my *Tannhäuser*, it positively became a dominating need, which thrust back each alien effort to withdraw myself from its despotic mastery.

This Lohengrin is no mere outcome of Christian meditation, but one of man's earliest poetic ideals; just as, for the matter of that, it is a fundamental error of our modern superficialism to consider the specific Christian legends as by any means original creations. Not one of the most affecting, not one of the most distinctive Christian myths belongs by right of generation to the Christian spirit, such as we commonly understand it: it has inherited them all from the purely human intuitions of earlier times, and merely molded them to fit its own peculiar tenets. To purge them of this heterogeneous influence, and thus enable us to look straight into the pure humanity of the eternal poem: such was the task of the more recent inquirer,* a task which it must necessarily remain for the poet to complete.

Just as the main feature of the *mythos* of the Flying Dutchman may be clearly traced to an earlier setting in the Hellenic Odyssey; just as this same Ulysses in his wrench from the arms of Calypso, in his flight from the charms of Circe, and in his yearning for the earthly wife of cherished home, em-

* The allusion is probably to Ludwig Feuerbach's *Essence of Christianity.*—Tr.

bodied the Hellenic prototype of a longing such as we find in Tannhäuser, immeasurably enhanced and widened in its meaning: so do we already meet in the Grecian *mythos*—nor is even this by any means its oldest form—the outlines of the myth of Lohengrin. Who does not know the story of Zeus and Semele? The god loves a mortal woman, and for sake of this love, approaches her in human shape; but the mortal learns that she does not know her lover in his true estate, and, urged by love's own ardor, demands that her spouse shall show himself to physical sense in the full substance of his being. Zeus knows that she can never grasp him, that the unveiling of his godhead must destroy her; himself, he suffers by this knowledge, beneath the stern compulsion to fulfill his loved one's dreaded wish: he signs his own death warrant, when the fatal splendor of his godlike presence strikes Semele dead.

Was it, forsooth, some priestly fraud that shaped this myth? How insensate, to attempt to argue from the selfish state-religious, caste-like exploitation of the noblest human longing, back to the origin and the genuine meaning of ideals which blossomed from a human fancy that stamped man first as man! 'Twas no *god*, that sang the meeting of Zeus and Semele; but *man*, in his humanest of yearnings. Who had taught man that a god could burn with love toward earthly woman? For certain, only man himself, who, however high the object of his yearning may soar above the limits of his earthly wont, can stamp it with the imprint of his human nature. From the highest sphere to which the might of his desire may bear him up, he finally can only long again for what is purely human, can only crave the taste of his own nature, as the one thing worth desiring.

What then is the inmost essence of this human nature, whereto the desire which reaches forth to farthest distance turns back at last, for its only possible appeasement? It is the *necessity of love*; and the essence of this love, in its truest utterance, is the *longing for utmost physical reality*, for fruition in an object that can be grasped by all the senses, held fast with all the force of actual being. In this finite, physically sure embrace, must not the god dissolve and disappear? Is not the mortal, who had yearned for God, undone, annulled? Yet is not love, in its truest, highest essence, herein revealed? Marvel, ye erudite critics, at the omnipotence of human minstrelsy, unfolded in the simple *mythos of the folk*! Things that all your understanding can not so much as comprehend are there laid bare to human feeling, with such a physically perfect surety as no other means could bring to pass.

The ethereal sphere, from which the god is yearning to descend to men, had stretched itself, through Christian longing, to inconceivable bounds of space. To the Hellenes, it was still the cloud-locked realm of thunder and the thunder-bolt, from which the lusty Zeus moved down, to mix with men in expert likeness: to the Christian, the blue firmament dissolved into an infinite sea of yearning ecstasy, in which the forms of all the gods were melted, until at last it was the lonely image of his own person, the yearning Man, that alone was left to greet him from the ocean of his fantasy. One primal, manifold-repeated trait runs through the sagas of those peoples who dwelt beside the sea or sea-embouching rivers: upon the blue mirror of the waters there draws nigh an unknown being, of utmost grace and purest virtue, who moves and wins all hearts by charm resistless; he is the embodied wish of the yearner who dreams of happiness in that far-off land he can not sense. This unknown being vanishes across the ocean's waves, so soon as ever questioned on his nature. Thus—so goes the story—there once came in a swan-drawn skiff, over the sea to the banks of the Scheldt, an unknown hero: there he rescued downtrod innocence, and wedded a sweet maiden; but since she asked him who he was and whence he came, he needs must seek the sea once more and leave his all behind.

Why this saga, when I learned it in its simplest outlines, so irresistibly attracted me that, at the very time when I had but just completed *Tannhäuser*, I could concern myself with naught but it, was to be made clearer to my feeling by the immediately succeeding incidents of my life.

6. Siegfried. *Turning point in Wagner's artistic development. Abandons history for myth*

EVEN during the musical composition of *Lohengrin*, midst which I had always felt as though resting by an oasis in the desert, two subjects had usurped my poetic fancy: they were Siegfried and Frederic Barbarossa.

Once again, and that the last time, did Myth and History stand before me with opposing claims; this while, as good as forcing me to decide whether it was a musical drama, or a spoken play, that I had to write. A closer narration of the conflict that lay behind this question, I have purposely reserved until this stage, because it was *here* first that I arrived at its definite answer, and thus at a full consciousness of its true nature.

Since my return to Germany from Paris, my favorite study had been that of ancient German lore. I have already dwelt on the deep longing for my native home that filled me then. This home, however, in its actual reality, could nowise satisfy my longing; thus I felt that a deeper instinct lay behind my impulse, and one that needs must have its source in some yearning other than merely that for the modern homeland. As though to get down to its root, I sank myself into the primal element of home, that meets us in the legends of a past which attracts us the more warmly as the present repels us with its hostile chill. To all our wishes and warm impulses, which in truth transport us to the future, we seek to give a physical token by means of pictures from the past, and thus to win for them a form the modern present never can provide.

In the struggle to give the wishes of my heart artistic shape, and in the ardor to discover what thing it was that drew me so resistlessly to the primal source of old home sagas, I drove step by step into the deeper regions of antiquity, where at last to my delight, and truly in the utmost reaches of old time, I was to light upon the fair young form of *man*, in all the freshness of his force. My studies thus bore me, through the legends of the Middle Ages, right down to their foundation in the old Germanic *mythos*; one swathing after another, which the later legendary lore had bound around it, I was able to unloose, and thus at last to gaze upon it in its chastest beauty. What here I saw, was no longer the figure of conventional history, whose garment claims our interest more than does the actual shape inside; but the real naked man, in whom I might spy each throbbing of his pulses, each stir within his mighty muscles, in uncramped, freest motion: the type of the true *human being*.

At like time I had sought this human being in history too. Here offered themselves relations, and nothing but relations; the human being I could see only in so far as the relations ordered him: and not as he had power to order *them*. To get to the bottom of these "relations," whose coercive force compelled the strongest man to squander all his powers on objectless and never-compassed aims, I turned afresh to the soil of Greek antiquity, and here, again, was pointed at the last to *mythos*, in which alone I could touch the ground of even these relations: but in that *mythos*, these social relations were drawn in lines as simple, plastic, and distinct as I had earlier recognized therein the human shape itself. From this side, also, did *mythos* lead me to this man alone, as to the involuntary *creator* of those relations, which, in their documento-monumental perversion, as the excrescences of history, as traditional fictions and established rights, have at last usurped dominion over man and ground to dust his freedom.

Although the splendid type of Siegfried had long attracted me, it first enthralled my every thought when I had come to see it in its purest human shape, set free from every later wrappage. Now for the first time, also, did I recognize the possibility of making him the hero of a drama; a possibility that had not occurred to me while I knew him only from the medieval *Nibelungenlied*. But at like time with him, had Friedrich I loomed on me from the study of our history: he appeared to me, just as he had appeared to the saga-framing German folk, a historical rebirth of the old pagan Siegfried.

When the wave of political commotion broke lately in upon us, and proclaimed itself at first, in Germany, as a longing for national unity, it could not but seem to me that Friedrich I would lie nearer to the folk, and be more readily understood, than the downright human Siegfried. Already I had sketched the plan for a drama in five acts, which should depict this Friedrich's life, from the Roncolian Diet down to his entry on the Crusade. But ever and again I turned in discontentment from my plan. It was no mere desire to mirror detached historical events that had prompted my sketch, but the wish to show a wide connexus of relations in such a fashion that its unity might be embraced in easy survey, and understood at once.

In order to make plainly understandable both my hero and the relations that with giant force he strives to master, only to be at last subdued by them, I should have felt compelled to adopt the method of *mythos*, in the very teeth of the historic material: the vast mass of incidents and intricate associations, whereof no single link could be omitted if the connection of the whole was to be intelligibly set before the eye, was adapted neither to the form nor to the spirit of drama. Had I chosen to comply with the imperative demands of history, then had my drama become an unsurveyable conglomerate of pictured incidents, entirely crowding out from view the real and only thing I wished to show; and thus, as artist, I should have met precisely the same fate in my drama as did its hero: to wit, I should myself have been crushed by the weight of the very relations that I fain would master—that is, portray—without ever having brought my purpose to an understanding; just as Friedrich could not bring his will to carrying out. To attain my purpose, I should therefore have had to reduce this mass of relations by *free* construction, and should have fallen into a treatment that would have absolutely violated history. Yet I could not but see the contradiction involved herein; for it was the main characteristic of Friedrich, in my eyes, that he should be a *historical* hero. If, on the other hand, I wished to dabble in mythical construction, then, for its ultimate and highest form, but quite beyond the modern poet's reach, I must go back to the unadulterated *mythos*, which up to now the folk alone has hymned, and which I had already found in full perfection —in the "Siegfried."

7. *Breaks with operatic conventions*

WHEN I knowingly and willingly gave up the "Friedrich," in which I had approached the closest to that political life, and —by so much the clearer as to what I wished—gave preference to the "Siegfried," I entered a new and most decisive period of my evolution, both as artist and as man: the period of *conscious artistic will* to continue on an altogether novel path, which I had struck with unconscious necessity, and whereon I now, as man and artist, press on to meet a newer world.

I have here described the influence that my possession with the spirit of Music exerted on the choice of my poetic stuffs, and therewith on their poetic fashioning. I have next to show the reaction that my poetic procedure, thus influenced, exercised in turn upon my musical expression and its form. This reaction manifested itself chiefly in two departments: in the *dramatic musical form* in general, and in the *melody* in particular.

Seeing that, onward from the said turning point of my artistic course, I was once for all determined by *the stuff*, and by that stuff as seen with the eye of Music, so in its fashioning I must necessarily pass forward to a gradual but complete upheaval of the traditional *operatic form*. This opera form was never, of its very nature, a form embracing the whole drama, but the rather an arbitrary conglomerate of separate smaller forms of song, whose fortuitous concatenation of arias, duos, trios, and so on, with choruses and so-called ensemble pieces, made out the actual edifice of opera. In the poetic fashioning of my stuffs, it was henceforth impossible for me to contemplate a filling of these ready-molded forms, but solely a bringing of the drama's broader object to the cognizance of the feeling.

In the whole course of the drama I saw no possibility of division or demarcation, other than the acts in which the place or time, or the scenes in which the dramatis personae change. Moreover, the plastic unity of the mythic stuff brought with it this advantage, that, in the arrangement of my scenes, all those minor details, which the modern playwright finds so indispensable for the elucidation of involved historical occurrences, were quite unnecessary, and the whole strength of the portrayal could be concentrated upon a few weighty and decisive moments of development. Upon the working out of these fewer scenes, in each of which a decisive mood was to be given its full play, I might linger with an exhaustiveness already reckoned for in the original draft; I was not compelled to make shift with mere suggestions, and—for sake of the outward economy—to hasten on from one suggestion to another; but with needful repose I could display the simple object in the very last connections required to bring it clearly home to the dramatic understanding.

Through this natural attribute of the stuff, I was not in the least coerced to strain the planning of my scenes into any preconceived conformity with given musical forms, since they dictated of themselves their mode of musical completion. In the ever surer feeling hereof, it thus could no more occur to me to rack with willful outward canons the musical form that sprang self-bidden from the very nature of these scenes, to break its natural mold by violent grafting in of conventional slips of operatic song. Thus I by no means set out with the fixed purpose of a deliberate iconoclast to destroy, forsooth, the prevailing operatic forms, of aria, duet, and so on; but the omission of these forms followed from the very nature of the stuff, with whose intelligible presentment to the feeling through an adequate vehicle, I had alone to do.

A mechanical reflex of those traditional forms still influenced me so much in my *Flying Dutchman*, that any attentive investigator will recognize how often there it governed even the arrangement of my scenes; and only gradually, in *Tannhäuser*, and yet more decisively in *Lohengrin*—accordingly, with a more and more practiced knowledge of the nature of my stuff and the means necessary for its presentment—did I extricate myself from that form-al influence, and more and more definitely rule the form of portrayal by the requirements and peculiarities of the stuff and situation.

8. Growing inwardness of his art, concluding with Tristan, *where only "inner movements of the soul" are depicted*

WITH *The Flying Dutchman* and all my following sketches I once for all forsook the realm of *history*, even in my choice of stuff, for that of *legend*. I may here dispense with pointing out to you the inner tendencies which guided that decision, and lay stress upon the influence exerted by this choice of stuff on the molding of the poetic and, in particular, the musical form.

All that detailed description and exhibition of the historico-conventional which is requisite for making us clearly understand the events of a given, remote historical epoch, and which the historical novelist or dramatist of our times has therefore to set forth at such exhaustive length—all this I could pass over. And thus not only for the poem, but in particular for the music, there was removed any compulsion to adopt a mode of treatment quite foreign to them, and above all quite impossible to music. The legend, in whatever age or nation it occurs, has the merit of seizing nothing but the purely human content of that age and nation, and of giving forth that content in a form peculiar to itself, of sharpest outline, and therefore swiftly understandable. A ballad, a refrain of the folk, suffices to acquaint us with this telling character in the twinkling of an eye. This legendary coloring, for the display of a purely human event, has in particular the real advantage of uncommonly facilitating the task I assigned to the poet above, the task of silencing the question "Why?" Just as through the characteristic scene, so also through the legendary tone, the mind is forthwith placed in that dream-like state wherein it presently shall come to full clairvoyance, and thus perceive a new coherence in the world's phenomena; a coherence it could not detect with the waking eye of every-day, wherefore it had ever asked about the why as though to conquer its abashedness in presence of the world's incompre-hensible, of that world which now becomes to it so clear and vividly intelligible. How music is at last fully to round this quickening spell, you now will lightly comprehend.

But even for the poet's manipulation of the stuff, its legendary character affords the essential advantage that whereas the simple sequence of the plot, so easily surveyable in all its outward bearings, renders it needless to linger by any outer explanation of its course, on the other hand the poem's far largest space can be devoted to exhibiting the inner springs of action, those inner soul motives which are finally and alone to stamp the action as a "necessary" one—and that through the sympathetic interest taken in those motives by our own inmost hearts.

In looking through my poems now placed before you, you will readily notice that I but very gradually grew conscious of the advantage just referred to, and but gradually learned to profit by it. Even the outward *volumen*, increasing with each poem, will afford you evidence of this. You will soon perceive that my initial bias against giving the poem a broader reach sprang chiefly from my keeping at first too much in eye the traditional form of opera music, which had hitherto made a poem impossible that did not allow of numberless word repetitions. In *The Flying Dutchman* my only care, in general, was to keep the plot to its simplest features, to ex-clude all useless detail such as the intrigues one borrows from common life, and in return to develop more fully those traits which were to set in its proper light the characteristic coloring of the legendary stuff, since here they seemed to me to altogether coincide with the idiosyncrasy of the inner motives of action; and to do this in such a way, that that color itself should be turned into action.

You perhaps will find the plot of *Tannhäuser* already far more markedly evolving from its inner motives. Here the decisive catastrophe proceeds without the least constraint from a lyric tournament of bards, in which no other power save the most hidden inner workings of the soul drives onward the decisive blow, and in such a manner that even this denouement's *form* belongs purely to the lyric element.

The whole interest of *Lohengrin* consists in an inner working within the heart of Elsa, involving every secret of the soul: the endurance of a spell of wondrous power for blessing, that fills her whole surrounding with the most persuasive sense of truth, hangs solely on her refraining from the question as to its *whence*. Like a cry from the inmost want of woman's heart, this question struggles loose—and the spell has vanished. You may guess how singularly this tragic "Whence?" concurs with that aforesaid theoretic "why?"

I too, as I have told you, felt driven to this "Whence and wherefore?" and for long it banned me from the magic of my art. But my time of penance taught me to overcome the question. All doubt at last was taken from me, when I gave myself up to the *Tristan*. Here, in perfect trustfulness, I plunged into the inner depths of soul events, and from out this inmost center of the world I fearlessly built up its outer form. A glance at the *volumen* of this poem will show you at once that the exhaustive detail-work which a historical poet is obliged to devote to clearing up the outward bearings of his plot, to the detriment of a lucid exposition of its inner motives, I now trusted myself to apply to these latter alone. Life and death, the whole import and existence of the outer world, here hang on nothing but the inner movements of the soul. The whole affecting action comes about for reason only that the inmost soul demands it, and steps to light with the very shape foretokened in the inner shrine.

Perhaps in the execution of this poem much will strike you as going too far into subtle (*intime*) detail; and even should you concede this tendency as permissible to the poet, you yet might wonder how he could dare hand over to the musician all this refinement of minutiae, for carrying out. In this you would be possessed by the same bias as led myself, when drafting *The Flying Dutchman*, to give its poem nothing but the most general of contours, destined merely to play into the hands of an absolute-musical working out. But in this regard let me at once make one reply to you: whereas the verses were there intended as an underlay for operatic melody, to be stretched to the length demanded by that melody through countless repetitions of words and phrases, in the musical setting of *Tristan* not a trace of word repetition is any longer found, but the weft of words and verses foreordains the whole dimensions of the melody, that is, the structure of that melody is already erected by the *poet*.

9. Spiritual crisis: Schopenhauer; the longing for death. Letter to Franz Liszt, December 16, 1854.

DEAR FRANZ,

I begin to find out more and more that you are in reality a great philosopher, while I appear to myself a harebrained fellow. Apart from slowly progressing with my music, I have of late occupied myself exclusively with a man who has come like a gift from heaven, although only a literary one, into my solitude. This is Arthur Schopenhauer, the greatest philosopher since Kant, whose thoughts, as he himself expresses it, he has thought out to the end. The German professors ignored him very prudently for forty years; but recently, to the disgrace of Germany, he has been discovered by an English critic. All the Hegels, etc., are charlatans by the side of him. His chief idea, the final negation of the desire of life, is terribly serious, but it shows the only salvation possible. To me of course that thought was not new, and it can indeed be conceived by no one in whom it did not pre-exist, but this philosopher was the first to place it clearly before me. If I think of the storm of my heart, the terrible tenacity with which, against my desire, it used to cling to the hope of life, and if even now I feel this hurricane within me, I have at least found a quietus which in wakeful nights helps me to sleep. This is the genuine, ardent longing for death, for absolute unconsciousness, total non-existence. Freedom from all dreams is our only final salvation.

In this I have discovered a curious coincidence with your thoughts; and although you express them differently, being religious, I know that you mean exactly the same thing. How profound you are! In your article about the *Dutchman* you

have struck me with the force of lightning. While I read
Schopenhauer I was with you, only you did not know it. In
this manner I ripen more and more. I play with art only to
pass the time. In what manner I try to amuse myself you will
see from the enclosed sheet.

For the sake of that most beautiful of my life dreams
Young Siegfried, I shall have to finish the *Nibelungen* pieces
after all; the *Valkyrie* has taken so much out of me that I
must indulge in this pleasure; I have got as far as the second
half of the last act. The whole will not be finished till 1856;
and in 1858, the tenth year of my Hegira, the performance
may take place, if at all. As I have never in life felt the real
bliss of love, I must erect a monument to the most beautiful
of all my dreams, in which, from beginning to end, that love
shall be thoroughly satiated. I have in my head *Tristan and
Isolde*, the simplest but most full-blooded musical conception;
with the "black flag" which floats at the end of it I shall cover
myself to die.

10. *Prelude to* Tristan *und* Isolde

AN old, old tale, exhaustless in its variations, and ever sung
anew in all the languages of medieval Europe, tells us of
Tristan and Isolde. For his king the trusty vassal had wooed
a maid he durst not tell himself he loved, Isolde; as his master's bride she followed him, for, powerless, she needs must do
the wooer's bidding. Love's goddess, jealous of her downtrod
rights, avenged herself: the love drink destined by the careful
mother for the partners in this merely political marriage, in
accordance with the customs of the age, the goddess foists on
the youthful pair through a blunder diversely accounted for;
fired by its draught, their love leaps suddenly to vivid flame,
and each avows to each that they belong to none save each
other. Henceforth no end to the yearning, longing, bliss, and
misery of love: world, power, fame, splendor, honor, knighthood, loyalty, and friendship, all scattered like a baseless
dream; one thing alone left living: desire, desire unquenchable,
longing forever rebearing itself—a fevered craving; one sole

redemption—death, surcease of being, the sleep that knows no waking!

Here, in music's own most unrestricted element, the musician who chose this theme as introduction to his love drama could have but one care: how to restrain himself, since exhaustion of the theme is quite impossible. So in one long breath he let that unslaked longing swell from first avowal of the gentlest tremor of attraction, through half-heaved sighs, through hopes and fears, laments and wishes, joy and torment, to the mightiest onset, most resolute attempt to find the breach unbarring to the heart a path into the sea of endless love's delight. In vain! Its power spent, the heart sinks back to pine of its desire—desire without attainment; for each fruition sows the seeds of fresh desire, till in its final lassitude the breaking eye beholds a glimmer of the highest bliss: it is the bliss of quitting life, of being no more, of last redemption into that wondrous realm from which we stray the furthest when we strive to enter it by fiercest force. Shall we call it death? Or is it not night's wonder world, whence—as the story says—an ivy and a vine sprang up in locked embrace o'er Tristan and Isolde's grave?

11. Negation of the will; Dante; Buddhism. Letter to Franz Liszt, June 7, 1855

A *Divina Commedia* it is to be? That is a splendid idea, and I enjoy the music in anticipation. But I must have a little talk with you about it. That *Hell* and *Purgatory* will succeed I do not call into question for a moment, but as to *Paradise* I have some doubts, which you confirm by saying that your plan includes choruses. In the Ninth Symphony the last choral movement is decidedly the weakest part, although it is historically important, because it discloses to us in a very naïve manner the difficulties of a real musician who does not know how (after hell and purgatory) he is to represent paradise. About this paradise, dearest Franz, there is in reality a considerable difficulty, and he who confirms this opinion is, curiously enough, Dante himself, the singer of Paradise, which in his

Divine Comedy also is decidedly the weakest part. I have followed Dante with deepest sympathy through the *Inferno* and
the *Purgatorio*; and when I 'emerged from the infernal slough,
I washed myself, as does the poet, with the water of the sea at
the foot of the Mountain of Purgatory. I enjoyed the divine
morning, the pure air. I rose step by step, deadened one passion after the other, battled with the wild instinct of life, till at
last, arrived at the fire, I relinquished all desire of life, and
threw myself into the glow in order to sink my personality in
the contemplation of Beatrice. But from this final liberation I
was rudely awakened to be again, after all, what I had been
before, and this was done in order to confirm the Catholic
doctrine of a God Who, for His own glorification, had created
this hell of my existence, by the most elaborate sophisms and
most childish inventions, quite unworthy of a great mind. This
problematic proof I rejected from the bottom of my soul, and
remained dissatisfied accordingly. In order to be just to Dante
I had, as in the case of Beethoven, to occupy the historic
standpoint; I had to place myself in Dante's time and consider
the real object of his poem, which, no doubt, was intended to
advocate a certain thing with his contemporaries—I mean the
reform of the Church. I had to confess that in this sense he
understood marvelously well his advantage of expressing himself in an infallible manner through means of popular and
generally accepted ideas. Before all, I cordially agreed with
him in his praise of the saints who had chosen poverty of their
own free will. I had further to admire even in those sophisms
his high poetic imagination and power of representation, just
as I admire Beethoven's musical art in the last movement of
his Ninth Symphony. I had further to acknowledge, with
deepest and most sublime emotion, the wonderful inspiration
through means of which the beloved of his youth, Beatrice,
takes the form in which he conceives the Divine doctrine; and
in so far as that doctrine teaches the purification of personal
egoism through love, I joyfully acknowledge the doctrine of
Beatrice. But the fact that Beatrice stands, as it were, on the
chariot of the Church, that, instead of pure, simple doctrine,
she preaches keen-witted ecclesiastic scholasticism, made her
appear to me in a colder light, although the poet assures us
that she shines and glows for ever. At last she became indifferent to me; and although as a mere reader I acknowledge
that Dante has acted appropriately, in accordance with his
time and his purpose, I should as a sympathetic co-poet have
wished to lose my personal consciousness, and indeed all con-

sciousness, in that fire. In that manner I should, no doubt, have fared better than even in the company of the Catholic Deity, although Dante represents it with the same art with which you, no doubt, will endeavor to celebrate it in your choruses. I faithfully record to you the impression which the *Divine Comedy* has made upon me, and which in the *Paradise* becomes to my mind a "divine comedy" in the literal sense of the word, in which I do not care to take part, either as a comedian or as a spectator.

The misleading problem in these questions is always how to introduce into this terrible world, with an empty nothing beyond it, a God Who converts the enormous sufferings of existence into something fictitious, so that the hoped-for salvation remains the only real and consciously enjoyable thing. This will do very well for the Philistine, especially the English Philistine. He makes very good terms with his God, entering into a contract by which, after having carried out certain points agreed upon, he is finally admitted to eternal bliss as a compensation for various failures in this world. But what have we in common with these notions of the mob?

You once expressed your view of human nature to the effect that man is "une intelligence, servie par des organes." If that were so, it would be a bad thing for the large majority of men, who have only "organs," but as good as no "intelligence," at least in your sense. To me the matter appears in a different light, viz.,—

Man, like every other animal, embodies the "will of life," for which he fashions his organs according to his wants; and amongst these organs he also develops intellect, *i.e.,* the organ of conceiving external things for the purpose of satisfying the desire of life to the best of his power. A *normal* man is therefore he who possesses this organ, communicating with the external world (whose function is perception, just as that of the stomach is digestion) in a degree exactly sufficient for the satisfaction of the vital instinct by external means. That vital instinct in *normal* man consists in exactly the same as does the vital instinct of the lowest animal, namely, in the desire of nourishment and of propagation. For this "will of life," this metaphysical first cause of all existence, desires nothing but to live—that is, to nourish and eternally reproduce itself—and this tendency can be seen identically in the coarse stone, in the tenderer plant, and so forth up to the human animal. Only the organs are different, of which the will must avail itself in the higher stages of its objective existence, in order to satisfy its more complicated, and therefore more disputed and less easily obtainable, wants. By gaining this insight, which is confirmed by the enormous progress of modern science, we understand at once the characteristic feature of the life of the vast majority of men, and are no longer astonished because they appear to us simply as animals; for this is the *normal* essence of man. A very large portion of mankind remains *below* this *normal* stage, for in them the complicated organ of perception is not developed even up to the capability of satisfying normal wants; but, on the other hand, although of course very rarely, there are *abnormal* natures in which the ordinary measure of the organ of perception—that is, the brain—is exceeded, just as nature frequently forms monstrosities in which *one organ* is developed at the expense of the others. Such a monstrosity, if it reaches the highest degree, is called *genius*, which at bottom is caused only by an abnormally rich and powerful brain. This organ of perception, which originally and in normal cases looks outward for the purpose of satisfying the wants of the will of life, receives in the case of an abnormal development such vivid and such striking impressions from outside that for a time it emancipates itself from the service of the will, which originally had fashioned it for its own ends. It thus attains to a "will-less"—*i.e.*, aesthetic—contemplation of the world; and these external objects, contemplated *apart from the will*, are exactly the ideal images which the *artist* in a manner fixes and reproduces. The sympathy with the external world which is inherent in this contemplation is developed in powerful natures to a permanent forgetfulness of the original personal will, that is to a *sympathy* with external things for their own sake, and no longer in connection with any personal interest.

The question then arises what we see in this abnormal state, and whether our sympathy takes the form of *common joy* or *common sorrow*. This question the true *men of genius* and the true *saints* of all times have answered in the sense that they have seen nothing but *sorrow* and felt nothing but *common sorrow*. For they recognized the *normal* state of all living things and the terrible, always self-contradictory, always self-devouring and blindly egotistic, nature of the "will of life" which is common to all living things. The horrible cruelty of this will, which in sexual love aims only at its own reproduction, appeared in them for the first time reflected in the organ of perception, which in its normal state had felt its subjection to the will to which it owed its existence. In this manner the organ of perception was placed in an abnormal sympathetic condition. It endeavored to free itself permanently and finally from its disgraceful serfdom, and this it at last achieved in the perfect negation of the "will of life."

This act of the "negation of will" is the true characteristic of the saint, which finds its last completion in the absolute cessation of personal consciousness; and all consciousness must be personal and individual. But the saints of Christianity, simple-minded and enveloped in the Jewish dogma as they were, could not see this, and their limited imagination looked upon that much-desired stage as the eternal continuation of a life, freed from nature. Our judgment of the moral import of their resignation must not be influenced by this circumstance, for in reality they also longed for the cessation of their individual personality, *i.e.*, of their existence. But this deep longing is expressed more purely and more significantly in the most sacred and oldest religion of the human race, the doctrine of the Brahmins, and especially in its final transfiguration and highest perfection, Buddhism. This also expounds the myth of a creation of the world by God, but it does not celebrate this act as a boon, but calls it a sin of Brahma which he, *after having embodied himself in this world,* must atone for by the infinite sufferings of this very world. He finds his salvation in the saints who, by perfect negation of the "will of life," by the sympathy with all suffering which alone fills their heart, enter the state of Nirwana, *i.e.*, "the land of being no longer." Such a saint was Buddha. According to his doctrine of the migration of souls every man is born again in the form of that creature on which he had inflicted pain, however pure his life might otherwise have been. He himself must now know this pain, and his sorrowful migration does not cease, until during an entire course of his new-born life he has inflicted pain on no creature, but has denied his own will of life in the sympathy with other beings. How sublime, how satisfying is this doctrine compared with the Judaeo-Christian doctrine, according to which a man (for, of course, the suffering *animal* exists for the benefit of man alone) has only to be obedient to the Church during this short life to be made comfortable for all eternity, while he who has been disobedient in this short life will be tortured for ever. Let us admit that Christianity is to us this contradictory phenomenon, because we know it only in its mixture with, and distortion by, narrow-hearted Judàism, while modern research has succeeded in showing that pure and unalloyed Christianity was nothing but a branch of that venerable Buddhism which, after Alexander's Indian expedition, spread to the shores of the Mediterranean. In early Christianity we still see distinct traces of the perfect negation of the "will of life," of the longing for the destruction of the world, *i.e.,* the cessation of all existence. The pity is that this deeper insight into the essence of things can be gained alone by the abnormally organized men previously referred to, and that they only can fully grasp it. In order to communicate this insight to others, the sublime founders of religion have therefore to speak in images, such as are accessible to the common normal perception. In this process much must be disfigured, although Buddha's doctrine of the migration of souls expresses the truth with almost perfect precision. The normal vulgarity of man and the license of general egoism further distort the image until it becomes a caricature. And I pity the poet who undertakes to restore the original image from this caricature. It seems to me that Dante, especially in the *Paradise,* has not succeeded in this; and in his explanation of the Divine natures he appears, to me at least, frequently like a childish Jesuit. But perhaps you, dear friend, will succeed better, and as you are going to paint a *tone* picture I might almost predict your success, for music is essentially the artistic, original image of the world. For the initiated no error is here possible. Only about the *Paradise,* and especially about the choruses, I feel some friendly anxiety. You will not expect me to add less important things to this important matter.

12. Overthrow of humanistic values; changes in The Ring. Letter to August Röckel, August 23, 1856

THE period which I have worked in obedience to my intuitions dates from *The Flying Dutchman. Tannhäuser* and *Lohengrin* followed, and if there is any expression of an underlying poetic motive in these works, it is to be sought in the sublime tragedy of renunciation, the negation of the will, which here appears as necessary and inevitable, and alone capable of working redemption. It was this deep underlying idea that gave to my poetry and my music that peculiar consecration, without which they would not have had that power to move profoundly which they have. Now, the strange thing is that in all my intellectual ideas on life, and in all the conceptions at which I had arrived in the course of my struggles to understand the world with my conscious reason, I was working in direct opposition to the intuitive ideas expressed in these works. While, as an artist, I *felt* with such convincing certainty that all my creations took their coloring from my feelings, as a philosopher I sought to discover a totally opposed interpretation of the world; and this interpretation once discovered, I obstinately held to it, though, to my own surprise, I found that it had invariably to go to the wall when confronted by my spontaneous and purely objective artistic intuitions. I made my most remarkable discovery in this respect with my Nibelung drama. It had taken form at a time when, with my ideas, I had built up an optimistic world, on Hellenic principles; believing that in order to realize such a world, it was only necessary for man to wish it. I ingeniously set aside the problem, why they did not wish it. I remember that it was with this definite creative purpose that I conceived the personality of Siegfried, with the intention of representing an existence free from pain. But I meant in the presentment of the whole Nibelung myth to express my meaning even more clearly, by showing how from the first wrongdoing a whole world of evil arose, and consequently fell to pieces in order to teach us the lesson that we must recognize evil and tear it up by the roots, and raise in its stead a righteous world. I was scarcely aware that in the working out, nay, in the first elaboration of my scheme, I was being unconsciously guided by a wholly different, infinitely more profound intuition, and that instead of conceiving a phase in the development of the world, I had grasped the very essence and meaning of the world itself in all its possible phases, and had realized its nothingness; the consequence of which was, that as I was true to my living intuitions and not to my abstract ideas in my completed work, something quite different saw the light from what I had originally intended. But I remember that once, toward the end, I decided to bring out my original purpose, cost what it might, namely, in Brünnhilde's final somewhat artificially colored invocation to those around her, in which, having pointed out the evils of possession, she declares that in love alone is blessedness to be found, without (unfortunately) making quite clear what the nature of that love is, which in the development of the myth we find playing the part of destructive genius.

To this extent was I led astray in this one passage by the interposition of my intellectual intention. Strangely enough, I was always in despair over this said passage, and it required the complete subversion of my intellectual conceptions brought about by Schopenhauer, to discover to me the reason of my dissatisfaction, and to supply me with the only adequate keystone to my poem* in keeping with the idea of the drama, which consists in a simple and sincere recognition of the true relations of things and complete abstinence from the attempt to preach any particular doctrine.

13. *Relation of* Tristan *to* The Ring

WITH the sketch of *Tristan und Isolde* I felt that I was really not quitting the mythic circle opened out to me by my Nibelungen labors. For the grand concordance of all sterling myths, as thrust upon me by my studies, had sharpened my eyesight for the wondrous variations standing out amid this harmony. Such a one confronted me with fascinating clearness in the relation of Tristan to Isolde, as compared with that of Siegfried to Brünnhilde.

Just as in languages the transmutation of a single sound forms two apparently quite diverse words from one and the same original, so here, by a similar transmutation or shifting of the time motif, two seemingly unlike relations had sprung from the one original mythic factor. Their intrinsic parity consists in this: both Tristan and Siegfried, in bondage to an illusion which makes this deed of theirs unfree, woo for another their own eternally predestined brides, and in the false relation hence arising find their doom. Whereas the poet of *Siegfried,* however, before all else abiding by the grand coherence of the whole Nibelungen myth, could only take in eye the hero's downfall through the vengeance of the wife who at like time

* This new version of the final verses of *Götterdämmerung* was later canceled as the first had been; the poem was allowed to finish without any trace of moral reflection and doctrine.—TR.

offers up herself and him: the poet of *Tristan* finds his staple matter in setting forth the love pangs to which the pair of lovers, awakened to their true relation, have fallen victims till their death. Merely the thing is here more fully, clearly treated, which even there was spoken out beyond mistake: death through stress of love—an idea which finds expression in Brünnhilde, for her part conscious of the true relation. What in the one work could come to rapid utterance only at the climax, in the other becomes an entire content, of infinite variety; and this it was that attracted me to treat the stuff at just that time, namely, as a supplementary act of the great Nibelungen myth, a *mythos* compassing the whole relations of a world.

14. Nibelungen myth considered as a "sketch for a drama," Summer 1848*

FROM the womb of night and death was spawned a race that dwells in Nibelheim (Nebelheim), that is, in gloomy subterranean clefts and caverns: Nibelungen are they called; with restless nimbleness they burrow through the bowels of the earth, like worms in a dead body; they smelt and smith hard metals. The pure and noble Rhinegold Alberich seized, divorced it from the waters' depth, and wrought therefrom with cunning art a Ring that lent him rulership of all his race, the Nibelungen: so he became their master, forced them to work for him alone, and amassed the priceless Nibelungen Hoard, whose greatest treasure is the Tarnhelm, conferring power to take on any shape at will, a work that Alberich compelled his own brother Reigin (Mime = Eugel) to weld for him. Thus armored, Alberich made for mastery of the world and all that it contains.

The race of giants, boastful, violent, ur-begotten, is troubled in its savage ease: their monstrous strength, their simple mother wit, no longer are a match for Alberich's crafty plans

---

* The composition and revision of the four *Ring* poems was not completed until December 1852; therefore this early sketch is not to be considered Wagner's final conception.—EDS.

of conquest: alarmed they see the Nibelungen forging wondrous weapons that one day in the hands of human heroes
shall cause the giants' downfall. This strife is taken advantage
of by the race of gods, now waxing to supremacy. Wotan bar-
gains with the giants to build the gods a burg from whence to
rule the world in peace and order; their building finished, the
giants ask the Nibelungen Hoard in payment. The utmost cunning of the gods succeeds in trapping Alberich; he must ransom his life with the Hoard; the Ring alone he strives to keep.
The gods, well knowing that in it resides the secret of all
Alberich's power, extort from him the Ring as well: then he
curses it; it shall be the ruin of all who possess it. Wotan
delivers the Hoard to the giants, but means to keep the Ring
as warrant of his sovereignty: the giants defy him, and Wotan
yields to the counsel of the three Fates (Norns), who warn
him of the downfall of the gods themselves.

Now the giants have the Hoard and Ring safe kept by a
monstrous Worm in the Gnita- (Neid-) Haide [the Grove of
Grudge]. Through the Ring the Nibelungs remain in thralldom, Alberich and all. But the giants do not understand to use
their might; their dullard minds are satisfied with having
bound the Nibelungen. So the Worm lies on the Hoard since
untold ages, in inert dreadfulness: before the luster of the new
race of gods the giants' race fades down and stiffens into impotence; wretched and tricksy, the Nibelungen go their way of
fruitless labor. Alberich broods without cease on the means of
gaining back the Ring.

In high emprise the gods have planned the world, bound
down the elements by prudent laws, and devoted themselves
to most careful nurture of the human race. Their strength
stands over all. Yet the peace by which they have arrived at
mastery does not repose on reconcilement: by violence and
cunning was it wrought. The object of their higher ordering of
the world is moral consciousness: but the wrong they fight
attaches to themselves. From the depths of Nibelheim the conscience of their guilt cries up to them: for the bondage of the
Nibelungen is not broken; merely the lordship has been reft
from Alberich, and not for any higher end; but the soul, the
freedom of the Nibelungen lies buried uselessly beneath the
belly of an idle Worm: Alberich thus has justice in his plaints
against the gods.

Wotan himself, however, cannot undo the wrong without
committing yet another: only a free will, independent of the
gods themselves, and able to assume and expiate itself the bur-

den of all guilt, can loose the spell; and in man the gods perceive the faculty of such free will. In man they therefore seek
to plant their own divinity, to raise his strength so high that,
in full knowledge of that strength, he may rid him of the gods'
protection, to do of his free will what his own mind inspires.
So the gods bring up man for this high destiny, to be the canceler of their own guilt; and their aim would be attained even
if in this human creation they should perforce annul themselves, that is, must part with their immediate influence
through freedom of man's conscience. Stout human races,
fruited by the seed divine, already flourish: in strife and fight
they steel their strength; Wotan's wish-maids shelter them as
shield-maids, as *Walküren* [valkyries] lead the slain-in-fight to
Walhall, where the heroes live again a glorious life of jousts
in Wotan's company.

But not yet is the rightful hero born, in whom his self-
reliant strength shall reach full consciousness, enabling him
with the free-willed penalty of death before his eyes to call his
boldest deed his own. In the race of the Wälsungen this hero
at last shall come to birth: a barren union is fertilized by
Wotan through one of Holda's apples, which he gives the
wedded pair to eat: twins, Siegmund and Sieglinde (brother
and sister), spring from the marriage. Siegmund takes a wife;
Sieglinde weds a man (Hunding); but both their marriages
prove sterile: to beget a genuine Wälsung, brother and sister
wed each other. Hunding, Sieglinde's husband, learns of the
crime, casts off his wife, and goes out to fight with Siegmund.
Brünnhilde, the Walküre, shields Siegmund counter to Wotan's
commands, who had doomed him to fall in expiation of the
crime; already Siegmund, under Brünnhilde's shield, is drawing sword for the death blow at Hunding—the sword that
Wotan himself once had given him—when the god receives
the blow upon his spear, which breaks the weapon in two
pieces. Siegmund falls. Brünnhilde is punished by Wotan for
her disobedience: he strikes her from the roll of the Walküren,
and banishes her to a rock, where the divine virgin is to wed
the man who finds and wakes her from the sleep in which
Wotan plunges her; she pleads for mercy, that Wotan will ring
the rock with terrors of fire, and so ensure that none save the
bravest of heroes may win her.

After long gestation the outcast Sieglinde gives birth in the
forest to Siegfried (he who brings Peace through Victory):
Reigin (Mime), Alberich's brother, upon hearing her cries,
has issued from a cleft and aided her: after the travail Sieg-

linde dies, first telling Reigin of her fate and committing the babe to his care. Reigin brings up Siegfried, teaches him smithery, and brings him the two pieces of the broken sword, from which, under Mime's directions, Siegfried forges the sword Balmung. Then Mime prompts the lad to slay the Worm, in proof of his gratitude.

Siegfried first wishes to avenge his father's murder: he fares out, falls upon Hunding, and kills him: only thereafter does he execute the wish of Mime, attacks and slays the giant Worm. His fingers burning from the Worm's hot blood, he puts them to his mouth to cool them; involuntarily he tastes the blood, and understands at once the language of the wood-birds singing round him. They praise Siegfried for his glorious deed, direct him to the Nibelungen Hoard in the cave of the Worm, and warn him against Mime, who has merely used him as an instrument to gain the Hoard, and therefore seeks his life. Siegfried thereon slays Mime, and takes the Ring and Tarnhelm from the Hoard: he hears the birds again, who counsel him to win the crown of women, Brünnhilde. So Siegfried sets forth, reaches Brünnhilde's mountain, pierces the billowing flames, and wakes her; in Siegfried she joyfully acclaims the highest hero of the Wälsung stem, and gives herself to him: he marries her with Alberich's ring, which he places on her finger. When the longing spurs him to new deeds, she gives him lessons in her secret lore, warns him of the dangers of deceit and treachery; they swear each other vows, and Siegfried speeds forth.

A second hero stem, sprung likewise from the gods, is that of the Gibichungen on the Rhine: there now bloom Gunther and Gudrun, his sister. Their mother, Grimhild, was once overpowered by Alberich, and bore him an unlawful son, Hagen. As the hopes and wishes of the gods repose on Siegfried, so Alberich sets his hope of gaining back the Ring on his hero offspring Hagen. Hagen is sallow, glum, and serious; his features are prematurely hardened; he looks older than he is. Already in his childhood Alberich had taught him mystic lore and knowledge of his father's fate, inciting him to struggle for the Ring: he is strong and masterful; yet to Alberich he seems not strong enough to slay the giant Worm. Since Alberich has lost his power, he could not stop his brother Mime when the latter sought to gain the Hoard through Siegfried; but Hagen shall compass Siegfried's ruin, and win the Ring from his dead body. Toward Gunther and Gudrun, Hagen is reticent—they fear him, but prize his foresight and experience: the secret of some marvelous descent of Hagen's, and that he is not his lawful brother, is known to Gunther: he calls him once an Elf-son.

Gunther is being apprised by Hagen that Brünnhilde is the woman most worth desire, and excited to long for her possession, when Siegfried speeds along the Rhine to the seat of the Gibichungs. Gudrun, inflamed to love by the praises he has showered on Siegfried, at Hagen's bidding welcomes Siegfried with a drink prepared by Hagen's art, of such potence that it makes Siegfried forget his adventure with Brünnhilde and marriage to her. Siegfried desires Gudrun for wife: Gunther consents, on condition that he help him win Brünnhilde. Siegfried agrees: they strike blood-brothership and swear each other oaths, from which Hagen holds aloof.

Siegfried and Gunther set out, and arrive at Brünnhilde's rocky fastness: Gunther remains behind in the boat; Siegfried for the first and only time exerts his power as Ruler of the Nibelungen, by putting on the Tarnhelm and thereby taking Gunther's form and look; thus masked, he passes through the flames to Brünnhilde. Already robbed by Siegfried of her maidhood, she has lost alike her superhuman strength, and all her runecraft has she made away to Siegfried—who does not use it; she is powerless as any mortal woman, and can only offer lame resistance to the new, audacious wooer; he tears from her the Ring—by which she is now to be wedded to Gunther—and forces her into the cavern, where he sleeps the night with her, though to her astonishment he lays his sword between them. On the morrow he brings her to the boat, where he lets the real Gunther take his place unnoticed by her side, and transports himself in a trice to the Gibichenburg through power of the Tarnhelm. Gunther reaches his home along the Rhine, with Brünnhilde following him in downcast silence: Siegfried, at Gudrun's side, and Hagen receive the voyagers.

Brünnhilde is aghast when she beholds Siegfried as Gudrun's husband: his cold civility to her amazes her; as he motions her back to Gunther, she recognizes the Ring on his finger: she suspects the imposture played upon her, and demands the Ring, for it belongs not to him, but to Gunther who received it from her: he refuses it. She bids Gunther claim the Ring from Siegfried: Gunther is confused, and hesitates. Brünnhilde: So it was Siegfried that had the Ring from her? Siegfried, recognizing the Ring: "From no woman I had it; my right arm won it from the giant Worm; through it am I the Nibelungen's lord, and to none will I cede its might."

Hagen steps between them, and asks Brünnhilde if she is certain about the Ring? If it be hers, then Siegfried gained it by deceit, and it can belong to no one but her husband, Gunther. Brünnhilde loudly denounces the trick played on her; the most dreadful thirst for vengeance upon Siegfried fills her. She cries to Gunther that he has been duped by Siegfried: "Not to thee —to this man am I wed; he won my favor."

Siegfried charges her with shamelessness: Faithful had he been to his blood-brothership—his sword he laid between Brünnhilde and himself: he calls on her to bear him witness. Purposely, and thinking only of his ruin, she will not understand him. The clansmen and Gudrun conjure Siegfried to clear himself of the accusation, if he can. Siegfried swears solemn oaths in confirmation of his word. Brünnhilde taxes him with perjury: All the oaths he swore to her and Gunther has he broken: now he forswears himself, to lend corroboration to a lie. Everyone is in the utmost commotion. Siegfried calls Gunther to stop his wife from shamefully slandering her own and husband's honor: he withdraws with Gudrun to the inner hall.

Gunther, in deepest shame and terrible dejection, has seated himself at the side, with hidden face: Brünnhilde, racked by the horrors of an inner storm, is approached by Hagen. He offers himself as venger of her honor: she mocks him, as powerless to cope with Siegfried: one look from his glittering eye, which shone upon her even through that mask, would scatter Hagen's courage. Hagen: He well knows Siegfried's awful strength, but she will tell him how he may be vanquished? So she who once had hallowed Siegfried, and armed him by mysterious spells against all wounding, now counsels Hagen to attack him from behind; for, knowing that the hero ne'er would turn his back upon the foe, she had left it from the blessing.

Gunther must be made a party to the plot. They call upon him to avenge his honor: Brünnhilde covers him with reproaches for his cowardice and trickery; Gunther admits his fault, and the necessity of ending his shame by Siegfried's death; but he shrinks from committing a breach of blood-brotherhood. Brünnhilde bitterly taunts him: What crimes have not been wreaked on her? Hagen inflames him by the prospect of gaining the Nibelung's Ring, which Siegfried certainly will never part with until death. Gunther consents; Hagen proposes a hunt for the morrow, when Siegfried shall be set upon, and perhaps his murder even concealed from

Gudrun, for Gunther was concerned for her sake: Brünnhilde's lust of vengeance is sharpened by her jealousy of Gudrun. So Siegfried's murder is decided by the three. Siegfried
and Gudrun, festally attired, appear in the hall, and bid them
to the sacrificial rites and wedding ceremony. The conspirators
feigningly obey: Siegfried and Gudrun rejoice at the show of
peace restored.

Next morning Siegfried strays into a lonely gully by the
Rhine, in pursuit of quarry. Three mermaids dart up from
the stream: they are soothsaying Daughters of the waters'
bed, whence Alberich once had snatched the gleaming Rhinegold to smite from it the fateful Ring: the curse and power
of that Ring would be destroyed, were it regiven to the
waters, and thus resolved into its pure original element. The
Daughters hanker for the Ring, and beg it of Siegfried, who
refuses it. (Guiltless, he has taken the guilt of the gods upon
him, and atones their wrong through his defiance, his self-
dependence.) They prophesy evil, and tell him of the curse
attaching to the ring: Let him cast it in the river, or he must
die today.

Siegfried: "Ye glibtongued women shall not cheat me of
my might: the curse and your threats I count not worth a hair.
What my courage bids me is my being's law; and what I do
of mine own mind, so is it set for me to do: call ye this curse
or blessing, it I obey and strive not counter to my strength."

The three Daughters: "Wouldst thou outvie the gods?"

Siegfried: "Show me the chance of mastering the gods,
and I must work my main to vanquish them. I know three
wiser women than you three; they wot where once the gods
will strive in bitter fearing. Well for the gods, if they take
heed that then I battle *with* them. So laugh I at your threats:
the ring stays mine, and thus I cast my life behind me." (He
lifts a clod of earth, and hurls it backward over his head.)

The Daughters scoff at Siegfried, who weens himself as
strong and wise as he is blind and bond slave: "Oaths has
he broken, and knows it not: a boon far higher than the
Ring he's lost, and knows it not: runes and spells were taught
to him, and he's forgot them. Fare thee well, Siegfried! A
lordly wife we know; e'en today will she possess the Ring,
when thou art slaughtered. To her! She'll lend us better
hearing."

Siegfried, laughing, gazes after them as they move away
singing. He shouts: "To Gudrun were I not true, one of you
three had ensnared me!" He hears his hunting comrades

drawing nearer, and winds his horn: the huntsmen—Gunther and Hagen at their head—assemble round Siegfried. The midday meal is eaten: Siegfried, in the highest spirits, mocks at his own unfruitful chase: But water game had come his way, for whose capture he was not equipped, alack! or he'd have brought his comrades three wild water birds that told him he must die today. Hagen takes up the jest, as they drink: Does he really know the song and speech of birds, then? Gunther is sad and silent.

Siegfried seeks to enliven him, and sings him songs about his youth: his adventure with Mime, the slaying of the Worm, and how he came to understand bird language. The train of recollection brings him back the counsel of the birds to seek Brünnhilde, who was fated for him; how he stormed the flaming rock and wakened Brünnhilde. Remembrance rises more and more distinct. Two ravens suddenly fly past his head.

Hagen interrupts him: "What do these ravens tell thee?" Siegfried springs to his feet. Hagen: "*I* rede them; they haste to herald thee to Wotan." He hurls his spear at Siegfried's back. Gunther, guessing from Siegfried's tale the true connection of the inexplicable scene with Brünnhilde, and suddenly divining Siegfried's innocence, had thrown himself on Hagen's arm to rescue Siegfried, but without being able to stay the blow. Siegfried raises his shield, to crush Hagen with it; his strength fails him, and he falls of a heap.

Hagen has departed; Gunther and the clansmen stand round Siegfried, in sympathetic awe; he lifts his shining eyes once more: "Brünnhilde, Brünnhilde! Radiant child of Wotan! How dazzling bright I see thee nearing me! With holy smile thou saddlest thy horse, that paces through the air dew-dripping: to me thou steer'st its course; here is there Lot to choose! Happy me thou chos'st for husband, now lead me to Walhall, that in honor of all heroes I may drink All-Father's mead, pledged me by thee, thou shining wish-maid! Brünnhilde! Brünnhilde! Greeting!" He dies. The men uplift the corpse upon his shield, and solemnly bear it over the rocky heights, Gunther in front.

In the Hall of the Gibichungs, whose forecourt extends at the back to the bank of the Rhine, the corpse is set down: Hagen has called out Gudrun; with strident tones he tells her that a savage boar had gored her husband. Gudrun falls horrified on Siegfried's body: she rates her brother with the murder; Gunther points to Hagen: He was the savage boar, the murderer of Siegfried.

Hagen: "So be it; an I have slain him, whom no other dared to, whatso was his is my fair booty. The Ring is mine!"

Gunther confronts him: "Shameless Elf-son, the Ring is mine, assigned to me by Brünnhilde: ye all, ye heard it."

Hagen and Gunther fight: Gunther falls. Hagen tries to wrench the Ring from the body—it lifts its hand aloft in menace; Hagen staggers back, aghast; Gudrun cries aloud in her sorrow; then Brünnhilde enters solemnly:

"Cease your laments, your idle rage! Here stands his wife, whom ye all betrayed. My right I claim, for what must be is done!"

Gudrun: "Ah, wicked one! 'Twas thou who brought us ruin."

Brünnhilde: "Poor soul, have peace! Wert but his wanton: his wife am I, to whom he swore or e'er he saw thee."

Gudrun: "Woe's me! Accursed Hagen, what badest thou me, with the drink that filched her husband to me? For now I know that only through the drink did he forget Brünnhilde."

Brünnhilde: "Oh, he was pure! Ne'er oaths were more loyally held, than by him. No, Hagen has not *slain* him; for Wotan has he marked him out, to whom I thus conduct him. And I, too, have atoned; pure and free am I: for he, the glorious one alone, o'erpowered me."

She directs a pile of logs to be erected on the shore, to burn Siegfried's corpse to ashes: no horse, no vassal shall be sacrificed with him; she alone will give her body in his honor to the gods. First she takes possession of her heritage; the Tarnhelm shall be burned with her: the Ring she puts upon her finger. "Thou froward hero, how thou held'st me banned! All my rune lore I bewrayed to thee, a mortal, and so went widowed of my wisdom; thou usedst it not; thou trustedst in thyself alone: but now that thou must yield it up through death, my knowledge comes to me again, and this Ring's runes I rede. The ur-law's runes, too, know I now, the Norns' old saying! Hear, then, ye mighty gods, your guilt is quit: thank him, the hero, who took your guilt upon him! To mine own hand he gave to end his work: loosed be the Nibelungs' thralldom, the Ring no more shall bind them. Not Alberich shall receive it; no more shall he enslave you, but he himself be free as ye. For to you I make this Ring away, wise sisters of the waters' deep; the fire that burns me, let it cleanse the evil toy; and ye shall melt and keep it harmless, the Rhinegold robbed from you to weld to ill and bondage. One only shall rule, All-Father thou in thy glory! As pledge of thine eternal might, this man I bring thee: good welcome give him; he is worth it!"

Midst solemn chants Brünnhilde mounts the pyre to Siegfried's body. Gudrun, broken down with grief, remains bowed over the corpse of Gunther in the foreground. The flames meet across Brünnhilde and Siegfried—suddenly a dazzling light is seen: above the margin of a leaden cloud the light streams up, showing Brünnhilde, armed as Walküre on horse, leading Siegfried by the hand from hence.

At like time the waters of the Rhine invade the entrance to the hall; on their waves the three water maids bear away the Ring and Helmet. Hagen dashes after them, to snatch the treasure, as if demented. The Daughters seize and drag him with them to the deep.

15. *Commentary on* The Ring. *Letter to August Röckel, January 25, 1854*

WE must learn *to die,* and to die in the fullest sense of the word. The fear of the end is the source of all lovelessness, and this fear is generated only when love itself begins to wane. How came it that this feeling which imparts the highest blessedness to all things living was so far lost sight of by the human race that at last it came to this: all that mankind did, ordered, and established was conceived only in fear of the end. My poem sets this forth. It reveals Nature in her undisguised truth, with all those inconsistencies which, in their endless multiplicity, embrace even directly conflicting elements. But it is not the repulse of Alberich by the Rhine daughters—that repulse was inevitable owing to their nature —that was the cause of all the mischief. Alberich and his Ring would have been powerless to harm the gods had they not themselves been susceptible to evil. Wherein, then, is the root of the matter to be sought? Examine the first scene between Wotan and Fricka, which leads up to the scene in the second act of *Die Walküre.* The necessity of prolonging beyond the point of change the subjection to the tie that binds them—a tie resulting from an involuntary illusion of love, the duty of maintaining at all costs the relation into which they have entered, and so placing themselves in hopeless opposition to the universal law of change and renewal, which governs the world of phenomena—these are the conditions which bring the pair of them to a state of torment and natural lovelessness.

The development of the whole poem sets forth the necessity of recognizing and yielding to the change, the many-sidedness, the multiplicity, the eternal renewing of reality and of life. Wotan rises to the tragic height of *willing* his own destruction. This is the lesson that we have to learn from the history of mankind: *to will what necessity imposes*, and ourselves bring it about. The creative product of this supreme, self-destroying will, its victorious achievement, is a fearless human being, one who never ceases to love: Siegfried. That is the whole matter. As a matter of detail, the mischief-making power, the poison that is fatal to love, appears under the guise of the gold that is stolen from Nature and misapplied—the Nibelungs' Ring, never to be redeemed from the curse that clings to it until it has been restored to Nature and the gold sunk again in the depths of the Rhine. But it is only quite at the end that Wotan realizes this, when he himself has reached the goal of this tragic career; what Loge had foretold to him in the beginning with a touching insistence, the god consumed by ambition had ignored. Later in Fafner's deed he merely recognized the power of the curse; it is only when the Ring works its destroying spell on Siegfried himself that he realizes that only by restoration of what was stolen can the evil be annulled, and he deliberately makes his own destruction part of the conditions on which must depend the annulling of the original mischief.

Experience is everything. Moreover, Siegfried alone (man by himself) is not the complete human being: he is merely the half; it is only along with Brünnhilde that he becomes the redeemer. To the isolated being not all things are possible; there is need of more than one, and it is woman, suffering and willing to sacrifice herself, who becomes at last the real, conscious redeemer: for what is love itself but the "eternal feminine" (*das ewig Weibliche*).

I do not agree with your criticisms with regard to a certain want of lucidity and distinctness of statement: on the contrary, I believe that a true instinct has kept me from a too great definiteness; for it has been born in on me, that an absolute disclosing of the intention disturbs true insight. What you want in drama—as indeed in all works of art—is to achieve your end, not by statement of the artist's intentions, but by the presentment of life as the resultant, not of arbitrary forces, but of eternal laws. It is just this that distinguishes my poetic material from all the poetical material which alone absorbs poets' minds at the present day.

For example, by insisting, as you do, that the intention of Wotan's appearance on the scene in "Young Siegfried" [*Siegfried*] should be more clearly defined, you are prejudicing in a marked manner the fateful element in the development of the drama, which to me is so important. After his farewell to Brünnhilde, Wotan is in all truth a departed spirit; true to his high resolve, he must now leave things alone, and renouncing all power over them, let them go as they will.

For this reason, he is now only the "Wanderer." Look well at him, for in every point he resembles us. He represents the actual sum of the Intelligence of the Present, whereas Siegfried is the man greatly desired and longed for by us of the Future. But we who long for him cannot fashion him; he must fashion himself and by means of our annihilation. Taken in this way, Wotan is, you must acknowledge, highly interesting; whereas he would seem to us most unworthy if he appeared as a subtle intriguer, which indeed he would be if he gave counsel apparently against Siegfried, though in reality favorable to Siegfried and consequently himself. That were a deception worthy of our political heroes, but not of my jovial god, bent on his own annihilation. Look at him in this juxtaposition to Siegfried in the third act. In presence of his impending destruction, the god has at last become so completely human that—contrary to his high resolve—there is once more a stirring of his ancient pride, brought about by his jealousy for Brünnhilde—his vulnerable point, as it has now become. He will, so to speak, not allow himself to be merely thrust aside; he chooses rather to fall before the conquering might of Siegfried. But this part is so little premeditated and intentional, that in a sudden burst of passion the longing for victory overpowers him, a victory, moreover, which he admits could have made him only more miserable. Holding the views I do, I could give only the faintest and subtlest indication of my design. Of course, I do not mean my hero to make the impression of a wholly unconscious creature: on the contrary, I have sought in Siegfried to represent my ideal of the perfect human being, whose highest consciousness manifests itself in the acknowledgment that all consciousness must find expression in present life and action.

The enormous significance that I attach to this consciousness, which can scarcely ever find adequate expression in mere words, will be quite clear to you in the scene between Siegfried and the Rhine daughters. Here we see that infinite wisdom has come to Siegfried, for he has grasped the highest truth and knows that death is better than a life of fear: knowledge of the Ring, too, has come to him, but he does not heed its power, for he has something better to do; he keeps it only as proof that he at least has never learned what fear means. Confess, in the presence of such a being the splendor of the gods must be dimmed.

What strikes me most is your question, "Why, seeing that the gold is restored to the Rhine, is it necessary that the gods should perish?" I feel certain that, at a good performance, the most simple-minded spectator will be left in no doubt on that point. Certainly the downfall of the gods is no necessary part of the drama regarded as a mere contrapuntal nexus of motives. As such, indeed, it might have been turned, twisted, and interpreted to mean any conceivable thing— after the manner of lawyers and politicians. No, the necessity for this downfall had to arise out of our own deepest convictions, as it did with Wotan. And thus it was all-important to justify this catastrophe to the feelings of the spectators; and it is so justified to anyone who follows the course of the whole action with all its simple and natural motives. When finally Wotan gives expression to this sense of necessity, he proclaims only that which we have all along felt must needs be. At the end of *Rhinegold* when Loge watches the gods enter Walhalla and speaks these fateful words: "They hasten toward their end who imagine themselves so strong in their might," he, in that moment, gives utterance only to our own conviction; for anyone who has followed the prelude sympathetically, and not in a hypercritical, caviling spirit, but abandoning himself to his impressions and feelings, will entirely agree with Loge.

And now let me say something to you about Brünnhilde. You misunderstand her, too, when you attribute her refusal to give the Ring up to Wotan to hardness and obstinacy. Can you not see that it was for love's sake that Brünnhilde sundered herself from Wotan and from all the gods, because where Wotan clung to schemes, she could only—love? Above all, from the moment Siegfried had awakened her she has no knowledge other than the knowledge of love. Now the symbol of this—after Siegfried's departure—is the Ring. When Wotan claims it from her, one thing only is present to her spirit— what it was that originally alienated her from him, her having disobeyed for love's sake; and this alone she is still conscious of, that for love she has renounced her godhead. She knows also that one thing alone is godlike, and that is love; therefore let the splendor of Walhalla fall in ruins, she will not give up the Ring (her love). Just consider how poor, avaricious, and common she would have stood revealed to us if she had refused the Ring because she had learned (possibly from Siegfried) of its magic, and the power of gold. Surely you do not seriously think such a thing of so grand a woman? But if you shudder because, being the woman she is, she should have preserved as a symbol of love just this Ring on which the curse lay, then you will have understood the curse of the Nibelungs in its most terrible and tragic significance; then you will admit the necessity of the whole of the last drama of "Siegfried's Death." That had to be compassed in order that the malign influence of the gold should be fully revealed. How did it come about that Brünnhilde yielded so readily to the disguised Siegfried? Simply because he had wrested the Ring from her, in which her whole strength lay. The terror, the fatality (*das Dämonische*) that underlie the whole of that scene seem entirely to have escaped you. Through the fire which it had been foreordained that none but Siegfried should pass, which actually none but he had passed, another has made his way to her with but little difficulty.

Everything totters around Brünnhilde, everything is out of joint; in a terrible conflict she is overcome, she is "forsaken of God." And moreover it is Siegfried in reality who orders her to share his couch; Siegfried whom she (unconsciously and thus with the greater bewilderment) almost recognizes, by his gleaming eye, in spite of his disguise. You must feel that something is being enacted that is not to be expressed in mere words—and it is wrong of you to challenge me to explain it in words.

16. Parsifal. *Letter to Mathilde Wesendonck, May 30, 1859*

PARSIFAL is bound to be another very nasty job. Considered strictly, *Amfortas* is the center and principal subject. There you have a pretty *Parsifal* tale at once. To myself of a sudden it has grown too appallingly clear: it is my Tristan of the third act with an inconceivable increase. The spear wound—haply yet another—in his heart, the poor man knows but one longing in his fearful anguish, that for death; to win to that uttermost cordial, again and again he craves the aspect of the Grail, if that at least might close his wound, since every other aid is impotent, nothing—nothing serves!—Yet again and again does the Grail but renew him this one thing, that he *cannot* die; its sight but multiplies his torments, adding un-dyingness to them. Now, the Grail, after *my* reading, is the cup of the Last Supper, wherein Joseph of Arimathea gathered the blood of the Saviour on the cross. Now see what a terrible import is gained by Amfortas' relation to this wonder cup; he, stricken with the selfsame wound, dealt him by the spear of a rival in a passionate love adventure—for his only sustenance must yearn for the boon of that blood which erst flowed from the Saviour's like spear wound, when, world-renouncing, world-redeeming, He pined world-suffering on the cross! Blood for blood, wound for wound—but from here to there what a gulf between this blood, this wound!

All transport, worship, ecstasy, at the wondrous presence of the chalice which reddens into soft entrancing radiance, new life is poured through all his veins—and death can not draw nigh him! He lives, relives, and more fiercely than ever the fatal wound ravens him, *his* wound! Devotion itself be-comes a torture! Where is an end to it, where redemption? Suffering of mankind through all eternity!—In the frenzy of despair might he turn entirely from the Grail, shut fast his eyes thereto? Fain would he, for a possibility of death, but —he has been appointed Guardian of the Grail himself. And no blind outer power appointed him—no! but since he was so worthy, since none had understood the marvel of the Grail so deeply and so inwardly as he; as even now his whole soul ever turns again toward that sight which withers him in adoration, blends heavenly unction with eternal ban!

And I'm to execute a thing like that, make music for it too? Let him do it who likes!

Someone may do it, who will manage just à la Wolfram;* that won't much matter, and after all may sound like something, perhaps even something quite pretty; but *I* take such things far too seriously. Look, if you please, on the other hand, how easy even Meister Wolfram made it for himself! Never mind his understanding simply nothing of the inner content; he strings incident to incident, adventure to adventure, turns the Grail motif into rare and curious happenings and pictures, fumbles around, and leaves the earnest seeker with the question what he really meant. To which his answer would have to be: Hm, I really don't know that myself, any more than the priest his Christianity, which he also mumbles at the altar without a notion what it is.

And that's the truth. Wolfram is an utterly unripe appearance, the blame for which must largely be laid on his barbaric, altogether mongrel era, hovering between primitive Christendom and the newer State. Nothing in that age could be carried right through; poetic depth immediately is merged in insubstantial fantastries. I am almost coming to agree with Frederick the Great, who, upon the Wolfram being handed him, told the publisher he musn't bother him with such rubbish!—Seriously, one must have so lived into the heart of a subject like this through its legend's sterling features, as I now have done with this Grail saga and then taken a bird's-eye glance at the way in which Wolfram represents the same thing to himself—which I also have done in skimming through your book—to be repelled at once by the poet's incapacity (with Gottfried van Strassburg's *Tristan* it already had gone much the same with me).

Take merely one point: among all the meanings given by the legends to the Grail, this superficial "penetrator" selects the one that has the very least to say. Certainly the identification of this marvel with a precious stone occurs in the earliest sources one can trace, namely in the Arabic of the Spanish Moors; for one observes, alas! that all our Christian legends have a foreign, pagan origin. In this case our onlooking Christians were amazed to learn that the Moors in the Kaaba

---

* Wolfram von Eschenbach, author of the medieval romance *Parzival*.

at Mecca (dating from the pre-Mohammedan religion) paid reverence to a wondrous stone (sun stone—or meteoric stone—indubitably fallen from the sky).

The Christians, however, soon framed the legends of its miraculous power *their own* way, and brought it into rapport with the Christian mythos; a proceeding simplified by the persistence of an ancient legend in the south of France, that Joseph of Arimathea once fled there with the sacred bowl of the Last Supper—which harmonizes perfectly with the enthusiasm of the early Christian age for relics. Sense and meaning thus entered at once, and with true rapture do I marvel at this splendid trait of Christian myth development which devised the most pregnant symbol ever yet invented as physical garb for the spiritual core of a religion!

Whom does it not thrill with the most affecting and sublimest feelings, to hear that that goblet whence the Saviour pledged his last farewell to his disciples—and wherein the Redeemer's deathless blood itself was gathered and preserved—is still extant, and the elect, the pure, may gaze at and adore its very self? How incomparable! And then the doubled meaning of one vessel, as chalice also at the holy eucharist—unquestionably the Christian cult's most lovely sacrament! Thence, too, the legend that the Grail (Sang Réal—hence San(ct) Gral) alone sustained its pious knighthood, and gave them food and drink at mealtimes. And all this so senselessly passed over by our poet who merely took his subject from the sorry French chivalric romances of his age and chattered gaily after, like a starling! Conclude from that to all the rest! Fine are none but single descriptions, the strong point of all the medieval poets: there visuality reigns finely felt, but their *whole* remains ever invertebrate.

Then think of all I should have to set about with Parsifal himself! For with him, too, Wolfram knows not what to do: his despair of God is absurd and unmotivated, still more unsatisfying his conversion; that matter of the "question" is too entirely flat and meaningless. Here, accordingly, I should have to invent just everything. Added to that is one more difficulty with Parsifal. As the longed-for saviour of Amfortas, he is wholly indispensable: but if Amfortas is to be set in the true light due him, he acquires such intensely tragic interest that it becomes well-nigh more than hard to let a second main interest crop up beside him; yet Parsifal must be accorded that main interest, unless he is merely to come on at the end as a damping *deus ex machina*. Consequently Parsifal's evolution, his sublimest purification, albeit predestined by his whole pensive, profoundly compassionate nature, has to be placed in the foreground once more. And for that I can choose no spacious outline, such as Wolfram had at disposal: I must so compress the whole into *three* main situations of drastic intent, that the deep and branching contents yet may stand forth sharp and clear; for, to operate and represent *thus*, when all's said, is *my* art.

PART VI

The Art of Performance

1. Conducting: relation of melody to tempo; establishing the correct tempo; the principle of modifying tempo; performing Beethoven's Ninth Symphony

I PROPOSE to relate my own experiences and judgment of a field of musical activity that has hitherto been left to routine for its practice, to ignorance for its criticism. To ratify my verdict I shall not appeal to conductors themselves, but to bandsmen and singers, as these alone have a right sense of whether they are being conducted well or badly; though they certainly can never decide the point until, for once in a most exceptional way, they really are well conducted. Moreover, I shall make no attempt at setting up a system, but merely jot down a series of personal observations, reserving to myself the right of continuing the same as occasion offers.

A correct conception of the melos alone can give the proper tempo: the two are indivisible; one conditions the other. And if I do not scruple to declare that by far the most performances of our classic instrumental works are seriously inadequate, I propose to substantiate my verdict by pointing out *that our conductors know nothing of proper tempo, because of their understanding nothing about song.* I have never met a single German *Kapellmeister* or musical conductor who could really *sing* a melody, let his voice be good or bad; no, music to them is an abstraction, a cross between syntax, arithmetic, and gymnastics; so that one may well conceive its votaries making capital teachers at a conservatoire or musical gymnasium, but never imagine them breathing life and soul into a musical performance.

To sum up in one word the question of a tone work's right performance, so far as depends on the conductor, it is this: Has he given throughout the proper *tempo?* for his choice and dictation of that tells us at once whether he has understood the piece or not. Upon closer acquaintance with the piece, the proper tempo will give the players almost of itself

301

a clue to the proper rendering, whilst that tempo itself is direct evidence of the conductor's acquaintance with the latter. How far from easy it is to determine the proper tempo, however, is shown by the fact that only through a knowledge of the correct rendering, in every respect, can that proper tempo itself be found.

Earlier musicians had so true a feeling of this, that Haydn and Mozart, for instance, mostly denoted their tempos in very general terms: "allegro," "adagio" and "andante," with the simplest qualifications, embrace well-nigh everything they thought needful in this regard. And going back to S. Bach, we find the tempo scarcely ever even indicated at all; which, in a truly musical sense, is quite the most correct. Bach told himself something like this: Whoever does not understand my theme and figuration, does not divine their character and expression, what will it profit him to be given an Italian sign of tempo?—To speak from my very own experience, I may state that I furnished my earlier operas—those played at the theatres—with downright eloquent directions for tempo, and fixed them past mistaking (as I thought) by metronomic cyphers. But whenever I heard of a foolish tempo in a performance of my *Tannhäuser,* for instance, my recriminations were always parried by the plea that my metronomic marks had been followed most scrupulously. So I saw how uncertain must be the value of mathematics in music, and thenceforth dispensed with the metronome; contenting myself with quite general indications for even the principal time measure, and devoting all my forethought to its *modifications,* since our conductors know as good as nothing of the latter. Now, these generalisms, in their turn, have lately worried and confused conductors, as I hear, especially owing to their being couched in German; for the gentlemen, accustomed to the old Italian labels, are all at sea as to what I mean by *mässig* (moderate) for instance. This complaint was recently made me by a *Kapellmeister* whom I lately had to thank for spinning out the music of my *Rheingold*—which had lasted two hours and a half at the rehearsals under a conductor instructed by myself—to three full hours, according to the report in the Augsburg *Allgemeine Zeitung.* Something similar was once told me in characterization of a performance of my *Tannhäuser,* namely, that the overture, which lasted just twelve minutes under my own conduct in Dresden, had here [Munich] been spun to twenty.

"Dragging," however, is not the forte of our strictly elegant conductors of latter days; quite the contrary, they manifest a fatal love for scurrying and hunting down. Thereby hangs a tale well-nigh sufficient in itself to summarize the newest, the so extremely fashionable goings-on in music.

Robert Schumann once complained to me, at Dresden, that Mendelssohn had quite ruined his enjoyment of the Ninth Symphony by the rapid pace at which he took it, particularly in the first movement. Myself I once heard Mendelssohn conduct a symphony of Beethoven's, at a concert rehearsal in Berlin: it was the Eighth (in F). I noticed that he would pick out a detail here and there— almost at random—and polish it up with a certain pertinacity; which was of such excellent service to the detail, that I wondered only why he didn't pay the same attention to other nuances: for the rest, this so incomparably buoyant symphony flowed down a vastly tame and chatty course. As to conducting, he personally informed me once or twice that a too slow tempo was the devil, and for choice he would rather things were taken too fast; a really good rendering was a rarity at any time; with a little care, however, one might gloss things over; and this could best be done by never dawdling, but covering the ground at a good stiff pace. Mendelssohn's actual pupils must have heard from the master a little more, and more in detail, to the same effect; for it can hardly have been a maxim confided to my ear alone, as I later have had occasion to learn its consequences, and finally its grounds.

Of the former I had a lively experience with the orchestra of the Philharmonic Society in London. Mendelssohn had conducted that band for a considerable period, and the Mendelssohnian mode of rendering had confessedly been raised into a fixed tradition; in fact, it so well suited the customs and peculiarities of this society's concerts that it almost seemed as if Mendelssohn had derived his mode of rendering from them. As a huge amount of music was consumed at those concerts, but only one rehearsal allowed for each performance, I myself was often obliged to leave the orchestra to its tradition, and thereby made acquaintance with a style of execution which forcibly reminded me at any rate of Mendelssohn's dictum to myself. The thing flowed on like water from a public fountain; to attempt to check it was out of the question, and every allegro ended as an indisputable presto. The labor of intervention was painful enough; for not until one had got the right and rightly shaded tempo did one discover the other sins of rendering that had lain swamped beneath the deluge. For one thing, the orchestra never played else but mezzoforte; neither a genuine forte, nor a true piano, came about. In important cases, as far as possible, I at last insisted upon the rendering that I myself deemed right, as also on the suitable tempo. The good fellows had nothing against it, and expressed sincere delight; to the public, too, it plainly seemed the thing: but the reporters flew into a rage, and so alarmed the committee that I once was actually asked to be so good as scurry the second movement of Mozart's Symphony in E-flat again, as one had always been accustomed to, and as Mendelssohn himself had done.

Finally the fatal maxim was put into so many words, when a very amiable elderly contrapuntist whose symphony I was to conduct, Mr. Potter (if I mistake not), implored me from his heart to take his andante downright fast, since he had great fears of its proving wearisome. I pointed out that, let his andante last as short as it might, it could not fail to weary if played without all finish and expression; whereas it might prove quite fascinating if its dainty, naïve theme were only rendered by the orchestra in somewhat the way I proceeded to hum it him, for that was surely what he meant when writing it. Mr. Potter was visibly touched, agreed with me, and merely advanced the plea that he had lost all habit of counting on such a style of orchestral delivery. On the evening itself, just after this andante, he pressed my hand for very joy.

I must keep on coming back to tempo for the present; for, as already said, 'tis the point where the conductor has to show himself worth his salt.

Manifestly, the correct speed for any piece of music can be determined only by the special character of its phrasing; to determine the former, we must have come to terms about the latter. The requirements of the phrasing, whether it leans chiefly toward legato tone (song) or more toward rhythmic motion (figuration), are the points that must determine the conductor as to which class of tempo he has to make preponderate.

Now, adagio bears the same relation to allegro as legato tone to figured motion. The legato tone lays down the law for the tempo adagio: here rhythm dissolves into the pure and self-sufficing, self-governing life of tone. In a certain subtle sense one may say that the pure adagio can not be taken slow enough: here must reign a rapt confidence in the eloquent persuasiveness of tone speech pure and simple; here the languor of emotion becomes an ecstasy; what the allegro expressed by a change of figuration is spoken here by infinite variety of modulated tone; the faintest change of harmony surprises us, the most remote progressions are prepared for and awaited on the tiptoe of suspense.

Not one of our conductors trusts himself to grant the adagio a proper measure of this its attribute; they start by hunting for some figuration or other, and trim their tempo to its hypothetic speed. Perhaps I am the only conductor who has dared take the adagio proper of the third movement of the Ninth Symphony at a pace in strict accordance with its character. This adagio is first contrasted with an alternating andante in triple time, as though to stamp its quite peculiar quality for anyone to see; but it doesn't restrain our conductors from so blotting out the character of each that nothing remains save the rhythmic interchange of common and triple time. Finally this movement—one of the most instructive in the present connection—supplies with its richly figured 12/8 time the plainest example of a refraction of the pure adagio character by a more pointed rhythmicizing of the figured accompaniment, now raised to self-dependence, while the cantilena still preserves its characteristic breadth. Here we have the focused image, so to speak, of an adagio which had erewhile yearned to melt into infinity; and just as an unshackled freedom to revel in expression by tone had earlier allowed the pace to oscillate between the gentlest laws, so now the firm-set rhythm of the figured ornament supplies the new law of adherence to one definite rate of motion—a law whose ultimate corollaries will be our law for the allegro's speed.

As the held note with its various modifications of length is the basis of all musical delivery, so the adagio—particularly through the logical development given it by Beethoven in this third movement of his Ninth Symphony—becomes the basis of all measurement of musical time. In a delicately discriminating sense, the allegro may be regarded as ultimate outcome of the pure adagio's refraction by a busier figuration. If one takes a closer look at the ruling motives in the allegro itself, one will always find them dominated by a singing quality derived from the adagio. Beethoven's most significant allegro movements are mostly governed by a root melody, belonging in a deeper sense to the character of the adagio; and hereby they obtain that *sentimental* import which distinguishes them so explicitly from the earlier, *naïve* order. Yet to the Beethovenian

the Mozartian

already bears no distant kinship, and neither with Mozart nor Beethoven does the allegro's true distinctive character appear till figuration entirely gains the upper hand of song: that is to say, until the reaction of rhythmic motion against legato tone is thorough and complete. This case is met the most frequently in closing movements modeled on the rondeau, of which the finales of Mozart's E-flat major, and Beethoven's A-major Symphony are very speaking specimens. Here purely rhythmic motion celebrates its orgies, so to say, and hence this kind of allegro cannot be taken sharp and brisk enough. But whatever lies between those two extremes is subject to the *laws of reciprocity*; and these laws can not be read with too much subtlety, for they are the same at bottom as those that modified legato tone itself into every conceivable nuance. And now that I am about to deal more searchingly with this *modification of tempo*—a thing not merely quite unknown to our conductors, but doltishly proscribed by them for reason of that nonacquaintance—the attentive reader will understand that we here are handling a positive life principle of all our music.

The main tempo of the Prelude to *Die Meistersinger* was inscribed by me as *sehr mässig bewegt,* meaning something the same as *allegro maestoso* in the older style of signature. No tempo stands more in need of modification than this, when maintained for any length, and especially when the thematic subjects are treated strongly episodically. It also is a favorite for the varied combination of motives of different types, because the broad symmetry of its 4/4 beat lends itself with great facility to the modifications required by such a treatment. Moreover, this medium "common time" is the most comprehensive of all; beaten in vigorous crotchets, it can represent a true alert allegro—and this is the real main tempo here meant by me, appearing at its swiftest in the eight bars leading from the march to the E-major:

 *etc.*

or it can be treated as a half-period composed of two 2/4 beats, and will then assume the character of a brisk scherzando, as at the entry of the theme in diminution:

or, again, it may even be interpreted as an *alla-breve* (2/2), and then express the older sedate andante proper (particularly employed in church music), which rightly should be marked by two moderately slow beats. In this last sense I have used it from the eighth bar after reentry of C-major for combining the principal march theme, now borne by the basses, with the second principal theme now sung in flowing rhythmic duplication by the violins and cellos:

 *etc.*

This second theme made its first appearance "diminished" and in pure 4/4 time:

There with the greatest softness in delivery it combines a passionate, almost a hasty character (somewhat of a clandestinely whispered declaration of love); since the passionate haste is sufficiently expressed by a greater mobility of figuration, to preserve the theme's chief characteristic, that of tenderness, the pace must necessarily be a little slackened, dropping to the utmost shade of gravity whereof the 4/4 beat is capable; and to bring this imperceptibly about (that is, without really effacing the fundamental character of the main tempo) a bar of *poco rallentando* introduces the phrase. Through the more restless nuance of this theme, which gains at last the upper hand,

and which, I have also marked expressly with "more passionate," it was easy for me to lead the tempo back to its original swifter motion; and this in turn was convertible into the aforesaid *andante alla breve,* for which I had only to resume a nuance of the main tempo already developed in the first exposition. The first development of the staid march theme, to wit, had terminated in a longish coda of cantabile character, which could be given proper breadth only if taken at that *tempo andante alla breve.* As this full-toned cantabile

was preceded by a fanfare in massive crotchets,

that change of tempo had obviously to enter with the cessation of the pure crotchet movement, that is to say, with the sustained dominant chord that introduces the cantabile. Now, as the broader minim-movement is here worked out to a long and animated climax, particularly as regards the modulation, I believed I could safely leave the pace to the conductor's common sense, since the mere execution of such passages will of itself put more fire into the tempo if only one yields to the natural feeling of the bandsmen; so surely did I count on this, as a conductor of some experience, that I thought it needless to indicate anything but the place where the original 4/4 beat is resumed, as suggested to every musical ear by the

return of the crotchet motion in the harmonies. In the conclusion of the prelude this broader 4/4 beat is just as obviously
called for by the re-entry of that sturdy marchlike fanfare,
with which the doubling of the figured ornament combines
to close the movement in precisely the same tempo as it had
begun.

As I have mentioned again and again in the preceding,
all attempts at modification of tempo in behalf of the rendering of classical, and particularly of Beethovenian music, have
been received with displeasure by the conductor guild of our
times. I have given circumstantial proofs that a one-sided
modification of tempo, without a corresponding modification
of tone production itself, affords prima-facie ground for
objections; on the other hand I have exposed the deeper-
lying cause of this one-sidedness, and thus have left those objections with nothing to fall back on save the incapacity and
general unfitness of our conductors themselves. It certainly
is a valid argument, that nothing could do more harm to the
pieces I have instanced than a willful introduction of random
nuances of tempo, which must at once throw wide the door
to the fantastic whims of every empty or conceited time-
beater aiming at effect, and in time would make our classical
music literature completely unrecognizable. To this, of course,
there is no reply, save that our music is in a very sad plight
when such fears can arise; since it is as good as saying that
one has no faith in the good sense of our artistic public,
against which those quips and quiddities would break in vain.

Performing Beethoven's Ninth Symphony

At a performance I lately conducted of this wondrous tone
work certain reflections touching what I deem the irremissible
distinctness of its rendering forced themselves so strongly on
me that I since have meditated a remedy for the ills I felt.
The result I now lay before earnest musicians, if not as an
invitation to follow my method, at least as a stimulus to
independent study.

In general, I draw attention to the peculiar position in which
Beethoven was placed as regards the instrumentation of his
orchestral works. He instrumented on exactly the same assumptions of the orchestra's capacity as his predecessors
Haydn and Mozart, notwithstanding that he vastly outstripped
them in the character of his musical conceptions. What we
may fitly define as *plastique*, in the grouping and distribution

of the various instrumental families, with Mozart and Haydn
had crystallized into a firm agreement between the character
of their conceptions and the technique of the orchestra as
formed and practiced until then. There can be nothing more
adequate, than a symphony of Mozart's and the Mozartian
orchestra: one may presume that to neither Haydn nor Mozart
there ever occurred a musical thought which could not have
promptly found expression in their orchestra. Here was
thorough congruence: the tutti with trumpets and drums
(only truly effective in the tonic), the quartet passage for
the strings, the harmony or solo of the wind, with the inevitable duo for French horns—these formed the solid groundwork not only of the orchestra but of the draft for all
orchestral compositions. Strange to relate, Beethoven also
knew no orchestra other than this, and he never went beyond
its employment on what then appeared quite natural lines.

It is astonishing what distinctness the master manages to
give to conceptions of a wealth and variety unapproached
by Haydn or Mozart, with identically the same orchestra. In
this regard his *Sinfonia eroica* remains a marvel not only of
conception, but also, and no less, of orchestration. Only, he
already here exacted of his band a mode of rendering which
it has been unable to acquire to this day: for the execution
would have to be as much a stroke of genius, on the orchestra's part, as the master's own conception of the score. From
this point then, from the first performance of the "Eroica,"
begin the difficulties of judging these symphonies, ay, the
hindrances to pleasure in them—a pleasure never really arrived at by the musicians of an older epoch. These works fell
short of full *distinctness* in achievement for the simple reason
that it no longer lay ensured in the use to which the orchestral
organism was put, as in the case of Haydn and Mozart, but
could be brought out by nothing save a positively virtuosic
exploit of the individual instrumentalists and their chief.

To explain: now that the opulence of his conceptions
required a far more complex material and a much more
minute distribution thereof, Beethoven saw himself compelled
to exact the most rapid change in force and expression from
one and the same orchestra player, after the fashion acquired
by the great virtuoso as a special art. For example the
characteristically Beethovenian crescendo, ending, not in a
forte, but in a sudden piano: this single nuance, so frequently
recurring, is still so foreign to most of our orchestral players
that cautious conductors have made their orchestra players

reverse the latter part of the crescendo into a sly diminuendo, to secure at least a timely entry of the piano. The secret of this difficulty surely lies in demanding from one and the same body of instruments a nuance that can be executed quite distinctly only when distributed between two separate bodies, alternating with one another. Such an expedient is in common practice with later composers, at whose disposal stands the increased orchestra of today. To them it would have been possible to ensure great distinctness for certain effects devised by Beethoven without any extravagant claims on the orchestra's virtuosity, merely through the present facilities of distribution.

Beethoven, on the contrary, was obliged to count on the same virtuosity in his band as he himself had before acquired at the pianoforte, where the greatest expertness of technique was simply meant to free the player from all mechanical fetters, and thus enable him to bring the most changeful nuances of expression to that drastic distinctness without which they often would make the melody appear only an unintelligible chaos. The master's last piano compositions, conceived on these lines, have first been made accessible to us by Liszt, and till then were scarcely understood at all. Exactly the same remark applies to his last quartets. Here, in certain points of technique, the single player has often to do the work of many, so that a perfect performance of a quartet from this period may frequently delude the hearer into believing he listens to more musicians than are really playing. Only at quite a recent date, in Germany, do our string quartets appear to have turned their virtuosity to the correct rendering of these wondrous works, whereas I remember hearing these same quartets performed by eminent virtuosi of the Dresden Kapelle, Lipinski at their head, so indistinctly that my quondam colleague Reissiger might hold himself justified in calling them pure nonsense.

The said distinctness rests, in my opinion, on nothing other than a drastic marking of the *melody*. I have shown elsewhere how it became possible to French musicians to discover the mode of rendering here required, before the Germans: the secret was that, adherents of the Italian school, they looked on melody, on song, as the essence of all music. Now, if true musicians have succeeded on this only rightful path, of seeking out and giving prominence to the melody, in finding the proper rendering for works of Beethoven's which erewhile seemed past understanding; and if we may hope that they will further be able to establish it as a normal standard, in the way already done so admirably by Bülow with Beethoven's pianoforte sonatas, then in the great master's necessitation to make his utmost of the technical means at hand—the pianoforte, the quartet, and finally the orchestra—we might perceive the creative impetus to a spiritual development of mechanical technique itself; and to this, in turn, we should owe a spiritualizing of execution never yet displayed by virtuosi. However, as I here am dealing with the Beethovenian orchestra and the main principle of ensuring its *melody,* I have now to consider an evil which at first seems well-nigh irremediable, since it contravenes that principle in a way no ever so spirited virtuosity can possibly amend.

Unmistakably, with the advent of Beethoven's deafness the aural image of the orchestra in so far faded from his mind that he lost that distinct consciousness of its dynamic values which now was so indispensable, when his conceptions themselves required a constant innovation in orchestral treatment. If Mozart and Haydn, with their perfect stability of orchestral form, never employed the soft wood instruments in a sense demanding of them an equal dynamic effect to that of the full "quintet" of strings, Beethoven on the contrary was often moved to neglect this natural proportion. He lets the wind and strings alternate with each other, or even combine, as two equally powerful engines of tone. With the manifold extension of the newer orchestra, it certainly is possible to do this most effectively today; in the Beethovenian orchestra it could be accomplished only on assumptions that have proved illusory.

True, that Beethoven succeeds at times in giving the woodwind the necessary incisiveness, through allying with it the brass: but he was so lamentably hampered by the structure of the "natural" horns and trumpets, the only ones then known, that their employment to reinforce the wood has been the very cause of those perplexities which we feel as irremovable obstacles to the plain emergence of the melody. The musician of today I have no need to warn of the last-named drawbacks in Beethovenian orchestration, for, with our now universal use of the chromatic brass, he will easily avoid them; I have merely to state that Beethoven was compelled suddenly to arrest the brass in outlying keys, or to let it sound a shrill note here and there, as the nature of the instrument permitted, utterly distracting one's attention from the melody and harmony alike.

As it surely is superfluous to produce a schedule in support

of this assertion, I shall proceed to instance the remedies
which I myself have tried in single cases where the obscuring
of the master's plain intention had at last become unbearable.
One obvious cure I have found in a general order to the
second horn, or second trumpet as the case may be, to play
the high note missing from the lower octave in passages such
as

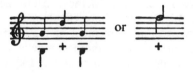

taking it thus:

which is quite easy of execution upon the chromatic instruments alone employed in our orchestras of today. This
simple expedient has in itself removed great obstacles. Less
easy is it to help, however, where the trumpets have dominated everything up to a certain point, and suddenly break
off for mere reason that the passage—though intended to be
as loud as ever—here strays into a key for which the natural
instruments have no corresponding interval. As example I
cite the forte passage in the andante of the C-minor Symphony:

and so on.

Here the trumpets and kettledrums, which for two bars long
have filled the whole with splendor, pause suddenly for close
upon two bars, then re-enter for a bar, and cease again for

over another. Owing to the character of these instruments the
hearer's attention is inevitably diverted to this color incident,
inexplicable on purely musical grounds, and therewith is distracted from the main affair, the melodic progress of the
basses. The only remedy I have been able to devise till now is
to rob those intermittent instruments of a portion of their
glare by ordering them to play less loudly, which at any rate
is advantageous to a greater distinctness in the melody of the
basses. As to the highly disturbing effect of the trumpets in
the first forte of the second movement of the Symphony in A,
however, I at last arrived at a more energetic resolve. Here
Beethoven had very rightly felt the necessity for the two trumpets, but unfortunately their simplicity of structure debarred
them from co-operating in the fashion needed: I made them
play the whole theme in unison with the clarinets. The effect
was so excellent that not one of the audience felt it other than
a gain, yet not as any change or innovation.

An equally thorough cure of a different though kindred
defect in the instrumentation of the second movement of the
Ninth Symphony, its great scherzo, I could never yet decide
upon, since I had always hoped to compass it by purely dynamic means. I refer to the passage, first in C, the second
time in D, which we must take as that movement's second
theme:

and so on.

Here the weak woodwinds, two flutes, two oboes, two clarinets, and two bassoons, have to assert a bold and trenchant
theme against the whole weight of the string quintet accompanying them in continual fortissimo with the four-octave
figure:

The support they receive from the brass is of the kind described above, that is, a "natural" note strewn here and there, which rather mars than aids the theme's distinctness. I challenge any musician to say with a clear conscience that he has ever plainly heard this melody in any orchestral performance, nay, that he would so much as know it if he had not spelled it from the score or played it from the pianoforte arrangement. Our usual conductors do not even seem to have hit upon the first expedient, that of considerably decreasing that *ff.* of the strings; for, whatever orchestra players I have got together for this symphony, they invariably began this passage with the utmost fury. That expedient I myself had always adopted, however, and believed it would prove successful enough if I could only get the woodwind doubled. But experience has never verified my theory, or most inadequately, since it demanded of the woodwind instruments a greater penetration of tone than consists with their character, at least in the present combination. If I had to conduct this symphony again, I can think of no better remedy for the undeniable indistinctness, if not inaudibility in which this extraordinarily energetic dance motif is lost, than to allot a quite definite share in the theme to at least the four horns. This might perhaps be done as shown.

We should then have to try whether the theme was now sufficiently strengthened to allow the string quintet to take the figure of accompaniment in the *ff.* prescribed by the master— a matter of no less importance; for Beethoven's present idea is clearly the same exuberance of spirits that leads to the unparalled excess at the return of the principal theme of the

and so on.

movement in D-minor, a thought which nowhere yet has
found expression but in the most original inventions of this
unique wonderworker. For this very reason I had already
deemed it a sorry makeshift to emphasize the wind by deadening the strings, as that must tame the passage's wild character
past recognition. So that my last advice would be, to go on
fortifying the theme of the "wind," even by bringing in the
trumpets, until it plainly pierces through and dominates the
strings' most strenuous fortissimo. The trumpets in fact are introduced at the passage's return in D, but alas! again, in a way
that merely blurs the woodwinds' theme; so that I here have
found myself compelled, as before, to enjoin on strings and
trumpets alike a characterless moderation. In deciding all such
points, the question is whether one prefers to go for some
time without hearing anything of the tone poet's intentions distinctly, or to adopt the best expedient for doing justice to
them. In this respect the audience of our concert rooms and
opera houses is certainly accustomed to a quite unconscious
act of self-denial.

For another drawback in the instrumentation of this Ninth
Symphony, arising from the selfsame grounds, I decided upon
a radical cure at the last performance I conducted. It concerns
the terrifying fanfare of the wind at the beginning of the last
movement. Here a chaotic outburst of wild despair pours forth
with an uproar which everyone will understand who reads this

passage by the notes of the woodwind, to be played as fast as possible, when it will strike him as characteristic of that tumult of tones that it scarcely lends itself to any sort of rhythmic measure. If this passage is plainly stamped with the ¾ beat; and if as usual, in the conductor's dread of a change of time, this is taken in that cautious tempo held advisable for the suceeding recitative of the basses, it necessarily must make an almost laughable effect. But I have found that even the boldest tempo not only left the unison theme of the "wind" still indistinct, but did not free the passage from the tyranny of a beat which here should certainly appear to be discarded. Again the evil lay in the intermittence of the trumpets, whilst it was impossible to dispense with them and yet observe the master's intentions. These clamorous instruments, compared with which the woodwind is little more than a hint, break off their contribution to the melody in such a way that one hears nothing but the following rhythm:

To give prominence to that kind of rhythm was in any case entirely outside the master's aim, as is plainly shown by the last recurrence of the passage, where the strings co-operate. Thus the limitations of the natural trumpets had here again prevented Beethoven from thoroughly fulfilling his intention. In a fit of despair quite suited to the character of this terrible passage, I took upon myself this time to make the trumpets join with the woodwind throughout, playing as follows:

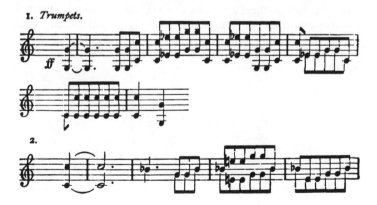

and so on.

At its later return the trumpets again took the passage as the first time.

Light was won: the fearsome fanfare stormed across us in all its rhythmic chaos, and we knew at last why the "Word" must come.

Harder than this *restitutio in integrum* of the master's intention was the finding of a remedy for cases where no mere reinforcement or completion, but an actual tampering with the structure of the orchestration, or even of the part writing, seems the only way to rescue Beethoven's melodic aim from indistinctness and misunderstanding.

For it is unmistakable that the limits of his orchestra—which Beethoven enlarged in no material respect—and the master's gradual debarment from the hearing of orchestral performances, led him at last to an almost naïve disregard of the relation of the actual embodiment to the musical thought itself. If in obedience to the ancient theory he never wrote

higher than   for the violins in his symphonies, whenever

his melodic intention took him above that point he had recourse to the well-nigh childish device of leaping down to the lower octave with the notes that would have overstepped it, heedless that he thereby broke the melodic train, nay, made it positively misleading. I hope that every orchestra already takes the phrase for the first and second violins and violas in the great fortissimo of the second movement of the Ninth Symphony, not as it is written,

from mere dread of the high B for the first violins, but as the melody requires:

I also presume the first flute can now take

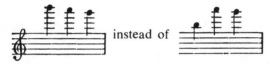

without alarm.

Though here and in many similar cases the remedy is easy enough, the really serious demands for more radical change occur in phrases for the wind where the master's principle of avoiding any violation of the compass accepted for an instrument, and quite particularly the flute, led him either utterly to distort the earlier melodic curve or to introduce this instrument with notes not contained in, and disturbing to, the melody. Now the flute, as extreme upper voice, inevitably arrests the ear so soon as ever it enters, and if the melody does not come out clearly in its notes it necessarily leads the ear astray. Of this ill effect our master appears to have grown completely heedless in course of time: for instance, he will give the melody to the oboe or clarinet in soprano, and, as if determined to introduce the upper register of the flute notwithstanding its incapacity to take the theme iself an octave higher, he assigns it notes outside the melody, thereby distracting our attention from the lower instrument. It is quite another matter when an instrumental composer of today, with the modern facilities, desires to make a principal motive in the middle and lower registers stand out beneath a canopy of higher voices: he strengthens the sonority of the deeper instruments in due degree, choosing a group whose distinct characteristics [of timbre] allow of no confusion with the upper instruments. Thus was I myself enabled in the Prelude to *Lohengrin*, for instance, plainly to sound the fully harmonized theme beneath instruments playing high above it all the while, and to make that theme assert itself against every movement of the upper voices.

But it is no question of this practice—to whose discovery great Beethoven himself first led the way, as to every other

genuine invention—when considering the indisputable hindrances whose removal we have now in view. Rather is it a
disturbing ornament, strewn in as if by chance, whose hurtful
effect on the melody's clearness we would fain tone down.
Thus I have never heard the opening of the Eighth Symphony
(in F) without my attention to the theme being troubled in
the sixth, seventh, and eighth bars by the unthematic entry of
the oboe and flute above the melody of the clarinet; whereas
the flute's participation in the first four bars, although not
strictly thematic, does not disguise the melody, because the
latter is here given utmost prominence by the mass of violins
in forte. But this evil of the woodwind is so serious in an
important passage of the first movement of the Ninth Symphony that I shall choose that instance as my principal text.

It is the eight-bar *espressivo* of the woodwind, beginning in
Breitkopf und Härtel's edition with the third bar of the nineteenth page, toward the end of the first section of the movement aforesaid, and returning in a similar fashion at bar three
of the fifty-third page. Who can declare that he has ever heard
this passage, with distinct perception of its melodic content, at
any of our orchestral performances? With that insight so peculiar to him, Liszt was the first to set this melody in its proper
light through his wonderful pianoforte arrangement of the
Ninth Symphony, among the rest; disregarding the mostly disturbing notes for the flute until it takes over the theme from
the oboe, he lowers that continuation a full octave, and thus
preserves the master's prime intention from all misunderstanding. According to Liszt these melodic phrases read as follows:

Now, it might seem presumptuous, and not in character with
Beethoven's instrumentation—which has its most legitimate
idiosyncrasies—if we here were to omit the flute altogether, or
employ it as mere unison reinforcement of the oboe. I should

therefore leave the flute part essentially as it stands, making it keep perfect faith with the melody only where it takes the lead, and instructing the player to subordinate both force and expression to the oboe where the latter claims our full attention. Accordingly, as continuation of its phrase in the upper octave, fifth bar,

the flute would have to play the sixth bar

not 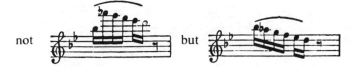 but

and thus the line of melody would be more correctly followed than was possible to Liszt with the technique of the pianoforte.

If we further were to effect one simple alteration in the second bar, making the oboe give the phrase in full, as it does in the fourth bar: thus

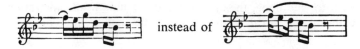 instead of

all we should need to give the whole passage its due pronounced expression, entirely lost at present, would be to somewhat slacken speed and observe the following nuances—which really are nothing but corollaries of the master's own notation:

In bars seven and eight, on the other hand, a fine and at last quite strong crescendo would suitably lead up to the expression with which to throw ourselves on the piercing accents of the following cadenza.

Where the passage returns in the movement's second section, in a different key and register, it will be much harder to bring about a like intelligibleness of its melodic content. Here, the clef being raised, the flute has necessarily the principal part to play; but as even *its* compass does not extend high enough, changes have been made in the melody that positively obscure it and contradict the sense expressed at like time by the other instruments. Let us compare the flute part in the score:

with the melody to be deciphered from a combination of the notes for the oboe, the clarinet, and the flute itself, answering to the earlier form at the close of the first section, namely:

After this comparison we can regard the written flute part only as a serious distortion of the musical thought, since it quite distracts us from the melody.

As a thorough restoration here seemed audacious, since it would have meant the changing of a whole interval twice over, namely, in the third bar of the flute

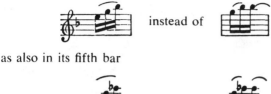 instead of

as also in its fifth bar

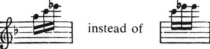 instead of

Liszt himself abstained from the bold attempt, and left the passage a melodic monster; as which it appears to everyone who attends our orchestral performances of this symphony, and here experiences a gap, that is, complete unclearness of the melody, for eight bars long. Having repeatedly suffered under the same distressing impression myself, I now should decide, upon occasion, to get these eight bars played by the flute and oboe in the manner following:

The second flute would have to be omitted from the fourth bar, but in the seventh and eighth, by way of partial compensation, the second oboe would play thus:

Beyond the nuances already recommended for the *espressivo*, in every second bar we should have to make the more strenuous   , to do justice to the variation in the melos; whilst a special *molto crescendo* would have to emphasize the last of the eight bars, thereby also setting in its true decisive light the desperate spring of the flute from G to the high F sharp:

which I here consider to be in thorough keeping with the master's real intention.

If we reflect of what unique importance it is to every musical message, that the melody shall hold us without cease, even though the art of the tone poet often parcels it into its tiniest fractions; and that the correctness of this melodic language can lag in no respect behind the logical coherence of a thought expressed in abstract word speech, without bewildering us by indistinctness as much as does an unintelligible sentence: then we must admit that nothing is so worth the utmost study as the attempt to clear the meaning of a phrase, a bar, nay more, a single note in the message handed down to us by a genius such as Beethoven's. For every transformation, however startling, of a being so eternally sincere, arises solely from the godlike ardor to lay bare to us poor mortals the deepest mysteries of its world view. As one should never quit a knotty passage of a great philosopher before one plainly understands it; and as, this rule neglected, the farther one reads the less one heeds the teacher, so one should never glide over a single bar of a tone poem such as Beethoven's without having distinctly grasped it—unless one proposes merely to beat time in the usual way of our well-appointed academic concertmongers, by whom I am quite prepared to find myself treated as a vain outrager of the sacredness of the letter.

Despite that fear, however, I cannot desist from the attempt to prove by a few more instances that a well-considered alteration of the letter, here and there, may promote a proper understanding of the master's intention.

So my next example shall be a nuance of dynamic expression that obscures its just intention in the carrying out. The stirring passage of the first movement (p. 13, Härtel's edition):

is immediately worked out by a triplication of the melodic thought of the first two bars, thus spreading the crescendo sen-

tence over six whole bars; of these the master gives the first
couple to a detachment of the wind to play quite piano, and
lets the real crescendo enter only with the third bar and the
accession of fresh wind instruments; finally, the third onset of
the same melodic thought is given to the now predominant
strings, with force emphatically increasing till it reaches a fortissimo at bar seven. Now, I have found that the crescendo
prescribed for the ascending figure of the strings in contrary
motion at the second onset of the wind [bar 3 of this six-bar
passage] was detrimental to an emphatic effect of the *più crescendo* of the violins at the third onset,

for it prematurely withdrew attention from the wind and its
none too forcible assertion of the main melodic thought, and
at like time made it difficult to give the thematic entry of the
violins [bar 5] its characteristic stamp, namely, the arrival of
the true crescendo. Here, where the evil is but slightly marked,
it might be altogether conquered by that discreet *poco crescendo* which, alas! is well-nigh unknown as yet to our orchestra players, but which must necessarily precede a *più
crescendo*; and one of my reasons for discussing this passage
at length, is to commend that important dynamic nuance to
special practice and adoption.

Even the most careful observance of that precept, however,
would not remedy the evil consequences of the master's
missed intention where the passage recurs in the last section of
this movement, since the dynamic disproportion of the alternate groups of instruments here makes it quite impossible to
treat with a gentle hand the nuances prescribed. This remark
applies in particular to the first two bars of the kindred passage on page 47 of the score, where the first violins with all the
other strings have to start a crescendo which the clarinet, taking it up with the answering phrase, is quite unable to carry
forward with due force and climax: here I have had to decide
on a total abandonment of the crescendo in the first two bars,
reserving it for the wind to execute, and that most energetically, in the two bars following; and this time, as it already
reaches an actual forte with the fifth bar, the strings may also
fearlessly support it. For the same reason of dynamic disproportion, at the further return of the passage with the last bar

of page 59 the first two bars must be taken quite piano; the two succeeding, with a strong crescendo by the wind, a weaker by the strings; and the latter will commence their real swell of sound with the last two bars before the "forte."

As I do not propose to dilate any longer on the character of Beethoven's nuances of expression, or on what appears to me their proper mode of execution; and as I believe that the care with which I have detailed my grounds for a rare amendment of the nuances prescribed by him will have justified my opinion of that mode: in this regard I have further to say only that the sense of these signs must be studied as thoroughly as the theme itself, since in them often lies the only guide to an understanding of the master's intention when conceiving the musical motive. Yet I may add that when I advocated a suitable modification of Beethovenian tempos in my earlier essay on "Conducting," I certainly had no idea of recommending the witty mode in which, as I have seriously been assured, a Berlin Upper *Kapellmeister* conducts those symphonies: to make them piquant, so it is said, certain passages are first played forte, next piano, as if in echo, at one time slower, at another faster; pranks that a *Kapellmeister's* flow of humor will dictate to him in the score of *The Figlia del Regimento* or *Martha*, for instance, but of which I should have been the last to dream when making my hardly explicable demands in favor of a proper rendering of Beethoven's music.

With the same motive, which has prompted all my efforts to elucidate the master's intentions, I finally have to discuss an extremely difficult passage in the vocal quartet, in which after long experience I have at last discovered the ill that robs this marvelous composition of a truly delightful effect at all performances. It is the last passage for the soloists at the symphony's close, the famous B-natural: "wo dein sanfter Flügel weilt." The reason of its general, nay, universal, failure does not consist in the height of the ascent for the soprano at its close, or the scarcely arduous intonation of the D-natural for the alto in the bar before the last: these difficulties are to be completely surmounted, on the one hand by a soprano with a fairly high compass, on the other by a really musical contralto with a knowledge of the harmonic situation. The real and radical hindrance to a pure and beautiful effect is to be found in the tenor part, which begins its figured motion a bar too soon, and thereby on the one hand mars the clearness of the joint delivery, whilst on the other it assigns the voice a task fatiguing under any circumstances, but here opposed to every law of normal respiration, and using up the singer's strength. If we analyze the passage from the entry of the $\frac{6}{4}$ chord with the signature B-natural (page 264 of the score), its exquisite melodic content resolves itself into a figured phrase for the soprano, taken up in turn by alto, tenor, and bass, in free imitation. Abstracting the voices that merely accompany this phrase, we find the master's intention distinctly expressed as follows:

and so on. However, at the phrase's second entry the tenor supports the alto throughout in sixths and thirds; so that when we reach the third bar, not only do we lose the import of the reappearance of the soprano's melismic figure in the tenor part, but the ear, having already been attracted to the latter voice, is deprived of the charm of a fresh entry. Besides the clouding of the master's intention, the effect of this glorious passage is further injured by the tenor's inability to take the two consecutive figured bars with the same ease as he certainly could the second of those bars alone. After mature deliberation I have therefore resolved to spare the tenor in future the difficult figure in support of the alto, preceding his main entry, and merely to allot him its essential harmonic notes; his part would then run thus:

I am convinced that every tenor who has struggled in vain to sing

will be very grateful to me, and now will render all the finer the melodic phrase belonging to himself. To give the latter full expression, I would commend to him the following dynamic nuance:

For a last remark I merely mention, without going into any further argument, that, when the admirable singer Betz most kindly undertook the baritone solo at the last performance I conducted of the Ninth Symphony, I induced him without any trouble, instead of

to start with the preceding bar and sing:

To our academic singers of the solid English oratorio school we may leave it, for all future time, to vent their "joy" in two strict crotchets.

2. *Acting: Performing* The Flying Dutchman. *The gestures, attitudes, and facial expressions to be used by the performer of the Dutchman's role in the long first monologue*

IN the first place I have to remind the conductor and *régisseur* of what I laid to their heart before, when dealing with the production of *Tannhäuser*, as regards the close accord between what passes in the orchestra and what passes on the stage. The ships and sea, in particular, demand from the *régisseur* an unusual amount of care: he will find all needful indications at the corresponding places of the pianoforte edition or full score. The opera's first scene has to bring the spectator into that mood in which it becomes possible for him to conceive the mysterious figure of the Flying Dutchman himself: it must therefore be handled with exceptional kindness; the sea between the headlands must be shown as boisterous as possible; the treatment of the ship cannot be naturalistic enough: little touches, such as the heeling of the ship when struck by an extra big wave (between the two verses of the Steersman's song) must be very drastically carried out. Special attention is demanded by the lighting, with its manifold changes: to make the nuances of storm in the First Act effective, a skillful use of painted gauzes, as far as quite the middle distance of the stage, is indispensable. However, as these remarks are not specially directed to the purely decorative aspect of the performance (for which I must refer to the scenario of this opera as produced in the Berlin playhouse) I content myself—as said —with pleading for an exact observance of my scattered scenic indications, and leave to the inventive powers of the scenepainter and machinist the method of their carrying out.

I therefore turn simply to the performers, and among these more particularly to the representant of the difficult principal role, that of the Dutchman. Upon the happy issue of this title role depends the *real* success of the whole opera: its exponent must succeed in rousing and maintaining the deepest pity; and this he will be able to, if he strictly observes the following chief characteristics.

His outward appearance is sufficiently notified. His first entry is most solemn and earnest; the measured slowness of his landing should offer a marked contrast with his vessel's weirdly rapid passage through the seas. During the deep trumpet notes (B-minor) at quite the close of the introductory scene he has come off board, along a plank lowered by one of the crew, to a shelf of rock on the shore; his rolling gait, proper to seafolk on first treading dry land after a long voyage, is accompanied by a wavelike figure for the violins and "tenors": with the first crotchet of the third bar he makes his second step—always with folded arms and sunken head; his third and fourth steps coincide with the notes of the eighth and tenth bars. From here on, his movements will follow the dictates of his general delivery, yet the actor must never let himself be betrayed into exaggerated stridings to and fro: a certain terrible repose in his outward demeanor, even amid the most passionate expression of inward anguish and despair, will give the characteristic stamp to this impersonation.

The first phrases are to be sung without a trace of passion (almost in strict beat, like the whole of this recitative), as though the man were tired out; at the words, declaimed with bitter ire, *"ha, stolzer Ozean,"* and so on (thou haughty ocean), he does not break as yet into positive passion: more in terrible scorn, he merely turns his head half-round toward the sea. During the ritornel after *"doch ewig meine Qual"* (but ever lasts my pain), he bows his head once more, as though in utter weariness; the words *"euch, des Weltmeers Fluthen,"* etcetera (to you, ye waves of earthly sea), he sings in this posture, staring blankly before him. For the mimetic accompaniment of the allegro, *"wie oft in Meeres tiefsten Grund,"* etcetera (how oft in ocean's deep abysm), I do not wish the singer to cramp too much his outer motion, yet he still must abide by my prime maxim, namely, however deep the passion, however agonized the feeling which he has to breathe into the voice part, he must for the present keep to the utmost calm in his outer bearing: a movement of the arm or hand, but not too sweeping, will suffice to mark the single more emphatic accents. Even the words *"Niemals der Tod, nirgends ein Grab!"* (Nor ever death, nowhere a grave!), which are certainly to be sung with the greatest vehemence, belong rather to the *description* of his sufferings than to a direct, an actual outburst of his despair: the latter he reaches only with what follows, for which the utmost energy of action must therefore be reserved.

With the repetition of the words *"diess der Verdammniss Schreckgebot!"* (This was my curse's dread decree!) he has somewhat inclined his head and his whole body: so he remains throughout the first four bars of the postlude; with the tremolo of the violins (E-flat) at the fifth bar he raises his face to heaven, his body still bent low; with the entry of the muffled roll of the kettledrum at the ninth bar of the postlude he begins to shudder, the down-held fists are clenched convulsively, the lips commence to move, and at last (with eyes fixed heavenward throughout) he starts the phrase *"Dich frage ich,"* etcetera (Of thee I ask). This whole, almost direct address to "God's angel," for all the terrible expression with which it is to be sung, must yet be delivered in the pose just indicated (without any marked change beyond what the execution necessarily demands at certain places): we must see before us a "fallen angel" himself, whose fearful torment drives him to proclaim his wrath against Eternal Justice.

At last, however, with the words *"Vergeb'ne Hoffnung,"* etcetera (Thou vainest hope) the full force of his despair finds vent: furious, he stands erect, his eyes still gazing heavenward, and with utmost energy of grief he casts all "futile hopes" behind: no more will he hear of promised ransom, and finally (at entry of the kettledrum and basses) he falls of a heap, as though undone.

With the opening of the allegro ritornel his features kindle to a new, a horrible last hope—the hope of world upheaval, in which he too must pass away. This closing allegro requires the most terrible energy, not only in the vocal phrasing but also in the mimic action; for everything here is unmasked passion. Yet the singer must do his best to give this whole tempo, despite its vehemence of phrasing, the semblance of a mere gathering of all his force for the final crushing outbreak at the words *"Ihr Welten! endet euren Lauf!"* etcetera (Ye worlds! now end your last career!). Here the expression must reach its loftiest pitch. After the closing words, *"ewige Vernichtung, nimm' mich auf!"* (Eternal Chaos, take me hence!) he remains standing at full height, almost like a statue, throughout the whole fortissimo of the postlude: only with the entry of the *piano*, during the muffled chant from the ship's hold, does he gradually relax his attitude; his arms fall down; at the four bars of *espressivo* for the first violins he slowly sinks his head, and during the last eight bars of the postlude he totters to the rock wall at the side; he leans his back against it and remains for long in this position, with arms tight-folded on the breast.

I have discussed this scene at so much length, in order to show in what sense I wish the Dutchman to be portrayed, and what weight I place on the most careful adapting of the action to the music. In a like sense should the performer take pains to conceive the whole remainder of his role. Moreover, this aria is also the hardest in all the part, and more especially since the public's further understanding of the subject depends upon the issue of this scene: if this monologue, in keeping with its aim, has thoroughly attuned and touched the hearer, the further success of the whole work is for the major part ensured—whereas nothing that comes after could possibly make up for anything neglected here.

In the ensuing scene with Daland the Dutchman retains at first his present posture. Daland's questions, from aboard ship, he answers with the faintest movement of his head. When Daland comes toward him on dry land, the Dutchman also advances to about the middle of the stage, with stately calm. His whole demeanor here shows quiet, restful dignity; the expression of his voice is noble, equable, without a tinge of stronger accent; he acts and talks as though from ancient habit: so often has he passed through like encounters and transactions; everything, even the seemingly most purposed questions and answers, takes place as if by instinct; he deals as though at bidding of his situation, to which he gives himself mechanically and without interest, like a wearied man. Just as instinctively again, his yearning for "redemption" reawakes; after his fearful outburst of despair he has grown gentler, softer, and it is with touching sadness that he speaks his yearning after rest. The question *"hast du eine Tochter?"* (Hast thou a daughter?) he still throws out with seeming calm; but suddenly the old hope (so often recognized as vain) is roused once more by Daland's enthusiastic answer: *"fürwahr, ein treues Kind"* (Ay! ay! a *faithful* child); with spasmodic haste he cries: *"sie sei mein Weib!"* (be *she* my wife!). The old longing takes him once again, and in moving accents (though outwardly calm) he draws the picture of his lot: *"ach, ohne Weib, ohne Kind bin ich"* (Ah! neither wife nor child have *I*). The glowing colors in which Daland now paints his daughter still more revive the Dutchman's old yearning for "redemption through a woman's truth," and in the duet's closing allegro the battle between hope and despair is driven to the height of passion—wherein already hope appears well-nigh to conquer.

At his first appearance before Senta, in the Second Act, the

Dutchman again is calm and solemn in his outer bearing: all his passionate emotions are strenuously thrust back within his breast. Throughout the lengthy first *fermata* he stays motionless beside the door; at the commencement of the drum solo he slowly strides toward the front; with the eighth bar of that solo he halts (the two bars *accelerando* for the strings relate to the gestures of Daland, who still stands wondering in the doorway, awaiting Senta's welcome, and impatiently invites it with a movement of his outstretched arms); during the next three bars for the drum the Dutchman advances to the extreme side-front, where he now remains without a motion, his eyes bent fixedly on Senta. (The recurrence of the figure for the strings relates to the emphatic repetition of Daland's gesture: at the pizzicato on the next *fermata* he ceases inviting her, and shakes his head in amazement; with the entry of the basses, after the *fermata*, he himself comes down to Senta.

The postlude of Daland's aria must be played in full: during its first four bars he turns to depart without further ado; with the fifth and sixth he pauses, and turns round again; the next seven bars accompany his byplay as he watches now the Dutchman, now Senta, half pleased, half curiously expectant; during the subsequent two bars for the double-basses he goes as far as the door, shaking his head; with the theme's resumption by the wind instruments he thrusts in his head once more, withdraws it vexedly, and shuts the door behind him—so that with the entry of the F-sharp chord for the "wind" he has disappeared for good. The remainder of the postlude, together with the ritornel of the following duet, is accompanied on the stage by total immobility and silence: Senta and the Dutchman, at opposite extremities of the foreground, are riveted in contemplation of each other. (The performers need not be afraid of wearying by this situation: it is a matter of experience that this is just the one which most powerfully engrosses the spectator, and most fittingly prepares him for the following scene).

The whole succeeding E-major section is to be executed by the Dutchman with complete repose of outer mien, however stirring the emotion wherewith he delivers his lines; only the hands and arms (and that most sparingly) must he employ to emphasize the stronger accents. Not until the two bars of the drum solo, before the following E-minor tempo, does he rouse himself, to draw somewhat closer to Senta: during the short ritornel he moves a few steps toward the middle of the stage, with a certain constraint and mournful courtesy. (I must here inform the conductor that experience has shown me I was mistaken in marking the tempo *un poco meno sostenuto*: the long preceding tempo, true enough, is somewhat slow at its commencement—particularly in the Dutchman's first solo— but little by little it instinctively freshens toward the close, so that with the entry of E-minor the pace must necessarily be somewhat restrained once more, in order to give at least the opening of this section its needful impress of decorous calm. The four-bar phrase, in fact, must be *slackened down* in such a manner that the fourth bar is played in marked *ritenuto*: the same thing applies to the first phrase now sung by the Dutchman.)

With the ninth and tenth bars, during the solo for the drum, the Dutchman again advances one, and two steps nearer to Senta. With the eleventh and twelfth bars, however, the time must be taken somewhat more briskly, so that at the B-minor, *"du könntest dich,"* etcetera, the tempo I really meant—moderato, certainly, but not quite so dragging—at last arrives, and is to be maintained throughout the section. At the *più animato*: *"so unbedingt, wie?"* the Dutchman betrays the animating effect which Senta's first real speech has wrought on him: with this passage he must already begin to show more visible agitation. But Senta's passionate interjection: *"o welche Leiden! Könnt' ich Trost ihm bringen!"* (What tale of grief! Oh, could I respite bring him!) stirs him to the depths of his being: filled with astonished admiration, he stammers out the half-hushed words: *"welch' holder Klang im nächtlichen Gewühl!"* (What gentle strains in Night's most raging storm!). With the *molto più animato*, he scarce can master himself any longer; he sings with the utmost fire of passion, and at the words: *"Allmächtiger, durch diese sei's!"* (Almighty, be't through *her!*) he hurls himself upon his knees. With the *agitato* (B-minor) he rises to his feet impetuously: his love for Senta displays itself at once in terror of the danger she herself incurs by reaching out a rescuing hand to him. It comes over him as a hideous crime, and in his passionate remonstrance against her sharing in his fate he becomes a human being through and through, whereas he hitherto had often given us but the grim impression of a ghost. Here, then, the actor must give to even his outer bearing the full impress of human passion; as if felled to the ground, he falls before Senta with the last words: *"nennst ew'ge Treue du nicht dein!"* (if troth of thine lasts not for aye!) so that Senta stands high above him, like his angel, as she tells him what *she* means by *troth.*

During the ritornel of the succeeding *allegro molto* the Dutchman lifts himself erect, in solemn exaltation: his voice is stirred to the sublimest height of victory. In all that follows there can be no more room for misunderstanding: at his last entry, in the Third Act, all is passion, pain, despair. Particularly do I exhort the singer not to drag the recitative passages, but to take everything in the most spirited, most stressful tempo.

The role of Senta will be hard to misread; one warning alone have I to give: let not the *dreamy* side of her nature be conceived in the sense of a modern, sickly sentimentality! Senta, on the contrary, is an altogether robust Northern maid, and even in her apparent sentimentality she is thoroughly naïve. Only in the heart of an entirely naïve girl, surrounded by the idiosyncrasies of northern nature, could impressions such as those of the ballad of the Flying Dutchman and the picture of the pallid seaman call forth so wondrous strong a bent, as the impulse to redeem the doomed: with her this takes the outward form of an active monomania such, indeed, as can be found only in quite naïve natures. We have been told of Norwegian maids of such a force of feeling, that death has come upon them through a sudden rigor of the heart. Much in this wise may it go, with the seeming "morbidness" of pallid Senta.

Nor must Eric be a sentimental whiner: on the contrary, he is stormy, impulsive, and somber, like every man who lives alone (particularly in the northern highlands). Whoever should give a sugary rendering to his *Cavatina* in the Third Act would do me a sorry service, for it ought instead to breathe distress and heartache. (Everything that might justify a false conception of this piece, such as its falsetto passage and final cadenza, I implore may be either altered or struck out). Further, I beseech the exponent of Daland not to drag his role into the region of the positively comic: he is a rough-hewn figure from the life of everyday, a sailor who scoffs at storms and danger for sake of gain, and with whom, for instance, the—certainly apparent—sale of his daughter to a rich man ought not to seem at all disgraceful: he thinks and deals, like a hundred thousand others, without the least suspicion that he is doing any wrong.

3. Singing: Ludwig Schnorr von Carolsfeld, Wagner's ideal Heldentenor; descriptions of his work in Tannhäuser and Tristan; Wagner's method of coaching a singing actor

OF the young singer Ludwig Schnorr of Carolsfeld I first heard through my old friend Tichatschek, who paid me a visit at Zurich in the summer of 1856, and directed my attention to the future of this highly talented young artist. The latter had just commenced his stage career at the Carlsruhe court theatre; by the director of that theatre, who likewise visited me in the summer of the following year, I was informed of Schnorr's especial predilection for my music, as also for the tasks I set before the dramatic singer. On that occasion we agreed that I should destine my *Tristan*, with whose conception I then was busied, for a first performance at Carlsruhe; for this purpose it was hoped that the Grand Duke of Baden, who was very kindly disposed toward me, would be able to overcome the difficulties which still stood in the way of my unmolested return to the dominions of the German Bund. From young Schnorr himself, a little later, I received a beautiful letter, with well-nigh passionate assurance of his devotion to me.

For reasons which contained a considerable element of vagueness, the realization of our preconcerted plan for the Carlsruhe performance of my *Tristan*, completed by me in the summer of 1859, was ultimately declared impossible. As to Schnorr himself, I was informed at the same time that, despite his great devotion to me, he considered it impossible to master the difficulties of the principal role, particularly in the last act. Moreover, his bodily health was represented to me as being in a critical condition: he was said to be suffering from an obesity that deformed his youthful figure. In particular the picture wakened in me by this last report was very dismal. When in the summer of 1861 I visited Carlsruhe at last, and the execution of the earlier scheme was broached anew by the grand duke—who throughout had retained his friendly feeling toward me—I was almost rebellious against

336

the management's offer to open negotiations for the part of Tristan with Schnorr, then engaged at the Dresden court theatre; I declared that I had no manner of wish to make the personal acquaintance of this singer, since I feared lest the grotesqueness of his figure, occasioned by his malady, might even blind me to his real artistic gifts.

Soon afterward a performance of my new work was projected at Vienna, but, as it in turn had not been made possible, I spent the summer of 1862 at Biebrich on the Rhine; thence I visited Carlsruhe for a performance of *Lohengrin*, in which Schnorr appeared as "guest." I went to it in secret, and had intended to let myself be seen by no one, for sake of concealing my presence from Schnorr; for, abiding by my renouncement of him, and in dread lest the terrifying accounts of his misshapenness should be more than realized by actual impression, I was anxious to avoid even making his personal acquaintance. That timorous mood of mine was swiftly altered.

Though the sight of this swan knight landing from a tiny shallop offered me the certainly somewhat estranging first impression of a youthful Hercules, yet his earliest entry placed me under the quite specific spell of the God-sent legendary hero in whose regard one asks not: How is he? but tells oneself: Thus is he! And indeed this instantaneous effect, piercing the very soul, can be compared with nothing but magic; I remember to have experienced it in my earliest youth with Schröder-Devrient, determining the cast of my whole life, and since then never so definitely and strongly as with Ludwig Schnorr at his entry in *Lohengrin*. In futher course of his rendering, I noticed certain tokens of unripeness of conception and execution; but even these afforded me the charm of unspoiled youthful purity, of a soil still virgin for the choicest flowers of artistic cultivation. The warmth and tender inspiration, shed from the wondrous love-filled eyes of this scarcely more than youth, forthwith assured me of the daemonic fire with which they once would flame; to me he rapidly became a being for whom, on account of his boundless talent, I fell into a tragical suspense. Directly after the First Act I sought out a friend, and commissioned him to beg of Schnorr an interview with me after the performance. And so it fell out: late in the evening the young giant came untired to my room at the hotel, and the bond was sealed; we had little need to talk, save jokes. But a longer meeting at Biebrich was arranged for the near future.

There by the Rhine we met for two happy weeks, to go

through my Nibelungen works and particularly the *Tristan* to our heart's content, accompanied at the pianoforte by von Bülow, who then was on a visit to me. Here everything was said and done, to bring about an intimate agreement as to each artistic interest that filled our minds. As regards his doubts of the executability of the Third Act of *Tristan*, Schnorr told me they had less arisen from any fear of over-taxing and exhausting the voice than from his inability to understand one single passage; but a passage which seemed to him the weightiest of all, namely, the curse on love, and especially the musical expression of the words "from sweet-ness and suffering, laughter and sorrow" (*aus Lachen und Weinen, Wonnen und Wunden*) and so on. I showed him how I had meant it, and what manner of expression, at any rate prodigious, I wanted given to this phrase. He swiftly under-stood me, recognized his mistake in imagining too quick a tempo, and now perceived that the resulting "rush" had been to blame for his failure to hit the right expression, and thus for his missing the meaning of the passage itself. I admitted that with this slower tempo I was certainly making a quite unwonted, perhaps a monstrous, demand on the singer's strength; but *that* he made utterly light of, and at once proved to me that precisely through this *ritenuto* he was able to render the passage to complete satisfaction.

To me that one feature has remained as unforgettable as instructive: the utmost physical exertion lost all its fatiguing-ness, owing to the singer's having grasped the right expression of the words; the spiritual understanding gave forthwith the strength to overcome the material difficulty. And this tender scruple had weighed for years on the young artist's conscience; his doubt of being able to reproduce a solitary passage had made him fear to match his talent against the whole task; to "cut" that passage—the ready expedient of our most cele-brated opera heroes—naturally could never occur to him, for he perceived in it the apex of the pyramid to which the tragic tendence of this Tristan towers up. Who can measure the hopes which took possession of me, now that this wondrous singer had passed into my life? We parted; and only after years, were new and strange destinies to bring us to-gether again for final solving of our problem.

Thenceforward my endeavors for a performance of *Tristan* went hand in hand with those for Schnorr's co-operation in it; they prospered only when a new-arisen, illustrious friend of my art granted me the Munich court theatre for that purpose. At the beginning of March, 1965, Schnorr arrived in Munich, upon a brief visit, for sake of discussing the needful preliminaries of our soon forthcoming project; his presence led to a performance of *Tannhäuser*, for the rest not specially prepared, in which he undertook the title role with a single stage rehearsal. I thus was limited to private conversation with him, for arranging with him his execution of this hardest of all my tasks for the dramatic singer.

In general, I told him of the dismal dissatisfaction I had experienced from the previous stage success of my *Tannhäuser*, owing to the principal part having never yet been properly rendered, nay, even comprehended. Its chief feature I defined to him as *utmost energy, of transport alike and despair,* with no halfway house between the moods, but abrupt and downright in its change. To fix the type for his portrayal, I bade him note the importance of the first scene with Venus; if the intended shock of this first scene hung fire, the failure of the whole impersonation needs must follow; for no jubilance of voice in the first finale, no girding and fury at the papal ban in Act III, could then avail to bring about the right impression.

My new working of this Venus scene, prompted by my recognition of just that importance and its insufficient definition in the earlier draft, had not as yet been put in rehearsal at Munich; Schnorr must therefore do his best, for the present, with the older version: the torturing conflict in Tannhäuser's soul being here still left more exclusively to the *singer,* all the more necessary would it be for him to give it due expression by the energy of his interpretation; and in my opinion he would accomplish this only if he took the whole scene as one long climax leading to the catastrophic cry, "My weal rests in *Maria!*" I told him, this *"Maria!"* must burst forth with such vehemence that the instantaneous disenchantment of the Venusberg, and the miraculous translation to his native valley, shall be understood at once as the necessary fulfillment of an imperative behest of feeling driven to the utmost resolution. With that cry he had taken the attitude of one transported into loftiest ecstasy, and thus he must remain, without a motion, his eyes rapt heavenward; ay, even until addressed by the knights who enter later, he must not quit the spot.

How to solve this task—already refused me by a very celebrated singer, a few years previously, as quite inexecutable —I would direct him at the stage rehearsal, placing myself beside him on the boards. There accordingly I took my

stand, close by his side, and, following the music and surrounding scenic incidents bar by bar, from the goatherd's
song to the departure of the pilgrims, I whispered him the
inner cycle of the entranced's emotions, from the sublimest
ecstasy of complete unconsciousness to the gradual wakening of his senses to their present environment, his ear being
first to return to life—while, as if to shield the wonder from
disturbance, he forbids his eye, now unchained from the
magic spell of Heaven's ether, to look as yet upon the homely
world of earth. The gaze fixed movelessly on high, merely
the physiognomic play of features, and finally a gentle
slackening of the body's rigid upright pose, betray the stir of
gained rebirth; till every cramp dissolves beneath the whelm-
ing miracle, and he breaks down at last in humbleness, with
the cry: "Almighty, to Thy name be praise! Great are the
wonders of Thy grace!" Then, with the hushed share he
takes in the pilgrims' chant, the look, the head, the whole
posture of the kneeling man, sink ever deeper; till choked
with sobs, and in a second, saving swoon, he lies prone,
unconscious, face to earth.

Continuing to prompt him in undertones, to a like effect,
I remained by Schnorr's side throughout the rehearsal. On
his part my hints and very brief directions were answered by
a fleeting glance, just as gentle, and of so heartfelt a sincerity
that, assuring me of the most marvelous concordance, it
opened for myself new insights into my own work; so that
through one example, at any rate unparalleled, I became
aware how fruitful to both sides may be the affectionate
communion of artists differently endowed, if only their gifts
are mutually and fully complemental.

After that rehearsal, not another word did we say about
Tannhäuser. Moreover, after the performance on the following
night scarce a word fell from our lips about it; especially
from mine no word of praise or recognition. Through my
friend's quite indescribably wonderful impersonation, of that
evening, I had gained a glimpse into my own creation such
as seldom, perhaps never, had been vouchsafed to an artist.
That fills one with a certain hallowed awe, in whose presence
it beseems one to observe a reverent silence.

With this one, this never repeated impersonation of
Tannhäuser, Schnorr had thoroughly realized my innermost
artistic aim; the daemonic in joy and sorrow had never
for one moment been lost from sight. The crucial passage
in the second finale, so often begged by me in vain: *"Zum*

Heil den Sündigen zu führen," and so on—obstinately omitted by every singer on plea of its great difficulty, by every *Kapellmeister* in virtue of the customary "cut"—for the first and unique time was it delivered by Schnorr with that staggering and thereby harrowing expression which converts the hero, of a sudden, from an object of abhorrence into the typic claimant of our pity. Through his frenzy of humiliation during the rapid closing section of the Second Act, and through his anguished parting from Elisabeth, his appearance as a man demented in Act III was properly prepared for: from this broken being the outburst of emotion was all the more affecting; till at last his renewed access of madness summoned the magic reapparition of Venus with well nigh the same daemonic cogence as the invocation of the Virgin, in Act I, had miraculously called back the Christian world of home and day. Schnorr was truly terrible in this last frenzy of despair, and I cannot believe that Kean or Ludwig Devrient in *Lear* could ever have attained a grander pitch of power.

The impression made upon the audience was most instructive to myself. Much, as the well-nigh speechless scene after the exorcising of the Venusberg, gripped it in the right sense, and provoked tumultuous demonstrations of general and undivided feeling. On the whole, however, I noticed mere stupefaction and surprise; in particular the quite new, such as that eternally omitted passage in the second finale, almost alienated people through upsetting their wonted notions. From one friend, not otherwise dullwitted, I positively had to hear that I had no right to get Tannhäuser represented my way, since the public as well as my friends had everywhere received this work with favor, and thereby had plainly pronounced the former reading—the tamer but pleasanter one, however it might dissatisfy myself—at bottom the more correct. My objection to the absurdity of such an argument was dismissed with an indulgent shrug of the shoulders, as much as to say, it made no difference.

In face of this general effeminacy, nay, debauchment, not only of the public taste, but even of the judgment of some of those with whom we came into closer contact, there was nothing for us but to possess our souls in patience; so we went on in our simple concord as to what was true and proper, quietly doing and working, without other expostulation than that of the artistic deed.

And that deed was preparing, with the return of my artistic ally at commencement of the ensuing April, and the beginning of our joint rehearsals for *Tristan*. Never has the most bungling singer or orchestra player let me give him such minute instructions as this hero who touched the highest mastership of song; with him the seemingly most paltry stubbornness in my directions found naught but gladdest welcome, for their sense he caught at once; so that I really should have deemed myself dishonest, if, haply not to seem too touchy, I had withheld the tiniest comment. The reason of it was that the ideal meaning of my work had already opened to my friend quite of itself, and truthfully become his own; not one fiber of this soul tissue, not the faintest hint of a hidden allusion had ever escaped him, had failed of being felt to its tenderest shade. Thus it was a mere question of accurately gauging the technical means of singer, musician, and mime, to obtain a constant harmony of the personal aptitude, and its individuality of expression, with the ideal object of portrayal. Whoso was present at these rehearsals must remember to have witnessed an artistic consentaneousness the like whereof he has never seen before or since.

Only as to the Third Act of *Tristan* did I never say a word to Schnorr, beyond my earlier explanation of the one passage which he had not at that time understood. Whereas throughout the rehearsals of Acts I and II I had kept both ear and eye intent upon my player, with the commencement of Act III I instinctively quite turned from sight of the death-wounded hero lying stretched upon his bed of anguish, and sat motionless upon my chair with half-closed eyes, to plunge myself within. At the first stage rehearsal the unwonted duration of my seeming utter listlessness would appear to have inwardly embarrassed Schnorr, for in course of the whole protracted scene, even at the singer's most impassioned accents, I never once faced toward him, nay, not so much as stirred; but when at last, after the curse on love, I reeled across and, bending down to throw my arms around the prostrate figure on the couch, I softly told the wondrous friend that no words could express my estimate of the ideal now fulfilled by him, his deep-brown eye shot fire like the star of love; a scarcely audible sob—and never did we speak another serious word about this final act. Just to intimate my feelings, I would simply allow myself some such jest as the following: a thing like this Act III was easy enough to write, but to be compelled to hear Schnorr sing it was hard indeed, and so I could not even bring myself to look.

In truth even yet, when jotting down these recollections

after three years' interval, it is impossible for me to express myself adequately about that achievement of Schnorr's as Tristan, which reached its summit in my drama's final act; and impossible, perhaps, for reason that it quite eludes comparison. Entirely at loss to furnish so much as an approximate idea thereof, I believe the only way to transfix that terribly fleeting miracle of musico-mimetic art will be to ask the genuine friends of my self and works, both now and in times to come, before all to take into their hands the score of this Third Act. They first would have to pay close heed to the orchestra, from the act's commencement down to Tristan's death, and follow carefully the ceaseless play of musical motives, emerging, unfolding, uniting, severing, blending anew, waxing, waning, battling each with each, at last embracing and well nigh engulfing one another; then let them reflect that these motives have to express an emotional life which ranges from the fiercest longing for bliss to the most resolute desire of death, and therefore required a harmonic development and an independent motion such as could never be planned with like variety in any pure symphonic piece, and thus, again, were to be realized only by means of instrumental combination such as scarce a purely instrumental composer had been compelled as yet to press into his service to a like extent. Now let them observe that, regarded in the light of opera, this whole enormous orchestra bears to the monologues of the singer—outstretched upon a couch, too—the mere relation of the accompaniment to a so-called solo: and they may judge for themselves the magnitude of Schnorr's achievement, when I call on every candid hearer of those Munich performances to testify that, from the first bar to the last, all attention, all interest was centered in the actor, the singer, stayed riveted to him, and never for a moment, for one single text word, did he lose his hold upon his audience, but the orchestra was wholly effaced by the singer,. or—to put it more correctly—seemed part and parcel of his utterance. Surely, to anyone who has carefully studied the score, I have said enough to signalize the incomparable artistic grandeur of my friend's achievement, when I add that already at the full rehearsal unbiased hearers had credited this very act with the most popular effect in all the work, and prophesied for it a general success.

In myself, while witnessing the public representations of *Tristan*, a reverent amaze at this my friend's titanic deed developed to a positive terror. To me it seemed at last a crime, to demand a frequent repetition of this deed, to enlist it perchance in the operatic repertoire; and, after Tristan's love curse in the fourth performance, I felt driven to declare definitely to those around me that this must be the last performance of *Tristan*, that I would not consent to its being given any more.

It may be difficult for me to make this feeling clearly understood. No anxiety about victimizing the physical forces of my friend entered into it, for any such consideration had been wholly silenced by experience. Anton Mitterwurzer, who, as Schnorr's colleague at the Dresden court theatre and his comrade, Kurwenal, in the Munich Tristan performances, evinced the most intelligent interest in the doings, and the deepest sorrow for the fate of our friend—that well-tried singer expressed himself most aptly in this regard: when his Dresden colleagues raised the cry that Schnorr had murdered himself with *Tristan*, he very shrewdly replied that a man like Schnorr, who had shown himself master of his task in the fullest sense, could never overtax his physical powers, since a victorious disposal of the latter was necessarily included in the spiritual mastery of the whole affair. As a matter of fact, neither during nor after the performances was there ever detected the smallest fatigue in his voice, or any other bodily exhaustion; on the contrary, whilst solicitude for their success had kept him in constant agitation *before* the performances, after each fresh success he was restored to the gayest of moods and the most vigorous carriage. It was the fruit of these experiences, very correctly estimated by Mitterwurzer, that led us earnestly to ponder, on the other hand, how it might be gathered for the establishment of a new style of musicodramatic rendering, a style in answer to the true spirit of German art. And here my encounter with Schnorr, now thriven to such an intimate alliance, opened a prospect full of unhoped promise for the outcome of our joint labors in the future.

The inexhaustibility of a genuinely gifted nature had thus become right plain to us, from our experiences with the voice of Schnorr. For that mellow, full, and brilliant organ, when employed as the immediate implement for achieving a task already mastered mentally, produced on us the said impression of absolute indefatigableness. What no singing master in the world can teach we found was only to be learned from the example of important tasks thus triumphed over. But what is the real nature of these tasks, for which our singers have not yet found the proper Style? Their first aspect is that of an unwonted demand upon the singer's physical endurance; and if the singing master is called in, he believes—and rightly, from his standpoint—that he must fly to mechanical devices for strengthening the organ, in the sense of absolutely denaturalizing its functions. In the first stages of its cultivation, as probably is inevitable, the voice is treated as a mere animal organ; but when, in further course of training, its musical soul is to unfold itself at last, standing specimens can alone supply the scheme of voice employment; therefore the whole remaining matter resolves itself into a question of the tasks proposed in them.

Now, the singing voice has hitherto been trained on none but the Italian model; there existed no other. Italian vocalism, however, was informed with the whole spirit of Italian music; at its prime its most thorough exponents were the castrati, since the spirit of this music made for merely sensuous pleasure, without a spark of nobler passion—whilst the voice of the adolescent male, the tenor, was scarcely then employed at all, or, as later, in a falsetto masking as the voice of the castrato. Yet, under the undisputed leadership of German genius, and particularly of Beethoven, more modern music has soared to the height and dignity of sterling art through this one thing: that, beyond the sensuously pleasurable, it has drawn the spiritually energetic and profoundly passionate into the orbit of its matchless expression. How then can the masculine voice, trained to the earlier musical tendence, take up the tasks afforded by our German art of nowadays? Cultivated for a mere material appeal to the senses, it here sees nothing but fresh demands on material strength and sheer endurance, and the modern singing master therefore makes it his principal aim to equip the voice to meet them. How erroneous is this procedure may be easily imagined; for any male singing organ merely trained for physical force will succumb at once, and bootlessly, when attempting to fulfill the tasks of newer German music, such as are offered in my own dramatic works, if the singer be not thoroughly alive to their *spiritual* significance.

The most convincing proof of this was supplied us by Schnorr himself; and, in illustration of the profound and total difference we here are dealing with, I shall cite my experience of that adagio passage in the second finale of *Tannhäuser* (*"zum Heil den Sündigen zu führen"*). If nature in our times has wrought a miracle of beauty in the manly vocal organ, it is the tenor voice of Tichatschek, which for forty years has retained its strength and roundness. Whoever heard him recently declaim in *Lohengrin* the story of the Holy Grail, in noblest resonance and most sublime simplicity, was touched and seized as by a living wonder. Yet in Dresden many years ago I had to strike out that passage from *Tannhäuser* after its first performance, because Tichatschek, then in fullest possession of his vocal force and brilliance, was unable, owing to the nature of his dramatic talent, to master the expression of that passage as *an ecstasy of humiliation,* and positively fell into physical exhaustion over a few high notes. Now, when I state that Schnorr not only delivered this passage with the most heartrending expression but brought out those same high notes of passionate grief with complete fullness of tone and perfect beauty, I certainly have no idea of ranking Schnorr's vocal organ above Tichatschek's, in any sense as though it surpassed the latter in natural power; but, as compared with this uncommon gift of nature, I claim for the voice of Schnorr just that aforesaid tirelessness in service of the spiritual understanding.

With the recognition of Schnorr's unspeakable import for my own artistic labors, a new springtime of hope had dawned upon my life. Now had been found the immediate ligament, to link my work with the present and make it fruitful. Here one might both teach and learn; the despaired of, scoffed at and reviled, it now could be made an art deed testifying of itself. The institution of a German style, for rendering and representing works of German spirit, became our watchword. And now that I had embraced this livening hope of a great but gradual advance, I openly declared myself against any speedy resumption of *Tristan*. With this performance, as with the work itself, we had taken too vast, nay, well nigh forlorn a leap across to the new, that still remained to be first won; rents and chasms yawned between, and they must be most diligently filled, to pave a highway for the needful comrades to escort us lonely ones to those far distant heights.

So Schnorr was to become our own. The foundation of a Royal School for Music and Dramatic Art was resolved on. The difficulties in the way of releasing the artist from his Dresden contract suggested to us the peculiar character of the position which we ourselves must offer him, to make it once for all a worthy one. Schnorr should retire altogether from the theatre and become teacher of our school, simply taking part in special, extraordinary stage performances, in confirmation of our course of study. This project thus involved the liberation of an artist, whose soul burned clear with noblest fire, from the common drudgery of the operatic repertoire; and what it meant for him, to have to languish in that service, could be felt by none more keenly than myself.

Have not the most inextricable, most torturing and most dishonoring molestations, cares and humiliations in my life proceeded from that one misunderstanding which, perforce of outer haps of life and outward semblance, held me up to the world, to every social and aesthetic relation contained therein, as just nothing but an "opera composer" and "operatic *Kapellmeister*"? If this singular *quid pro quo* was bound to bring eternal confusion into all my relations with the world, and particularly into my demeanor toward its claims upon myself, one certainly cannot make light of the sufferings which the young, deep-souled, and nobly earnest artist had to endure in his position of "opera singer," in his subjection to a theatric code devised against refractory heroes of the wings, in his obedience to the orders of uncultured and overbearing official chiefs.

Nature meant Schnorr for a musician and poet; like myself, he took up the special study of music after receiving a general education in the sciences; and very probably he would already have followed a road both outwardly and inwardly akin to mine, had there not early developed in him that organ whose exhaustlessness was to serve for fulfillment of my most ideal wants, and thus to associate him directly with my life career, as complemental counterpart of my own tendence. But behold! our modern culture had nothing to offer him save theatrical engagements, the post of "tenor," in much the same way as Liszt became a "pianoforte player."

Now at last, protected by a prince most graciously disposed to my ideal of German art, our culture was to be grafted with the shoot* whose growth and fruitage would have fertilized the soil for genuinely German deeds of art; and truly it was time that rescue were afforded to the downcast spirit of my friend. Here lay the hidden worm that sapped the man and artist's buoyant life force. This became plainer and plainer to me, as to my astonishment I remarked the passionate, nay, furious intensity with which he jibbed at misdemeanors in the traffic of the stage, things that are always happening in

* The proposed music school at Munich is meant.—EDS.

this blend of bureaucratic priggishness and comediantic want of conscience, and therefore are not felt at all by those concerned. Once he complained to me: "Ah! it's not my acting and singing that take it out of me in *Tristan*, but the provocations in between; my lying quietly upon the boards, after the sweating fever of excitement in the great scene of the last act—that's what kills me. In spite of all my complaints, I haven't been able to get them to screen the stage from the terrible draft that pours like ice across my rigid body and chills me to death, while the gentlemen behind the wings trot out the latest scandal of the town!" As we had noticed no symptoms of a catarrhal cold, he gloomily hinted that such chills had other, more dangerous, results with him.

In the last days of his Munich stay his excitability took an ever darker tinge. Finally he appeared on the boards once more, as Eric in *The Flying Dutchman*, and played that difficult episodic role to our highest admiration; nay, he positively made us shudder by the singular moody vehemence wherewith—in strict accordance with the wish I had expressed to him—he portrayed the sorrows of this young Norweigan hunter, making his hapless love break out in flames of lurid fire. Only, by a word or two he betrayed to me that night a deep dissatisfaction with all his surroundings. Moreover, he seemed suddenly invaded by doubts as to the feasibility of our cherished hopes and plans; he appeared unable to comprehend how, with this prosaic, utterly unsympathetic, nay, spitefully hostile environment that lay in ambush for us, one could entertain a serious thought of doing good work. And it was with bitter grudge that he received pressing orders from Dresden to return by a given day, for a rehearsal of *Il Trovatore* or *The Huguenots*.

From this dismal anxious mood, in which I shared at last myself, we were set free again by the last glorious evening we ever spent together. The king had a private audience in the Residenz theatre, for which he had commanded the performance of various excerpts from my works. From each of *Tannhäuser, Lohengrin, Tristan, Das Rheingold, Die Walküre, Siegfried*, and finally *Die Meistersinger*, a characteristic piece was rendered by singers and full orchestra, under my personal direction. Schnorr, who here heard many a new thing of mine for the first time, and further sang "Siegmund's Liebeslied," "Siegfried's Schmiedelieder," Loge in the *Rheingold* morsel, and finally Walther von Stolzing in the larger fragment from *Die Meistersinger*, with entrancing power and beauty—Schnorr felt as if lifted above all cares of life, upon his return from half an hour's interview to which he had been graciously invited by the king, who attended our performance quite alone. Boisterously he threw his arms around me: "God! how thankful I am for this evening!" he cried, "Eh! now I know what makes your faith so firm! Be sure, between this heavenly king and you, I too shall turn to something splendid!"

So again we bade goodbye to serious talk. We took tea together in a hotel; tranquil gaiety, friendly faith, sure hope were the mainsprings of our well-nigh purely joking conversation. "Well, well!" the word went, "tomorrow, once more, to the ghastly masquerade! Then soon set free for ever!" Our speedy au revoir was a thing so certain in our minds that we held it superfluous, nay, quite out of place, even to say farewell. We parted in the street, as at our customary good night; next morning my friend departed quietly for Dresden.

About a week after our scarcely heeded parting, Schnorr's death was telegraphed to me. He had sung at one more stage rehearsal, and had had to rebuke his colleagues for expressing their surprise that he really was left with any voice. Then a terrible rheumatism had seized his knee, leading to a fever that killed him in a very few days. Our preconcerted plans, the representation of *Siegfried*, his anxiety lest folk attribute his death to an overexertion with *Tristan*, these were the thoughts that had occupied his lucid, and at last his waning consciousness.

With Bülow, I hoped to reach Dresden in time for the interment of our beloved friend: in vain; it had been necessary to commit his body to the earth a few hours before the time appointed; we arrived too late. In brilliant July sunshine, be-bannered Dresden was shouting its welcome to the crowds streaming in for the General Festival of German Singers. The coachman, hotly urged by me to reach the house of death, had great difficulty in forcing his way through the throng, and told me that upwards of 20,000 singers had come together.

Ay!—said I to myself—*The* singer has but just gone!

Posthaste we turned our backs on Dresden.

PART VII

Bayreuth

1. The founding of the Festspielhaus; Wagner's speech on the occasion; the design of the theatre; hidden orchestra, perspective arrangement, stage space

THE remoter future—should my work be then still living —cannot be spared a knowledge of the circumstances which have hindered my work from becoming a full-fledged deed, from that decisive meeting* to the present day. Now that I and my unusual artistic project had been placed in broad daylight, it really appeared as if all the ill-will that had lurked before in ambush was determined to make an open attack in full force. Indeed, it seemed as though no single interest, of all those represented by our press and our society, was not stung to the quick by the composition and plan of production of my work. To stay the disgraceful direction taken by this feud in every circle of society, which recklessly assailed alike protector and protected, I could but decide to strip the scheme of that majestic character which my patron had accorded it, and turn it into a channel less provocative of universal wrath.† Indeed, I even tried to divert public attention from the whole affair by spending a little hard-won rest on the completion of the score of my *Meistersinger*, a work with which I should not appear to be quitting the customary groove of performance at the theatre.

But, for all its favorable reception by the public, the experiences I made with the fate of this very work, on the

---

* Wagner's first meeting with Ludwig II of Bavaria.—EDS.

† In rendering the latter half of this sentence I have been obliged to paraphrase it slightly, to make its meaning clearer. What our author alludes to is obviously the grandiose project entertained by Ludwig II in 1865, of building a monumental theatre for the *Ring*, to be connected by a bridge across the Isar with a new avenue extending to the royal palace in Munich. This plan fell through, as is commonly known, owing to the bitter jealousy of courtiers, place hunters, and the press. In fact it was not until 1871, after the epoch-making reconsolidation of Germany, that Richard Wagner's hopes of getting even a "provisional theatre" built for his work, no matter in what German "nook," revived at all.—TR.

one hand, on the other with the spirit of our German stage, determined me to hold unflinchingly aloof from any further dealings with the latter. Owing to the peculiar nature of the German sense of art, whoever has had serious dealings with the German theatre in the hope of meeting some power of discrimination, some support by an energetic expression of will, on the part of public taste, must have perceived at once that his efforts were totally fruitless and could stir up only strife against himself. Thus nothing could persuade me to take a share in the attempts at performing single sections of my larger work, though I myself had taken the first step thereto in my earlier bending to the storm. I am even ignorant of the exact way in which those attempts fell out, since my friends fully recognized that I should be spared a report of the details.*

Through the sacrifice herein involved, however, it became possible for me to obey the first command of my exalted benefactor: *Complete thy work!* Arrived once more in that peaceful refuge whence I once had gazed upon the soundless world of Alps while mapping out that overweening plan, remote from every clamor I was at last to be permitted to bring its composition to an end.

Now the same faithful guardian who watched over the completion of my work has also made it possible for me to tread in hope and confidence the path that shall lead to its performance in the mode first planned. For if a whole community once set itself against the mandate of one master mind, with a work completed under shelter of this mighty one I now have found a fresh community to whom, by its own will, to commit the realization of that scheme.

In search for the ideal side of German nature, I necessarily must turn to the community of executant artists, before the so-called public. Here I began with the musician proper [i.e. the orchestra player], and won encouragement from his ready apprehension of the right, so soon as duly shown him. Next to him, though far more encased in bad habits, I found the musical mime; who, with any real talent, at once perceives and gladly treads his art's true sphere, if but the right example is held up before him.

Arguing from these two hopeful symptoms, I then inferred

---

* *Das Rheingold* and *Die Walküre* were produced in Munich on September 22, 1869, and June 26, 1870, respectively.—Tr.

that an excellent performance by the artists could scarcely lack intelligent acceptance; and thus my further task was to awake the presentiment of such a higher satisfaction in all whose help I needed to promote my scheme. If alike by setting the example of good performances, as by supplying the key to artistic problems first clearly worked out by myself, I shall have roused the active attention of a sufficient number of the German public to enable me to reach my goal—in *that* I must recognize the "new community" I had to find.

WITH the appeal I published to the friends of my art, to join me in the undertaking I had planned, I was addressing in the strictest sense a question to an unknown quantity, with whose constitution I was first to gain acquaintance from its answer.

Only to a handful of more intimate friends did I express my views as to the precise mode in which a solid form might be given to the interest I asked for. The youngest of these friends, the exceptionally talented and energetic Karl Tausig, embraced the matter as a task peculiarly falling to himself: together with a lady of distinguished rank and earnestly inclined toward my art, he sketched the plan of obtaining for my enterprise a sufficient number of patrons to subscribe the sum we estimated as the minimum required for building a provisional theatre, equipping a first-class stage with faultless scenery, and compensating the artists who were to be specially selected and assembled for our performances; a sum amounting to three hundred thousand thalers, to be collected in patronage subscriptions of three hundred thalers each [about $219,150 and $219.00]. Hardly had he begun to set his scheme in motion when a sudden death removed him from us in his thirtieth year. Deeply awed, to me the question erst addressed to a "community" had now become a question to Fate.

The little band of friends, so seriously lessened, worked on undaunted in the spirit of the friend deceased; a man of sovereign power was won as patron, and unexpected readiness displayed itself among less powerful, ay, even among the powerless, to raise for me a new and vital power through association. At Mannheim, with the support of comrades just as earnestly disposed, a pre-eminently active friend of my art and tendencies—a gentleman till then unknown to me in person—called into life a union for the furtherance of my published project; a union which boldly took the name of "Richard Wagner Verein," and bore it in defiance of all scoffers. Its example soon was copied: under the same title a second *Verein* arose in Vienna, and similar societies were quickly formed in an ever-increasing number of German cities. Nay, from across the German frontiers, from Pesth and Brussels, London and at last New York, unions of like name and tendence conveyed to me their promises and greetings.

It then appeared high time for me to make the needful preparations for carrying out my enterprise. Already in the spring of 1871 I had chosen Bayreuth for my goal, after a quiet visit of inspection: all idea of using the famous opera house of the margraves I abandoned as soon as I had seen its interior; but the character and situation of the kindly city were all that I had wished for. So I repeated my visit in the winterly late autumn of that year; this time to open direct negotiations with the Bayreuth town authorities themselves. I have no need here to reiterate the earnest thanks I owe those true and honored men; in excess of every expectation, their courteous hospitality now gave my daring enterprise the friendly soil whereon to thrive in common with my livelong home. An unrivaledly beautiful and extensive freehold, hard by the town itself, was bestowed upon me for erection of the theatre I had in mind. Having arranged the structural scheme with a man of eminent experience and proved inventiveness in the internal disposition of theatres,* I agreed with him to commit to an equally practiced architect† the preparation of the further plans and execution of the provisional building. And thus, despite the many difficulties occasioned by the unusual nature of our task, we were able to announce to our friends and patrons the 22nd of May in the year 1872‡ as the date for laying the foundation stone.

For this event I conceived the notion of giving my supporters an artistic reward for their trouble of meeting at Bayreuth, in the shape of as perfect a performance as possible of Beethoven's great Ninth Symphony. The simple invitation which I addressed to our best orchestras, choirs, and famous soloists sufficed to procure me a body of such

---

* Wilhelm Neumann, of Berlin; perhaps, however, the reference is to Karl Brand of Darmstadt, the expert stage machinist who had so much to do with the building of a theatre in which the stage was the main consideration.—TR.

† Brückwald, of Leipzig.—TR.

‡ R. Wagner's birthday.—TR.

admirable executants as scarcely ever can have been assembled for a similar purpose.

This first success was of most encouraging augury for the future prospering of the grand theatrical performances themselves. It set all concerned in so excellent a temper, that even the drenching storm which maimed the rites of laying the foundation stone was unable to damp our spirits. In the capsule to be buried in that stone we placed a message from the illustrious defender of my best endeavors, together with various records and a verse indited by myself:

"Hier schliess' ich ein Geheimniss ein,
da ruh' es viele hundert Jahr':
so lange es verwahrt der Stein,
macht es der Welt sich offenbar."*

To the assembly itself I addressed the following speech.†

"My Friends and valued Helpers!

"Through you I today am placed in a position surely never occupied before by any artist. You believe in my promise to found for the Germans a theatre of their own, and give me the means to set before you a plain delineation of that theatre. For this is to serve, in the first place, the provisional building whose foundation stone we lay today. When we see each other on this spot once more, that building shall greet you, that building in whose characteristics you will read at once the history of the idea which it embodies. You will find an outer shell constructed of the very simplest material, which at best will remind you of those wooden structures which are knocked together in German towns for gatherings of singers and the like, and pulled down again as soon as the festival is over. How much of this building is reckoned for endurance shall become clearer to you when you step inside. Here too you will find the very humblest material, a total absence of

---

* A secret here I deep have lain,
for centuries there may it rest:
while e'er the stone shall this contain,
its meaning may the world attest!—TR.

† This address, originally intended for the ceremony itself, was actually delivered to the great gathering in the old opera house at Bayreuth after the return of the little party that had braved the elements to assist in laying the stone. The performance of the Ninth Symphony was given later in the day.—TR.

embellishment; perchance you will be surprised to miss even
the cheap adornments with which those wonted festal halls
were made attractive to the eye. In the proportions and
arrangement of the room and its seats, however, you will
find expressed a thought which, once you have grasped it,
will place you in a new relation to the play you are about
to witness, a relation quite distinct from that in which you
had always been involved when visiting our theatres. Should
this first impression have proved correct, the mysterious entry
of the music will next prepare you for the unveiling and
distinct portrayal of scenic pictures that seem to rise from
out an ideal world of dreams, and which are meant to set
before you the whole reality of a noble art's most skilled
illusion. Here at last you are to have no more provisional
hints and outlines; so far as lies within the power of the
artists of the present, the most perfect scenery and miming
shall be offered you.

"Thus my plan; which bases what I just have called the
enduring portion of our edifice on the utmost possible
achievement of a sublime illusion. Must I trust myself to
lead this artistic exploit to complete success, I take my
courage solely from a hope engendered by despair itself.
I trust in the German spirit, and hope for its manifestment
in those very regions of our life in which, as in our public
art, it has languished in the sorriest travesty. Above all I trust
in the spirit of German music, for I know how glad and
bright it burns in our musicians so soon as e'er a German
master wakens it within them; and I trust in our dramatic
mimes and singers, for I have learned that they could be as
if transfigured to new life when once a German master led
them back from idly playing at a harmful pastime, to true
observance of their lofty calling. I trust in our artists, and
aloud I dare to say it on a day which, at my simple friendly
bidding, has gathered round me so select a host of them from
points so distant in our fatherland: when, self-forgetful for
very joy in the artwork, they presently shall sound their festal
greeting to you with our great Beethoven's wonder symphony,
we all may surely tell ourselves that the work we mean to
found today will also be no cheating mirage, though we
artists can vouch only for the sincerity of the idea it is to
realize.

"But to whom shall I turn, to ensure the ideal work its solid
lastingness, the stage its monumental shrine?

"Of late our undertaking has often been styled the erection of a 'national theatre at Bayreuth.' I have no authority to accept that title. Where is the 'nation,' to erect itself this theatre? When the French National Assembly was dealing with the state subvention of the great Parisian theatres a little while ago, each speaker warmly advocated the continuance, nay, the increase of their subsidies, since the maintenance of these theatres was a debt not merely due to France, but to Europe which had accustomed itself to receiving from them its laws of intellectual culture. Can we imagine the embarrassment, the perplexity into which a German parliament would fall, had it to handle a similar question? The debates perhaps would terminate in the comforting conclusion that our theatres required no national support at all, since the French National Assembly had already provided for *their* needs too. In the best event our theatre would be treated as the German Reich was treated in our various *Landtags* but a few years back: namely, as a pure chimera.

"Though a vision of the true German theatre has built itself before my mental eye, I have had promptly to recognize that I should be abandoned from both within and without, were I to step before the nation with that scheme. Yet I may be told that, though one man might not be believed, the word of many would perhaps find credence: that one really might succeed in floating a gigantic limited company, to commission an architect to rear a sumptuous fabric somewhere or other, which one then might dub a 'German National Theatre' in full confidence that a German national theatric art would spring up in it of itself. All the world now pins its faith to a continual, and in our latter days an extremely rapid 'progress,' without any clear idea of what we are advancing toward, or the kind of step we are marching; but those who brought a really new thing to the world have never been asked what relation they bore to this "progressive" surrounding, that met them with naught but obstacles and opposition. On a holiday like this we shall not recall the undisguised complaints, the deep despair of our very greatest minds, whose labors showed the only veritable progress; but perhaps you will allow the man you honor today with so unusual a distinction, to express his heartfelt joy that the thought of a single individual has been understood and embraced in his lifetime by so large a number of friends as your gathering here and now attests.

"I had only you, the friends of my peculiar art, my deeds

and labors, for sympathizers with my projects: only asking your assistance for my work, could I approach you. To be able to set that work intact and pure before those who have shown their serious liking for my art in spite of all adulteration and defacement—this was my wish; to you I could impart it sans presumption. And solely in this almost personal relation to you, my friends and helpers, can I see the present ground on which to lay the stone to bear the whole ambitious edifice of our noblest German hopes. Though it be but a provisional one, in that it will resemble all the German's outward form for centuries. 'Tis the essence of the German spirit to build from within: the eternal God lives in him, of a truth, before he builds a temple to His glory. And that temple will proclaim the inner spirit to the outer eye in measure as that spirit has matured its amplest individuality. So I shall call this stone the talisman whose power shall unseal to you the hidden secrets of that spirit. Let it now but bear the scaffolding whose help we need for that illusion which shall clear for you life's truest mirror, and already it is firmly, truly laid to bear the prouder edifice whene'er the German folk desires, in its own honor, to enter its possession with you. So be it consecrated by your love, your benisons, the gratitude I bear you, all of you, who have sped, enheartened, given to and helped me!—Be it consecrated by the spirit that inspired you to hear my call; that filled you with the courage, taunts unheeding, to trust me wholly; that found in me a voice to call you, because it dared to hope to recognize itself within your hearts: the German Spirit, that shouts to you across the centuries its ever young Good morrow."

I scarcely need relate the course of that fair feast whose tenor I believe the speech above sufficiently expresses. With it was begun a deed that can endure the scoffs and calumnies of all to whom its underlying thought must forever stay incomprehensible, as is only to be expected of those who hang about life's marketplace to glean the fodder for an ephemeral art or literary existence. However hard our undertaking prove, my friends and I will therein merely recognize the selfsame hardships that have weighed for years, for centuries, upon all healthy evolution of a culture truly native to the German. Whoever has followed with sympathy my demonstrations of those hardships, as viewed from my particular standpoint, will not require me to explain them once again. My hopes in this regard, however, I here will finally denote by one sole name, that "Bayreuth" which has already become a byword for something unknown or misinterpreted, by the one side, and awaited with fond expectance by the other.

For what our not always very brilliant wags had formerly made merry over with the senseless term a *Zukunftsmusik* (music of the future) has now exchanged its cloudy shape for the solid masonry of "Bayreuth." The cloud has found a resting place, whereon to take material form. The "theatre of the future" is no longer the "preposterous idea" I tried to force on our standing court and city theatres for sake, we shall say, of becoming general music director or even general intendant;* but (perhaps because I nowhere saw a chance of getting appointed?) I now appear to wish to graft my notion on a definite locale, which therefore must be reckoned with. This is the little, out-of-the-way, forgotten Bayreuth. It thus must be allowed, in any case, that I had no desire to frame my undertaking with the glitter of a crowded capital—which would not have come so hard to me as some profess to fancy.† But whether those wits direct their jests at the place's smallness or the extravagance of the idea it stands for, they cannot do away with its localization of what was but a thought before, and I accept the sneer with greater satisfaction than was possible to me with that idiotic *Zukunftsmusik*. If my friends were able to adopt the latter designation of their tendences with the same pride as the valiant Netherlanders once wore their nickname "Gueux" [beggars], I willingly adopt "Bayreuth" as a title of good omen, a collective term for all the life that gathers now from widest circles round the realizing of the artwork I had planned.

Who, buffeted from place to place, attains the spot he chooses for his final rest, examines all its signs for happy augury. If my Hans Sachs in *Die Meistersinger* lauds Nuremberg as lying in the heart of Germany, with still more right I now could claim that kindly lot for Bayreuth. Hither once stretched the vast Hercynian wild, in which the Romans ne'er set foot; to this day its memory lingers with us in the appellation Frankenwald, that wood whose gradual uprooting we may trace in countless names of places showing "Rod" or "Reut."

* As the music historian in Brockhaus' *Konversationslexikon* has recently insinuated.—R. WAGNER.

† In his *Richard Wagner* Mr. H. S. Chamberlain tells us that a society in Berlin offered the master "a million" ($243,500) in 1873, if he would transfer his project to that city, and that a similar offer reached him from Chicago.—TR.

Of the name "Bayreuth" itself there are two different explanations. Here the Bavarians (*Bayern*) are said to have cleared the forest and made a habitation, their *Herzogs* (dukes) having once upon a time received the land from the King of the Franks: this theory flatters a certain sense of historical justice, restoring the land, after many a change of rulers, to those to whom it owed a portion of its earliest culture. Another, a more skeptical explanation declares that we here have simply the name of an ancient castle, situated "near the clearing" (*beim Reuth*). In either case we keep the "Reuth," the place reclaimed from waste and made productive; reminding us of the "Rütli" of old Switzerland*—to gain an ever-fairer, nobler meaning from the name.

The land became the Franconian Mark [borderland] of the German Reich against the fanatical Czechs, whose more peaceable Slavonic brethren had already settled in it and so enhanced its culture that many local names still bear alike the Slavic and the German stamp; here first were Slavs transformed to Germans, without a sacrifice of idiosyncrasy, and amicably shared the fortunes of a common country. Good witness of the German spirit's qualities! After a long dominion over this mark the burgraves of Nuremberg took their road to the Mark of Brandenburg, to found in time the royal throne of Prussia, and finally the German Empire. Though the Romans had never pushed so far, yet Bayreuth was not left without Romanic culture. In the Church it stoutly threw aside the yoke of Rome; but the old city, burned so oft to ashes, assumed the garment of French taste at bidding of parade-struck princes: an Italian built its great opera house, one of the most fantastic monuments of the rococo style. Here flourished ballet, opera, and comedy. Yet the burgomaster of Bayreuth "affected"—as the high dame herself expressed it—to address his welcome to the sister of Frederick the Great in honest *German*.

From these few traits who might not paint a picture of the German character and history, a picture which enlarged would mirror back the German realm itself? A rugged soil, tilled by the most diverse of tribal settlers, with local names often scarce intelligible, and distinctly recognizable through nothing, at the last, but its victorious loyalty to the German language. The Roman Church imposed on it her Latin, Gallic

* Where Tell and his companions met to found Swiss freedom. —TR.

culture her French; the scholar and the gentleman used none but foreign lingo, yet that bumpkin of a burgomaster still "affected" to speak his *Deutsch*. And *Deutsch* it after all remained. Eh! and looking closer at that scene between the Bayreuth burgomaster and the Prussian princess, we see that not only was German spoken here, but one even affected a "purified" German; which must have much annoyed the lofty dame, as in her meeting with the Empress of Austria the two ladies had been unable to understand one another in German, through the opposing rankness of the only patois known to each. Thus we here find German *culture* too: plainly the educated burgesses of Bayreuth took an active interest in the reawakening of German literature, enabling them to follow the unparalleled upsoaring of the German spirit, the feats of Winckelmann, Lessing, Goethe, and finally Schiller; so that at last the town itself produced a far-famed contribution to the culture of that spirit, in the works of its native Friedrich Richter—self-styled "Jean Paul" in mirthful irony—whilst the folly of high quarters, disowning home for foreign dictates and French influences, fell victim to a ghastly impotence.

To whom must not the strangest thoughts have flocked, when he took his seat on that 22nd of May, 1872, in the selfsame place once filled by the margrave's court and guests, great Frederick himself at their head; from the selfsame stage that once had offered these a ballet, an Italian opera, or French comedy, to hear the forces of that marvelous Ninth Symphony unchained by German orchestra players gathered to the feast from every district of the Fatherland? When at last from those tribunes where gold-laced trumpeters had blown the banal fanfare, for reception of their mightinesses by a fawning household, impassioned German singers cried to the assembly now, "Embrace, ye millions!"—before whom did there not float a living vision of the sounding triumph of the German spirit?

This meaning was it granted me to attach to our inaugural feast without dissent; and to all who kept it with us the name Bayreuth has come to mean a precious memory, a stirring thought, a pregnant motto.

In sooth it needed such a motto, to hold out in daily war against the undermining of the German nation by a deeply alien spirit.

The question "What is German?" has long and earnestly engaged me. Forever it would shape itself anew: did I deem it answerable for certain in the one form, straightway it stood before me in another, till I often gave it up in utter doubt. A patriot driven to undisguised despair, the wonderful Arnold Ruge, at last pronounced the German "despicable." Who once has heard that awful word cannot prevent it coming back to him in moments of revulsion, and it perhaps may then be likened to those potent drugs which doctors use to fight a deadly malady: for it speedily brings home to us that we ourselves are "the German," the German who recoils in horror from his own degenerate image; he perceives that only to himself is this degeneration visible as such—and what else could have made that knowledge possible, save the indomitable consciousness of his own true nature? No trick can now deceive him any more; no longer can he dupe himself with pleasant words, cajole himself with semblances; over him they have lost all power. In no accepted phase of life, no current form, can he recognize Germanism, but where it often positively sins against that form. Even his language, that one hallowed birthright of his race, laboriously preserved and handed new to him by greatest spirits, he sees insensately abandoned to the openest abuse; he sees how almost every preparation is on foot to verify the boastful saying of the President of the North American States, that soon but *one* tongue will be spoken over all the earth—which, taken literally, can mean only a universal jargon blended of all ingredients, whereto the modern German may at any rate flatter himself on having already furnished a right handsome contribution.

Whoso had shared with me these painful thoughts must alike have felt the power of the promise, "Embrace, ye millions!" upon that day in the strange rococo opera-house at Bayreuth, and perchance divined that the saying of General Grant might fulfill itself in another way than loomed before the esteemed American.

It surely also dawned on everyone that the redeeming German word, in the sense of the great master of tones, required another dwelling place than that Franco-Italian opera house, to become a concrete plastic deed. And hence we laid upon that day the foundation of a building with whose peculiarities I now shall try to familiarize the reader, foreshadowing by their very character the *example* of what I long have yearned for as a meet and fitting habitation for the German spirit.

To explain the plan of the festival theatre now in course of erection at Bayreuth I believe I cannot do better than to begin with the need I felt the first, that of rendering invisible the mechanical source of its music, to wit the orchestra; for this one requirement led step by step to a total transformation of the auditorium of our neo-European theatre.

The reader of my previous essays already knows my views about the concealment of the orchestra, and, even should he not have felt as much before, I hope that a subsequent visit to the opera will have convinced him of my rightness in condemning the constant visibility of the mechanism for tone production as an aggressive nuisance. In my article on Beethoven I explained how fine performances of ideal works of music may make this evil imperceptible at last, through our eyesight being neutralized, as it were, by the rapt subversion of the whole sensorium. With a dramatic representation, on the contrary, it is a matter of focusing the eye itself upon a picture; and that can be done only by leading it away from any sight of bodies lying in between, such as the technical apparatus for projecting the picture.

Without being actually covered in, the orchestra was therefore to be sunk so deep that the spectator would look right over it, immediately upon the stage; this at once supplied the principle that the seats for the audience must be ranged in gradually ascending rows, their ultimate height to be governed solely by the possibility of a distinct view of the scenic picture. Our whole system of tiers of boxes was accordingly excluded; beginning at the walls beside the stage itself, their very height would have made it impossible to prevent their occupants looking straight down into the orchestra. Thus the arrangement of our rows of seats acquired the character obtaining in the antique amphitheatre: yet the latter's actual form, with arms stretched out on either side beyond the full half-circle, could not be seriously thought of; for the object to be plainly set in sight was no longer the chorus in the orchestra, surrounded for the greater part by that ellipse, but the "scene" itself; and that "scene," displayed to the Greek spectator in the merest low relief, was to be used by us in all its depth.

Hence we were strictly bound by the laws of *perspective*, according to which the rows of seats might widen as they mounted higher, but must always keep their front toward the stage. From the latter forward the *proscenium*, the actual framing of the scenic picture, thus necessarily became the starting point of all further arrangements. My demand that the orchestra should be made invisible had at once inspired the genius of the famous architect* whom I was first privileged to consult in the matter with a scheme for the empty space between the proscenium and the front row of seats: this space—which we called the "mystic gulf," because it had to part reality from ideality—the master framed in a second, a wider proscenium, from whose relation to the narrower proscenium proper he anticipated the singular illusion of an apparent throwing back of the scene itself, making the spectator imagine it quite far away, though he still beholds it in all the clearness of its actual proximity; while this in turn gives rise to the illusion that the persons figuring upon the stage are of larger, superhuman stature.

The success of this arrangement would alone suffice to give an idea of the spectator's completely changed relation to the scenic picture. His seat once taken, he finds himself in an actual "theatron," that is, a room made ready for no purpose other than his looking in, and that for looking straight in front of him. Between him and the picture to be looked at there is nothing plainly visible, merely a floating atmosphere of distance, resulting from the architectural adjustment of the two proscenia; whereby the scene is removed as it were to the unapproachable world of dreams, while the spectral music sounding from the "mystic gulf," like vapors rising from the holy womb of Gaia beneath the Pythia's tripod, inspires him with that clairvoyance in which the scenic picture melts into the truest effigy of life itself.†

* Gottfried Semper.—Tr.

† As to the scandalous thrusting forward of this picture, so that the spectator can almost touch it, I recently expressed myself in my *Glance at the German Operatic Stage of Today*; I have only to add that, to my sincere relief, I found that this evil had already been felt by a builder of theatres—though, to my knowledge, by this one alone—namely, the architect of the playhouse at Mannheim. So far as possible in the present theatre, he had isolated the scenic picture by abolishing the proscenium boxes and leaving in fact an empty recess at either side, behind a second proscenium. But unfortunately the orchestra occupying this space was unconcealed, and the towering boxes still jutted hard on the proscenium; whereby the good effect was lost, nothing remaining but the excellence of the builder's idea. Governed by an equally proper feeling, the artistic intendant of the Dessau court theatre kept the proscenium mostly in half-light, to throw the picture back as by a rim of shadow; which had the additional advantage that, finding themselves but poorly lighted in the extreme foreground, the performers preferred to stay in the vivid relief of the middle distance.—R. Wagner.

A difficulty arose in respect of the side walls of the auditorium: unbroken by any tiers of boxes, they presented a flat expanse, to be brought into no plausible agreement with the rows of seats. The famous architect at first entrusted with the task of building the theatre in monumental fashion had all the resources of his art to draw upon, and made so admirable a use of the noblest renaissance ornament that the bare surface was transformed into a perpetual feast for the eye. For our provisional theatre at Bayreuth we had to renounce all idea of a like adornment, which has no meaning unless the material itself be precious, and were once more faced with the question how to treat these walls that stood at variance with the actual space for holding the audience.

A glance at the first of the plans . . . shows an oblong narrowing toward the stage, as the space to be employed for the spectators, bounded by two unsightly wedges that widen as they approach the proscenium. While the side walls flanking these wedges were obliged to be rectangular because of the structural requirements of the building, and although the space thus left on either hand could conveniently be utilized for stairways giving access to the seats, the visual effect of the whole would have been ruined by those two empty corners. Now, to mask the blanks immediately in front of our double proscenium, the ingenuity of my present adviser had already hit on the plan of throwing out a third and still broader proscenium.

Seized with the excellence of this thought, we soon went further in the same direction, and found that, to do full justice to the idea of an auditorium narrowing in true perspective toward the stage, we must extend the process to the whole interior, adding proscenium after proscenium until they reached their climax in the crowning gallery, and thus enclosing the entire audience in the vista, no matter where it took its place. For this we devised a system of columns, answering to the first proscenium and broadening with the blocks of seats they bounded; at once they cheated us of the square walls behind them, and admirably hid the intervening doors and steps. With that we had settled all our internal arrangements. . . .

As we were building a merely provisional theatre, and therefore had only to keep in view its inner fitness for its end, we might congratulate ourselves on being relieved, for the present, of the task of furnishing our edifice with a beautiful exterior in architectural harmony with the inner idea. Had we even been supplied with nobler material than our estimates allowed of, we should have shrunk in terror from the task of erecting a monumental pile, and been obliged to look around us for assistance such as we could scarcely anywhere have found just now. For here presented itself the newest, the most individual problem, and, since it could never yet have been attempted, the most difficult for the architect of the present (or the future?) day.

Our very poverty of means, however, compelled us to think of nothing but the sheer objective fitness of our building, the absolutely essential for our aim: and aim and object here resided in the inner relation of the auditorium to a stage of the largest dimensions necessary for mounting perfect scenery. Such a stage requires to be of three times the height it presents to the spectator, since its scenery must be able to be raised alike and lowered in its full extent. Thus from floor to roof the stage needs twice the height required by the auditorium. If one consults this utilitarian need alone, the outcome is a conglomerate of two buildings of totally different form and size. To mask the disproportion of these two buildings as much as possible, most architects of our newer theatres have considerably increased the height of the auditorium, and above that, again, have added rooms for scenepainting and sundry managerial purposes—though such rooms have generally been found so inconvenient that they are very seldom used. Moreover, one could always fall back on the expedient of adding another tier or two of boxes, even allowing the topmost gallery to lose itself high up above the opening for the stage, since it was meant only for the poorer classes, upon whom one thought nothing of inflicting the inconvenience of a bird's-eye view of the goings-on below them in the parterre. But these tiers are banished from *our* theatre, nor can an architectural need dictate that we should lift our gaze on high, above blank walls, as in the Christian dome.

Now, by treating in the very baldest way our task of erecting an outwardly artless and simply provisional theatre, to be placed on a high and open site, I believe we have at like time reduced the problem itself to its plainest terms. It now lies naked and distinct before us, the tangible diagram, so to speak, of what a theatric structure should outwardly express if it have no common, but an altogether ideal purpose to reveal. The main body of this structure thus represents the infinitely complex apparatus for scenic performances of the greatest possible perfection of technique: its annex, on the other hand, consists of little more than a covered forecourt, in which to accommodate those persons for whom the performance is to become a visual play.

There it may stand, on the fair hill by Bayreuth.

2. "Parsifal *at Bayreuth*," *final festival in 1882: acting technique, scenery, rehearsals*

As our dedication feasts of nowadays retain their popularity chiefly through the attendant so-called "church wake," I believed that my only course, in setting the symbolic love feast of my Grail Knights before a modern opera public, would be to think of the *Bühnenfestspielhaus* as this time hallowed for the picturing of so sublime a rite. . . . Whoever had the mind and eye to seize the character of all that passed within the walls of that house during those two months, both the productive and the receptive, could not describe it otherwise than as governed by a consecration that shed itself on everything without the smallest prompting. Experienced managers asked me after the authority presiding over this so amazingly accurate execution of every scenic, musical, and dramatic detail upon, above, below, behind, and before the stage; I cheerfully replied that it was Anarchy, for all did what they *would*, to wit, the right.

And so it was: each understood the whole, and the object aimed at by the whole. No one thought too much expected of him, no one too little offered him. Success was to each of greater moment than applause, to receive which from the audience in the wonted evil manner was deemed obnoxious; whilst the lasting interest of our visitors rejoiced us as a testimony to the correctness of our estimate of our own efforts. Fatigue we knew not; though the influence of well-nigh continuously dull and rainy weather was most depressing, everyone declared himself relieved at once when he set to work in the theatre. If the author of all the labors transferred to his artistic friends and comrades was often haunted by the presage of a scarcely avoidable lassitude, each nightmare was swiftly dispelled by a hearty assurance of the highest spirits from all concerned.

Disputes about rank were impossible where six singers of so-called "first roles" had undertaken the unnamed leadership of Klingsor's flower maidens, while their followers were played with the greatest alacrity by representatives of every branch. Had there really been need of an example for the actors of the principal parts—it could have been given them by the artistic unanimity of those magic flower maidens. They were foremost in fulfilling one of the weightiest requirements, which I had to make the pivot of a proper rendering: that passionate accent which modern stage singers have acquired from the operatic music of our day, breaking every melodic line without distinction, was to be interdicted here. I was understood at once by our fair friends, and soon their coaxing strains took on an air of childlike naïvete that, touching through a matchless intonation, was utterly opposed to that idea of sensual seduction which certain people had presupposed as the composer's aim. I do not believe that so magical a maiden grace has ever been displayed by song and gesture, as our lady artists gave us in this scene of *Parsifal*.

To turn this magic to a *consecration* imbuing the whole stage festival soon became the earnest care of all engaged in the rehearsals and performances; and what unwonted demands were thus made upon style will be evident if we reflect that the strongly passionate, the fierce, nay, savage, had to be expressed according to its natural character in single portions of the drama. The difficulty of the task thereby imposed on the leading actors was ever more apparent to us. Before all else we had to adhere to the greatest distinctness, especially of speech: a passionate phrase must have a confusing, and may have a forbidding, effect if its logical tenor remains unseized; but to seize it without effort we must be enabled to understand plainly the smallest link in the chain of words at once: an elided prefix, a swallowed suffix, or a slurred connecting syllable destroys that due intelligibleness forthwith. And this self-same negligence directly extends to the melody, reducing it through disappearance of the musical particles to a mere trail of isolated accents, which, the more passionate the phrase, at last become sheer interjections; the weird, nay, the ridiculous effect whereof we feel at once when they strike on our ear from some distance, without a vestige left of the connecting links.

If in our study of the Nibelungen pieces six years back the singers already were urged to give precedence to the "little" notes, before the "big," it was solely for sake of that distinctness; without which both drama and music, speech and melody, remain equally un-understandable, and are sacrificed to that trivial operatic effect whose employment on my own dramatic melody has called forth such confusion in our musical so-called "public opinion" that nothing but this indispensable distinctness can clear it up. But that involves complete abandonment of the false pathos fostered by the mode of rendering condemned.

Violent outbursts of poignant passion, the natural vents of a deeply tragical subject, can produce their harrowing effect only when the standard of emotional expression which they exceed is observed in general. Now we deemed this moderation best ensured by a wise economy in the use of breath and plastic movement. In our practices we became aware of the clumsy waste of breath, in the first place, committed in most of our opera singing; for we soon discovered what a single well-placed breath could do toward giving a whole sequence of tones its proper sense, both melodic and logical. Simply by a wise restraint and distribution of force we—naturally—found it so much easier to render justice to what I have termed the "little" notes, which, lying lower for the most part, yet form important links in speech and melody; and just because the advantage of rounding off the entire phrase in one respiration forbade us to squander too much breath on the higher notes, which stand forth of themselves. So we were able to keep long lines of melody unbroken, however great the play of color in their feeling accents—eloquent instances whereof I may recall to our hearers with Kundry's lengthy narration of Herzeleide's fate, in the second act, and Gurnemanz' description of Good Friday's magic in the third.

In close connection with the advantage of a wise economy in the expenditure of breath, for the effectual understanding of the dramatic melody, we recognized the need of ennobling the plastic movements by a most conscientious moderation. Those screams, which are almost the only thing heard of the tune in our common operatic style, have always been accompanied by violent movements of the arms, employed at last so uniformly that they have lost all meaning and can but give the innocent spectator the absurd impression of a marionette. By all means, the conventional deportment of our well-bred classes would be out of place in a dramatic portrayal, especially when it is raised by music to the sphere of ideal pathos: here we no longer want etiquette, but the natural grace of sublimity. With the great distance often unavoidable in our theatres, the modern actor is precluded from depending on a mere play of features for his desired effect, and the mask of paint with which he combats the bleaching glare of the footlights allows him little but an indication of the general character, not of the hidden movements of the inner soul. In musical drama, however, the all-explaining eloquence of the harmonic tone-play affords an incomparably surer and more convincing means of effect than possibly can stand at service of the mere mimic; and dramatic melody intelligibly delivered, as set forth above, makes a nobler and more distinct impression than the most studied discourse of the best-skilled physiognomist, when it is least impeded by those artifices which alone can help the latter.

On the other hand the singer seems more directed than the mime to plastic movements of the body itself, and particularly of those vehicles of feeling, the arms; yet in the use of these we had to abide by the selfsame law that kept the stronger accents of the melody in union with its particles. Whereas in operatic pathos we had accustomed ourselves to throwing wide our arms as if calling for help, we found that a half-uplifting of one arm, nay, a characteristic movement of the hand, the head, was quite enough to emphasize a somewhat heightened feeling, since a powerful gesture can have a truly staggering effect only when emotion bursts at last its barriers like a force of nature too long held back.

The singer's law for shifting place is commonly an inconsiderate routine, as his most strenuous attention is claimed by the frequently serious difficulties of his purely musical task; but we soon discovered how much was accomplished toward raising our dramatic performance above the operatic level by a careful ordering of his paces and his standing still. As the main affair of older opera was the monologic aria, which the singer was almost compelled to fire into the face of the audience, so to say, the notion arose that even in duets, trios, nay, whole general musters, the so-called ensembles, everyone must discharge his part into the auditorium from a similar position. As walking was thus altogether precluded, the arms were set in that almost continuous motion of whose impropriety, nay, absurdity, we had already grown aware.

Now, if in genuine musical drama the *dialogue*, with all its amplifications, becomes the unique basis of dramatic life; and therefore if the singer no longer has aught to address to the audience, but all to his interlocutor—we could but see that the usual alignment of a pair of duetists robbed their impassioned talk of all dramatic truth: for they either had to tell the audience at large what was meant for one another, or to show it nothing but their profile, with the resulting indistinctness both of speech and acting. To vary the monotony, one generally had made the two singers cross each other and change places, during an orchestral interlude. But the alertness of the dialogue itself supplied us with the aptest change of posture; for we had found that the sharper accents at close of a phrase or speech occasioned a movement of the singer, which had only to take him about one step forward and he was placed with his back half turned to the audience but his face shown full to his partner, as if in expectation of an answer; whilst the other need merely take about one step back, to begin his reply, and he was in the position to address his colleague—who now stood diagonally in front of him—without being turned from the audience.

By this and similar devices we were able to save the stage picture from ever standing stock-still, and to win from all the changeful motives, offered alike by solemn earnestness and graceful mirth, that animation which alone can give a drama its due import of an action true to life.

Yet, for all our technical provisions and agreements, and all the special talent of the artists, which alone could give them real effect, such fair success could never have been compassed if the musical and scenic elements had not contributed their own full share from every side. As regards the scenery in its widest sense, the first thing to claim our solicitude was a fitness in the costumes and decorations. Here much had to be invented, needless as it might seem to those accustomed to catering for the love of pomp and entertainment by a skillful combination of all the tried effects of opera. As soon as it came to the question of a costume for Klingsor's magic flower maidens, we found nothing but models from ballet or masquerade: the now so favorite court carnivals, in particular, had betrayed our most talented artists into a certain conventional lavishness of ornament that proved quite futile for our object, which was to be attained only on lines of ideal naturalness. These costumes must completely harmonize with Klingsor's magic garden itself, and we had to be quite sure that, after many attempts, we had found the right motive for this floral majesty, unknown to physical experience, before we could introduce into it living female forms that seemed to spring quite naturally from out its wizard wealth. Then with two of those giant flower bells that decked the garden in their rich profusion we had the costume for our magic maiden; to give the last touch to her attire, she had only to snatch up one of the glowing flower cups all strewn around, to tilt it childlike on her head—and, forgetting each convention of the opera ballet, we might take the thing as done.

Though our utmost diligence was spent on giving the height of solemn dignity to the ideal temple of the Grail, whose model could be taken only from the noblest monuments of Christian architecture, yet the splendor of this sanctuary of a divinest halidom was by no means to be extended to the costume of its knights themselves: a noble Templar-like simplicity arrayed their figures with a picturesque severity, yet human grace. The significance of the kingship of this brotherhood we sought in the original meaning of the word "king" itself, as head of the race, a race here chosen to protect the Grail: nothing was to distinguish him from the other knights, save the mystic import of the lofty office reserved for him alone, and his sufferings understood by none.

For the funeral of the first king, Titurel, a pompous catafalque had been suggested, with black velvet drapery suspended from on high, whilst the corpse itself was to be laid out in costly robes of state with crown and scepter, somewhat as the King of Thule had often been depicted to us at his farewell drink. We resigned this grandiose effect to a future opera, and abode by our undeviating principle of reverent simplicity.

Only on one point had we to make a tiresome compromise, on this occasion. By a still inexplicable misreckoning, the highly gifted man to whom I owe the whole stage mounting of the *Parsifal*, as formerly of the Nibelungen pieces—and who was torn from us by sudden death before the full completion of his work*—had calculated the speed of the so-called *Wandeldekoration* (moving scenery) in the first and third acts at more than twice as fast as was dictated in the interest of the dramatic action. In this interest I had never meant the passing of a changing scene to act as a decorative effect, however artistically carried out; but, at hand of the accompanying music, we were to be led quite imperceptibly, as if in a dream, along the "pathless" adits to the Gralsburg; whose legendary inaccessibility to the non-elect was thus, withal, to be brought within the bounds of dramatic portrayal. When we discovered the mistake, it was too late so to alter the unusually complicated mechanism as to reduce the scenes to half their length;

* Karl Brandt.—Tr.

for this time I had to decide not only on repeating the orchestral interlude [Act I] in full, but also upon introducing tedious
retardations in its tempo: the painful effect was felt by us all,
yet the mounting itself was so admirably executed that the
entranced spectator was compelled to shut one eye to criticism.

For the third act, however—though the moving scene had
been carried out by the artists in an almost more delightful,
and quite a different manner from the first—we all agreed that
the danger of an ill effect must be obviated by complete omission; and thus we had a fine occasion to marvel at that spirit
which possessed all sharers in our artwork: the amiable and
talented artists who had painted these sets which would have
formed the principal attraction in any other stage performance—themselves consented, without the faintest umbrage, to
this second so-called moving scenery being entirely discarded
this time, and the stage concealed for a while by the curtain.
Moreover they gladly undertook to reduce the first moving
scenery by one-half for the performances of next year, and to
alter the second so that we should neither be fatigued and distracted by a lengthy change, nor need to have the scene cut
short by closure of the curtain.

To have had my hints and wishes so intimately understood
in this last department, which I might call that of "scenic
dramaturgy," was the great good fortune of my association
with the excellent son of that lamented friend to whom almost
exclusively I owe the construction of our festival house and its
stage apparatus. This young man evinced so plain a consciousness of the ideal aim in all the technical knowledge and practical skill acquired through his father's vast experience, that I
wish only that I could find his like in the stricter sphere of
musical dramaturgy, on whom to devolve one day my burdensome and lonely office.

On this latter field, alas! all is still so new, and hidden by the
dust of bad routine, that experiences such as those we lately
reaped in common through our study of *Parsifal* can be compared only with a breath of fresh air to the choking, or a flash
of light in darkness. Here indeed no experience could help us
as yet to a swift understanding, but inspiration—that *Weihe!*
—creatively supplied the place of years of conscious practice
of the right. This was shown by the progress of the repetitions;
their excellence did not succumb to any chilling of the first
day's warmth, as usual at our theatres, but markedly increased.
As with the scenic-musical work on the stage, this might have

been especially observed in the so decisive purely musical work of the orchestra. If I there was helped to fair success by intelligent and devoted friends who self-sacrificingly took duties given to none but inferiors elsewhere, we here were taught how much the German orchestra player's sense of beauty and fine feeling is susceptible of, when he knows himself released for a time from incompatible demands upon his faculties, to give his whole mind to the solving of higher tasks, imposed elsewhere in haste. Brought into thorough concord with the singers by the proved acoustics of its installation, our orchestra attained a beauty and spirituality of expression already sadly missed by every hearer who returns to the gorgeous opera houses of our great cities and has to suffer from their primitive arrangements for the band.

Thus even the influence of our surrounding optic and acoustic atmosphere bore our souls away from the wonted world; and the consciousness of this was evident in our dread at the thought of going back into that world. Yes, *Parsifal* itself had owed its origin and evolution to escape therefrom! Who can look, his lifetime long, with open eyes and unpent heart upon this world of robbery and murder, organized and legalized by lying, deceit, and hypocrisy, without being forced to flee from it at times in shuddering disgust? Whither turns his gaze? Too often to the pit of death. But him whose calling and his fate have fenced from that, to him the truest likeness of the world itself may well appear the herald of redemption sent us by its inmost soul. To be able to forget the actual world of fraud in this true-dream image will seem to him the guerdon of the sorrowful sincerity with which he recognized its wretchedness. Was he to help himself with lies and cheating, in the evaluation of that picture? [*To the artists*] You all, my friends, found that impossible; and it was the very truthfulness of the exemplar which he offered you to work upon, that gave you too the blessed sense of world escape; for you could but seek your own contentment in that higher truth alone. And that you found it was proved me by the hallowed grief of our farewell, when after all those noble days the parting came. To us all it gave the surety of another joyful meeting.

My salutations now for that!

3. *The Staging of* Tristan and Isolde *by Appia*

IF we stop to analyze the heightened state of our nervous sensibilities during a performance of *Tristan and Isolde*, we realize that this is further intensified by one peculiar circumstance: nothing in any stage setting is capable of complementing the immense emotional tension produced by the dramatic action of the opera and no effort of imagination on our part is capable of counteracting the inadequacy of any performance that we are likely to witness. This is confirmed by the fact that if we close our eyes the stage setting can be dispensed with; only the actor-singers induce us to open our eyes again. If on the other hand we study the score in order to find a clue to the manner in which the opera should be staged, we find none of any special importance other than what Wagner has indicated in his brief stage directions. Of course, the site and epoch of the play can suggest a thousand things to us. The memory of certain parts of the score, such as many of the string passages, suggest a form of scenic investiture that might equal in intensity the drama's musical expressiveness. But if we plan this and that, we find in the end that we have not come any nearer the essential drama of the opera and that despite our best efforts its dramatic line, which should determine the form of the stage setting, remains persistently and entirely alien to it.

This occurs because the two are fundamentally irreconcilable: the action involved is entirely an inner, a purely spiritual one. Tristan and Isolde are in conflict with the external world and elect to die. The attempt is aborted and they are thrown back into a life where they no longer belong. There is no need for the scenic designer to visualize this outer life, these purely external surroundings, for two reasons: firstly, because Wagner as a playwright is not interested in them, and his concentration on the inner, or spiritual, drama of the play would in any case have prevented him from doing so. What is dramatized at the outset is a conflict in the souls of Tristan and Isolde. Later on, in the dramatic action of the play there is no longer any conflict with the external world in which they find themselves. This will have become a vain phantom when they call upon death again. What possible relation, we ask ourselves, can stage setting have in a drama of this sort? Nevertheless, *Tristan* is a work written for the theatre, intended for the stage, and one that can be realized only in performance.*

The audience sees a dramatic performance which obviously involves the inner spiritual drama described above. But Wagner's indications as to how the work should be staged are restricted to a minimum, leaving the designer free to exploit any number of possibilities. The essential action is communicated to the spectator's ear with the convincing

---

* *Translator's Note*: Adolphe Appia's scenario for the staging of *Tristan and Isolde* is an appendix to his volume *Die Musik und die Inscenierung* (Music and Stage Setting), published in Munich in 1899. The manuscript was originally written in French. The only publisher interested being a German one, it was unfortunately translated into a particularly clumsy German that is a complete compendium of all the worst faults that German style is capable of displaying. The problem of translation is therefore an almost insuperable one. The meaning has often to be guessed at, whole sentences rephrased in order to become at all intelligible. Any certainty that the original meaning has been accurately captured is often unattainable. However, this translation, which might more strictly be termed a paraphrase, does convey, I think, Appia's technical and artistic ideas with sufficient clearness to show their epoch-making quality.

The kind of dramatic and atmospheric lighting here indicated, the subtle fluctuation of light used to emphasize and heighten dramatic action (the text motivating the light cues), has now become a traditional technique of modern staging in almost any serious production. But this kind of "light plot" was unheard of until Appia described it at a date when the mechanical apparatus to control stage lighting with the necessary fluency and subtlety had not yet been perfected. Although Appia had never staged an opera nor, I believe, even a play at the time his book was written, his visualization is so complete and specific that a director then or today could design and direct a performance of *Tristan* in all its essential details using the outlines indicated in his book. It would undoubtedly be a far more dramatically expressive performance than any modern opera stage has ever offered us. This outline, as well as the entire book, is the measure of Appia's genius as an innovator and originator of a characteristic technique of modern production.

I have discussed Appia's relation to the modern stage in my book *The Stage Is Set*, specifically in Part III, Chapter 4, "Aesthetic Principles, The Ideas of Adolphe Appia."

A typewritten copy of the French manuscript of *Die Musik und die Inscenierung*—the original manuscript is at the University of Geneva—is available to readers in the Theatre Collection of the New York Public Library. Unfortunately, this appendix is not included.—LEE SIMONSON.

clarity and freedom peculiar to the kind of poetic music drama that Wagner has made possible. At the same time the spectator's eye comes in contact with a purely arbitrary scenic scheme. Even if this seems a fortunate state of affairs at first glance, in practice it will be found that the consequences are not. The balance of sight and sound, which is the very essence of music drama, is disturbed and the drama itself is liable to degenerate into a chaos of sensory impressions. It is essential for the spiritual conflict involved that some form of representation be found which allows it to be successfully dramatized. Therefore the problem of the scene designer is not to reconcile the inner and the outer drama or the opera itself, but to establish their relation in a way which will make their import clear. Moreover the audience can be made directly aware of the inner or spiritual action involved only by some form of scenic investiture which is based upon the dramatic line of the play.

What method of stage setting should be adhered to in a drama where the physical setting, the outer world it embodies, is so essentially unimportant?—Unquestionably, the utmost simplification of all of its decorative and pictorial elements.— The illusory nature of this phantom world which surrounds Tristan and Isolde is precisely what must be established by the stage setting, from the beginning of the second act on, sustained of course by the music itself which divests both Tristan and Isolde of any contact with an actual world. The unreal, phantom nature of the world, for such it has become to them, in itself explains their need to escape its unreality in death. In so far as we make the spectator aware of how unimportant the physical stage setting is in comparison to the inner spiritual action, we induce him vicariously to become a part of this inner spiritual drama. The essential thing then becomes the purely inner, poetic, musical expressiveness of the play, and the balance between inner and outer drama can be maintained by a form of stage setting which underlines this relationship.

Wagner in *Tristan* allows us to share the emotional life of his hero much more completely and more intensely than in any of his other dramas. Despite this fact we can find no visual equivalent for this experience as spectators. On the one hand the members of the audience are spectators and at the same time they remain, so to speak, blind supernumeraries. The fundamental principle on which the staging of *Tristan and Isolde* should be based is this: *The audience must see the world of the protagonists as they themselves see it.* Naturally, this cannot be taken literally. But nevertheless the statement indicates clearly enough the spirit in which the scenic designer must work if the essential spirit of this masterpiece is to be visualized. He must aim at the utmost simplicity and be careful to avoid a single superfluous detail even in the scenes that do not seem to lend themselves to such simplification. Let us therefore begin with the second act:

When Isolde enters she is aware of only two things: Tristan's absence and the torch (last glimmer of the first act) which motivates this absence. The warm summer night arching over the lofty trees of the castle park is no longer factual reality for Isolde. These shimmering distances to her eyes are simply the empty and terrifying space that separates her from Tristan. At the same time, in spite of the agony of her desire, there burns in the depth of her soul a flame which transmutes all the powers of nature and miraculously makes them a harmonious whole. Only the torch remains obviously exactly what it is—a sign, a symbol which keeps her from the man she loves.

When she extinguishes the torch she destroys this barrier. She nullifies this inimical space. Time stops. In identifying ourselves with her we marvel at the extinction of these two inimical elements. Finally, the obliteration is complete. Time, space, the echoes of the natural world surrounding her, the ominous torch, everything is wiped out. Nothing exists, for Tristan is in Isolde's arms.

Time, that has stopped, takes on a fictitious continuity for the audience as music. And space—what remains of that for us who have not drunk the potion?

Like the hero and heroine we experience nothing more except this ecstasy of being together. The passion that is burning in their souls seems to us, as to them, much more real than their corporeal presences. And the rhythm of the music draws us deeper and deeper into the secret world in which their union is eternally consummated. Only one thing shocks us: we can still see them. We become painfully aware that we are forced to see these two who no longer really exist. As the phantoms of the material world appear again to us at the same time that they become apparent once again to the two lovers, when these two, who have transcended the corporeal world, once again come into contact with it, we feel as though we had practiced a deception on them, and were part of a conspiracy.

How will the stage designer embody all this so that the spectator in the course of this act does not rationalize what has happened, does not analyze it intellectually, but is carried away by its inner emotional surge?

On the basis of this analysis let me indicate point by point the following method of staging:

Picture of the stage at the rise of the curtain: A great torch at stage center. The somewhat narrow stage space is filled with enough light so that the actors can be distinctly seen, without dimming the brilliance of the torch and above all without dimming the shadows which this source of light casts. The forms which demarcate the stage setting are seen only hazily. The quality of the light veils them in an atmospheric blur. A few barely visible lines in the stage setting indicate the forms of trees. Gradually the eye becomes accustomed to this: above, it becomes aware of the mass of a building in front of which one perceives a terrace.

During the entire first scene Isolde and Brangaene stay on this terrace, and between them and the foreground one senses a declivity, the forms of which one cannot identify clearly. When Isolde extinguishes the torch the entire setting is enveloped in a monotonous half-light in which the eye loses itself without being arrested by a single definite shape. Isolde, as she flies toward Tristan, is enveloped in mysterious shadow which intensifies the impression of death that the right half of the stage has already induced in us. During the first ecstasy of their encounter both remain on the terrace. At its climax (page 136,* piano 8°, ff.° in orch. *Mein!*) we perceive that they come toward us imperceptibly from the upper terrace and by means of a barely noticeable ramp reach a lower platform farther in the foreground. This platform, the ramp leading from the terrace to it, and another incline which leads to the forepart of the stage itself, make an uneven terrain on which the glowing dialogue of the scene that follows takes place.

Then, when their desire is sufficiently appeased, when a single idea possesses them and when we become increasingly aware of the death of time, only then do they reach the foreground of the stage where (pages 161–162) we perceive for the first time a bench that awaits them. The whole mysterious half-lighted space of the stage becomes still more uniform

---

* Page references throughout the text refer to the vocal-piano score by Richard Kleinmichel published by G. Schirmer, New York.—Eds.

in tint. The structural forms are blotted out in the shadow of the background and even the different planes of the stage floor are no longer visible.

Whether as a result of our visual reactions induced by the gleam of the torch and the shadows it casts, or whether because our eye has followed the path that Tristan and Isolde have just traversed, however that may be, we become aware of how tenderly they are enfolded by the world about them. During Brangaene's song the light grows still dimmer. Even the figures of the actors no longer have any clear definition. Finally, when passion awakes once more, grows and threatens by its overwhelming power to annihilate any scenic investiture that might be given it, at this moment (page 193, first ff.° in the orch.) a pale red light strikes at stage right in the background. King Mark and his men-at-arms break in upon the scene. Slowly, cold and colorless, the dawn begins. The eye begins to recognize the general forms of the stage setting and the painted flats that suggest them become clear and hard in quality for the first time. With the greatest effort at self-control Tristan comes back to contact with the world once again, challenging Melot, who betrayed him, to a duel.

In the setting, now cold in color and hard as bone, only one spot is veiled from the dawning day and remains soft and shadowy: the bench at the foot of the terrace.

In order to indicate this projected form of stage setting more clearly and to amplify the accompanying sketches, I add the following detailed description of the stage setting.

The terrace which cuts through the stage at an angle goes from stage left, meets the stage right flats which are farther upstage, and loses itself in the night of the backdrop. This terrace should be at least two meters higher than the stage floor. The left side of this terrace for about one-third of the width of the stage is bounded by a wall. This wall slopes gradually toward the foreground, and at the left forms an angle which bounds the stage setting from there to the proscenium. From the left third of the stage to the extreme point on stage right two ramps lead from the terrace to the foreground and incorporate a fairly large platform that extends at a slight angle toward the left side of the stage: *

The actual foreground in consequence is very restricted as it is bounded on one side by the corner of the terrace and its

---

* *Note*: Right and left throughout seem to be from the audience's point of view.

supporting wall and on the other does not extend beyond the descent from the terrace which occupies more than half the width of the stage. The building which flanks the terrace spreads from the torch, which is about stage center, to stage left where it follows the line of the terrace and of the entire setting from there to the proscenium.

On stage right the setting remains open. One can distinguish the silhouettes of dark trees which bound it at that point. Their barely indicated foliage serves to mask the sky borders. At the foot of the terrace is a bench with the corner of the wall forming its back. This bench at the left quarter of the stage serves to balance the descent leading from the terrace and seems also to overlook the open right side of the stage setting even though this is not actually possible. The torch is fastened to the wall of the building between the gate and a small flight of stairs the outline of which detaches itself from the background. This torch must be placed quite high so that for the majority of the audience it makes a brilliant contrast not with the building but with the background. The general coloring of the stage picture is vague. The walls and a part of the stage seem to be overgrown with moss and ivy. The various platforms must be painted so as to seem as far as possible a unit, and they are only noticeable as the actors move on or across them.

The lines which indicate the top of the stage setting must not be anything like a symmetrical arch of branches and leaves, but rather lean toward the left side somewhat in the fashion of an arbor. At the right side they must extend upward with as much definition as possible so that this half of the stage keeps its essential characteristic: the left half, a refuge and resting place completely confined, the right side an opening leading out into the unknown.

The following notes demonstrate how the actors can use the platforms indicated in the stage setting.

Up to page 122 Isolde and Brangaene use only the middle of right side of the terrace and do not come beyond stage center. At her cry, *"Dien Werk? O thoer'ige Magd,"* Isolde reaches the left side of the terrace and sings (page 122) at the edge of the boundary wall, that is, directly above the bench in the foreground. She returns to stage center only to extinguish the torch. I have already indicated that at ff.° page 136 the two protagonists leave the terrace and imperceptibly draw near the audience, until they reach the platform. Page 141 with the words *"Dem Tage!"* Tristan is at the outer left end of the upper ramp in the middle of the stage, the same spot that later, page 158, *"um einsam in oeder Pracht,"* Isolde will occupy, and Melot also, during the entire closing scene. From this position Tristan faces right. During page 136 he gradually but not too noticeably reaches the lower ramp, page 149, ascends to the platform, and, page 150, to the upper ramp leading to the terrace while Isolde, same page, *"O eitler Tageskuecht,"* stands opposite him on the lower ramp with her back to the extreme left of the stage as if to prevent Tristan from leaving by this exit. On page 154, *"da daemmert mild,"* Tristan, who is turned slightly left, reaches the platform between the two ramps, turns toward the audience, and on page 155, *"O Heil dem Trank,"* is on the lower ramp, as near the audience as the arrangement of the stage permits. Isolde remains on the central platform between the two ramps, and on page 158, *"um einsam,"* is at stage center at the extreme left of the upper ramp. With her cry *"O nun waren wir Nachtgeweihte,"* Tristan, who is on the lower ramp and nearer the audience, turns slightly toward Isolde, that is, to stage left. They approach each other gradually during pages 159–161 and on pages 161–162 descend to the stage left foreground where they remain until the end of the act.

Kurvenal breaks in in order to bring Tristan news of his betrayal. At the outset he does not advance beyond the upper terrace, and only at the appearance of Mark and his men-at-arms does he descend to the lower ramp. The king himself remains on the platform between the two ramps until the end of the act. His men group themselves on the terrace above. Melot is stage center at the end of the upper level, and the audience sees him between Kurwenal and the king, although he is much farther upstage. As Tristan challenges him, he leaps upon the platform and from there to the ramp on which Tristan falls.

In the setting of the second act the arrangement of the platforms is of chief importance. Of course, lighting must give the stage setting a definition as well as the necessary envelopment by which the essential character of the setting is established. However, in relation to the actors the lighting plays a comparative negative role, whereas in the third act it constitutes the principal element of the setting, and the painting of the setting is reduced to the barest minimum.

When Tristan awakes he does not at first know where he is. When he is told, he does not understand. The name of the castle, its location are matters of complete indifference to him. The plaintive shepherd's tune that awakes him does not give him the slightest clue. When he tries to express what he feels he is conscious only of the light which disturbs him and a desire for the darkness in which he sees refuge. He connects Isolde with these two sensations because Isolde is brought back to him with the dawning day. In this blinding daylight he must "seek, see and find" her, but nevertheless it is this daylight which, like the ominous torch in Act II, separates her from him. But as he learns that Isolde is coming, indeed that she is near, the castle becomes a reality for him; it commands the sea and from it one can see on the horizon the ship that carries Isolde. In this fever of desire the idea takes shape: Tristan, who from his bier cannot even see the sea, sees the ship.

Now the melody that awakened him speaks to him more distinctly than all his visions.

His desire remains importunate. His fever heightens it. And the pitiless sunlight that will not let it die offers no possibility of appeasement. In a paroxysm of despair Tristan once more is shrouded in darkness. He loses consciousness.

What awakens him is not a melancholy lament or even the belated, inimicable light of day. No. Out of the depth of the night a miraculous ray reaches him. Isolde is near; she is at his side.

After this heavenly vision we become aware of reality again.

The sinking sun, the blood of his wound are only further symbols of his ecstasy: they must flood the castle. "She, who will forever heal his wound . . ." she nears . . . her voice is heard. . . . But in order to reach her the torch must be extinguished—Tristan falls lifeless in Isolde's arms.

The lovely, radiant light of day, which has been in reality their illusion, sinks slowly into the sea and with its last rays surrounds the protagonists with a wreath of blood.

The role which lighting has to play in this act is therefore clearly indicated. As long as light is only a source of suffering for Tristan, he must not be directly touched by it. As soon as he is able to accept its reality and use it as a medium for his visions it illuminates his face.

This is the entire scenic problem of the act, and determines the way both the setting and its arrangement are to be used.

In order to achieve this effect the area of light must be greatly limited and a great deal of space left for shadows.

Under these circumstances it would appear as though the scenery were totally unimportant. However, in order to provide the right background for the light, the setting must be carefully planned, and because the setting has only this function there cannot be much choice as to how the site of the action is to be realized. I trust that no one will think me either arbitrary or fantastic if I attempt to give it definite shape.

The walls of the castle, which bound the setting at stage left as well as upstage and from there extend toward stage right, must surround Tristan as a screen might surround a sick person. The scenery downstage right must seem to indicate the end of this screen, so that it seems almost as though one had removed part of the screen to enable the audience to see the stage. The two ends of this screen leave a wide view of the sky and are connected with the stage floor by a bounding wall.

To the general outline of this as indicated, one needs only to add the barest essentials, namely, to cover the skyborders and to provide a sufficient motivation for the shadow which covers the castle courtyard. But in order to make the play of light on the stage floor vibrant, the stage platforms should be arranged in the following manner. The entire length of the wall at stage left is reenforced by a buttress-like support which gives it a more definite accent without disturbing its simplicity. From its base the stage floor descends slightly, then rises again, in order to form the roots of the gigantic trees under which Tristan lies. From these roots the stage floor sinks, but this time to a lower level, so that from this tree to the lower right there seems to be a path leading from the castle door in the background toward the foreground. The approach from the sea which is near the wall is also slightly raised. Using this construction the stage becomes a plane sloping from left to right, so that the light coming from stage right, always at a declining angle, eventually hits the base of the buttress wall.

What also has to be planned with greatest care is the general outline of the setting which contrasts with the brilliance of the sky, and here the greatest simplicity must be preserved. The high point, from which Kurwenal can watch the horizon, must be incorporated in the wall at the right side of the stage, but downstage so that it does not obviously break the unity of line and at the same time keeps Kurwenal throughout as an expressive silhouette. It is obvious that the sea must not be visible to any of the audience, that no horizon is seen between the wall and the sky, and that the arch of the sky is unbroken blue without clouds.

In order that Tristan may be illuminated by a natural play of light, he is placed opposite the open sky and surrounded with as few accessories as possible. Stage properties would only destroy the unity of the setting as conceived. Kurwenal has simply thrown a cloak between a few protruding tree roots and places Tristan there, thus improvising an inconspicuous resting place where the wounded Tristan is stretched out.

To add any more details to this picture, already adequately indicated, is needless. Let us then refer to the score in order to to see how the lighting in the act is to be schemed.

On page 253 the growing light begins to play around Tristan's feet. On page 256 it reaches his belt; on page 259 it grazes his face; on pages 261–262 he is entirely immersed in light; on page 263 the light spills over his immediate surroundings. On pages 261–275 the light is at its high point. Nevertheless the stage is never brightly lighted, for the wall, which cuts off the sky in the background, continues to throw deep shadows in the castle yard and also on the path leading up to it. Beginning page 275, the light is the color of the sunset. But this rapidly dims during the singing of pages 276–282; the animated scene (pages 284–288) plays in relative darkness, so that details are no longer recognizable; in contrast the foreground is bathed in blood-red light which continues to grow in intensity.

The stage platforms which form the base of the wall can be advantageously used for the combat (pages 288–289). Kurwenal comes into the light as he is wounded, and collapses near Tristan. None of Mark's men-at-arms or any of Kurwenal's leave the area of shadow. The greatest care must be taken in regard to the cast shadows in this last scene, so that Mark and Brangaene, who have their backs to the source of light, become dark silhouettes without, however, casting a shadow on Tristan or Isolde. Kurwenal falls in the shadow cast by Tristan. From page 294 on, the light dims more and more until the forms of the stage setting become twilight silhouettes. The curtain falls on a scene, quiet and monotonous in color, in which the eye distinguishes nothing except the last rays of the sunset playing above Isolde's pale countenance.

It is probable that the notes on the scenery, added to the

score by Wagner, are meant to be taken as nothing more than a brief comment on the setting rather than as a scheme to be literally followed. For it is obvious that Wagner in describing the stage setting has done so not from the point of view of the actor but from the essential poetic content of the act. It seems almost as if Wagner had attempted to find scenic forms outside the score.

In these last two acts of *Tristan and Isolde* stage lighting and the general structure of the setting have reduced scene-painting to a minimum. The designer has had to give painting itself no particular function. On the contrary, his task has been to reduce its importance so that it is wholly subordinate as an element of the background. But in the first act we are part of the outer life of the hero and heroine, and we can be aware of its tragic import only if it is completely visualized. If, in the succeeding acts, we want to reduce this actual world to the simplest forms that can express it we must, in contrast, in the first act establish not only its actuality but express as well the quality which in the end makes it an illusion from which the protagonists can flee.

In this respect the scenery of the first act offers a golden opportunity.

In the twilight of her tent Isolde tries, head in her pillow, to evade the reality she dreads. But an echo of this hated life meets her ear. Beside herself, she jumps to her feet. The song of the sailors seems to her almost a personal insult. The lying evasion of her retreat lies heavy upon her. She fairly suffocates under the folds of her tent; and finally, when the actuality of the situation forces itself upon her, she decides to confront it, triumph over it. At her command the curtains of the tent open.

The wind blows into the open tent. Isolde gazes and gazes, saturates her eyes with this light whose radiance means nothing more to her than what it symbolizes. It condones Tristan's betrayal. For the only reality to her is the world which she grows conscious of in his presence. Spellbound, she regards him, but she cannot bear this passive role long. As it becomes increasingly impossible for her to evade the issue, she decides to take part in it. Tragic conflict is imminent. Isolde must await its advent silently, and the curtains of the tent close again at the moment when this duplicity of Isolde becomes insupportable.

The music seems to have been muffled by these conflicting

alternatives. She, the consort of an immensely powerful ruler, did not know what to do with her golden opportunity. Now, in the quiet twilight of her tent, her emotions overflow. The world of actuality beats against its walls like breaking waves, but of what importance is that? The curtains will not open again until Tristan and Isolde have denied the reality of the situation that they enact, until their momentary attempt to dominate it will force from them the passionate outcry of their deepest moment of suffering. The implications of their deed will no longer be obvious to them. The curtains of Isolde's tent, therefore, in the most literal sense of the words, constitute the boundary between the inner and outer drama of the play. The essential action of the play is materialized by them plastically and dramatically, both from the point of view of the subtlest demands of the score and the simplest implications of the actual space to be utilized.

Nothing remains for the stage designer except to emphasize the contrasts of these two parts of the stage. With every means at his command he must emphasize the dramatic symbolism of the entire setting. In Isolde's tent, where most of the act takes place, nothing occurs except what serves to express Isolde's inner conflict. To be sure, Brangaene has the traditional role of the confidante, but this role is transmuted by its musical treatment. She is nothing more than a dramatic expedient to lessen the improbability of too lengthy monologues and exchanges of sentiments between the leading personages. The music makes her a mere voice whose import is much more than that of a conventional personage whose only function is to elicit replies. Therefore her presence is justified in this inner shrine, in this refuge. The curtains of the tent are like eyelids which close or open upon outer actuality.

The lighting of this part of the stage must be very uniform and so arranged that there are no cast shadows. The footlights, even though used at minimum intensity, must show the forms of the actors' features clearly. The light outside the tent must throw as many and as varied shadows as possible, so that, in contrast with the tent, it becomes the arena of the actual world. Within the tent the few necessary properties, such as furniture and other objects, must have the least definition possible. The expressiveness of the light must reach its high point in the open part of the stage. At the same time the construction of the stage setting must be such that the unification of the actors and the total stage picture is furthered. The role that painting plays in the stage setting can be clearly deduced from the above.

When these essential conditions are fulfilled, the general arrangement of the stage picture is unimportant. But these general conditions entail certain consequences; for example, the sea and sky must not be visible when the curtains of the tent are closed; when at the beginning of the act Brangaene opens one of the flaps of the tent in order to look overboard the spectator must get the impression of the outer world entirely by means of the brilliance of the light beyond, which only touches Brangaene's feet, but not strongly enough to throw a shadow on the floor of the tent. The ship can be easily indicated by a few characteristic lines of rigging, for the ship itself is so clearly indicated by the score that the heaping up of nautical details on the part of the scene designer must seem like a clumsy repetition of the text. (Note: which is unfortunately always the case when this act is staged.)

When the curtains of the tent are opened for the first time (pages 14–15) the outer light, being almost vertical in direction, does not cross the threshold of the tent. On page 99, when they are opened for the second time, the angle of light is more acute, as it is late afternoon. The light then pours a golden flood across the foreground and casts shadows in the direction of the audience. All the details of the stage setting are obliterated; only one portion is emphasized and dominates the stage picture: the personages who are awaiting the arrival of the king and the group standing opposite them. The first, particularly Tristan and Isolde, show as backlighted silhouettes, as they are hit by the low-angled light coming from stage rear. The other group, as they are not standing between the light and the audience, are much more brightly lighted and the details of this group are much more definitely seen.

Let us sum up the role that the stage setting plays in *Tristan and Isolde*. In the first act it dramatizes in the most tangible way the conflict which eventually becomes an inner and a spiritual one in the lives of the two protagonists. The lighting plays the same negative role in Isolde's tent that it does as far as the actual setting is concerned in the second act. Outside the curtains of the tent it indicates the entire arena of conflict and prepares for the dramatic contrast which the subsequent stage pictures provide.

In the second act the greatest simplification of the stage

setting is essential. However, in order to preserve its connection with the dramatic action it becomes, as indicated by the roles of the actors, a highly expressive arrangement of stage levels unified by the lighting which has the further purpose of dramatizing the action involved.

In the third act the lighting is dominant, and determines everything else in the scenic scheme. Light and shadow in the course of the drama achieve the same significance as a musical motif which, once stated and developed, has an infinite range of variation. Tristan's agony is sufficient motivation for carrying this kind of lighting to its greatest degree of expressiveness; and the audience, overwhelmed vicariously by the spiritual tragedy of the hero and heroine would be disturbed by any form of stage setting which did not incorporate this element of design. The audience would really suffer for lack of the kind of staging I have indicated, because it needs to get through its eyes a kind of impression which, up to a given point, can equal the unexampled emotional power of the score. Light is the only medium which can continuously create this impression and its use is motivated and justified by the score itself.

One can see that for the staging of *Tristan* the important thing is the pictorial ensemble, and this short résumé that I have given is proof of this fact. A stage designer who has sufficient sensibility to accept the kind of subordination that music drama demands of him thereby proves that he is cultured enough to avoid any obvious errors of taste.

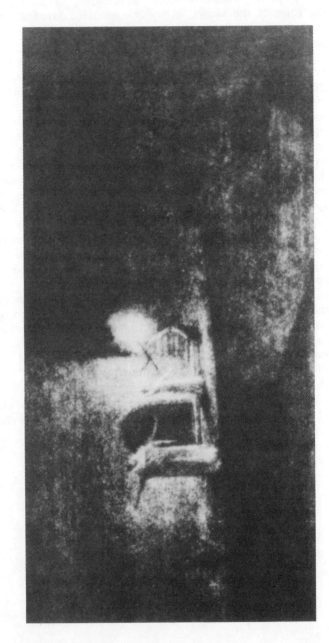

ADOLPHE APPIA. Design of 1896 for *Tristan and Isolde*, Act II

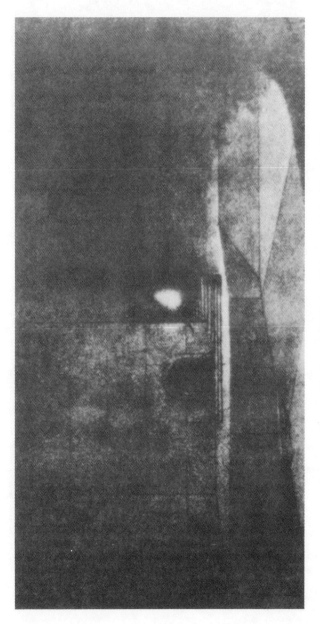

ADOLPHE APPIA. Design of 1923 for *Tristan and Isolde*, Act II

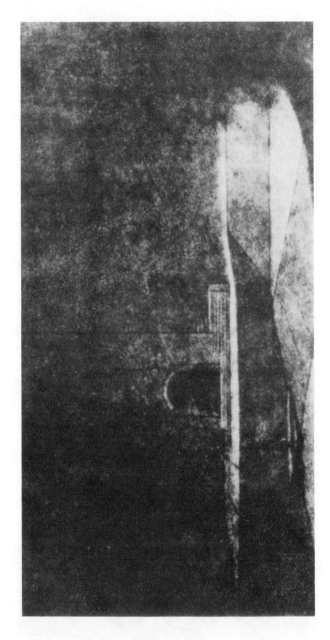

ADOLPHE APPIA. Design of 1923 for *Tristan and Isolde*, Act II

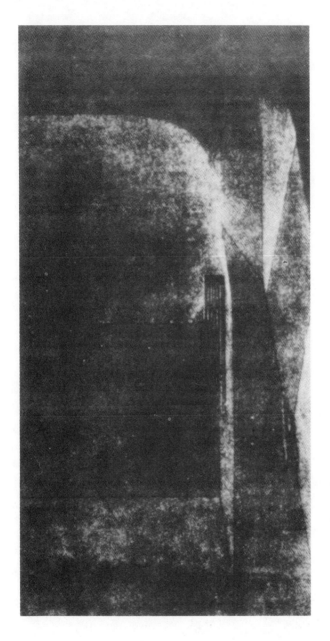

ADOLPHE APPIA. Design of 1923 for *Tristan and Isolde*, Act II

PART VIII

Politics

1. On state and religion:* State guarantees stability: basic Wahn of political life is patriotism; public opinion; the king and religion; dogma and allegory; the function of art

A highly-prized young friend† desires me to tell him whether, and if so in what way, my views on *state* and *religion* have changed since the composition of my art writings in the years 1849 to 1851.

It is precisely here, however, where everyone considers he has a right to his opinion, that a definite utterance becomes more and more difficult the older and more experienced one grows. For here is shown again what Schiller says: *"Ernst ist das Leben, heiter ist die Kunst"* (Life is earnest, art is gay). Perhaps, however, it may be said of me that, having taken art in such special earnest, I ought to be able to find without much difficulty the proper mood for judging life. In truth I believe the best way to inform my young friend about myself will be to draw his foremost notice to the earnestness of my artistic aims; for it was just this earnestness that once constrained me to enter realms apparently so distant as state and religion. What there I sought was really never aught beyond my art—that art which I took so earnestly, that I asked for it a basis and a sanction in life, in state, and lastly in religion. That these I could not find in modern life impelled me to search out the cause in my own fashion; I had to try to make plain to myself the tendence of the state, in order to account for the disdain with which I found my earnest art ideal regarded everywhere in public life.

But it certainly was characteristic of my inquiry that it never led me down to the arena of *politics* proper; that is to say, the politics of the day remained as entirely untouched by me, as, despite the commotion of those times, they never truly touched myself. That this or that form of government,

* Written in the winter of 1864–1865.—EDS.
† Refers to Ludwig II of Bavaria.—EDS.

the jurisdiction of this or that party, this or that alteration in the mechanism of our state affairs, could furnish my art ideal with any veritable furtherance, I never fancied; therefore whoever has really read my art writings must rightly have accounted me unpractical; but whoever has assigned me the role of a political revolutionary, with actual enrollment in the lists of such, manifestly knew nothing at all about me, and judged me by an outer semblance of events which haply might mislead a police officer, but not a statesman. Yet this misconstruction of the character of my aims is entangled also with my own mistake: through taking art in such uncommon earnest, I took life itself too lightly; and just as this avenged itself upon my personal fortunes, so my views thereon were soon to be given another tinge. To put the matter plainly, I had arrived at a reversal of Schiller's saying, and desired to see my earnest art embedded in a gladsome life; for which Greek life, as we regard it, had thus to serve me as a model.

From all my imaginary provisions for the entry of the artwork into public life, it is evident that I pictured them as a summons to self-collection from amid the distractions of a life which was to be conceived, at bottom, merely as a gladsome occupation, and not as a fatiguing toil. Hence the political movements of that time did not attract my serious attention until they touched the purely social sphere, and thus appeared to offer prospects of the realization of my ideal premises—prospects which, I admit, for some time occupied my earnest thought. The line my fancy followed was an organization of public life in common, as also of domestic life, such as must lead of itself to a beauteous fashioning of the human race. The calculations of the newer Socialists therefore lost my sympathy from the moment they seemed to end in systems that took at first the repellent aspect of an organization of society for no purpose other than equally allotted toil. However, after sharing the horror which this aspect kindled in aesthetically cultured minds, a deeper glance into the proposed condition of society made me believe I detected something very different from what had hovered before the fancy of those calculating Socialists themselves. I found to wit that, when equally divided among all, actual *labor*, with its crippling burthen and fatigue, would be downright done away with, leaving nothing in its stead but an *occupation*, which necessarily must assume an artistic character of itself. A clue to the character of this occupation, as substitute for actual labor, was offered me by husbandry, among other things; this, when plied by every member of the parish, I conceived as partly developed into more productive tillage of the garden, partly into joint observances for times and seasons of the day and year, which, looked at closer, would take the character of strengthening exercises, ay, of recreations and festivities. Whilst trying to work out all the bearings of this transformation of one-sided labor, with its castes in town and country, into a more universal occupation lying at the door of every man, I became conscious on the other hand that I was meditating nothing so intensely new, but merely pursuing problems akin to those which so dearly had busied our greatest poets themselves, as we may see in *Wilhelm Meisters Wanderjahre.* I, too, was therefore picturing to myself a world that I deemed possible, but the purer I imagined it, the more it parted company with the reality of the political tendencies of the day around me; so that I could say to myself, My world will never make its entry until the very moment when the present world has ceased— in other words, where Socialists and politicians came to end, should *we* commence: I will not deny that this view became with me a positive mood: the political relations of the beginning of the bygone 'fifties kept everyone in a state of nervous tension, sufficient to awake in me a certain pleasurable feeling which might rightly seem suspicious to the practical politician.

Now, on thinking back, I believe I may acquit myself of having been sobered from the aforesaid mood—not unlike a spiritual intoxication—first and merely through the turn soon taken by European politics. It is an attribute of the poet, to be riper in his inner intuition of the essence of the world than in his conscious abstract knowledge: precisely at that time I had already sketched, and finally completed, the poem of my *Ring des Nibelungen.* With this conception I had unconsciously admitted to myself the truth about things human. Here everything is tragic through and through, and the will, that fain would shape a world according to its wish, at last can reach no greater satisfaction than the breaking of itself in dignified annulment. It was the time when I returned entirely and exclusively to my artistic plans, and thus, acknowledging life's earnestness with all my heart, withdrew to where alone can "gladsomeness" abide.

My youthful friend will surely not expect me to give a categorical account of my later views on politics and state:

under any circumstances they could have no practical importance, and in truth would simply amount to an expression
of my horror of concerning myself professionally with matters
of the sort. No; he can merely be wishful to learn how things
so remote from its ordinary field of action may shape themselves in the brain of a man like myself, cut out for nothing
but an artist, after all that he had gone through and felt.
But lest I might appear to have meant the above as a dis-
paragement, I must promptly add that whatever I might have
to put forward would strictly and solely be a witness to my
having arrived at a full valuation of the great, nay, terrible
earnest of the matter. The artist, too, may say of himself,
"My kingdom is not of this world"; and, perhaps more than
any artist now living, I may say this of myself, for very
reason of the earnestness wherewith I view my art. And that's
the hardship of it; for with this beyond-the-worldly realm of
ours we stand amid a world itself so serious and so careworn that it deems a fleeting dissipation its only fitting refuge,
whereas the need for earnest elevation has quite become a
stranger to it.

Life is earnest, and has always been so.

Whoever would wholly clear his mind on this, let him
but consider how in every age, and under ever freshly shaped,
but ever self-repeating forms, this life and world have spurred
great hearts and spacious minds to seek for possibility of its
bettering; and how 'twas always just the noblest, the men
who cared alone for others' weal and offered willingly their
own in pledge, that stayed without the slightest influence
on the lasting shape of things. The small success of all such
high endeavors would show him plainly that these world
improvers were victims to a fundamental error, and demanded
from the world itself a thing it cannot give. Should it even
seem possible that much might be ordered more efficiently
in man's affairs, yet the said experiences will teach us that
the means and ways of reaching this are never rightly pre-
determined by the single thinker; never, at least, in a manner
enabling him to bring them with success before the knowledge of the mass of men.

Upon a closer scrutiny of this relation, we fall into
astonishment at the quite incredible pettiness and weakness
of the average human intellect, and finally into shamefaced
wonder that it should ever have astonished us; for any
proper knowledge of the world would have taught us from
the outset that blindness is the world's true essence, and not

knowledge prompts its movements, but merely a headlong impulse, a blind impetus of unique weight and violence, which procures itself just so much light and knowledge as will suffice to still the pressing need experienced at the moment. So we recognize that nothing really happens but what has issued from this not far-seeing will, from this will that answers merely to the momentarily experienced need; and thus we see that practical success, throughout all time, has attended only those politicians who took account of nothing but the momentary need, neglecting all remoter, general needs, all needs as yet unfelt today, and which therefore appeal so little to the mass of mankind that it is impossible to count on its assistance in their ministration.

Moreover, we find personal success and great, if not enduring, influence on the outer fashioning of the world allotted to the violent, the passionate individual, who, unchaining the elemental principles of human impulse under favoring circumstances, points out to greed and self-indulgence the speedy pathways to their satisfaction. To the fear of violence from this quarter, as also to a modicum of knowledge thus acquired of basic human nature, we owe the *state*. In it the need is expressed as the human will's necessity of establishing some workable agreement among the myriad blindly grasping individuals into which it is divided. It is a contract whereby the units seek to save themselves from mutual violence, through a little mutual practice of restraint.

As in the nature-religions a portion of the fruits of the field or spoils of the chase was brought as offering to the gods, to make sure of a right to enjoy the remainder, so in the state the unit offered up just so much of his egoism as appeared necessary to ensure for himself the contentment of its major bulk. Here the tendence of the unit naturally makes for obtaining the greatest possible security in barter for the smallest possible sacrifice: but to this tendence, also, he can give effect only through equal-righted fellowships; and these diverse fellowships of individuals equally entitled in their groups make up the parties in the state, the larger owners striving for a state of permanence, the less favored for its alteration. But even the party of alteration desires nothing beyond the bringing about a state of matters in which it, too, would wish no further change; and thus the state's main object is upheld from first to last by those whose profit lies in permanence.

Stability is the intrinsic tendence of the state. And rightly;

404 WAGNER ON MUSIC AND DRAMA

for it constitutes withal the unconscious aim in every higher human effort to get beyond the primal need: namely, to reach a freer evolution of spiritual attributes, which is always cramped so long as hindrances forestall the satisfaction of that first root need. Everyone thus strives by nature for stability, for maintenance of quiet; ensured can it be, however, only when the maintenance of existing conditions is not the preponderant interest of one party only. Hence it is in the truest interest of all parties, and thus of the state itself, that the interest in its abidingness should not be left to a single party. There must consequently be given a possibility of constantly relieving the suffering interests of less favored parties; in this regard the more the nearest need is kept alone in eye, the more intelligible will be itself, and the easier and more tranquillizing will be its satisfaction. General laws in provision of this possibility, whilst they allow of minor alterations, thus aim alike at maintenance of stability; and that law which, reckoned for the possibility of constant remedy of pressing needs, contains withal the strongest warrant of stability, must therefore be the most perfect law of state.

The embodied voucher for this fundamental law is the *monarch*. In no state is there a weightier law than that which centers its stability in the supreme hereditary power of one particular family, unconnected and uncommingling with any other lineage in that state. Never yet has there been a constitution in which, after the downfall of such families and abrogation of the kingly power, some substitution or periphrasis has not necessarily, and for the most part necessitously, reconstructed a power of similar kind. It therefore is established as the most essential principle of the state; and as in it resides the warrant of stability, so in the person of the king the state attains its true ideal.

For, as the king on one hand gives assurance of the state's solidity, on the other his loftiest interest soars high beyond the state. Personally he has naught in common with the interests of parties, but his sole concern is that the conflict of these interests should be adjusted, precisely for the safety of the whole. His sphere is therefore equity, and where this is unattainable, the exercise of grace. Thus, as against the party interests, he is the representative of purely human interests, and in the eyes of the party-seeking citizen he therefore occupies in truth a position well-nigh superhuman. To him is consequently accorded a reverence such as the highest citizen would never dream of distantly demanding for himself; and here, at this summit of the state where we see its ideal reached, we therefore meet that side of human apperception which, in distinction from the faculty of recognizing the nearest need, we will call the power of *Wahn*.* All those, to wit, whose simple powers of cognizance do not extend beyond what bears upon their nearest need—and they form by far the largest portion of mankind—would be unable to recognize the importance of a royal prerogative whose exercise has no directly cognizable relation with their nearest need, to say nothing of the necessity of bestirring themselves for its upholding, nay, even of bringing the king their highest offerings, the sacrifice of goods and life, if there intervened no form of apperception entirely opposed to ordinary cognizance.

This form is Wahn.

Before we seek to gain intelligence of the nature of Wahn from its most wondrous phrases, let us take for guide the uncommonly suggestive light thrown by an exceptionally deep-thinking and keen-sighted philosopher of the immediate past upon the phenomena, so puzzling in themselves, of animal instinct.

The astounding "aimfulness" in the procedures of insects, among whom the bees and ants lie handiest for general observation, is admittedly inexplicable on the grounds that account for the aimfulness of kindred joint procedures in human life; that is to say, we cannot possibly suppose that these arrangements are directed by an actual knowledge of their aimfulness indwelling in the individuals, nay, even of their aim. In explanation of the extraordinary, ay, the self-sacrificing zeal, as also the ingenious manner, in which such animals provide for their eggs, for instance, of whose aim and future mission they cannot possibly be conscious from experience and observation, our philosopher infers the exist-

---

* *Wahn-Vermögen.* As the word *Wahn* is frequently used in these pages, and is absolutely untransferable, I shall mostly retain it as it stands. It does not so much mean an "illusion" or "delusion," in general, as a "semiconscious *feigning*" (such as the "legal fiction"), a "dream," or a "symbolic aspiration"—its etymological kinship being quite as near to "fain" as to "feign"; but the context will leave the reader in no doubt as to its particular application in any sentence. It will be remembered that *Wahn* plays an important part in Hans Sachs' monologue in *Die Meistersinger*, Act III; the poem of that drama, containing the *Wahn* monologue in a somewhat more extended form than its ultimate version, had already been published in 1862.—Tr.

ence of a Wahn that feigns to the individual insect's so scanty intellectual powers an end which it holds for the satisfaction of its private need, whereas that end in truth has nothing to do with the individual, but with the species.

The individual's egoism is here assumed, and rightly, to be so invincible that arrangements beneficial merely to the species, to coming generations, and hence the preservation of the species at cost of the transient individual, would never be consummated by that individual with labor and self-sacrifice, were it not guided by the fancy (Wahn) that it is thereby serving an end of its own; nay, this fancied end of its own must seem weightier to the individual, the satisfaction reapable from its attainment more potent and complete, than the purely individual aim of everyday, of satisfying hunger and so forth, since, as we see, the latter is sacrificed with greatest keenness to the former. The author and incitor of this Wahn our philosopher deems to be the spirit of the race itself, the almighty will-to-life supplanting the individual's limited perceptive faculty, seeing that without its intervention the individual, in narrow egoistic care for self, would gladly sacrifice the species on the altar of its personal continuance.

Should we succeed in bringing the nature of this Wahn to our inner consciousness by any means, we should therewith win the key to that else so enigmatic relation of the individual to the species. Perhaps this may be made easier to us on the path that leads us out above the state. Meanwhile, however, the application of the results of our inquiry into animal instinct to the products of certain constant factors of the highest efficacy in the human state—factors unbidden by any extraneous power, but arising ever of their own accord —will furnish us with an immediate possibility of defining Wahn in terms of general experience.

In political life this Wahn displays itself as *patriotism*. As such it prompts the citizen to offer up his private welfare, for whose amplest possible ensurement he erst was solely concerned in all his personal and party efforts, nay, to offer up his life itself, for ensuring the state's continuance. The Wahn that any violent transmutation of the state must affect him altogether personally, must crush him to a degree which he believes he never could survive, here governs him in such a manner that his exertions to turn aside the danger threatening the state, as 'twere a danger to be suffered in his individual person, are quite as strenuous, and indeed more eager than in the actual latter case; whereas the traitor, as also the churlish realist, finds it easy enough to prove that, even after entry of the evil which the patriot fears, his personal prosperity can remain as flourishing as ever.

The positive renunciation of egoism accomplished in the patriotic action, however, is certainly so violent a strain that it cannot possibly hold out for long together; moreover the Wahn that prompts it is still so strongly tinctured with a really egoistic notion that the relapse into the sober, purely egoistic mood of everyday occurs in general with marked rapidity, and this latter mood goes on to fill the actual breadth of life. Hence the patriotic Wahn requires a lasting symbol, whereto it may attach itself amid the dominant mood of everyday—thence, should exigence again arise, to promptly gain once more its quickening force; something like the colors that led us formerly to battle, and now wave peacefully above the city from the tower, a sheltering token of the meeting place for all, should danger newly enter. This symbol is the king; in him the burgher honors unaware the visible representative, nay, the live embodiment of that same Wahn which, already bearing him beyond and above his common notions of the nature of things, inspirits and ennobles him to the point of showing himself a patriot.

Now, what lies above and beyond patriotism—that form of Wahn sufficient for the preservation of the state—will not be cognizable to the state burgher as such, but, strictly speaking, can bring itself to the knowledge of none save the king or those who are able to make his personal interest their own. Only from the kinghood's height can be seen the rents in the garment wherewithal Wahn clothes itself to reach its nearest goal, the preservation of the species, under the form of a state fellowship. Though patriotism may sharpen the burgher's eyes to interests of state, yet it leaves him blind to the interest of mankind in general; nay, its most effectual force is spent in passionately intensifying this blindness, which often finds a ray of daylight in the common intercourse of man and man.

The patriot subordinates himself to his state in order to raise it above all other states, and thus, as it were, to find his personal sacrifice repaid with ample interest through the might and greatness of his Fatherland. Injustice and violence toward other states and peoples have therefore been the true dynamic law of patriotism throughout all time. Self-preservation is still the real prime motive force here, since the quiet, and thus the power, of one's own state appears securable in no way other than through the powerlessness of other states, according to Machiavelli's telling maxim: "What you don't wish put on yourself, go put upon your neighbor!" But this fact that one's own quiet can be ensured by nothing but violence and injustice to the world without must naturally make one's quiet seem always problematic in itself: thereby leaving a door forever open to violence and injustice within one's own state too.

The measures and acts which show us violently disposed toward the outer world can never stay without a violent reaction on ourselves. When modern state-political optimists speak of a state of international law, in which the [European] states stand nowadays toward one another, one need point only to the necessity of maintaining and constantly increasing our enormous standing armies, to convince them, on the contrary, of the actual lawlessness of that state. Since it does not occur to me to attempt to show how matters could be otherwise, I merely record the fact that we are living in a perpetual state of war, with intervals of armistice, and that the inner condition of the state itself is not so utterly unlike this state of things as to pass muster for its diametric opposite. If the prime concern of all state systems is the ensurance of stability, and if this ensurance hinges on the condition that no party shall feel an irresistible need of radical change; if, to obviate such an event, it is indispensable that the moment's pressing need shall always be relieved in due season; and if the practical common sense of the burgher may be held sufficient, nay alone competent, to recognize this need: on the other hand we have seen that the highest associate tendence of the state could be kept in active vigor only through a form of Wahn; and as we were obliged to recognize that this particular Wahn, namely, that of patriotism, neither was truly pure nor wholly answered to the objects of the human race as such—we now have to take this Wahn in eye, withal, under the guise of a constant menace to public peace and equity.

The very Wahn that prompts the egoistic burgher to the most self-sacrificing actions can equally mislead him into the most deplorable embroglios, into acts the most injurious to quiet.

The reason lies in the scarcely exaggerable weakness of the average human intellect, as also in the infinitely diverse shades and grades of perceptive faculty in the units who, taken all together, create the so-called *public opinion*. Genuine respect for this public opinion is founded on the sure and certain observation that no one is more accurately aware of the community's true immediate life needs, or can better devise the means for their satisfaction, than the community itself; it would be strange indeed, were man more faultily organized in this respect than the dumb animal. Nevertheless we often are driven to the opposite view, if we remark how even for this, for the correct perception of its nearest, commonest needs, the ordinary human understanding does not suffice—not, at least, to the extent of jointly satisfying them in the spirit of true fellowship: the presence of beggars in our midst, and even at times of starving fellow creatures, shows how weak the commonest human sense must be at bottom.

So here we already have evidence of the great difficulty it must cost to bring true reason into the joint determinings of man; though the cause may well reside in the boundless egoism of each unit, which, outstripping far his intellect, prescribes his portion of the joint resolve at the very junctures where right knowledge can be attained through nothing but repression of egoism and sharpening of the understanding—yet precisely here we may plainly detect the influence of a baneful Wahn. This Wahn has always found its only nurture in insatiable egoism; it is dangled before the latter from without, however, to wit, by ambitious individuals, just as egoistic, but gifted with a higher, though in itself by no means high degree of intellect. This intentional employment and conscious or unconscious perversion of the Wahn can avail itself of none but the form alone accessible to the burgher, that of patriotism, albeit in some disfigurement or other; it thus will always give itself out as an effort for the common good, and never yet has a demagogue or intriguer led a folk astray without in some way making it believe itself inspired by patriotic ardor. Thus in patriotism itself there lies the holdfast for misguidance; and the possibility of keeping always handy the means of this misguidance, resides in the artfully inflated value which certain people pretend to attach to public opinion.

What manner of thing this public opinion is should be best known to those who have its name forever in their mouths and erect the regard for it into a positive article of religion. Its self-styled organ in our times is the "press": were she candid, she would call herself its generatrix, but she prefers to hide her moral and intellectual foibles—manifest enough to every thinking and earnest observer—her utter want of independence and truthful judgment, behind the lofty mission of her subservience to this sole representative of human dignity, this public opinion, which marvelously bids her stoop to every indignity, to every contradiction, to today's betrayal of what she dubbed right sacred yesterday. Since, as we else may see, every sacred thing seems to come into the world merely to be employed for ends profane, the open profanation of public opinion might perhaps not warrant us in arguing to its badness in and for itself: only, its actual existence is difficult, or well-nigh impossible to prove, for *ex hypothesi* it cannot manifest as such in the single individual, as is done by ever other noble Wahn; such as we must certainly account true patriotism, which has its strongest and its plainest manifestation precisely in the individual unit. The pretended vicegerent of "public opinion," on the other hand, always gives herself out as its will-less slave; and thus one never can get at this wondrous power, save—by making it for oneself. This, in effect, is what is done by the press, and that with all the keenness of the trade the world best understands, industrial business. Whereas each writer for the papers represents nothing, as a rule, but a literary failure or a bank-rupt mercantile career, *many* newspaper-writers, or all of them together, form the awe-commanding power of the *press*, the sublimation of public spirit, of practical human intellect, the indubitable guarantee of manhood's constant progress. Each man uses her according to his need, and she herself expounds the nature of public opinion through her practical behavior—to the intent that it is at all times havable for gold or profit.

It certainly is not so paradoxical as it might appear, to aver that with the invention of the art of printing, and quite certainly with the rise of journalism, mankind has gradually lost much of its capacity for healthy judgment: demonstrably the plastic memory, the widespread aptitude for poetical conception and reproduction, has considerably and pro-gressively diminished since even written characters first gained the upper hand. No doubt a compensatory profit to the general evolution of human faculties, taken in the very widest survey, must be likewise capable of proof; but in any case it does not accrue to us immediately, for whole generations—including most emphatically our own, as any close observer must recognize—have been so degraded through the abuses practiced on the healthy human power of judgment by the manipulators of the modern daily press in particular, and consequently through the lethargy into which that power of judgment has fallen, in keeping with man's habitual bent to easygoingness, that, in flat contradiction of the lies they let themselves be told, men show themselves more incapable each day of sympathy with truly great ideas.

The most injurious to the common welfare is the harm thus done to the simple sense of equity: there exists no form of injustice, of onesidedness and narrowness of heart, that does not find expression in the pronouncements of "public opinion," and—what adds to the hatefulness of the thing—forever with a passionateness that masquerades as the warmth of genuine patriotism, but has its true and constant origin in the most self-seeking of all human motives. Whoso would learn this accurately has but to run counter to "public opinion," or indeed to defy it: he will find himself brought face to face with the most implacable tyrant; and no one is more driven to suffer from its despotism than the monarch, for very reason that he is the representant of that selfsame patriotism whose noxious counterfeit steps up to him, as "public opinion," with the boast of being identical in kind.

Matters strictly pertaining to the interest of the king, which in truth can only be that of purest patriotism, are cut and dried by his unworthy substitute, this public opinion, in the interest of the vulgar egoism of the mass; and the necessitation to yield to its requirements, notwithstanding, becomes the earliest source of that higher form of suffering which the king alone can personally experience as his own. If we add hereto the personal sacrifice of private freedom which the monarch has to bring to "reasons of state," and if we reflect how he alone is in a position to make purely human considerations lying far above mere patriotism—as, for instance, in his intercourse with the heads of other states —his personal concern, and yet is forced to immolate them upon the altar of his state, then we shall understand why the legends and the poetry of every age have brought the tragedy of human life the plainest and the oftenest to show in just the destiny of kings.

In the fortunes and the fate of kings the tragic import of the world can first be brought completely to our knowledge. Up to the king a clearance of every obstacle to the human will is thinkable, so far as that will takes on the mold of state, since the endeavor of the citizen does not outstep the satisfaction of certain needs allayable within the confines of the state. The general and statesman, too, remains a practical realist; in his enterprises he may be unlucky and succumb, but chance might also favor him to reach the thing not in and for itself impossible, for he ever serves a definite, practical aim. But the king desires the ideal, he wishes justice and humanity; nay, wished he them not, wished he naught but what the simple burgher or party leader wants—the very claims made on him by his office, claims that allow him nothing but an ideal interest, by making him a traitor to the idea he represents, would plunge him into those sufferings which have inspired tragic poets from all time to paint their pictures of the vanity of human life and strife.

True justice and humanity are ideals irrealizable: to be bound to strive for them, nay, to recognize an unsilenceable summons to their carrying out, is to be condemned to misery. What the throughly noble, truly kingly individual directly feels of this, in time is given also to the individual unqualified for knowledge of his tragic task, and solely placed by nature's dispensation on the throne, to learn in some uncommon fashion reserved for kings alone: upon the height allotted to it by an unavoidable destiny, the vulgar head, the ignoble heart that in a humbler sphere might very well subsist in fullest civic honor, in thorough harmony with itself and its surroundings, here falls into a dire contempt, far-reaching and long-lasting, often in itself unreasoning, and therefore to be accounted well-nigh tragic. The very fact that the individual called to the throne has no personal choice, may allow no sanction to his purely human leanings, and needs must fill a great position for which nothing but great natural parts can qualify, foreordains him to a superhuman lot that needs must crush the weakling into personal nullity. The highly fit, however, is summoned to drink the full, deep cup of life's true tragedy in his exalted station. Should his construction of the patriotic ideal be passionate and ambitious, he becomes a warrior chief and conqueror, and thereby courts the portion of the violent, the faithlessness of fortune; but should his nature be noble-minded, full of human pity, more deeply and more bitterly than every other is he called to see the futility of all endeavors for true, for perfect justice.

To him more deeply and more inwardly than is possible to the state citizen, as such, is it therefore given to feel that in man there dwells an infinitely deeper, more capacious need than the state and its ideal can ever satisfy. Wherefore as it was patriotism that raised the burgher to the highest height by him attainable, it is *religion* alone that can bear the king to the stricter dignity of manhood.

Religion, of its very essence, is radically divergent from the state. The religions that have come into the world have been high and pure in direct ratio as they seceded from the state, and in themselves entirely upheaved it. We find state and religion in complete alliance only where each still stands upon its lowest step of evolution and significance. The primitive nature religion subserves no ends but those which patriotism provides for in the adult state; hence with the full development of patriotic spirit the ancient nature religion has always lost its meaning for the state. So long as it flourishes, however, so long do men subsume by their gods their highest practical interest of state; the tribal god is the representant of the tribesmen's solidarity; the remaining nature gods become penates, protectors of the home, the town, the fields, and flocks. Only in the wholly adult state, where these religions have paled before the full-fledged patriotic duty, and are sinking into inessential forms and ceremonies; only where "fate" has shown itself to be political necessity—could true religion step into the world. Its basis is a feeling of the unblessedness of human being, of the state's profound inadequacy to still the purely human need. Its inmost kernel is denial of the world—that is, recognition of the world as a fleeting and dreamlike state [of mind] reposing merely on illusion—and struggle for redemption from it, prepared for by renunciation, attained by faith.

In true religion a complete reversal thus occurs of all the aspirations to which the state had owed its founding and its organizing: what is seen to be unattainable here, the human mind desists from striving for upon this path, to ensure its reaching by a path completely opposite. To the religious eye the truth grows plain that there must be another world than this, because the inextinguishable bent to happiness cannot be stilled within this world, and hence requires another world for its redemption. What, now, is that other world? So far as the conceptual faculties of human understanding reach, and in their practical application as intellectual reason, it is quite impossible to gain a notion that shall not clearly show itself as founded on this selfsame world of need and change: wherefore, since this world is the source of our unhappiness, that other world, of redemption from it, must be precisely as different from this present world as the mode of cognizance whereby we are to perceive that other world must be different from the mode which shows us nothing but this present world of suffering and illusion.

In patriotism we have already seen that a Wahn usurps the single individual prompted merely by personal interests, a Wahn that makes the peril of the state appear to him an infinitely intensified personal peril, to ward off which he then will sacrifice himself with equally intensified ardor. But where, as now, it is a question of letting the personal egoism, at bottom the only decider, perceive the nullity of all the world, of the whole assemblage of relations in which alone contentment had hitherto seemed possible to the individual; of directing his zeal toward free-willed suffering and renunciation, to detach him from dependence on this world: this wonder-working intuition—which, in contra-distinction from the ordinary practical mode of ideation, we can apprehend only as Wahn—must have a source so sublime, so utterly incomparable with every other, that the only notion possible to be granted us of that source itself, in truth, must consist in our necessary inference of its exist-ence from this its supernatural effect.

Whosoever thinks he has said the last word on the essence of the Christian faith when he styles it an attempted satisfac-tion of the most unbounded egoism, a kind of contract wherein the beneficiary is to obtain eternal, never-ending bliss on condition of abstinence and free-willed suffering in this relatively brief and fleeting life, he certainly has defined there-with the sort of notion alone accessible to unshaken human egoism, but nothing even distantly resembling the Wahn-transfigured concept proper to the actual practicer of free-willed suffering and renunciation. Through voluntary suffering and renunciation, on the contrary, man's egoism is already practically upheaved, and he who chooses them, let his object be whate'er you please, is thereby raised already above all notions bound by time and space; for no longer can he seek a happiness that lies in time and space, e'en were they figured as eternal and immeasurable. That which gives to him the superhuman strength to suffer voluntarily must itself be felt by him already as a profoundly inward happiness, incogniz-able by any other, a happiness quite incommunicable to the world except through outer suffering; it must be the measure-lessly lofty joy of world-overcoming, compared wherewith the empty pleasure of the world conqueror seems downright null and childish.

From this result, sublime above all others, we have to

infer the nature of the divine Wahn itself; and, to gain any sort of notion thereof, we have therefore to pay close heed to how it displays itself to the religious world overcomer, simply endeavoring to reproduce and set before ourselves this conception of his in all its purity, but in nowise attempting to reduce the Wahn itself, forsooth, to terms of *our* conceptual method, so radically distinct from that of the religious.

As religion's highest force proclaims itself in *faith,* its most essential import lies within its *dogma.* Not through its practical importance for the state, that is, its moral law, is religion of such weight; for the root principles of all morality are to be found in every, even in the most imperfect, religion, but through its measureless value to the individual does the Christian religion prove its lofty mission, and that through its dogma. The wonderous, quite incomparable attribute of religious dogma is this: it presents in positive form that which on the path of reflection, and through the strictest philosophic methods, can be seized in none but negative form. That is to say, whereas the philosopher arrives at demonstrating the erroneousness and incompetence of that natural mode of ideation in power whereof we take the world, as it commonly presents itself, for an undoubtable reality, religious dogma shows the other world itself, as yet unrecognized; and with such unfailing sureness and distinctness, that the religious, on whom that world has dawned, is straightway possessed with the most unshatterable, most deeply blessing peace.

We must assume that this conception, so indicibly beautifying in its effect, this idea which we can rank only under the category of Wahn, or better, this immediate vision seen by the religious, to the ordinary human apprehension remains entirely foreign and unconveyable, in respect of both its substance and its form. What, on the other hand, is imparted thereof and thereon to the layman, to the people can be nothing more than a kind of allegory; to wit, a rendering of the unspeakable, impalpable, and never understandable through [their] immediate intuition, into the speech of common life and of its only feasible form of knowledge, erroneous per se. In this sacred allegory an attempt is made to transmit to wordly minds the mystery of the divine revelation; but the only relation it can bear to what the religious had immediately beheld is the relation of the day-told dream to the actual dream of night. As to the part the most essential of the thing to be transmitted, this narration will be itself so strongly tinctured with the impressions of ordinary daily life, and through them so distorted, that it neither can truly satisfy the teller—since he feels that just the weightiest part had really been quite otherwise—nor fill the hearer with the certainty afforded by the hearing of something wholly comprehensible and intelligible in itself.

If, then, the record left upon our own mind by a deeply moving dream is strictly nothing but an allegorical paraphrase, whose intrinsic disagreement with the original remains a trouble to our waking consciousness; and therefore if the knowledge reaped by the hearer can at bottom be nothing but an essentially distorted image of that original, yet this [allegorical] message, in the case both of the dream and of the actually received divine revelation, remains the only possible way of proclaiming the thing received to the layman. Upon these lines is formed the dogma; and this is the revelation's only portion cognizable by the world, which it therefore has to take on authority, so as to become a partner, at least through faith, in what its eye has never seen. Hence is faith so strenuously commended to the folk: the religious become a sharer in salvation through his own eye's beholding, feels and knows that the layman, to whom the vision itself remains a stranger, has no path to knowledge of the divine except the path of faith; and this faith, to be effectual, must be sincere, undoubting, and unconditional, in measure as the dogma embraces all the incomprehensible, and to common knowledge contradictory-seeming, conditioned by the incomparable difficulty of its wording.

The intrinsic distortion of religion's fundamental essence, beheld through divine revelation, that is to say, of the true root essence incommunicable per se to ordinary knowlege, is hence undoubtedly engendered in the first instance by the aforesaid difficulty in the wording of its dogma; but this distortion first becomes actual and perceptible from the moment when the dogma's nature is dragged before the tribune of common casual apprehension. The resulting vitiation of religion itself, whose holy of holies is just the indubitable dogma that blesses through an inward faith, is brought about by the ineluctable requirement to defend that dogma against the assaults of common human apprehension, to explain and make it seizable to the latter. This requirement grows more pressing in degree as religion, which had its primal fount within the deepest chasms of the world-fleeing heart, comes once again into a relation with the state.

The disputations traversing the centuries of the Christian religion's development into a Church and its complete metamorphosis into a state establishment, the perpetually recurring strifes in countless forms anent the rightness and the rationality of religious dogma and its points, present us with the sad and painfully instructive history of an attack of madness. Two absolutely incongruous modes of view and knowledge, at variance in their entire nature, cross one another in this strife, without so much as letting men detect their radical divergence: not but that one must allow to the truly religious champions of dogma that they started with a thorough consciousness of the total difference between their mode of knowledge and that belonging to the world; whereas the terrible wrong, to which they were driven at last, consisted in their letting themselves be hurried into zealotism and the most inhuman use of violence when they found that nothing was to be done with human reason, thus practically degenerating into the utmost opposite of religiousness.

On the other hand the hopelessly materialistic, industrially commonplace, entirely un-Goded aspect of the modern world is debitable to the counter eagerness of the common practical understanding to construe religious dogma by laws of cause and effect deduced from the phenomena of natural and social life, and to fling aside whatever rebelled against that mode of explanation as a reasonless chimera. After the Church, in her zeal, had clutched at the weapons of state jurisdiction, thus transforming herself into a political power, the contradiction into which she thereby fell with herself—since religious dogma assuredly conveyed no lawful title to such a power— was bound to become a truly lawful weapon in the hands of her opponents; and, whatever other semblance may still be toilsomely upheld, today we see her lowered to an institution of the state, employed for objects of the state machinery; wherewith she may prove her use, indeed, but no more her divinity.

But does this mean that religion itself has ceased?

No, no! It lives, but only at its primal source and sole true dwelling place, within the deepest, holiest inner chamber of the individual—there whither never yet has surged a conflict of the rationalist and supranaturalist, the clergy and the state. For *this* is the essence of true religion: that, away from the cheating show of the daytide world, it shines in the night of man's inmost heart, with a light quite other than the world-sun's light, and visible nowhere save from out that depth.

'Tis thus indeed! Profoundest knowledge teaches us that only in the inner chamber of our heart, in nowise from the world presented to us without, can true assuagement come to us. Our organs of perception of the outer world are merely destined for discovering the means wherewith to satisfy the individual unit's need, that unit which feels so single and so needy in face of just this world; with the selfsame organs we cannot possibly perceive the basic oneness of all being; it is allowed us solely by the new cognitive faculty that is suddenly awakened in us, as if through grace, so soon as ever the vanity of the world comes home to our inner consciousness of any kind of path.

Wherefore the truly religious knows also that he cannot really impart to the world on a theoretic path, forsooth through argument and controversy, his inner beatific vision, and thus persuade it of that vision's truth; he can do this only on a practical path, through *example*, through the deed of renunciation, of sacrifice, through gentleness unshakable, through the sublime serenity of earnestness that spreads itself o'er all his actions. The saint, the martyr, is therefore the true mediator of salvation; through his example the folk is shown, in the only manner to it comprehensible, of what purport must that vision be, wherein itself can share through faith alone, but not yet through immediate knowledge. Hence there lies a deep and pregnant meaning behind the folk's addressing itself to God through the medium of its heart-loved saints; and it says little for the vaunted enlightenment of our era that every English shopkeeper for instance, so soon as he has donned his Sunday coat and taken the right book with him, opines that he is entering into immediate personal intercourse with God. No: a proper understanding of that Wahn wherein a higher world imparts itself to common human ideation, and which proves its virtue through man's heartfelt resignation to this present world, alone is able to lead to knowledge of man's most deep concerns; and it must be borne in mind, withal, that we can be prompted to that resignation only through the said example of true saintliness, but never urged into it by an overbearing clergy's vain appeal to dogma pure and simple.

This attribute of true religiousness, which, for the deep reason given above, does not proclaim itself through disputation, but solely through the active example—this attribute, should it be indwelling in the king, becomes the only revelation, of profit to both state and religion, that can bring the two into relationship. As I have already shown, no one is more compelled than he, through his exalted, well-nigh super-human station, to grasp the profoundest earnestness of life; and—if he gain this only insight worthy of his calling—no one stands in more need, than he, of that sublime and strengthening solace which religion alone can give. What no cunning of the politician can ever compass, to him, thus armored and equipped, will then alone be possible: gazing out of that world into this, the mournful seriousness wherewith the sight of mundane passions fills him, will arm him for the exercise of strictest equity; the inner knowledge that all these passions spring only from the one great suffering of unredeemed mankind, will move him pitying to the exercise of grace. *Unflinching justice, ever-ready mercy—here is the mystery of the king's ideal!* But though it faces toward the state with surety of its healing, this ideal's possibility of attainment arises not from any tendence of the state, but purely from religion. Here, then, would be the happy trysting place where state and religion, as erst in their prophetic days of old, met once again.

We here have ascribed to the king a mission so uncommon, and repeatedly denoted as almost superhuman, that the question draws near: How is its constant fulfillment to be compassed by the human individual, even though he own the natural capacity for which alone its possibility is reckoned, without his sinking under it? In truth there rules so great a doubt as to the possibility of attaining the kingly ideal, that the contrary case is provided for in advance in the framing of state constitutions. Neither could we ourselves imagine a monarch qualified to fulfill his highest task, saving under conditions similar to those we are moved to advance when seeking to account for the working and endurance of everything uncommon and unordinary in this ordinary world. For, when we regard it with closer sympathy, each truly great mind—which the human generative force, for all its teeming productivity, brings forth so vastly seldom—sets us a-wondering how 'twas possible for it to hold out for any length of time within this world, to wit, for long enough to acquit itself of its tale of work.

Now, the great, the truly noble spirit is distinguished from the common organization of everyday by this: to *it* every, often the seemingly most trivial, incident of life and world intercourse is capable of swiftly displaying its widest correlation with the essential root phenomena of all existence, thus of showing life and the world themselves in their true, their terribly earnest meaning. The naïve, ordinary man—accustomed merely to seizing the outmost side of such events, the side of practical service for the moment's need—when once this awful earnestness suddenly reveals itself to him through an unaccustomed juncture, falls into such consternation that self-murder is very frequently the consequence. The great, the exceptional man finds himself each day, in a certain measure, in the situation where the ordinary man forthwith despairs of life. Certainly the great, the truly religious man I mean, is saved from this consequence by the lofty earnest of that inner ur-knowledge of the essence of the world which has become the standard of all his beholdings; at each instant he is prepared for the terrible phenomenon: also, he is armored with a gentleness and patience which never let him fall a-storming against any manifestation of evil that may haply take him unawares.

Yet an irrecusable yearning to turn his back completely on this world must necessarily surge up within his breast, were there not for him—as for the common man who lives away a life of constant care—a certain distraction, a periodical turning aside from that world's earnestness which else is ever present to his thoughts. What for the common man is entertainment and amusement must be forthcoming for him as well, but in the noble form befitting him; and that which renders possible this turning aside, this noble illusion, must again be a work of that man-redeeming Wahn which spreads its wonders wherever the individual's normal mode of view can help itself no further. But in this instance the Wahn must be entirely candid; it must confess itself in advance for an illusion, if it is to be willingly embraced by the man who really longs for distraction and illusion in the high and earnest sense I mean. The fancy-picture brought before him must never afford a loophole for resummoning the earnestness of life through any possible dispute about its actuality and provable foundation upon fact, as religious dogma does. No, it must exercise its specific virtue through its very setting of the conscious Wahn in place of the reality. This office is fulfilled by *art*; and in conclusion I therefore point my highly loved young friend to art, as the kindly life savior who does not really and wholly lead us out beyond this life, but, within it, lifts us up above it and shows it as itself a game of play; a game that, take it ne'er so terrible and earnest an appearance, yet here again is shown us as a mere Wahn picture, as which it comforts us and wafts us from the common truth of our distress.

The work of noblest art will be given a glad admittance by my friend, the work that, treading on the footprints of life's earnestness, shall soothingly dissolve reality into that Wahn wherein itself in turn, this serious reality, at last seems nothing else to us but Wahn: and in his most rapt beholding of this wondrous Wahn play, there will return to him the indicible dream picture of the holiest revelation, with clearness unmistakable—that same divine dream picture which the disputes of sects and churches had made ever more incognizable to him, and which, as well-nigh unintelligible dogma, could end only in his dismay. The nothingness of the world, here is it harmless, frank, avowed as though in smiling: for our willing purpose to deceive ourselves has led us on to recognize the world's real state without a shadow of illusion.

Thus has it been possible for me, even from this earnest sally into the weightiest regions of life's earnestness, and without losing myself or feigning, to come back to my beloved art. Will my friend in sympathy understand me, when I confess that first upon this path have I regained full consciousness of art's serenity?

2. German art and German policy:* German and French civilizations contrasted; development of the German nation; the Romantic movement; the decline of German art; need for the German princes to support German art; German union

I

IN his admirable *Inquiry into the European Balance of Power*,† Constantin Frantz closes with the following paragraph his exposition of the influence, outspoken in the Napoleonic propaganda, of French politics upon the European system of states:

* Written in the autumn of 1867.—EDS.
† *Untersuchungen über das europäische Gleichgewicht*, published in Berlin, 1859.—TR.

"But it is on nothing else than the power of French civilization that this propaganda rests; without that, itself would be quite powerless. To extricate ourselves from the tyranny of that materialistic civilization is therefore the only effectual dam against this propaganda. And this is precisely the mission of Germany; because Germany, of all Continental countries, alone possesses the needful qualities and forces of mind and spirit to bring about a nobler culture, against which French civilization will have no power any more. Here would you have the rightful German propaganda, and a very essential contribution to the re-establishment of European equipoise."

We place this saying of one of the most comprehensive and original political thinkers and writers—of whom the German nation might well be proud, had it only learned to listen to him—at the head of a series of inquiries to which we are incited by the certainly not uninteresting problem of the relation of art to politics in general, of German art endeavors to the struggle of the Germans for a higher political standing in particular. The first glance reveals this particular relation as of so peculiar a kind, that it seems worth while to proceed from *it* to a comparative examination of that more general relation—worth while for rousing the Germans to a noble sense of self-reliance, since the universal import of even this particular relation, while it meets the efforts of other nations in a conciliatory temper, at like time very evidently assigns to the qualities and development of just the German spirit the pre-eminent calling to that work of reconciliation.

That art and science pursue their own path of evolution, of efflorescence and decay, completely aside from the political life of a nation, must have been the conclusion of those who have paid their chief attention to art's Renaissance amid the political relations of the expiring Middle Ages, and have deemed impossible to accord to the downfall of the Roman Church, to the prevalence of dynastic intrigues in the Italian states, as also to the tyranny of the ecclesiastical Inquisition in Spain, any furthersome connection with the unparalleled artistic flourishing of Italy and Spain at the same epoch.

That present-day France is standing at the head of European civilization, and yet betrays the deepest bankruptcy of truly spiritual productivity, is a fresh apparent contradiction: here, where splendor, power, and acknowledged supremacy over almost every other land and nation in every conceivable form of public life are undeniable facts, the best spirits among this people, that accounts itself so eminently spiritual, despair of ever mounting from the mazes of the most degrading materialism to any sort of outlook on the beautiful. If one is to grant the justice of the never-ceasing French laments about the restriction of the nation's political freedom (and people flatter themselves with assigning this as the only ground for the ruin of the public art taste), these laments might still be met, and not without good reason, by a reference to those flowering periods of Italian and Spanish art when outward luster and decisive influence upon the civilization of Europe went hand in hand with so-called political thralldom, pretty much as now is the case in France. But, that at no epoch of their luster have the French been able to produce an art even distantly approaching the Italian, or a poetic literature of equal standing with the Spanish, must have a special reason of its own. Perhaps it may be explained through a comparison of Germany with France at a time of the latter's greatest splendor and the former's deepest downfall. There Louis XIV, here a German philosopher [Leibnitz] who believed he must recognize in France's brilliant despot the chosen ruler of the world: indisputably an expression of the German nation's deepest woe! At that time Louis XIV and his courtiers set up their laws even for what should rank as beautiful, beyond which, at the real heart of the matter, the French under Napoleon III have not as yet exceeded; from that time dates the forgetting of their native history, the uprooting of their saplings of a national art of poetry, the havoc played with the art and poesy imported from Italy and Spain, the transformation of beauty into elegance, of grace into decorum.

Impossible is it for us to discover what the true qualities of the French people might have engendered of themselves; it has so completely divested itself of these qualities, at least in so far as concerns its "civilization," that we can no longer argue as to how it would have borne itself without that transformation. And all this happened to this people when it was at a high stage of its splendor and its power, when, forgetting itself, it took its likeness from its princes; with such determinant energy did it happen, this civilized form of its impressed itself so indelibly upon every European nation, that even today one can picture nothing else but chaos, in an emancipation from that yoke, and the Frenchman would rightly think he had lapsed into utter barbarism if he swung himself from out the orbit of his civilization.

If we consider the positive murder of freedom involved in

this influence, which so completely dominated the most original German ruler-genius of latter times, Frederick the Great, that he looked down upon everything German with downright passionate contempt, we must admit that a redemption from the manifest bankruptcy of European manhood might be deemed of moment not unlike the deed of shattering the Roman world dominion and its leveling, at last quite deadening civilization. As there a total regeneration was needed of the European folk blood, so here a rebirth of the folk spirit might be required. And indeed it seems reserved for the selfsame nation from whom that regeneration once proceeded to accomplish this rebirth as well; for demonstrably, as scarce another fact in history, the resurrection of the German folk itself has emanated from the German spirit, in fullest contrast to the "Renaissance" of the remaining culture folks of newer Europe—of whom in the French nation's case at least, instead of any resurrection, an un-exampledly capricious transformation on mere mechanical lines, dictated from above, is equally demonstrable.

At the very time when the most gifted German ruler could not look beyond the horizon of that French civilization without a shudder, this rebirth of the German folk from its own spirit, a phenomenon unparalleled in history, was already taking place. Of it Schiller sings:

> No Augustan age's flower,
> No Medici's bounteous power,
>   Smiled upon our German Art;
> She was never nursed in luster,
> Opened wide her blossoms' cluster
>   Ne'er for royal princes' mart.

To these eloquent rhymes of the great poet we will add in humdrum prose that, when we talk of the rebirth of German art, we are speaking of a time at which, on the other hand, the German folk was scarcely recognizable outside its royal families; that, after the unheard-ruin of all civic culture in Germany through the Thirty Years' War, all right, nay, all capacity to move in any walk or sphere of life lay in the prince's hands alone; that these princely courts, in which alone the might and even the existence of the German nation found expression, behaved themselves with almost scrupulous conscientiousness as threadbare imitations of the French king's court; and we shall have a commentary, at any rate challenging earnest meditation, to Schiller's strophe. If we arise from that meditation with a feeling of pride in the German spirit's indomitable force; and if, encouraged by this feeling, we may dare assume that even now, despite the well-nigh unbroken influence of French civilization upon the public spirit of European peoples, this German spirit stands facing it as a rival equally endowed at bottom then, to mark the situation's political significance withal, we might frame the following brief antithesis:

French civilization arose without the people, German art without the princes; the first could arrive at no depth of spirit because it merely laid a garment on the nation, but never thrust into its heart; the second has fallen short of power and patrician finish because it could not reach as yet the courts of princes, not open yet the hearts of rulers to the German spirit.

The continued sovereignty of French civilization would therefore mean the continuance of a veritable estrangement between the spirit of the German folk and the spirit of its princes; it thus would be the triumph of French policy, aiming since Richelieu at European hegemony, to keep this estrangement on foot, and make it total: just as that statesman made use of the religious strifes and political antagonisms between princes and empire [or "Realm"—*Reich*] for founding French supremacy, so, under the changed conditions of the age, it would be bound to be the persistent care of gifted French dictators to employ the seductive influence of French civilization, if not to subjugate the remaining European peoples, at least openly to control the spirit of German courts.

Complete success attended this means of subjugation in the past century, where with a blush we see German princes snared and alienated from the German folk by presents of French ballet dancers and Italian singers, just as savage Negro princes are beguiled today with strings of beads and tinkling bells. How to deal with a folk from whom its indifferent princes have at last been actually kidnapped we may see by a letter of the great Napoleon to his brother, whom he had appointed King of Holland: he reproached him with having given way too much to the national spirit of his subjects, whereas, had he better Frenchified the country, the emperor would have added to his kingdom a slice of northern Germany, *"puisque c'eût été un noyau de peuple, qui eût dépaysé davantage l'esprit allemand, ce qui est le premier but de ma politique,"* as the sentence runs in the letter in question. Here stand naked, face to face, this *"esprit allemand"* and French civilization: between the two the German princes, of whom that noble strophe of Schiller's sings.

Clearly, then, it is worth while to inspect the closer relations of this German spirit with the princes of the German people: it well might give us serious pause. For we are bound some day to reach a point, in the contest between French civilization and the German spirit, where it will become a question of the continuance of the German princes. If the German princes are not the faithful guardians of the German spirit; if, consciously or unconsciously, they help French civilization to triumph over that German spirit, so woefully misprised and disregarded by them, then their days are numbered, let the fiat come from here or there. Thus we are fronted with an earnest question, of world-historical moment; its more minute examination will plainly teach us whether we err when, from our standpoint, that of German art, we assign to it so great and grave a meaning.

II

It is good, and most encouraging for us, to find that the German spirit, when with the second half of last century it raised itself from its deepest decay, did not require a new birth, but merely a resurrection; across two desert centuries it could stretch its hands to the selfsame spirit, which then strewed wide its lusty seeds through all the Holy Roman Empire of the German nation, and whose effect upon even the plastic shape of Europe's civilization we can never deem of small account if we remember that the beautiful, the manifoldly individual, the imaginative German costume of those days was adopted by every European nation. Look at two portraits: here Dürer, there Leibnitz; what a horror at the unhappy period of our downfall is awakened in us by the contrast!

Hail to the glorious spirits who first felt deep this horror, and cast their gaze across the centuries to recognize themselves once more! Then was found that it had not been drowsiness that plunged the German folk into its misery; it had fought its war of thirty years for its spiritual freedom; that was won, and though the body was faint with wounds and loss of blood, the mind stayed free, even beneath French full-bottomed wigs. Hail Winckelmann and Lessing, ye who, beyond the centuries of native German majesty, found the German's ur-kinsmen in the divine Hellenes, and laid bare the pure ideal of human beauty to the powder-bleared eyes of French-civilized mankind! Hail to thee, Goethe, thou who hadst power to wed Helena to our Faust, the Greek ideal to the German spirit! Hail to thee, Schiller, thou who gavest to the reborn spirit the stature of the "German stripling" (*des deutschen Jünglings*), who stands disdainful of the pride of Britain, the sensuous wiles of Paris! Who was this *deutsche Jüngling*? Has anyone heard of a French, an English *Jüngling*? And *yet* how plain and clear beyond mistake, we understand this "German *Jüngling*"! This stripling, who in Mozart's virginal melodies beshamed the Italian capons; in Beethoven's symphony grew up to courage of the man, for dauntless, world-redeeming deeds! And this stripling it was who threw himself at last upon the battlefield when his princes had lost everything—empire, country, honor; to reconquer for the folk its freedom, for the princes e'en their forfeit thrones. And how was this *Jüngling* repaid? In all history there is no blacker ingratitude than the German princes' treachery to the spirit of their people; and many a good, a noble and self-sacrificing deed of theirs will it need to atone for that betrayal. We hope for those deeds, and therefore let the sin be told right loudly!

How was it possible that the princes should have passed in total silence the incomparably glorious resurrection of the German spirit, not even have thence derived the smallest change in their opinion of their people's character? How explain this incredible blindness, which absolutely knew not so much as how to use that infinitely stirring spirit for the furthering of their dynastic policy?

The reason of the German heart's perversity in these highest regions of the German nation, of all places, lies certainly both deep and far away; in part, perchance, in just the universal scope of German nature. The German Reich was no narrow national state, and far as heaven from what hovers nowadays before the longing fancy of the weaker, downtrod, and dissevered races of the nation. The sons of German kaisers had to learn no less than four distinct European languages, to fit them for due converse with the members of the Reich. The fortunes of all Europe were assembled in the political forecast of the German kaiser's court; and never, even at the empire's lowest ebb, did this dispensation wholly change. Only, the imperial court at Vienna, through its weakness over against the Reich, at last was rather led by Spanish and Romish interests than exercised its influence over them; so that at its most fateful era the Reich was like an inn in which the host no longer, but the guests make out the reckoning.

Whilst the Viennese court had thus completely fallen into the Romo-Spanish rut, at its only substantial rival, the court of Berlin, the mastering tendence was that of French civilization, which had already fully drawn into its groove the courts of lesser princes, the Saxon at their head. By the fostering of art these courts, at bottom, meant nothing more than the procuring a French ballet or an Italian opera; and, taken strictly, they have not advanced one step beyond the notion till this day. God knows what would have become of Goethe and Schiller if the first, born well-to-do, had not won the personal friendship of a minor German prince, the Weimar wonder, and eventually been enabled in that position to provide to some extent for Schiller! Presumably they would not have been spared the lot of Lessing, Mozart, and so many another noble spirit. But the *deutsche Jüngling* was not the man to need the "smile of princes," in the sense of a Racine or a Lully: he was called to throw aside the "curb of rules," and as there, so here in the people's life, to step forth a liberator from oppression.

This calling was recognized by an intelligent statesman at the time of utmost want; and, when all the red-tape armies of our monarchs had been utterly routed by the holder of French power—invading no longer as a curled and frizzled civilizer, but as a ravenous lord of war; when the German princes were no longer servants to mere French civilization, but vassals to French political despotism: then was it the German *Jüngling* whose aid was invoked, to prove with weapons in his hand the mettle of this German spirit reborn within him. He showed the world its patent of nobility. To the sound of lyre and sword* he fought its battles. Amazed, the Gallic caesar asked why he no longer could beat the Cossacks and Croats, the Imperial and Royal Guards? Per-

---

* An allusion to Körner's patriotic songs, as set to music by Weber in September, 1814. These songs were the means of arousing the utmost patriotic enthusiasm among the youths and younger men of Germany.—Tr.

haps his nephew is the only man on all the thrones of Europe who really knows the answer to that question: he knows and *fears* the German *Jüngling*. Learn ye to know him too, for ye should *love* him!

But in what consisted the huge ingratitude wherewith the German princes recompensed the saving deeds of this German spirit? They were rid of the French oppressors; but French civilization they enthroned again, to hug its leading strings as ever. Merely the great-grandsons of that Louis XIV were to be installed in power once more; and indeed it looks as if their only care besides was to enjoy their ballet and their opera in peace again. To these regained delights they merely added one thing: fear of the German spirit. The *Jüngling* who had rescued them must pay for having shown his undreamed power. A more lamentable misunderstanding, than that which now prevailed throughout a whole half-century in Germany twixt folk and princes, history would find it hard to point to; and yet that misunderstanding is the only decent shadow of an excuse for the ingratitude exhibited.

If the German spirit had erewhile stayed unnoticed merely out of lethargy and corrupted taste, now, when its strength had proved itself upon the battlefield, the rulers confounded it with the spirit of the French Revolution—for everything had really to be looked at through French spectacles. The German stripling who had doffed his soldier's uniform and, in lieu of the French tailcoat, had reached back to the old-German gown was soon considered a Jacobin who devoted his time at German universities to nothing less than universal schemes of regicide. Or is this taking the kernel of the misunderstanding a shade too literally? So much the worse, if we are to suppose that the spirit of German rebirth indeed was grasped correctly, and hostile measures taken against it of set purpose.

With deep sorrow must we confess that ignorance and knowledge here appear to stand not all too wide apart; for that would mean that the deplorable consequences of a purposely fostered misunderstanding could be explained on none but the lowest grounds of lax and vulgar love of pleasure. For how did the *deutsche Jüngling* bear himself, returning home from war? Assuredly he strove to bring the German spirit into active efficacy in life itself; but no meddling with actual politics was his object; no, nothing but the renewing and strengthening of personal and social morality. Plainly is this

spoken in the founding of the *Burschenschaft*.* It well became
the young fighters of the nation's battles to take strong arms
against the savage brawls and hectorings of German student
life, to put down debauchery and drunkenness; on the other
hand, to institute a strenuous and systematic training of the
body, to do away with cursing and swearing, and to crown
true piety of heart with the vow of noble chastity. French
civilization had found the degenerate mercenaries of the
Thirty Years' War besotted with the vices here attacked: to
polish down and tinker up that rawness, with its aid, to the
princes seemed sufficient for all time. But now the German
youth itself designed to earn the praise erewhile bestowed
by Tacitus upon the *deutsche Jüngling*. What other people
has a similar event to show in all the history of its culture?

Truly a quite unparalleled phenomenon. Here was nothing
of that gloomy, tyrannous asceticism which at times has

---

* According to Brockhaus' *Conversations-Lexikon*, the first
Burschenschaft (from *Bursch*, a "fellow, youngster"—one might
say, a "scrub") was founded at Jena University, on June 12, 1815,
partly by students who had fought in the War of Liberation, partly
by members of the old university *Landsmannschaften*. Its motto
was "Honor, Freedom, Fatherland." Its objects were those stated
above, and its example was soon followed by almost every university in Germany proper. In two or three years' time a general
conclave, with annual sittings, was formed from among these
Burschenschaften, under the name of *Burschentag*. At this sort of
minor parliament the chief business from 1827 to 1831 was a
dispute between the so-called *Germanen*, a more practically political party, and the *Arminen* (henceforth in a minority) who made
chiefly for an *ideal* unity of the Fatherland and its attainment by
means of the original objects of the *Burschenschaft*. Already after
Kotzebue's murder by a German student in March, 1819, the
Burchenschaft had been denounced, and some of its members
"examined" for "demagogism"; but after the "Frankfort Attempt"
of 1833 (a rising in which certain students had taken part) the
legal prosecutions became numerous; sentences of death, etc. were
passed, though nothing more severe than personal imprisonment—
which had a trick of being quite severe enough—was really put
into execution. In later years milder counsels appear to have
prevailed again, on both sides.

The *Landsmannschaften* date almost as far back as the universities themselves. In these the members were enrolled according
to what one may call subnational districts—at least the divisions
were given territorial names—with all the evil consequences of
inflaming local, or at least sectional, animosity. At the time when
Wagner was at the Leipzig University, both species of groups seem
to have co-existed, an interesting account whereof will be found
in a note on the "Corps Saxonia" in Glasenapp's Appendix to the
third edition of his *Leben Richard Wagner's*.—Tr.

passed across Romantic peoples and left no trace behind: for this youth was—wonderful to say!—devout without being churchly. It is as though the spirit of Schiller, the tenderest and noblest of his ideal creations, here meant to take on flesh and blood upon a soil of ancient home. The social and political development to which it could not but have led, if the princes had only understood this youthful spirit of their folk, is surely past our rating high enough, our imagining its beauty. The aberrations of the unadvised were soon made use of for its ruin. Taunts and persecution tarried not to nip its flower in the bud. The old *Landsmannschaften* system, with all its vicious and deranging influence on youth, was given another lease of life, to oppose and ridicule the *Burschenschaft*; till at last, when the certainly not unintentionally aggravated blunders had begun to take a sinister and passionate character, the time had come for instructing the criminal courts to put a violent end to this German "league of demagogues."

The only thing left over from the time of Germany's revival was the military organization retained by Prussia; with this last remnant of the German spirit, uprooted everywhere else, the Prussian crown won the battle of Königgrätz,* to all the world's amazement, after the lapse of half a century. So great was the terror at this host in every European Ministry of War, that an anxious longing needs must seize the French commander in chief himself [Marshal Niel], regarded as the mightiest of them all, to introduce a something like this *Landwehr* into his so rightly famous army. We have seen, not long ago, how the whole French people kicked against the thought. So that French civilization has not accomplished what the downtrod German spirit so quickly and so lastingly succeeded in: the formation of a true folk army. As makeweight, it is busying itself with the invention of new weapons [*chassepots*], breechloaders and infantry cannon. How will Prussia reply to that? Likewise by perfecting her armor, or —by putting to good use the knowledge of its true means of power, at present not to be learned from it by any European people?—Since that memorable battle, on whose eve the fiftieth anniversary of the founding of the German *Burschenschaft* was celebrated, a great turning point has arrived, and

* Commonly, but erroneously, known in England and France as the Battle of Sadowa, in which Prussia inflicted a crushing defeat upon Austria, July 3, 1866.—Tr.

an immeasurably weighty resolution stands at halt: almost it looks as if the Emperor of the French more profoundly judges this importance than the governments of German princes seem to do. One word from the victor of Königgrätz, and a new power stands erect in history, whereagainst French civilization will pale its fires for ever.

Let us look closer at the consequences of what we have called that treachery to the German spirit, and see what since, in the course of a full half-century, has become of the seeds of its then so entrancingly hopeful bloom; in what manner German art and learning, which once had summoned forth the fairest phases of the people's life, have worked upon the evolution of this people's noble qualities since they were accounted and treated as foes to the quiet, or at all events the ease, of German thrones. Perhaps this survey may lead us to a plainer knowledge of the sins committed; and we then shall try mildly to think of them as failings, as to which we should merely have to stipulate for betterment, and not for expiation, when we finally admonish to a genuinely redeeming, inner union of the German princes with their folks, their imbuement with the veritable German spirit.

III

If one takes for granted that times of great political upsoaring are necessary to force the mental qualities of a people to high florescence, one is faced with the question: How is it, on the contrary, that the German War of Liberation was plainly followed by a terribly rapid falling off from the previous steady rise? Two issues are included in the answer, one showing us the dependence, the other the independence, of a nation's artistic genius on the actual stage of its political life. No doubt, the birth of even a great art genius must stand in some connection with the spirit of his time and nation; but if we don't propose to seek at random for the secret bonds of that connection, we certainly shall not do wrongly to leave to Nature her own mystery, and confess that great geniuses are born by laws we cannot fathom. That no genius, such as those the middle of last century brought forth in rich variety, was born in the beginning of the present century has certainly nothing strictly to do with the political life of the nation.On the other hand, that the high stage of mental receptivity whereto the artistic genius of the German rebirth had lifted us, so quickly settled down

again, that the folk allowed its ample heritage to be reft from
it well-nigh untasted—this, at any rate, may be explained by
the spirit of reaction from the fervor of the war of freedom.

That the womb of German mothers at that time conceived
for us no greater poets than Houwald, Müllner, and their
compeers may belong to the inscrutable secret of Nature;
but that these minor talents should have abandoned the free
highways of their great German fathers, to wander with quite
childish insipidity in a mournful imitation of misunderstood
Romanic models, and that these wanderings should have met
with actual consideration, allows us to argue with much
certainty to a mournful spirit, a mood of great depression, in
the nation's life. Nevertheless, in this mutual mood of mourning there lingered still a trace of spiritual freedom; one might
say, the exhausted German spirit was helping itself as best
it could. The true misery begins when it was to be helped
along in another fashion.

Indisputably the most decisive effect of the spirit of
German rebirth upon the nation itself had finally been exerted
from the theatre, through dramatic poetry. Whoever pretends
(as impotent literati are so found of doing nowadays) to
deny to the theatre a most preponderant share in the art
spirit's influence upon the ethical spirit of a nation, or even
to belittle it, simply proves that he himself stands quite
outside this genuine interaction, and deserves notice neither
in literature nor in art. For the theatre, had Lessing begun the
war against French tyranny, and for the theatre great Schiller
brought that war to fairest victory. The whole aim of our
[two] great poets was to give their poems their first, their
true, convincing life through the theatre; and all their intervening literature, in its truest sense, was merely an expression
of that aim. Without finding in the existing theatre a technical
development even somewhat preparatory for the high tendence
of German rebirth, our great poets were driven regardlessly
onward in advance of such development, and their legacy was
bequeathed to us on express condition that we first made it
truly ours.

If, then, no genius such as Goethe and Schiller was born
to us any more, it now was the very task of the reborn German spirit rightly to tend their works and thus make ready
for a long florescence, which Nature necessarily would have
followed with the bringing forth of new creative geniuses:
Italy and Spain once lived to see this reciprocity. Nothing

more would have been needed than to set the theatre in train duly to celebrate the deeds of Lessing's fight and Schiller's victory.

But as the youthful idealism of the *Burschenschaft* was parried by the vicious tendence of the old *Landsmannschaften,* so, with an instinct owned only by those whose subjects are profoundly helpless, the rulers took possession of this theatre, to withdraw the wondrous platform of the German spirit's noblest deeds of freedom from just the influence of that spirit's self. How does a skillful general prepare the enemy's defeat? By cutting off its communications, its commissariat. Napoleon the Great *"dépaysait"* the German spirit. From the heirs of Goethe and Schiller one took the theatre. Here opera, there ballet: Rossini, Spontini, the Dioscuri of Vienna and Berlin, who behind them dragged the Pleiades of German restoration.

Yet here, too, the German spirit was to try to break itself a path; if verse was dumb, yet tune rang out. The fresh, sweet breath of the youthful German breast, still heaving with noble aspiration, breathed out of glorious Weber's melodies; a new life of wonders was won for German feeling; with cheers the German folk received its *Freischütz,* and now seemed minded to throng anew the French-restored magnificence of the intendant-ruled court theatres—there, too, to conquer and to vivify. We know the long-drawn torments which the nobly popular German master suffered for his crime of the Lützow-hunters' melody,* and whereof at last he pined away and died.

The most calculating wickedness could not have gone to work more cleverly, than here was done, to demoralize and slay the German art spirit; but no less horrible is the supposition that perchance sheer stupidity and trivial love of pleasure, on the potentates' part, achieved this havoc. After the lapse of half a century the result is palpable enough, in the general state of spiritual life among the German people: 'twere a lengthy task, to follow it through all its strangely complex phases. We propose to offer later our contribution to that task, from several points of view. For our present purpose let it suffice to indicate the fresh-won power, over the German spirit, of a civilization which since has taken so

* In August, 1820, Weber was serenaded by the Göttingen students with his song *"Lützow's wilder Jagd,"* the words by Körner. Lützow had been allowed in 1813 to form a "free corps," which soon won celebrity for its dash and spirit in the War of Liberation; it was joined by Körner, Jahn, Friesen, and so on.—Tr.

fearfully demoralizing a turn in its own country that noble minds beyond the Rhine are casting glances, longing for redemption, across to us. From what they then behold, to their amazement, we best may gather how matters really stand with ourselves.

The Frenchman disgusted with his own civilization has read the book of Madame de Staël on Germany, let us say, or Benjamin Constant's report on the German theatre; he studies Goethe and Schiller, hears Beethoven's music, and believes he cannot possibly be mistaken if he seeks in close and accurate acquaintance with German life both consolation and a hope for his own people's future also. "The Germans are a nation of high-souled dreamers and deep-brained thinkers." Madame de Staël found stamped on Schiller's genius, upon the whole evolution of German science, the influence of Kant's philosophy.

What is there for the Frenchman of today to find with us? He will merely discover the remarkable consequences of a philosophic system once nursed in Berlin,* and now brought into thorough world renown under cover of the famous name of German philosophy; a system which has succeeded in so incapacitating German heads for even grasping the problem of philosophy, that it since has ranked as the correct philosophy to have no philosophy at all. Through such an influence he will find the spirit of all the sciences so altered that, in regions where the German's earnestness had made itself proverbial, superficiality, running after effect, and positive dishonesty—no longer in the discussion of any problems, but in personal bickerings mixed with calumnies and intrigues of every species—almost alone supply the foodstuff for our book mart, which itself has become a simple monetary speculation of the booksellers.

Luckily he will find, however, that the real German public, just like the French, reads no more books at all, but gains its information almost solely from the journals. In these latter he will find with sorrow that, even in an evil sense, the process is no longer German—as at least is the case with the wranglings of the university professors; for he will here observe the final consummation of a jargon that has more and more departed from resemblance to the German language. In all these manifestations of publicity he will also note the obvious trend toward forsaking any connection with the

---

* That of Hegel; whereof Feuerbach's was an offshoot.—TR.

nation's history, so highly honorable to the German, and "operating" a certain European dead level of the vulgarest interests of everyday, whereon the ignorance and fatuity of the journalist may frankly make its comfortable confession, so fondly flattering to the folk, of the uselessness of thorough culture.

To the Frenchman, amid such circumstances, the remains of the German people's love for reading and writing won't rank of special value; rather will he deem the people's mother wit and native common sense thereby endangered. For if he has been revolted in France by the nation's practical materialism, he will scarcely comprehend why this evil should be theoretically instilled into the German folk through a journalistic propaganda based on the most unspiritual conclusions of an arrogantly shallow nature-science; seeing that, upon this path, even the presumable results of naïve practice are made unfruitful.

Our guest next turns to German art, remarking in the first place that the German knows nothing by that name but painting and sculpture, with architecture perhaps thrown in. From those days of the German rebirth he recalls the fair, the noble beginnings of a development of the German art spirit on this side too: yet he perceives that what was meant in grand and genuine earnest by the noble Peter Cornelius, for instance, has now become a flippant pretext which flings its heels for mere effect, just the same as science and philosophy; but as far as effect is concerned, our Frenchman knows that none can beat his friends at home.

Onward to poetic literature. He believes he is reading the journals again. Yet no! Are these not books, and books of nine internally consecutive volumes? Here must be the German spirit; even if most of these books are mere translations, yet here at last must come to light what the German really is, apart from Alexandre Dumas and Eugène Sue? He undoubtedly is something else, to boot: a trader on the name and fame of German greatness! Everything bristles with patriotic assurances, and "German," "German," so tolls the bell above the cosmopolitan synagogue of the "up-to-date." 'Tis so easy, this "German"! It comes quite of itself, and no wicked Academy looks us up and down; nor is one exposed to the constant chicane of the French author, who for a solitary linguistic solecism is dismissed forthwith by all his colleagues with the cry that he can't write French.

But now to the theatre! There, in the daily, direct communion of the public with the intellectual leaders of its nation, must assuredly come out the spirit of the thoughtful German people, so self-conscious in the practice of its morals; the people of whom a certain Benjamin Constant had assured the Frenchman that it did not need French rules, since the seemly was a thing inherent in the inwardness and pureness of its nature. It is to be hoped our visitor won't make his first acquaintance with our Schiller and Goethe at the theatre, as in that case he could never comprehend why he had lately been erecting statues to the former in the squares of all our cities; or he would be led to suppose that it was in order to have done with the excellent, worthy man and his undeniable services, in some right handsome way, for good and all.

In particular, in his encounter with our great poets on the stage, he would be astounded at the extraordinarily dragging tempo in the recitation of their verses, for which he would feel bound to seek a stylistic ground until he became aware that this drawling arises merely from the actor's difficulty in following the prompter; for this mimetic artist has plainly not the time to commit his verses properly to memory. And the reason soon grows obvious enough; for one and the same actor, in course of the year, has to offer nearly all the products of the theatric literature of every age and every people, of every genre and every style—about the most remarkable collection one can anywhere find—to the subscribing public of the German theatre. With this unheard extension of the duties of the German mime, it naturally is never taken into consideration *how* he shall fulfill his task: both critics and public have got far beyond that. The actor is therefore compelled to found his popularity upon another quarter of his doings: the "up-to-date" is always bringing him something to set him in his congenial, his "self-intelligible" element; and here again, as in the case of literature, is found the help of the peculiar modern traffic of the newest German spirit with French civilization.

As Alexandre Dumas was Germaned there, so here the Parisian stage caricature is "localized"; and in measure as its new "locale" compares with Paris does this main support of the German theatre's repertory cut a presentable figure on our stage. A surprising awkwardness of the German's adds its quota to all this, producing complications which must awake in our French visitor the thought that the German far outstrips the Parisian in frivolity: what goes on in Paris really quite beyond the pale of good society, in the smaller hole-and-corner theatres, he will see reproduced in our most stylish of court theatres, with vulgar loutishness to boot, and set before the exclusive circles of society without a scruple, naked and unashamed, as the newest piece of drollery; and this is found quite as it should be.

Recently we lived to see Mdlle. Rigolboche—a person only explicable by means of Paris, and advertised in monster type as the Parisian "cancan-dancer"—summoned to perform at a Berlin theatre the dances which she there had executed, by special agreement with the well-known ballet caterers, for enlivening the most disreputable rendezvous of the traveling world;* moreover a gentleman of high position in the Prussian aristocracy, and in the habit of patronizing the world of art, paid her the honor of fetching her away in his carriage. This time we had our knuckles rapped for it in the Parisian press: for the French felt rightly shocked to see how French civilization looked without the French *décorum*. Indeed, we may conclude that it is a simple feeling of decency on the part of those peoples who were erewhile influenced by the German spirit, that now has turned them quite away from us and thrown them wholly into the arms of French civilization: the Swedes, Danes, Dutch, our blood-related neighbors, who once had stood in innermost spiritual communion with us, now draw their requirements in the way of art and intellect direct from Paris, as they very properly prefer at least the genuine articles to the counterfeits.

But what will our French visitor feel when he has feasted upon this spectacle of German civilization? To be sure, a desperate homesickness for at least the French decorum; and in that feeling, pondered well, there is won a new and most effectual engine of French supremacy, against which we may find it very hard to shield ourselves. If nevertheless we mean to make the attempt, let us proceed to test with care, and without a shred of idle overweening, the resources haply still remaining to us.

IV

To the intelligent Frenchman, whom we have just seen reviewing the present physiognomy of intellectual life in Germany, we yet might speak a final word of comfort— namely, that his eye had merely skimmed the outer atmo-

---

* 1867 was the year of the French International Exhibition.— TR.

sphere of true German spiritual life. That was the sphere wherein one let the German spirit struggle for a semblance of power and public agency: once it quite desisted from that struggle, corruption might naturally also lose all power over it. It will be both saddening and of profit, to seek that spirit out within its home, where once, beneath the stiff peruke of a Sebastian Bach, the powdered locks of a Lessing, it planned the wonder temple of its greatness. It says nothing against the German spirit's capacity, but merely against the intelligence of German policy, if there, in the depths of German individuality with its so universal aptitudes, a fund of gold lies buried without the power of bearing interest to the public life.

Repeatedly in the last few decades have we reaped the strange experience that German publicity has been first directed to minds of foremost rank in the German nation by the discoveries of foreigners. This is a beautiful feature, of deep significance, however shaming to German policy: if we weigh it well, we shall find therein an earnest admonition to German policy to do its duty and thus ensure for the whole family of European nations that healing which none of them is able to originate from its own spirit. Ever since the regeneration of European folk blood, considered strictly, the German has been the creator and inventor, the Romanic the modeler and exploiter: the true fountain of continual renovation has remained the German nature. In this sense, the dissolution of the "Holy Roman Empire of the German Nation" gave voice to nothing but a temporary preponderance of the practically realistic tendence in European culture; if this latter now has reached the abysm of sordidest materialism, by a most natural instinct the nations turn back to the fount of their renewing; and, strange to say, they there find the German Reich itself in an almost inexplicable state of suspended animation, yet not a victim to advanced decay, but engaged in a very obvious inner struggle toward its noblest resurrection.

Let us leave it to men of practical judgment to deduce from the efforts last indicated the outlines of a truly German policy, and here content ourselves, in keeping with our theme, with addressing our attention—aloof from that department of the German's public spiritual life which has been devastated by official misunderstanding—to the persistence of the German spirit in pursuing its peculiar line of evolution, albeit abandoned to the anarchy of its own initiative; for thus we may haply light upon the point where both directions of public life might fitly meet in a concord full of promise for the eventual raising of that hidden treasure.

More easily to reach that point, let us therefore seek the manifestations of the German spirit where they still perceptibly impinge upon publicity; and here, too, we shall meet with unexceptionable evidence of the German spirit's pertinacity, its reluctance to give up again a thing once grasped. The strictly federative spirit of the German has never thoroughly denied itself: even in the days of its deepest political downfall it has proved for all time, through the dogged maintenance of its princely dynasties against the centralizing tendence of the Habsburg kaiserdom, the impossibility of absolute monarchy in Germany. Ever since the uprousing of the folk spirit in the War of Liberation, this ancient federative bent has entered life again in every sort of form; where it showed itself the best equipped for life, in the associations of perfervid German youth, it was looked upon at first as hostile to monarchic ease, and violently repressed; yet no one could prevent its forthwith transferring itself to every sphere of spiritual and practical social interests.

But here again we are called to melancholy reflection, when we find ourselves compelled to admit that the wonderful vitality of the German spirit of association has never yet succeeded in gaining an actual influence upon the fashioning of public spirit. In truth, on every field of science, of art, of common social interests, we see the essence of German organization still hampered with much the kind of impotence that cleaves, for instance, to our *Turnvereins* [gymnastic unions] and their aimings at a general arming of the people, as against the standing troops, or to our chambers of deputies, copied from French and English models, as against the governments. With sorrow the German spirit therefore recognizes that even in these self-flattering manifestations it does not in truth express itself, but merely plays a piteous game of make-believe.

And finally what must make this in-itself-so-encouraging appearance of German unionism quite odious is that the selfsame spirit of gain and outer effect which we before discovered as reigning in all our official art publicity has been allowed to get the mastery of the German nature's manifestations on this side too: where everyone is so glad to dupe himself about his powerlessness for sake of at least doing something, and willingly acclaims the barrenest function as splendid productivity if only one is gathered together in good round numbers, there we may next expect to see a company in shares brought out to keep the thing afloat; and the true heir and administrator of European civilization will soon put in an appearance here, as everywhere else, with a Bourse speculation on *Deutschthum* and "German Solidness."

That no associations of ever so sensible heads can bring into the world a genius or a genuine work of art is patent enough: but that in the present state of public intellectual life in Germany they are not even equal to bringing knowably before the nation the works of genius, which naturally are begotten quite outside their sphere, they demonstrate by the mere fact of the art abodes, in which the works of the great masters of the German rebirth might be represented for the people's culture, being altogether withdrawn from their influence and turned into a nurseryground for the ruin of German art taste. Here on the side of art, as there on the side of politics, is irrefutable proof how little the German spirit has to await from all this mass of unions, radically German as may be their underlying principle.

Yet precisely in their case may we show the plainest, how, with one right step from the region of power, the most fruitful relation might be established for the good of all. For this we will refer once more to the *Turnvereins,* merely coupling with them the no less numerously supported *Schützenvereins* [rifle unions]. Sprung from a desire to exalt the folk spirit, their present agency—viewed from the ideal side—serves rather to narcotize that spirit, seeing that it is given a pretty toy to play with, and, especially when the fire of eloquence rules high at the yearly banquet of the founders' festival, is flattered into the belief that in this guise it really *is* of some account, that the welfare of the Fatherland hangs out-and-out on *it*; whereas, from the practical side, these unions serve the advocates of our standing troops for just as irrefragable a proof that it would be impossible to institute a reliable army upon the basis of folk-arming.

Now, the example of Prussia has already shown how the above contradictions may be almost completely adjusted: on the practical side, that of compassing a whole people's preparedness for war, the problem may be considered completely solved by the Prussian military organization; nothing lacks but on the ideal side, as well, to give the weaponed folk the ennobling sense of the true value of its arming and its readiness for action. It certainly is characteristic that the last

great victory of the Prussian host was ascribed by its com-
manders to other, to newer counsels, in the sense of returning
to the principle of a standing army pure and simple, whereas
all Europe took in eye the *Landwehr*'s constitution as the
origin of that success and an object for most serious meditation.

In that a very accurate knowledge of an army's needs, in
the way of organization, is assuredly at bottom of the Prussian
monarch's estimate—in itself a perhaps not quite unbiased
one—it would not be difficult to discover in what relation
the whole system of folk unions should stand to organizations
proceeding from the governments in order to help forward a
state of matters expedient from every point of view and, in
our opinion, conducive to true and general salvation. For,
that a host, to be at all times fit for service, needs a specially
practiced nucleus such as only the newer army discipline can
perfect, is just as undeniable as it would be preposterous to
want to train a country's whole able-bodied population for
absolutely professional soldiers—an idea whereat the French,
as known, were lately so horror-struck. On the other hand
the government has only to present to German unionism, in
every branch of public life therein involved, just what has
been brought to meet folk arming in the constitution of the
Prussian Army—namely, the effective earnestness of organization, and the example of the real professional soldier's valor
and endurance—to extend to the dilettantism of a male
population merely playing with firearms the strengthening
hand of universal welfare.

Now, we ask what an unheard, what an incommensurable
wealth of quickening organizations might not the German
state include within it, if *all* the various leanings toward true
culture and civilization, as exhibited in German unionism,
were drawn, in due analogy with the example of Prussian
military organization, into the only sphere of power to further
them, into that sphere in which the governments at present
hold themselves close-hedged by their bureaucratism?

As we here proposed to deal with politics merely in so far
as, in our opinion, they bear upon the German art spirit, we
leave it to other inquiries to yield us more precise conclusions
as to the political development of the German spirit, when
brought into that leavening union with the spirit of the German princes which we desire. If we reserve to ourselves, however, a further discussion of the German spirit's artistic
aptitudes, both social and individual, upon the lines of the

root idea last broached—we beg, for all our later researches on that domain, to carry over the result of this preliminary disquisition in something like the following sentence:

Universal as the mission of the German folk is seen to have been, since its entrance into history, equally universal are the German spirit's aptitudes for art; the rebirth of the German spirit, which happened in the second half of the preceding century, has shown us an example of the activation of this universality in the weightiest domains of art; the example of that rebirth's evaluation to the end of ennobling the public spiritual life of the German folk, as also to the end of founding a new and truly German civilization, extending its blessings e'en beyond our frontiers, must be set by those in whose hands repose the political fortunes of the German people: for this it needs nothing but that the German princes should themselves be given that right example from their own midst.

List of Sources

Except for the letters and the essay by Appia, all the material has been taken from *Richard Wagner's Prose Works*, translated by William Ashton Ellis, 8 vols., London, 1895–1899. Volume and page numbers refer to this translation. Dates in parentheses are dates of writing.

Pages	*Source*
	CULTURAL DECADENCE OF THE NINETEENTH CENTURY
37-41	Art and Revolution (1849). I: 41-47
41-43	A Communication to My Friends (1851). I: 351-54
43-45	The Vienna Opera House (1863). III: 366-68
45-46	Zukunftsmusik (1860). III: 332-33
46-51	*Tannhäuser* in Paris (1861). III: 351-52, 353-58
51-59	Judaism in Music (1850). III: 79, 84, 85, 86, 87-95, 99-100
59-62	Art and Revolution. I: 37-41
62-63, line 12	Zukunftsmusik. III: 306-307
63, line 13-page 64	Art and Revolution. I: 52, 52-53, 53-56, 59-60, 64-65
69-74	The Revolution (1849). VIII: 232-38
	THE GREEK IDEAL
77-78	Art and Revolution. I: 32-33
78-87	The Art-Work of the Future (1849). I: 139-41, 164-67, 134-36, 74-77
87-91	Opera and Drama (1850–1851). II: 153-56, 191
91, line 17-line 24	Zukunftsmusik. III: 312
91-92	Opera and Drama. II: 224
	THE ORIGINS OF MODERN OPERA, DRAMA, AND MUSIC
95-121	Opera and Drama. II: 24-28, 36-46, 48, 82-87, 87-99
121-24	The Art-Work of the Future. I: 149-53